The Era of Transitional Justice

The Era of Transitional Justice: The Aftermath of the Truth and Reconciliation Commission in South Africa and Beyond explores a broad set of issues raised by political transition and transitional justice through the prism of the South African TRC. South Africa constitutes a powerful case study of the enduring structural legacies of a troubled past, and of both the potential and limitations of transitional justice and human rights as agents of transformation in the contemporary era. South Africa's story has wider relevance because it helped to launch constitutional human rights and transitional justice as global discourses; as such, its own legacy is to some extent writ large in post-authoritarian and post-conflict contexts across the world. Based on a decade of research, and in an analysis that is both comparative and interdisciplinary, Paul Gready maintains that transitional justice needs to do more to address structural violence – and in particular poverty, inequality and social and criminal violence – as these have emerged as stubborn legacies from an oppressive or war-torn past in many parts of the world. Organised around four central themes – new keyword conceptualisation (truth, justice, reconciliation); re-imagining human rights; engaging with the past *and* present; remaking the public sphere – it is an argument that will be of considerable relevance to those interested in the law and politics of transitional societies.

Paul Gready is Professor of Applied Human Rights and Director of the Centre for Applied Human Rights at the University of York (UK).

Transitional Justice
Series Editor: Kieran McEvoy
Queen's University Belfast

The study of justice in transition has emerged as one of the most diverse and intellectually exciting developments in the social sciences. From its origins in human rights activism and comparative political science, the field is increasingly characterised by its geographic and disciplinary breadth. This series aims to publish the most innovative scholarship from a range of disciplines working on transitional justice related topics, including law, sociology, criminology, psychology, anthropology, political science, development studies and international relations.

Titles in this series:

Transitional Justice, Judicial Accountability and the Rule of Law
Hakeem O. Yusuf (2010)

The Era of Transitional Justice: The Aftermath of the Truth and Reconciliation Commission in South Africa and beyond
Paul Gready (2010)

The Era of Transitional Justice

The Aftermath of the Truth and
Reconciliation Commission in
South Africa and beyond

Paul Gready

Routledge
Taylor & Francis Group

a GlassHouse book

First published 2011
by Routledge
2 Park Square, Milton Park, Abingdon, Oxon, OX14 4RN

Simultaneously published in the USA and Canada
by Routledge
270 Madison Avenue, New York, NY 10016

A GlassHouse book

Routledge is an imprint of the Taylor & Francis Group, an informa business

© 2011 Paul Gready

Typeset in Baskerville by
Taylor & Francis Books
Printed and bound in Great Britain by
CPI Antony Rowe, Chippenham, Wiltshire

All rights reserved. No part of this book may be reprinted or reproduced or utilised in any form or by any electronic, mechanical, or other means, now known or hereafter invented, including photocopying and recording, or in any information storage or retrieval system, without permission in writing from the publishers.

British Library Cataloguing in Publication Data
A catalogue record for this book is available from the British Library

Library of Congress Cataloging in Publication Data
Gready, Paul.
The era of transitional justice : the aftermath of the truth and reconciliation commission in South Africa and beyond / Paul Gready.
  p. cm.
Includes bibliographical references.
1. South Africa. Truth and Reconciliation Commission.
2. Truth commissions–South Africa–Evaluation. 3. Apartheid–South Africa. 4. Human rights–South Africa.
5. South Africa–Politics and government. I. Title.
DT1974.2.G74 2011
968.06–dc22   2010013550

ISBN13: 978-0-415-58116-5 (hbk)
ISBN13: 978-0-203-84193-8 (ebk)

Contents

Acknowledgements		vi
	Introduction	1
1	Truth as genre	20
2	From social truth to rights-based participation	61
3	Justice past	93
4	Justice present	117
5	Speaking truth to reconciliation	156
6	Reconciliation, relationships and the everyday	195
	Conclusion	231
Interviewees		240
Bibliography		242
Index		266

Acknowledgements

This book has been a long time coming. The first interviews for it, or more accurately for a rather different book, were conducted in 1998. As usual, over time I have incurred four kinds of debt, from respectively: those who gave me money, those who talked to me, those who read and discussed what I wrote, and those who kept me sane.

In the first category, a Leverhulme Research Fellowship in 2004–5 allowed me to dedicate the best part of a year to researching and writing the book. Earlier awards from the Nuffield Foundation's Social Science Small Grant Scheme (for an initial set of interviews about the TRC) and Economic and Social Research Council (for work on magistrates) were also invaluable. Two grants from the University of London's Central Research Fund helped me to keep going back to South Africa.

In the second category I have incurred many debts and made many friends. Rather than single out individuals, I will simply refer you to the list of interviewees that appears at the end of the book (with the caveat that the list does not feature all those interviewed; in all I conducted well over 70 interviews during the decade in which I researched the book). My thanks also go to the various organisations with which I have worked and come into contact over the years.

Third, I owe a debt of gratitude to those who read and commented on parts or all of the book. My biggest debts in this regard are to Ron Dudai and Brian Phillips, fellow transitional justice addicts, who read the whole manuscript and commented with great critical insight and care. They made the book better than it would otherwise have been. I would like to thank staff and students at my current workplace, the Centre for Applied Human Rights at the University of York (UK), and my previous home, the Centre for International Human Rights at the Institute of Commonwealth Studies, University of London, for shaping my ideas and arguments over the years. A particular vote of thanks is due to my colleague at both institutions, Lars Waldorf, another transitional justice specialist, with whom I have shared many valuable discussions. I am also grateful to Lucy Harding for her meticulous work on the manuscript proofs.

Finally, those who kept me sane. Anashri Pillay read and commented on chapters, but also accompanied me on much of the journey. I would not have had it any other way.

Versions or sections of several chapters have previously appeared in journals or edited books, and reappear here with the requisite permissions:

'Telling Truth? The Methodological Challenges of Truth Commissions', in F. Coomans, F. Günfeld and M. Kamminga (eds) *Methods of Human Rights Research*, Maastricht Series in Human Rights, Intersentia: Antwerp, 2009, 159–85 (Chapter 1).

'Novel Truths: Literature and Truth Commissions', *Comparative Literature Studies* 46 (1), 2009: 156–76 (Chapters 2 and 5).

'The Public Life of Narratives: Ethics, Politics, Methods', in M. Andrews, C. Squire and M. Tamboukou (eds) *Doing Narrative Research*, Sage: London, 2008, 137–50 (Chapter 2).

'Culture, Testimony and the Toolbox of Transitional Justice', *Peace Review* 20 (1), 2008: 41–48 (Chapters 2 and 5).

My nephews – Joshua, Simeon and Reuben – have been lobbying me for years to dedicate a book to them. The deal was that I would do so when they expressed a bursting desire to actually read the book. I would be lying if I claimed they were spending sleepless nights waiting for this book, but I have capitulated. This book is for them. It is also for my mother who, with my father, taught me about human rights without ever using the term.

Introduction

South Africa is at a crossroads. Its post-apartheid achievements have been extraordinary (democracy, peace), but on the dark side of transition lies a more problematic reality, partly informed by the legacy of apartheid: poverty and inequality, social and criminal violence, an HIV/AIDS pandemic, and xenophobia. As such, South Africa constitutes a powerful case study of the enduring structural legacies of a troubled past, and of both the potential and limitations of transitional justice and human rights as agents of transformation in the contemporary era. South Africa's story has broader relevance because it helped to launch constitutional human rights and transitional justice as global discourses; its own legacy is to some extent writ large in post-authoritarian and post-conflict contexts across the world.

Transitional justice, a set of tools designed to address the legacies of a troubled past, is a creature of compromise; as such, truth commissions are its emblematic intervention. The ideal makes way for the possible, although it never stops asking the possible for more. In South Africa the compromises were of a kind familiar to peace processes in many parts of the world, as it became the exemplar of a new global compact that both facilitates and places constraints upon the changes associated with political transition. A negotiated settlement paved the way for majoritarian democracy and elections; a truth commission and an amnesty provision eased the passage; past gross violations of human rights received attention while enduring structural violence (poverty and inequality, violent crime) became the most enduring legacy of the past; and neo-liberalism trumped more redistributive economic policies. These compromises can be defended as necessary and midwives to the birth of something verging on the miraculous, or as midwives to a still-birth, as majority hopes for a better future were betrayed and the extraordinary all too swiftly became ordinary. Compromises have to be made, but which compromises, who is compromised, and what is the role of transitional justice and human rights in facilitating or contesting compromise?

Beginnings

This book started out as an inquiry into the keywords of the South African transition (truth, justice, reconciliation) as the main body of the Truth and

Reconciliation Commission's (TRC's) work came to a close in 1998. The TRC was the first truth commission to make a significant contribution to understandings of these terms, but their conceptual insights were post-hoc rationalisations for a politically informed mandate and working methods often devised on the hoof.[1] To provide just one example, the Commission's fourfold categorisation of truth – factual or forensic truth, personal and narrative truth, social or 'dialogue' truth, and healing and restorative truth (TRC 1998, Vol. 1: 110–14) – was ground-breaking, but was not coherently reflected in its work and report. The conceptual schema arose out of the hearings and research rather than informing them. Put simply, this is bad social science. The lesson is: consider your objectives, define your keywords, then design your institution accordingly. Alongside the lack of conceptual clarity, and the generally under-theorised nature of much work on transitional justice, I was also struck at the outset by the almost complete absence of evaluations of transitional justice mechanisms. Why, for example, were truth commissions being rolled out across the world, often citing the South African experience as inspiration, when there was so little sense of their impacts, what constituted success and how success should be measured?

So this is where I began, intending to write a book which would explore three central concerns. (1) Truth commissions are based on weak conceptual foundations, informed by an inadequate understanding of their foundational keywords – truth, justice, reconciliation – and the relationships between these keywords. (2) They have become a core component within the growing repertoire of transitional justice mechanisms with relatively little evaluation of their success, or clarity about what might constitute success. (3) Without greater conceptual clarity and rigorous evaluation there is a danger that the role and impacts of truth commissions will be exaggerated, misidentified or even negative. Much to my chagrin, important work has been done on these issues as I toiled on the book. In the South African setting, empirical research has mapped the impacts of the TRC (Chapman and van der Merwe 2008; Gibson 2004; Sarkin 2004).[2] On a broader canvas, keywords have been subjected to wide-ranging critique, chiefly on the grounds of the excessive claims made in their name (on truth, Mendeloff 2004; on justice/trials, Fletcher and Weinstein 2002), while research has also charted public and victim/survivor attitudes towards various transitional justice keywords and interventions.[3]

Tentative forays into evaluation have occurred. Recent 'how to' guides for truth commissions from Amnesty International (2007) and the Office of the United Nations High Commissioner for Human Rights (OHCHR 2006) provide relevant benchmarks – such as the need for consultation, political independence, procedural fairness and adequate powers (subpoena, search and seizure, witness protection, etc.) – which constitute the minimum preconditions for effectiveness. Hayner (2002: 252) identifies three criteria for evaluation relating to process (participation, engagement); product (the quality of the report and its recommendations); and impact (official and perpetrator response, report dissemination and acceptance, the implementation of recommendations).

Commissions can also be evaluated against their own mandates, against the fulfilment of certain human rights (rights to truth, justice, reparations), and/or on their victim-centred credentials. Nevertheless, while there have been evaluations of the TRC, and evaluation is an emerging frontier in transitional justice work more generally, evaluations remain an endangered species, and there is still little agreement about how to measure impacts (on who or what?) or on what constitutes success.[4]

So as the literature evolved and my focus followed suit, what, in the end, is this book about? It is not primarily a book about the TRC itself – the literature on the work of the Commission is extensive (Boraine 2000; Posel and Simpson 2002; Ross 2003; R. Wilson 2001). It is also not an impact assessment or evaluation, nor does it develop a tool for such endeavours. Two-by-two the chapters of the book retain the keywords format as an organising principle, and as a means of entering the arc of transitional justice debates, in the belief that the theorisation of these foundational terms remains both weak and crucial. The South African TRC is used as an entry-point to illuminate keywords of relevance to all transitional contexts and more recent turns in transitional justice debates (e.g. towards victim-centred approaches, reparations and restorative processes; towards local justice mechanisms). My analysis is both more interdisciplinary (chiefly exploring the interface between cultural studies and politics) and more comparative than other commentaries. The former allows the influence of the TRC to be traced beyond well-trodden paths, in literature and public culture as well as in legislation, for example; while the latter situates the TRC in global patterns of influence (the liberal peace; response templates to transitional crime). Based on an extensive literature review, a decade of research on the TRC, and well over 70 qualitative interviews, an interdisciplinary and comparative analysis helps to support the assertion that transitional justice and human rights need to do more to address structural violence, and in particular poverty/inequality and social and criminal violence, as these have emerged as stubborn legacies from an oppressive or war-torn past in many parts of the world. The key questions, of course, are: How? What levels of ambition, and indeed humility, are needed? And to what extent does South Africa offer an entry-point to generalisable challenges and solutions? Before outlining my arguments in response to these questions, more background is required.

What, for starters, is an official truth commission? (Unofficial truth projects (Bickford 2004) are also discussed in the analysis that follows, but their official counterparts have largely set the terms of debate). It is possible to distil the core characteristics of official commission down to (1) a focus on the past; (2) their origins at the point of transition away from war or authoritarian rule; (3) the investigation of patterns of abuses and specific violations committed over a period of time, rather than a single event; (4) a focus on violations of human rights, and sometimes of humanitarian norms as well; (5) a temporary, short-term life-span, usually culminating in the production of a report with recommendations; (6) official status, as commissions are sanctioned, authorised or empowered by the state (and sometimes by armed opposition groups, in the context of a peace accord); and (7) a victim-centred approach (Hayner 2002: 14, 17, see 14–23;

Quinn and Freeman 2003: 1119). The clean lines of this ambition are troubled by the political, economic and moral compromises inherent in transitional contexts. Commissions navigate the fault-line between the possible and the ideal, politics and human rights, between their own soft power and the hard(er) power of the state, and between their twin tasks of documenting the past and transforming the future.

More detailed background on the workings of the TRC will be provided in the chapters that follow; here a briefer introduction is sufficient. The Promotion of National Unity and Reconciliation Act (No. 34 of 1995), the TRC's founding Act, provided it with its primary tasks which were, in short, (1) establishing as complete a picture as possible of the gross violations of human rights in the past through investigations and hearings, (2) facilitating the granting of amnesty to those who met the relevant legal requirements, (3) establishing the fate or whereabouts of victims, restoring dignity by giving victims the opportunity to relate their own accounts, and recommending reparations, and (4) compiling a comprehensive report with findings and recommendations (Section 3:1 (a–d)). The promotion of national unity and reconciliation were broader objectives. Three committees – the Amnesty Committee, Human Rights Violations Committee (HRVC) and Reparation and Rehabilitation Committee – structured the TRC and underscored its priorities. The Commission focused on gross violations of human rights, defined as 'bodily integrity rights' (killing, abduction/'disappearance', torture or severe ill-treatment) (see TRC 1998, Vol. 1: 60–65, which outlines both the legislative basis for this emphasis and the TRC's own narrow interpretation of 'severe ill-treatment'). Among its most important innovations were a unique, individualised amnesty provision, in which amnesty for specific acts was made conditional on full disclosure and political motive, and sector hearings focusing on institutions and social groups.

The main portion of the Commission's work began in 1996 and was completed in 1998, with the finalisation of the first five volumes of its report (TRC 1998, Vols 1–5). Two further contributions followed: a special volume dedicated to victims (TRC 2002, Vol. 7), and a codicil report which documented material from the late-finishing amnesty process (TRC 2003, Vol. 6). The TRC gained unprecedented international attention through the place of apartheid in the international political imagination, high-profile commissioners (such as Archbishop Desmond Tutu, the TRC's chairperson), public victim and amnesty hearings, innovative institutional arrangements, widespread media coverage and excellent access to materials on the worldwide web.[5]

Truth commissions have gone global in the aftermath of the TRC. One estimate suggests that by mid-2004, 35 truth commissions had been established worldwide, and that momentum is building around this particular trend in political globalisation (Sikkink and Booth Walling 2006: 308–10). The South African TRC, its (former) staff and its philosophy occupy a particular place in this proliferation. The TRC is repeatedly acknowledged as source and inspiration in the transitional justice and truth commission literature. Quinn and

Freeman (2003: 1121), for example, note that it 'marked a turning point in global awareness about truth commissions – no commission is today better known around the world'. This is not to say that there is no competition in the transitional justice agenda-setting stakes. Sikkink and Booth Walling (2006) make a persuasive case for Argentina as the initiator of a 'justice cascade'. It has been home, over time, to the first important truth commission, initial trials of members of the military juntas, the overturning of amnesty provisions and, therefore, the idea that multiple transitional justice mechanisms can cohabit in productive ways. Nevertheless, few would contest the claim that the South African TRC remains the first among equals in the truth commission collective, and one of the key engines for what might be called the era of transitional justice.

Contexts

The era of transitional justice has three core characteristics: transitional justice (1) as an 'industry'; (2) as marked by a shift in ethos from substitution (choosing one mechanism rather than another, say truth commissions rather than trials) to complementarity (best captured by holistic approaches to the field), and the strategic challenge of intervention prioritisation and/or indivisibility; and (3) as a case study of the ambiguities of contemporary globalisation.

To say that transitional justice has become an industry is both a compliment and a warning. Cycles of boom and bust, as new ideas inspire hope, excessive ambition and then disappointment, are all too familiar in the annals of non-governmental organisations (NGOs), intergovernmental agencies such as the United Nations (UN) and bilateral donors. In the case of transitional justice and truth commissions, it is time to pause for thought. When countries in the new millennium throw off the shackles of authoritarian rule or conflict, the marketplace of options is crowded with the wares of transitional justice. 'How to' guides both restate ideals and draw on the lessons of past experience. Within the UN there has been a recent flurry of activity, providing overview guidance for transitional justice and truth commissions,[6] and related normative clarification.[7] Also on the market are more specific guides on aspects of transitional justice work, from archives (Peterson 2005) to memorialisation (Barsalou and Baxter 2007; Brett *et al.* 2008; Naidu 2004, 2004a). The key agents of dissemination have been a number of powerful Northern NGOs and academic centres,[8] often working with local and regional partners.[9] A proliferation of academic initiatives dedicated to the subject's study, training courses, e-mail listservs, a blizzard of commentary of various kinds, and a recently launched academic journal focusing on the topic (the *International Journal of Transitional Justice*) complete the picture.

Transitional justice has well and truly arrived. Its success raises questions such as whether effectiveness claims are backed up by evidence, and about whether transitional justice is now led by an epistemic community (an international, knowledge-based, elite professional and donor network) rather than locally rooted victim–survivor or social movements. Repeated calls for local control and adaptation should not overlook the power that an industry such as this has on the repertoire of options imagined and on donor purse strings. Some observers are sanguine about this reality:

> Although there had been some discussion within Sierra Leone about the importance of a truth commission prior to its establishment, the idea was obviously borrowed from elsewhere. It seems open to question whether Sierra Leone would have organised a truth commission had this not been prompted and encouraged by the 'international community'.
> (Schabas 2006: 39)

Maturation into an industry has been accompanied by a growing tendency to adopt holistic understandings of transitional justice. First, it is common practice now to define transitional justice extremely broadly, to include some or all of the following: criminal prosecutions, truth-telling, reparations, and institutional reform as core interventions; but also commemorative practices, educational reform, reconciliation initiatives, and more. Second, keywords are also viewed through the holistic prism. For example, much recent commentary on the peace versus justice debate – prioritising an end to violence versus prosecutions and the rule of law – seeks to move beyond a standoff between the two. It does so by arguing that justice and accountability should include judicial and non-judicial measures, and look to the future as well as to the past (criminal accountability; truth commissions; reparations; reform of the security and judicial sectors; demobilisation and integration of ex-combatants; and indigenous or community based-justice) (Hayner 2009). Similarly, peace is understood to span both negative peace (prioritising an end to violence) and positive peace (addressing the underlying causes of violence). The danger is that definitions become too broad to be meaningful. Third, in the shift from substitution to complementarity, interventions are seen in both/and more, rather than either/or, terms. While in the past it was often assumed that truth commissions would be a compromise where trials could not take place, now it is argued that the two can, and should, coexist (Roht-Arriaza and Mariezcurrena 2006). One influential framing of such holism is the 'ecology model' of social reconstruction (Fletcher and Weinstein 2002; Stover and Weinstein 2004). This approach suggests interventions at multiple levels of society – state, community, individual – and spanning fields as diverse as the rule of law and justice, security, education for democracy, economic development and reconciliation.

Such definitions usefully move beyond legal responses to include wider political and social processes, and can serve to integrate official, top-down mechanisms and unofficial, local, community or grassroots initiatives. That trade-offs are not always inherent in decision-making processes and more than one intervention can be required in circumstances where none standing alone would succeed (interventions may be mutually constitutive) are useful ways of reshuffling the transitional justice pack. Yet transitional justice is the art of imperfect solutions and difficult choices, in the context of competition for finite resources and delicate political dynamics. While we now know more about what should be done, we still know relatively little about how these objectives might be achieved. If necessary, how should interventions be prioritised so that they are sequenced over time, rather than traded off against one another in a zero-sum scenario?

Bosire (2006) in a piece with the suggestive title 'Overpromised, Underdelivered: Transitional Justice in Sub-Saharan Africa', argues that strengthening state institutions should be seen as a precondition or entry-point for successful transitional justice measures in this part of the world. Without functioning institutions little will be achieved. In transitional justice circles this domain is normally consigned to the wish-list of potential outcomes (via truth commission recommendations, for example), rather than as a necessary enabling condition. Other familiar sequencing cum trade-off challenges include the fact that perpetrators often receive benefits (amnesty; demobilisation, disarmament and reintegraion programmes) before victims, or in circumstances where victims receive nothing (prosecutions, reparations); the complex question of whether transformation precedes reconciliation or vice versa; and the role of unofficial, local interventions vis-à-vis official, top-down counterparts (laying foundations, complementing, substituting, critical engagement).

To this reservation I would add another: Should transitional justice be taking on more when it is far from clear that it can successfully achieve its original, far more modest, remit (truth, justice)? Holism both is a reaction to past shortcomings and runs the risk of reproducing them on a broader canvas. Keyword conceptualisation, for example, remains weak. While it is important to interrogate linkages between keywords, many analyses slide into a mire where justice, for example, entails pretty much everything. It is a sleight of hand to overcome what were previously seen as tensions – truth versus justice, peace versus justice – by defining the terms indistinguishably. Finally, holism is characteristic of the era of transitional justice in that while it is not unreflective, its criticisms are of the 'more work' variety; they anticipate the industry doing more, not less. In sum, the embrace of holism means that contemporary transitional justice encompasses an array of interventions (bringing in constituencies and skills beyond mainstream transitional justice and human rights); and is grappling with questions of timing, prioritisation, sequencing and interrelationships.

Finally, to understand the era of transitional justice we also need to interrogate transitional justice as a case study of the fault-lines within globalisation. Globalisation influences the manner in which ideas travel. In truth, the reach of the industry is uneven, with the majority of truth commissions having taken place in the Americas and Africa. Only one has set up shop in North Africa or the Middle East (Morocco, 2004). Recent analyses of the spread of transitional justice discourse have drawn on 'the boomerang pattern' (Keck and Sikkink 1998: 12–13) and 'spiral model' (Risse *et al.* 1999) as a feature of transnational advocacy network operations. Both models link the local and the global, with actors as diverse as NGOs, supportive states and international institutions putting pressure on recalcitrant states, notably in relation to human rights concerns. Civil society organisations and NGOs within and outside a given country are thereby instrumental in changing state behaviour and in the spread of international norms. Three examples illustrate ways in which these ideas have gained a hold in transitional justice debates.

First, the notion of the 'justice cascade' (Sikkink and Booth Walling 2006; also see Lutz and Sikkink 2001) makes the case that accountability for past human rights abuses is spreading through the increased use of trials and truth commissions. Powerful insider–outsider coalitions in Argentina have been at the forefront of innovation within this cascade. Similar processes are at work in the second example, Roht-Arriaza's (2005: 208–24) 'Pinochet effect'. The Pinochet case brought to the fore the role of diasporas and lawyers as transnational actors, and the fact that processes of accountability have been both domesticated in Chile and 'spiralled on' in the external states from where pressure came for change (for example, raising the question of Spain's own past). A third example explores the influence of the South African TRC on the Greensboro TRC in the United States. Tarrow (2005: 183–200) argues that such transmission requires diffusion, brokerage, mobilisation and certification (by authorities). Brokerage – which 'acts as a transnational hinge that communicates and adapts an external practice to new sites and situations' (190) – is highlighted as of particular importance to the spread of transitional justice norms (a specific broker cited is the International Center for Transitional Justice [ICTJ]). In all these examples, processes of political globalisation are cast in a positive light.

My argument about globalisation is of a different order. To be sure, transitional justice and truth commissions are now a strand characterising political globalisation, an inevitable part of the international call and response characterising conflict and authoritarian aftermaths. The more troubling dynamic is how they are interwoven with other strands of globalisation. Globalisation as a whole is forging transitions and democracies characterised by continuity as well as change, by structures of inequality and patterns of conflict that are reconfigured rather than brought to an end. Little wonder that there is now recognition that many transitions are stalled and without a clearly defined end-point (Carothers 2002). By focusing on political violence, civil–political rights abuses and the past to a greater extent than criminal or social violence, socio-economic rights and the present, the transitional justice tool-kit does little to challenge, for example, the impacts of neo-liberal economics and/or rising levels of violent crime and punitive responses to such crime. Limits are placed on structural change in new democracies, and within these limits the danger is that the marginalised are remarginalised. Holistic understandings of transitional justice too rarely extend to a critique of these other facets of globalisation that profoundly shape transitional realities. The question ultimately is whether transitional justice has become the conscience of transitional globalisation without troubling its essential characteristics.

Arguments

Four main arguments anchor the chapters that follow. They are rooted in but seek to extend beyond the South African experience, and suggest ways in which transitional justice and truth commissions can make a stronger contribution to structural transformation.

Conceptualising keywords

To recap, time and again for the TRC, conceptualisation was a post-hoc attempt to rationalise an existing mandate and manner of working. Weak conceptualisation of truth, justice and reconciliation still bedevils transitional justice debates. The current trend for holistic definitions often renders the terms virtually identical in their scope and interventionary ambition. This book uses the TRC as a prism through which to offer fresh, and transferable, insights into the meaning of each keyword. Coherent conceptualisation of keywords needs to inform the design of interventions, rather than following in their wake.

In the *truth* camp two claims are made. First, truth needs to be linked to genre, and in particular attempts to combine the genres of state inquiry, human rights report and official history in truth commission work and reporting. Second, there is a need to go beyond social or 'dialogue' truth and a focus on procedural liberalism to rights-based participation (Friedman 2006). Developed in, but enduring beyond, the transitional context, a culture of rights-based participation is the only way to ensure that a once-articulated voice will be twice and three times heard. The main *justice*-related argument is that the transitional moment needs an integrated justice agenda, in which backward-looking transitional justice measures mesh with criminal justice interventions focusing on the present and future. Social and criminal violence, and repressive responses to such violence, are currently relatively untroubled by transitional justice interventions. This moment is characterised by contradictions and mixed messages (amnesty for the apartheid-era killer; harsh punitive responses for the car hijacker) which undermine attempts to build respect for the rule of law. Drawing on Das and Kleinman (2002: 3–4), the chapters on *reconciliation* argue that this term entails, on the one hand, acts of public voicing from the previously marginalised and violated, folding into the broader demand for political recognition and a renegotiated citizenship. This strand of reconciliation is inextricably linked to rights-based participation. On the other hand, reconciliation requires the 'repair of relationships in the deep recesses of family, neighbourhood, and community'. Reconciliation is the work of (re)constructing relationships through enlightened processes, and is therefore embedded in everyday life.

Reimagining human rights

Here three main claims are made, each illustrating that transitional justice is, or could be, at the forefront of reimagining how we think about human rights.

First, truth commissions need to work with a broader definition of human rights. The TRC worked with a narrow, impoverished conceptualisation of human rights, thereby sidelining the different reality that could have been discovered by highlighting economic, social and cultural rights abuses and the indivisibility between these and civil–political rights. While some subsequent commissions have adopted a more inclusive approach (Peru, Sierra Leone, Timor Leste, Liberia, Kenya) much more work needs to be done on operationalising this agenda. The TRC also overlooked the range of identity positions made available by human rights discourse. It is, and has always been, a dual discourse of violence and violations (victims, perpetrators), and of idealism and just resistance (dating back to the natural rights tradition). While this second tradition was overlooked by the TRC, and is often neglected even in mainstream human rights, an affirmation of collective self-reliance, resistance and the role of the 'righteous' would tell a fuller account of the past and provide suggestive identity coordinates for reconciliation and a more unified future.

Second, hybridity – in forms of analysis, design of interventions, etc. – is a defining characteristic of more holistic transitional justice work, and is increasingly a feature of human rights practice in general as it moves into adjacent fields such as development, public health and environmental protection. As such, human rights must find productive ways to cohabit with other moral vocabularies and ways of working. Transitional justice, in forms as diverse as truth commissions and memorialisation, is informed but not completely monopolised by human rights, and as such is a driving force behind an important contemporary shift in the human rights movement.

The third way in which human rights needs to be reimagined also represents a new wave of thinking: human rights is a way of balancing law and politics, and balancing interests and weighing values, as well as making absolute claims and right-versus-wrong adjudications. Human rights provide a vocabulary for articulating, and then prioritising, the principles and demands at stake. Because of the context of compromise, transitional justice is one of the main fields in which this vision of rights is taking shape. The importance of victims' rights has come to the fore, for example, contesting a perceived emphasis on the rights of perpetrators (due process, etc.). A similar rebalancing has occurred to tackle non-state actors as human rights violators, as well as the state. While such processes are essential to a rebalancing and new politics of human rights, they do not require the abandonment of principle (for example, dealing with both sides does not mean morally equating both sides). Ignatieff (2001: 9–10) captures the balancing act:

> Human rights activism means taking sides, mobilizing constituencies powerful enough to force abusers to stop. As a consequence, effective human rights activism is bound to be partial and political. But at the same time, human rights politics is disciplined or constrained by moral universals. The role of moral universalism is not to take activists out of politics but to get

activists to discipline their partiality – their conviction that one side is right – with an equal commitment to the rights of the other side.

Engaging the past and present

Truth commissions require a more sophisticated understanding of the relationship between the past and present, continuity and change. First, government priorities quickly shift from redressing the past to building the future, and therefore a failure to engage with political concerns and volatile new policy agendas in the present (for example, relating to violent crime, poverty, race and xenophobia in South Africa) can result in instant obsolescence. Second, there is a need to more clearly link challenges in the present to structural continuities with the past. Finally, an anticipatory faculty is important because the past often affects the present not as straightforward repetition – as suggested by the cry 'never again' – but in modified, evolving ways, through complex processes of continuity and change. For example, violence in South Africa was localised, privatised and depoliticised, rather than brought to an end. In a pattern duplicated in other transitional contexts, it is clear that as political violence folds into criminal and social violence, embedded authoritarian responses from the state and society can easily become a backlash against human rights which targets criminals and the marginal poor rather than, or as well as, political opponents. More success is likely if the past's impact on the present is conceptualised beyond prevailing clichés – such as drawing a line under the past.

If truth commissions are to more fully describe the human rights legacies of the past, and fulfil their prevention ambitions, they need to engage with the past and the present, and to be more critical of the past's ongoing presence in the present. For practitioners, the past–present, continuity–change continuum requires that attention be paid to prioritising, sequencing and integrating interventions; to evolving relationships with the government; shifting patterns of violence and violation; support for and backlashes against human rights; and more.

Remaking the public sphere

This book argues that truth commissions are most importantly acts of public description (reports, public hearings) and constituency-building (through rights-based participation). It is in these two areas that commissions can have their most significant and wide-ranging influence. While remaining attentive to individuals, commissions should map the past with broad brush strokes, thereby holding up a mirror to the many and not the few and to structures of violence and not simply symptoms. Entry-points will have to be found to highlight more general patterns, but reflecting the indivisibility of rights is imperative. Documentation needs to be accompanied by dissemination. The TRC, largely through its public hearings, provides an opportunity to examine the ripple effects of a commission in the public sphere and civil society, beyond the rarefied circulations and 'fetishisation' of (often not widely read) reports (Cohen 1995) and (invariably very unevenly implemented) recommendations.[10] While public hearings may not always be possible, for example because of security concerns, a portfolio of ways is being developed by truth commissions to enhance the impacts of their public description work (ranging from popular summaries of reports to accompanying photographic exhibitions).

Moving on to participation and constituency-building, the TRC inspired a range of civil society initiatives and cultural production that mimicked, reworked and contested its methods and ethos. And yet this book argues that to really remake the public sphere, and facilitate political recognition and citizenship, requires a move beyond debate or 'dialogue' truth to rights-based participation. Such participation ideally needs to be enshrined in constitutional law, as it is in South Africa, and to extend to sensitive issues about which new dispensations are likely to remain ambiguous (human rights, economic redistribution, the rules of the political game). The TRC largely failed to create links between democratic principles and participation on the one hand and the legacies and contingencies of power on the other, in such a way that the former became an enduring challenge to the latter. A sustainable platform for marginalised voices in public decision-making constitutes the true meaning of democratic consolidation. While truth commissions alone cannot deliver this outcome, they can identify it as a priority and make a contribution to its realisation – to do so they need to rethink their interactions with civil society.

Contents

The first two chapters of the book unpack the keyword truth. Beyond the familiar strands of truth inquiry – *truth as acknowledgement, truth as justice, naming names, patterns versus individuals, amnesty for truth* – the first chapter maps a new conceptual understanding of truth: *truth as genre*. Many of the strengths and weaknesses of truth commissions can be traced to the fact that they constitute an imperfectly realised hybrid genre, comprising the state inquiry, human rights report and official history. I argue that each of the three genres carries a different objective, namely speaking truth to reconciliation (state inquiry), to power (human rights report), and to context and meta-narrative ([official] history).

Which genre comes to the fore, where, when and how, matters profoundly. State inquiries, for example, seek to legitimise the state and governmental agendas, while for the human rights report it is international human rights law that is the source of legitimacy. Which genre prevailed had implications for the degree to which the TRC critiqued the past actions of the ANC, or undermined the fragile early post-1994 consensus around political reconciliation and the Government of National Unity by critiquing all relevant parties. Further, the TRC was affected by micro dynamics within genres. An uneasy relationship between official history, academic history and public history concerning interpretation and ownership of the past, for example, shaped its work: to repair, establish and/or democratise the past?

Ultimately, the TRC failed to achieve a hybrid or synthetic coherence. Rather, genre status changed over time and through different sections of the organisation and report. An initial focus, at least within sections of the TRC, on narrative and history was overtaken midstream by an emphasis on quantitative methodology and making findings, by the investigative repertoires of the state inquiry and, in particular, human rights. The outcome of this act of colonisation by human rights, narrowly conceived (both substantively, as civil–political rights, and methodologically, as quantitative analysis), was that a decontextualised truth provided a partial critique of power. In particular, it highlighted what had already changed most (gross civil and political abuses) and not what had changed least (economic and social rights concerns). It is argued that this was not just an act of colonisation by human rights, but also an act of colonisation within human rights. Other ways of understanding human rights are available. The challenge, therefore, is how to render truth commissions generically coherent.

Nevertheless, the TRC's fourfold definition of truth and unique engagement with national and international publics (public hearings, media coverage) did challenge report and recommendation 'fetishisation' within human rights discourse. It provided possibilities for future truth conceptualisations to explore the intersection of processes, products and impacts. Given these arguments, the TRC's influence on social or 'dialogue' truth deserves special attention. Chapter 2 examines the significant degree of civil society participation in, and transparency surrounding, the work of the TRC (examples include the drafting of and lobbying around its founding legislation, the selection of commissioners, victim/survivor and mental health support structures, and policy on gender issues), but also important and revealing exceptions to this rule (policies governing amnesty, prosecutions and reparations). It suggests that the TRC provides an emblematic case study of the opportunities and challenges associated with reworking relationships between civil society and a new democratic state, within the new political culture of transition.

The TRC influenced the public sphere by shaping the values and discourse of democratic debate, thereby making a contribution to procedural liberalism. But the public sphere construed in this way should not be idealised. Significant deliberative and material inequalities remain, for example, while the influence of the media is widely recognised as a 'double-edged sword'. The need for publicity that is both comprehensive and balanced can be a challenge, with the media often proving a difficult partner in the quest for truth, justice and reconciliation. The chapter concludes with a case study of the mixed potential of social truth, exemplified by the power *and* vulnerability of testimony in a globalised public sphere. Oral testimony, in an era in which media coverage is increasingly global in reach, moves between the private and the public, the personal and the political, and between South and North. With voice comes power; the loss of control over representations in human rights reports, books, the media or elsewhere, can mark a return to powerlessness. The chapter examines TRC testimonies that took on an unanticipated and often uncomfortable public life, and responses by actors, such as victim/survivor organisations, reasserting control over their lives and stories by complementing the subaltern voice with a subaltern method.[11] Such initiatives epitomise attempts to forge a sustainable rights-based participation.

The argument, in a nutshell, is that for voice to really matter requires (1) control over voice, and its representation, interpretation and dissemination, and (2) rights-based participation. Such participation offers a means of linking official, top-down interventions with unofficial, local, community or grassroots counterparts, truth commissions and processes of democratisation, and powerful articulatory moments with more enduring forms of public decision-making. Scaling up interventions and sustainability usually requires a combination of top-down and bottom-up approaches. By not taking this route, the TRC imperilled its symbolic and procedural impacts. To take this route, participation, and the preconditions for participation, need to be prioritised in both truth commission activities and their recommendations.

Debates about transitional justice are dominated by past legacies. Chapters 3 and 4 argue that policies for, and understandings of, justice in the transitional era must engage with both the past *and* the present, transitional justice *and* criminal justice.

Chapter 3 examines two facets of the TRC's interaction with justice. First, it explores the TRC's complex relations with the criminal justice system (the theory and practice of the amnesty provision and prosecutions; day-to-day operations; mutual critique and competition as well as cooperation and support). Second, it analyses the TRC's own conceptualisations and reconceptualisations of justice. The TRC sought to address the critique that the amnesty provision, although individualised and conditional, still sanctioned impunity, largely by proposing social and restorative justice as alternatives to retributive justice. But, again, these were post-hoc rationalisations for an amnesty provision forged as part of a negotiated, political compromise, rather than forms of justice that seriously informed the amnesty policy and design of the TRC. A window of opportunity for rethinking understandings of justice during the transitional moment was not exploited to the full as the components of the TRC's conversation with justice failed to achieve conceptual coherence or any real weight. Debates about justice have proliferated, but with the TRC as a minor voice on the margins. A further reason for this is that the past as past has been overwhelmed by the past in the present, and in particular rising levels of criminal and social violence.

Chapter 4 moves from a consideration of 'justice past' to engage with 'justice present'. Both violence itself and responses to it are heavily informed by the past. In a South African context, Simpson (2001, 2002, 2004) has most cogently argued that the evaluation of transitional justice mechanisms such as the TRC must be placed in the context of the linked challenges posed by justice in transition and violence in transition. Patterns of violence and social conflict are reconfigured rather than being brought to an end. Violent crime that may appear new is often in reality rooted in ongoing experiences of social marginalisation, political exclusion and economic exploitation. By focusing on political violence the TRC cleansed the past, on both sides of the political divide, of antisocial elements; overlooked the criminalisation of politics and a politicisation of crime under apartheid; and dramatically reduced its potential impact on the present and ongoing violence and human rights concerns. Separating crime and politics requires the ability, beyond crime and violence, to secure influence, access status, derive subsistence and resolve disputes in civil society, public institutions and political processes. Truth commissions need to contribute to this parting of the ways rather than assume or celebrate its completion.

The chapter identifies patterns of continuity and change in transitional violence in South Africa (organised crime, vigilantism, warlords, ex-combatants, taxi violence), drawing on rich empirical research conducted by the Centre for the Study of Violence and Reconciliation (CSVR); and similar patterns in progressive and more repressive state and public responses to crime (instrumental authoritarianism, legal fetishism, paralegality, restorative justice), drawing on the work of the International Council on Human Rights Policy (2003) and Panizza (1995). Crime during transition assumes importance as a genuine problem, through public perceptions of crime and criminality, and in a symbolic or metaphorical guise. It becomes a key indicator of political dissatisfaction that can threaten the deepening of democracy and the entrenchment of human rights protections. Often, resorting to hard-line measures not only harks back to the past but also takes the form of a state and societal backlash against human rights. Such policies sit uneasily with amnesty provisions for past human rights abuses. In many countries, including South Africa, policies addressing transitional crime combine more liberal measures involving state and civil society collaboration (community policing, police training, external oversight mechanisms, restorative justice projects) and hard-line, non-consultative measures. This again suggests new opportunities and challenges for civil society–state relations, as roles are renegotiated in a dynamic policy environment. A key tension during transitions, therefore, is a struggle over the balance between more authoritarian and more progressive responses to crime and violence. Truth commissions must enter this debate. The argument of the two justice-based chapters, in short, is that a coherent approach to justice, past *and* present, is needed to reduce policy contradictions and perceptions of injustice, and rebuild faith in the rule of law while deepening democracy.

Chapters 5 and 6 focus on the last of the keyword triumvirate: reconciliation. None of the other keywords has been the subject of quite so much undeserved hype or castigation as reconciliation. It has a role to play, but a modest one. The first of these chapters explores the links between truth-telling and reconciliation. It analyses the TRC's conceptualisation of reconciliation (privileging individual or interpersonal and national reconciliation), and assumptions underpinning, as well as criticisms of, the speaking truth to reconciliation paradigm. The chapter argues that a truth template shaped the debates launched by the TRC in this arena. The truth template framed a debate, consisting of five interrelated strands. (1) Life stories were structured around instances of, and responses to, violence, but with diverging definitions and understandings of violence and violation (gross human rights abuse or structural violence, focusing on the apartheid era or a longer history of colonisation and dispossession?). (2) Past and present coexisted; and (3) the private, secret and censored, and the public, similarly, were characterised by a troubled coexistence rather than the new sweeping away the old. (4) The new order's speaking truth to reconciliation cohabited with a more contestual paradigm of speaking truth to power. Both voices are essential to longer-term demands for political recognition and citizenship from the marginalised. (5) Contests emerged over post-apartheid and post-TRC identities and self-identification (victim or survivor; singular or multiple identities; the direction and dynamics of identity transformation). A privileging of the victim within truth-telling, and the rise of cultures of victimhood, are analysed as an example of a truth template debate.

Drawing on this conceptual framework, the chapter documents the many sites of truth-telling that have engaged with the truth template, in turn appropriating, modifying and critiquing the notion of speaking truth to reconciliation. Support groups, memorialisation and public culture in the form of novels are marshalled as case studies and explored in depth. The TRC's success has been to inspire and legitimise these sites that have the potential to assist the TRC in achieving some of its goals, but also to nurture counter-discourses.

Chapter 6 moves on to the second component of reconciliation: relationships. The first section of the chapter formulates a definition of reconciliation as the work of (re)constructing relationships through enlightened processes. The ultimate goal is a series of reorientations that can only be achieved in the thick textures of everyday life: reorientations from the extraordinary, spectacular and individual to the ordinary and social process; from binary to multidimensional identities and ways of viewing the world; from suffering to living; from the past (rediscovery) to the present and future (creation); and, finally, towards a preparedness to embrace risk. The often overlooked risk of reconciliation is premised on costly signalling between parties, embracing openings on to an unpredictable future, and the necessity of transformative change. Apology and forgiveness are discussed as one example of the risk hypothesis.

The second half of the chapter applies this theory of reconciliation to two case studies, selected to explore structural relationships at community and economic levels, i.e. levels largely neglected by the TRC. Community reconciliation is investigated through the case study of a restorative justice mediation project undertaken by CSVR in Bonteheuwel, Cape Town. This is of interest because it illuminates the potential of interventions focusing on process, relationships and the everyday, highlights the still fractured nature of many post-apartheid communities (notably due to allegations of informing, poverty and crime), and both adopts and critiques the restorative justice agenda of the TRC. Enforced coexistence is not a characteristic of the final case study, economic reconciliation, and as such it poses particular challenges for relational reconciliation. Even here I argue that if the necessary will exists, an innovative mapping of relationships, responsibilities and appropriate channels of redress have a contribution to make to economic reconciliation and redistribution. Ultimately, this requires acknowledgement of broad-based responsibility and similarly framed redistribution and redress. Economic reconciliation faces formidable obstacles: the global meta-discourses that shape post-conflict continuity and change (neo-liberalism, a focus on civil and political rights, the liberal peace); the ANC's market-led economic policies and the inequalities still scarring South Africa; and the TRC's neglect of socio-economic rights alongside its troubled reparations policy. The chapter suggests both why and how economic and social rights should be addressed in transitional contexts, specifically by truth commissions. Land reform and separation policies are explored to chart the dangers and opportunities in more detail. The warning, ultimately, is a stark one: either poverty is relational, a shared responsibility, or it will become the subject of political struggles and adversarial relationships.

By way of conclusion, I return to the main arguments developed in the book by posing four questions for the era of transitional justice and human rights. The questions are: (1) Do human rights 'occupy the field of emancipatory possibility' (Kennedy 2002: 108)? (2) Is there a danger of co-option, and if so by what or whom? (3) Is too much or too little being attempted? And (4) Can the prioritisation/sequencing and interlinking of interventions be mapped on to patterns of continuity and change in transitional societies?

Notes

1 Insights into the extent to which the TRC's methodology was improvised are not hard to find. For example, references are made to numerous changes to the statement form or protocol for victims (TRC 1998, Vol. 1: 138–39), and to slowly emerging and changing definitions, for example as to what constituted a gross violation of human rights or who would be classified as a victim (Buur 2001: 166–67; 2003: 151–53). International lessons-learning processes mean there is less reason now for truth commissions to falter in this way, or at least to quite this extent.

2 The volume edited by Chapman and van der Merwe uses a range of qualitative and quantitative methodologies, including transcript analysis from hearings, to evaluate the TRC process and specifically its impact on victims and survivors. Gibson draws on public opinion surveys, exploring the TRC's impact on all South Africans, to test the hypothesis that truth leads to reconciliation, with the latter defined as interracial reconciliation, political tolerance, support for the principles of human rights and the legitimacy of political institutions. The former study is significantly more critical than the latter. Sarkin's work constitutes the most comprehensive available analysis of the TRC's amnesty process and transcripts. Two shorter evaluations are worth mentioning, Simpson (2002) and Stanley (2001), as they situate their assessments of the TRC in a wider context, notably the high levels of social and criminal violence and enduring poverty and inequality of the transitional present.

3 The International Center for Transitional Justice (ICTJ), often in collaboration with the Human Rights Center at the University of California, Berkeley, has been involved in a number of such surveys: Iraq 2004; Northern Uganda 2005 and 2007; Aceh, Indonesia 2008; Nepal 2008; Eastern Democratic Republic of Congo 2008 – and the resulting publications are available on its website: www.ictj.org. Also see the Afghanistan Independent Human Rights Commission (2005); Lundy and McGovern (2006), on Northern Ireland; Office of the United Nations High Commissioner of Human Rights (OHCHR) (2007), on Northern Uganda; and Stover and Weinstein (2004), on Rwanda and the former Yugoslavia. Snapshots of public attitudes are useful but also, given the volatility of political circumstances and attitudes in transitional contexts, somewhat limited. Among the most compelling research in this field is Penal Reform International's (PRI's) longitudinal research on the *gacaca* courts in Rwanda (*gacaca* courts are a significantly modified, local conflict resolution mechanism mobilised by the Rwandan government to help process the enormous number of post-1994 genocide suspects). Since 2002, this research has provided insights into the evolution of a unique transitional justice intervention, and public attitudes to the intervention; see www.penalreform.org/

4 Fletcher *et al.* (2009: 169) write: 'Certainly, the claims by advocates that transitional justice responses lead to peace and reconciliation appear at this point to represent hopes for a happy ending and not evidence-based policies on which the international community can count.' Four further points about the dark art of evaluation require attention. First, evaluation tools are likely to draw on, but modify, established models in fields like development, where monitoring and evaluation methodologies are far more advanced than they are in human rights. Second, evaluation raises its own challenges, from the danger of it becoming a technical, quantitative checklist rather than a more qualitative and political engagement with process and context, to whether to prioritise process or outcomes. Third, timing matters. Certain impacts register quickly, while others emerge slowly over time. Snapshot evaluations, like snapshot analyses of public attitudes, are only a first step; longitudinal surveys are needed. Finally, the empirically grounded transitional justice research agenda is currently damagingly skewed; people are much more likely to be asked what they would like from transitional justice than what they have received from it. This imbalance needs to be rectified.

5 The TRC website is now housed on the website of the Department of Justice and Constitutional Development: www.doj.gov.za/trc

6 The Rule of Law and Transitional Justice in Conflict and Post-Conflict Societies, Report of the Secretary General, UN Doc. S/2004/616, August 2004; and the OHCHR has produced a series of rule-of-law tools for post-conflict states, covering interventions such as truth commissions, prosecution initiatives, vetting and reparations. These are available at www.ohchr.org. Also see Amnesty International's *Truth, Justice and Reparation: Establishing an Effective Truth Commission* (Amnesty International 2007).

7 Including, notably, the Updated Set of Principles for the Protection and Promotion of Human Rights through Action to Combat Impunity, UN Doc. E/CN.4/2005/102/Add.1, February 2005; and the Basic Principles and Guidelines on the Right to a Remedy and Reparation for Victims of Gross Violations of International Human Rights Law and Serious Violations of International Humanitarian Law, adopted and proclaimed by UN General Assembly resolution 60/147 of 16 December 2005, UN Doc. A/RES/60/147.

8 The international hub for such actors is the United States, with the International Center for Transitional Justice (ICTJ), the Human Rights Center at the University of California, Berkeley, the United States Institute of Peace (USIP) and the American Association for the Advancement of Science (AAAS) to the fore. ICTJ, for example, provided organisational support to, and the staff who wrote, several of the OHCHR rule-of-law tools, and have themselves produced many similar guides.

9 Such as the Centre for the Study of Violence and Reconciliation (CSVR) in South Africa.
10 Recommendations are often hastily conceived, address a buffet of concerns based on very uneven expertise, and struggle to insert themselves into a rapidly changing policy environment. The challenges facing recommendations are likely to increase if truth commissions expand their remit into economic, social and cultural rights. As a result, recommendations should (1) secure the truth commission's own legacy (archives, etc.); (2) restate broad human rights and social justice principles at a time when they may be under siege; and (3) anticipate the challenges of the future and the ways in which the past will endure into the medium- and long-term future. Cross-referencing the recommendations of others should also be emphasised, as truth commissions are one voice in the chorus of transitional human rights debates (UN treaty bodies, regional human rights courts, local and international NGOs) and should position themselves as such.
11 By using the term 'subaltern' I mean to prioritise the agency of the oppressed and marginalised, notably as makers and recorders of history.

Chapter 1

Truth as genre

Transitional truths

Truth commissions contain various different but interlinking strands of truth inquiry, with similarly configured implications for methods, objectives and prioritised interests. Several of these strands are briefly detailed in the first section of this chapter – *truth as acknowledgement, truth as justice, naming names, patterns vs individuals, amnesty for truth*. Others are dealt with in later chapters (*truth and reconciliation* in Chapter 5; *apology as truth* in Chapter 6). The main subject of this chapter, however, is an attempt to go beyond these insights by mapping a new conceptual understanding of truth – *truth as genre*. Truth as genre provides a means of acknowledging and interrogating truth commission work across diverse methods, objectives and interests. Many of the strengths and weaknesses of official truth commissions can be traced to the fact that they constitute an imperfectly realised hybrid genre, spanning the state inquiry, human rights report and official history.

One of the most frequently cited conceptualisations of truth is *truth as acknowledgement*. The important distinction between knowledge (factual truth) and acknowledgement, attributed to Thomas Nagel (Aspen Institute 1989), is based on the premise that although certain truths may already be widely known they have often previously been officially denied or rationalised. There is value, therefore, both in establishing factual knowledge and in having knowledge sanctioned as official truth. Such acknowledgement affirms the reality of painful experience. It also reconfigures unequal and unaccountable relations of power as the state owns responsibility for its actions (albeit often under a different government), thereby healing the rift between private and social memory on the one hand and official denial and lies on the other.

A distinction can usefully be made between official acknowledgement (by the government of the day) and public acknowledgement (the formation of a more shared collective or societal memory of the past). To the extent that the TRC helped forge a greater consensus about certain broad truths – apartheid was a crime against humanity; both the apartheid state and its opponents committed abuses – it can be argued that it also helped to create a stronger collective memory and public acknowledgement of the past (Gibson 2004: 68–116, 156–66). Asking rather more of acknowledgement, Cohen (1995: 39–56) argues that human rights information-work has been more geared to transforming ignorance into knowledge than to thinking about transforming knowledge into acknowledgement. The desired response is surely for knowledge to be publicly acknowledged *and* acted upon (also see Cohen 2001: 222–77). The TRC was less successful in achieving acknowledgement in this fuller sense.

While truth commissions are often understood to sacrifice justice for truth, there are also a plethora of claims that truth, as acknowledgement or otherwise, constitutes (1) a stepping-stone towards greater justice, and (2) a form of justice (*truth as justice*).

Truth commissions can facilitate justice and help build the rule of law in various ways. Commissions have forwarded case files to prosecutors or the courts and provided evidence to support court proceedings (notably in the trials of leaders of the former military juntas in Argentina, to establish the identity of perpetrators through investigations in Chile, and at the international level in the charges brought against General Pinochet).[1] In 1998, the TRC handed a list of more than 300 names to the National Prosecuting Authority (NPA), requesting further investigations with a view to prosecution. Commissions have also investigated judicial complicity in abuse, and recommended sanctions against perpetrators (including prosecutions), reparations for victims/survivors and judicial reform (Hayner 2002: 86–106). Public truth-telling in hearings and reports can marshal the naming of perpetrators as a modest form of censure and as the basis of further possible judicial and non-judicial action. Truth in these guises can be construed as countering injustice, if in somewhat hushed tones.

A second argument is that truth intersects with justice most powerfully in transitional contexts by contributing to a public debate about the nature of justice, moving thinking out of the criminal justice/retributive trenches and on to suggestive, new terrain (see Chapters 3 and 4). Phelps writes of the TRC:

> the hearings were a public enactment of a radical kind of justice, justice that returns dignity to those who have been victimized; justice that gives back the power to speak in one's own words and to shape the experience of violence into a coherent story of one's own, thereby allowing for a renewed (or new) sense of autonomy and sense of control; justice that allows victims, in hearing stories from other victims, to locate their personal stories in a larger cultural story; justice that corrects the erroneous message communicated by the system of apartheid – that these people of color are unworthy – the message corrected not in the official language and setting of the legal system, but in public space that belongs to the people.
>
> (Phelps 2004: 111, see 52–128)

More concretely, consider the following quote about truth and justice from Irene Mxinwa, mother of one of the Guguletu Seven, who were killed in a police ambush in Guguletu, Cape Town, in March 1986. Here she is talking about her experience of testifying at a Human Rights Violations (HRV) hearing:

> [The TRC] created a safe environment where we can actually feel that we are human beings and we have dignity, we have a name, we have a face ... The kind of questions they put to us were really helpful and helping questions, so that we can be able to remember our story and if we make a mistake they wouldn't become impatient with you ... [T]he way the hearings were conducted and the way that the truth came out, you could actually see and feel justice.
> (Interview 30/7/1998)

Justice can be forged in properly constituted processes of change; in this case truth-telling, in and of itself, constituted a form of justice. This lesson needs to be writ large in transitional justice handbooks: how things are done (processes) matters as much as more conventional objectives (outcomes). Further, victim/survivor conceptualisations of keywords can resonate with the holistic definitions outlined in the introduction.

A further window on the truth as justice paradigm is *naming names* (Hayner 2002: 107–32). Truth commissions have adopted different, and often highly contested, policies on naming perpetrators, with some choosing to name (El Salvador, South Africa, Sierra Leone) but the majority not. The issue raises questions about what kind of procedures and methodologies truth commissions should adopt.

Formal naming, usually in reports, constitutes a finding of moral or political responsibility, not a legal judgment of guilt, and it is generally agreed that the lesser punishment of naming, possibly bringing with it a degree of public shaming and stigma, requires fewer due process protections. Nevertheless, naming pits the due process rights of alleged perpetrators against the right to truth of victims and survivors. How can the correct rights balance be struck? Other factors, of course, influence policies on naming, including mandate specifications; political pressures and possible impacts on a fragile peace; security and witness/perpetrator safety considerations; and the fact that the profile of those named can appear arbitrary. The outcome of naming can be negative, as in El Salvador where a blanket amnesty followed swiftly in the wake of the commission's report. Naming, in short, entails a balancing of, but not a moral equivalence between, victim/survivor and perpetrator rights, and needs to be a politically informed, strategic decision (is it likely to be effective?) as well as a moral one (is it the right thing to do?).

The South African TRC took the already complex issue of naming into new territory (du Toit 1999; Sarkin 1996, 2004: 92–97; TRC 1998, Vol. 1: 90–92), partly because hearings, crucially its victim hearings, were public and widely covered by the media, but also because it combined hearings with both the making of findings in its report and an amnesty process.[2] Names were cited in all these settings. Several court cases clarified the due process or procedural rules of the TRC (and specifically the meaning of Section 30 of the Promotion of National Unity and Reconciliation Act [No. 34 of 1995]), ultimately ensuring that the hearings and the final report became bogged down in a hugely time- and resource-intensive exercise of providing those to be named with reasonable prior notice and sufficient information to enable them to make representations and respond. In both arenas naming was curtailed as a result. Caught between competing demands – victim/survivor versus perpetrator rights; due process requirements, a mandate to make findings, reporting functions and therapeutic goals – the TRC struggled to find a coherent policy response to this issue that adequately respected the centrality of victims/survivors in its work.

Before leaving the issue of naming, one final, often overlooked point needs to be made. That is the importance of naming both victims/survivors *and* perpetrators in human rights documentation, where information and security concerns allow. While neither form of naming is done widely or consistently, as Bronkhorst (1998) notes, the potential implications of rectifying this situation are significant:

> If human rights organisations produce extensive or exhaustive lists of victims for each situation, they stress the principle that each individual victim is a life as valuable as that of any other person. In naming the names of perpetrators, they render individuals accountable for crimes committed, instead of sketching only the more elusive patterns of violations.
> (Bronkhorst 1998: 472)

The TRC report's incomplete list of victim names (TRC 1998, Vol. 5: 26–107) and scattered, disconnected references to victims in its various volumes were later complemented by a special volume dedicated to victims (TRC 2002, Vol. 7). This volume names and features short summary findings for the 22,025 people classified as victims by the TRC. Despite multiple challenges (omissions, truncation, formalisation) the naming of victims and the reclamation of a space for their stories can be seen as a form of acknowledgement – even if its impact was diminished by the fact that plans to send each named victim a copy of this report have not been realised. Victim recognition and self-recognition, facilitated by naming, direct quotations and life summaries, holds out the powerful promise that some at least will be 'mended by the mention' (Weschler 1990: 74).

The privileging of individual names and stories can clash with an emphasis on investigating patterns of abuse (*patterns vs individuals*). It is the highlighting of patterns, providing an authoritative account of the abuses of a particular era or regime (also called the 'global' truth), that is widely seen as a key role of truth commissions, and one that sets commissions apart from trials.

An article by Chapman and Ball (2001) takes a strong position on where truth commission priorities should lie (also see Chapman and Ball 2008). They state:

> it is our view that truth commissions are far better suited to pursue what we have termed 'macro-truth', the assessment of contexts, causes, and patterns

of human rights violations, than 'micro-truth' dealing with the specifics of particular events, cases, and people.

(Chapman and Ball 2001: 41)

The authors are critical of the TRC for focusing too much on the latter and too little on the former. They, and others, applaud the Guatemalan Commission for Historical Clarification (CEH) for its greater success at establishing macro-truths, even arguing that a mandate prohibiting it from naming perpetrators, although widely criticised, became a strength because it encouraged the CEH to examine broader issues such as the institutions and social structures that fostered violence (13). A number of claims are made by Chapman and Ball to support their argument: it is the big picture that is often most incomplete and victims also want systemic truths; commissions are not particularly good at investigating individual cases; micro-truths should mainly be left to the courts; commissions should prioritise the objective over the subjective dimensions of truth, outcomes (reports) over process (hearings); and responsibility should be attributed at the macro level too, focusing on institutions, parties, structures, policies, ideologies and patterns of abuse (41–43).

It is the case, as the TRC illustrated, that truth commissions are ill equipped to investigate potentially thousands of individual victim/survivor or perpetrator cases. The TRC's investigation unit, for example, predominantly provided corroboration rather than new information for victims/survivors. Pigou (2002: 37) states that probably over 90 per cent of people who appeared before the TRC did not receive meaningful new information about their cases. This was not simply a resource question: greater priority was given to making perpetrator findings and to the amnesty process. If investigations and reports may well in the main have to resort to illustrative or representative examples – 'window cases' in the TRC's jargon – to highlight patterns or important events, ways can also be found to name names, and summarise and acknowledge each and every individual victim/survivor story (see TRC 2002, Vol. 7).

The focus on patterns of abuse clearly matters, but it is also important to be honest about what a privileging of patterns means. To leave individual cases to the courts means that for the overwhelming majority nothing further will happen. To conclude, after outlining the argument detailed above, that findings should be 'victim-centered, telling the story from their point of view and validating their experiences' (Chapman and Ball 2001: 43) is somewhat disingenuous. Many victims/survivors want information about or acknowledgement of their particular experiences; their truths are particular truths. Others yearn to get beyond 'bad apple' exculpations to situate their experiences within broader policies of abuse. Both levels of analysis, in short, are necessary. The methodological challenge of synthesis spans the genres that are the subject of analysis in this chapter – state inquiry, human rights report, official history – and indeed the social sciences as a whole: how to integrate, while giving appropriate attention to, individual experiences *and* broader patterns alongside structural concern?

One of the unique features of the TRC was that it placed an amnesty process within the remit of a truth commission, and sought to link amnesty to the wider project of truth-telling and truth-gathering by making full disclosure one of the conditions for amnesty (*amnesty for truth*). Truth commissions, and other mechanisms, set up after the TRC have also experimented with amnesty for truth provisions. In Timor Leste, the CAVR (Commission for Reception, Truth and Reconciliation), through its Community Reconciliation Process, included a procedure enabling immunity from criminal and civil liability for less serious crimes, contingent upon factors such as full disclosure, a public apology, and fulfilling the terms of a Community Reconciliation Agreement (Burgess 2006). The Liberian TRC could recommend amnesty for perpetrators of, and accomplices in, less serious crimes if certain conditions were met, including full disclosure and remorse, while in Colombia under the Justice and Peace Law members of illegal armed groups who agree to demobilise are offered reduced sentences in exchange for confessions about human rights violations and reparations for their victims (Colombia's law is not linked to a truth commission). The Kenyan Truth Justice and Reconciliation Commission can also recommend amnesty for those who make a full disclosure about less serious and economic crimes.

A common problem for truth commissions, and truth generation, is the lack of cooperation from perpetrators (Hayner 2002: 39, 113–14). The participation of perpetrators in the South African TRC's truth-gathering was encouraged by a twin strategy, the carrot of amnesty for truth and the stick of potential prosecutions and civil claims (Sarkin 2004).[3] Given the impossibility of comprehensive prosecutions, such an amnesty provision may well have been the only available route to truth for many. Amnesty applications provided insights into particular events, and the roles, structures, modes of operation and links between key perpetrator groups and institutions, as well as perpetrator perspectives and motives, thereby helping to frame preventive recommendations. They were at the forefront of resolving killings and 'disappearance' cases and, therefore, exhumations; and even cracked complex killings resulting from security force infiltration of the liberation movements.[4]

However, the amnesty for truth equation also faced a range of challenges, which can be summarised as institutional problems, procedural shortcomings and the partiality of amnesty's truth.[5] Institutional problems arose from the fact that the Amnesty Committee was within but also one step removed from the TRC – insisting on 'an "arm's length" relationship' (TRC 2003, Vol. 6: 85) – composed of lawyers, and dominated by a legal ethos, a narrow, legal approach to truth and a less overt focus on victims/survivors. Institutional schisms, which influenced the methodology and goals of truth collection, and poor information flows between different parts of the Commission, hampered coherent truth collection.

The truth dividend was also diminished by a range of procedural issues (Sarkin 2004; interview 11/4/2005). The designated track of decision-making (the more numerous and cursory in chambers or administrative decisions dismissing cases that did not meet the formal conditions for amnesty and granting amnesty in less serious cases; or public amnesty hearings in cases involving gross violations of human rights); weak investigative capacity; uneven legal representation; the presence or otherwise of victims at the hearings; a narrow focus on incidents rather than contexts, on direct perpetration rather than its indirect counterpart (giving orders, devising policy); and decisions generally lacking explanation and rationale – all go to the heart of truth concerns, in particular the extent to which applicants' versions of events were fleshed out and adequately tested.

Finally, and partly as a result of institutional and procedural shortcomings, amnesty's truth was profoundly partial. Most crucially, the number of 'real' amnesty applications was in fact very small indeed (1,646). The TRC in its final, codicil report miscalculates the total number of amnesty applications (as 7,115, whereas the figure more usually cited now is 7,116), and fails to provide a comprehensive table of data (for useful tables see Coetzee 2003: 193–94; Foster *et al.* 2005: 14, 21; and Sarkin 2004: 126). A total of 293 members of the apartheid-era security forces applied for amnesty; most of these were from members of the security branch, while very few indeed (31 in total) were South African Defence Force (SADF) members (TRC 2003, Vol. 6: 182–83). Similarly, there were only 109 applications from Inkatha Freedom Party (IFP) supporters and members – the IFP is a Zulu-based party which with the support of the apartheid government fought a war against the ANC and its allies in the 1980s and into the 1990s (TRC 2003, Vol. 6: 340). Most amnesty applicants were black; the majority came from criminals in prison trying to depict their crimes as political, rather than 'real' applicants; among political protagonists, African National Congress (ANC)-aligned applicants dominated. At face value, this is a very bizarre picture of apartheid era violence and perpetration.

Three further examples are illustrative of the contours of partiality. First, few leaders applied for amnesty; foot-soldier truths predominated. Reasons for this include the impact of previous indemnity and related provisions, a misunderstanding of and political party opposition to the amnesty provision, and a simple disbelief that criminal or civil cases would ensue (see Chapter 3). Second, amnesty truth coverage was uneven, not only within and across the main players and over time, but certain abuses were virtually untouched by the amnesty process (torture, sexual abuse, apartheid state violations committed outside South Africa in neighbouring states, the disclosure of informers). The latter was dealt with on the basis of secrecy, and the confidential submission of lists of informers by the state and the ANC. Finally, applicants unsurprisingly told strategic truths, adapting their applications to meet the conditions for amnesty by privileging formal organisations rather than more informal features of violence, and political motives rather than alternatives such as racism and crime. Many felt dissatisfied with the perpetrator label; told narrowly corroborative and sanitised accounts of events; and were unapologetic for their actions: 'The much vaunted truth of amnesty hearings was often the truth of unrepentant serial murderers who still felt that their war was a just one' (R. Wilson 2001: 25).

The amnesty provision, operating under enormous resource and time pressures, uncovered important truths. But the profile of these truths, and inconsistencies on almost any given issue, impacted on the fullness of disclosure, on other facets of the TRC's mandate (was it 'victim-centred'?) and on various forms of truth detailed above (e.g. *patterns vs individuals*). Many victims/survivors failed to obtain new information here too, and much more could have been done to integrate the amnesty process into the micro and macro truth-gathering agendas of the TRC.

This briefly sketched background points to the complexity of the truth assignment for truth commissions. The absence of over-arching conceptualisations of the keyword truth is indicative both of this complexity and of the under-theorised nature of truth commission work and scholarship. This chapter outlines one such conceptualisation, truth as genre, which attempts to address inclusively a range of functions truth is expected to serve in truth commissions and transitional contexts.

Truth as genre

The truth commission report is a new genre of document in human rights and transitional politics, 'a new or incipient genre on the world scene' (Taylor 1994: 201). The truth established by official commissions is forged in the coming together of three tributary genres: the state inquiry, the human rights report and the official history. Although sharing substantially overlapping methodologies, some divergences of method and significant differences in the objectives of and interests prioritised by these tributary genres feed the potential and shortcomings of truth commissions. The main argument of this chapter is that the truth of truth commissions is undermined by a genre confusion that needs to be more rigorously understood and theorised before confusion can become complementarity and coherence.

The TRC faced this challenge in a stark form owing to the breadth of its mandate. The Promotion of National Unity and Reconciliation Act (No. 34 of 1995) outlined the truth-objectives of the TRC in the following terms in Section 3 (1) (a):

> [to establish] as complete a picture as possible of the causes, nature and extent of the gross violations of human rights which were committed during the period from 1 March 1960 to the cut-off date, including the antecedents, circumstances, factors and context of such violations, as well as the motives and perspectives of the victims and of the persons responsible for the commission of the violations, by instituting investigations and holding hearings.

The mandate required a focus on individual victims and perpetrators as well as broader patterns, and on facts informed by understanding and interpretation (motives, perspectives, antecedents, causes and context). Comments from TRC staff speak to the challenge of operationalising such a mandate:

> For as long as the nature of truth commissions remains undefined at this deeper level [of conceptual frameworks], the reports they produce are likely

to be problematic. Drawing on a variety of models and methodologies – the commission of inquiry, the courtroom, the archive, the psychological counselling room, the statistical graph, even the theatre – the South African TRC and its report satisfied neither lawyer, historian, psychologist nor statistician.

(Cherry *et al.* 2002: 34)

Taking a step back, it is useful at the outset to explore the meaning and role of 'discourse' and 'genre' as concepts. Discourse refers to the notion of 'language use in institutional, professional or more general social contexts' (Bhatia 2004: 3). By genre, I mean 'language use in a conventionalized communicative setting in order to give expression to a specific set of communicative goals of a disciplinary or social institution, which give rise to stable structural forms' by imposing constraints through language, texts, discourse and context (23). In the human rights field, Cohen (1995) describes a discourse as a 'way of talking and working', stating that a discourse has two components: knowledge ('a way of constructing and talking about a particular subject') and power ('a set of preferred strategies for policy and intervention') (3). He identifies seven human rights discourses – diplomatic, legalistic, political-philosophical, interventionist, monitoring, social scientific and the educational (3–17) – and stresses that most human rights organisations use a variety of discourses in their work. In the analysis that follows, genre is understood as a purposive communicative form, whereas discourse is a language of work and action.

If we identify, with Bhatia (2004), reporting genres as an example of a 'genre colony' (57–59), the communicative purpose of which is 'reporting on events' (81–82), the state inquiry, human rights report and official history can all be placed within such a colony. More interesting is the idea that part of colony formation is colonisation and 'a process whereby generic resources are exploited and appropriated to create hybrid' forms (58). In this process certain genres can dominate and hence colonise others. The truth commission report is such a hybrid genre – drawing on a legal, human rights-based mandate, the organisational culture and powers of a state inquiry, a broadly cross-cutting set of research methodologies, a diverse skill and personnel base (by disciplinary background, professional experience, ideological persuasion), and subject to often competing expectations (that it will give a voice to victims, identify human rights perpetrators and map related violations, legitimise the new state/government, write a revisionist national, official history). Underpinning all of these concerns are questions about colonisation, and whether a hybrid outcome has internal coherence.

State inquiry

The TRC was a state inquiry in the sense that it was established by the state, or more precisely by parliament and its enactment of the Promotion of National Unity and Reconciliation Act (No. 34 of 1995), which bestowed upon the

Commission its mandate and powers. The State President appointed the commissioners in consultation with the cabinet of a Government of National Unity, which included the National Party and Inkatha Freedom Party (IFP), following an extensive public nomination and selection process.[6] In the academic literature, state inquiries are normally understood to perform a range of political functions (Gilligan and Pratt 2004). The primary function and desired legacy is that of legitimacy, and specifically enhanced state legitimacy. In times of crisis, controversy and change, in which they are themselves usually complicit, states turn to such inquiries to educate the populace, frame public discourse and official policy, and provide closure and signal a break from the past. Periods of turmoil can be assuaged by the inquiry function of social repair. But alongside these anticipated and desired functions, as a manifestation of Falk's (2004) 'law of unintended effects', such inquiries can take on a life of their own and rub against the grain of expectation. This section examines in turn the TRC as part of a South African tradition of state inquiries, the TRC's two official regimes of truth (speaking truth to reconciliation and truth as objectivity), and how these regimes of truth both complemented one another and clashed over time.

South Africa has a long history of state inquiries, and it is revealing to place the TRC within this chronology and context. In a text that is strangely overlooked in the South African transitional justice literature, Ashforth (1990) analyses what he calls the 'Grand Tradition' of twentieth-century commission reports following inquiries into what was at the time the central feature of state and society formation in South Africa: what the ruling order termed 'the Native Question'.[7] Ashforth's (1–21) description of these commissions resonates with the already mentioned template of state inquiry functions and, perhaps more surprisingly given the markedly different political contexts, provides certain striking similarities with the TRC. For example, the commissions shared a desire to depoliticise and reconceptualise a controversial issue; a totalising approach to the problem and its solution; a mode of operation as 'reckoning schemes of legitimation'; a need to recast acceptable difference within society and thereby provide the conditions of possibility for politics; a process of state formation through and against an 'other' (previously 'the Native Question', in the new era 'the past'); and an evolution through the stages of investigation, report (initiating a dialogue between state and society) and archive (as reports enter a dialogue with history). This analysis suggests that official truth commissions could usefully be studied as one episode in an ongoing history of state inquiries within any given country.

While there is continuity within the family of state inquiries, there is also change. Ashforth contrasts the commission of inquiry with the torture chamber, as 'theatres of power' operating within different 'regimes of truth', but both serving as 'symbolic rituals aiding in the establishing and reproducing the power of modern states' (Ashforth 1990: 7). Commissions 'signify and in part establish a possibility of dialogue based on reason', while torture 'helps establish a realm of silence based on fear' (7). The TRC's public hearings, particularly for victims, epitomised the listening state, as a means of seeking to legitimise a new democratic dispensation. Yet what is unique about truth commissions, including the TRC, is that the relationship between the two theatres of power and regimes of truth is so proximate, continually played out within their hearings and activities, most powerfully through transformative processes of reversal between victim/survivor and torturer/perpetrator and between silence and voice.

Ashforth anticipates certain limitations of the TRC when he describes commission reports as representing 'the state speaking the "truth" about itself; a "truth" which frequently reveals the limits of the possible within a particular structure of state' (Ashforth 1990: 6). An endnote continues: 'The political essence of these limits concerns the question of who may speak (and in what ways) within an authoritatively recognized claim to be heard'. Commissions of inquiry through their authorisation of an official voice open up but also close off avenues for speech and dialogue. The 'limits of the possible' are likely to be less constrained in transitions characterised by regime change (South Africa) than in those with regime continuity (e.g. on public inquiries in Northern Ireland, see Hegarty 2003; and Rolston and Scraton 2005). Even in the former cases, and in processes intended to give voice to the previously voiceless, there are those who may not be heard as the state speaks the truth about itself.

Much of the literature on state inquiries, including Ashcroft's valuable contribution, is saturated with Foucault's insights on the institutional production of truth and power:

> Each society has its regime of truth, its 'general politics' of truth: that is, the types of discourse which it accepts and makes function as truth; the mechanisms and instances which enable one to distinguish true and false statements, the means by which each is sanctioned; the techniques and procedures accorded value in the acquisition of truth; the status of those who are charged with saying what counts as truth.
>
> (Foucault 1991: 73)

Post-apartheid South Africa developed a new official regime of truth: speaking truth to reconciliation became a privileged discourse and the TRC, for a time, was the primary site of production and sanction. Speaking truth to reconciliation, in short, was grounded in the provision of an officially sanctioned testimonial space, predominantly for victims of human rights violations. This space was both framed in a discourse of forgiveness, catharsis and healing, and linked to a broader nation-building project. Speaking truth to reconciliation, however, coexisted with a second regime of truth characteristic of the state inquiry: truth as objectivity.

If 'truth as objectivity' is the state inquiry's paradigmatic regime of truth and ideology of legitimation (Mongia 2004: 751), then the inquiry can be understood as a mechanism and set of rules, procedures, discourses and personnel generating a sense of objectivity. This outcome is forged through various modalities, such as the methodologies established for the production of truth, the use of expert knowledge, the selection of a broadly representative range of commission members,[8] and often considerable powers (notably, for the TRC, strong powers to subpoena witnesses, and of search and seizure). This regime of truth is evident in inquiry processes and products. Augmented by an official status and sanctioned to make (usually non-binding) recommendations, the state inquiry speaks truth with power.

Drawing the various strands of this analysis together, we can conclude that the state inquiry both uncovers and constitutes the truth; and like all truth commissions, the TRC described, investigated and produced the past (Mongia 2004: 752). The TRC's particular production of truth was governed by its interpretation of what constituted gross violations of human rights, a preference for even-handedness over partisanship, and so on. While such framing was wrapped in the cloak of objectivity and impartiality through reference to founding Acts, mandates, methodologies, human rights law and the need for balance, it also spoke to the desired objective of truth serving power, in this instance speaking truth to reconciliation. In this way the TRC's two regimes of truth were often marshalled to serve the same end.

If state inquiries are a form of 'politics by other means', political agendas shape inquiry truths in complex ways. A common criticism levelled at the TRC is that when truth and reconciliation, or truth as objectivity and speaking truth to reconciliation, clashed, the TRC frequently prioritised the latter for essentially political reasons. In cases where the TRC stepped back from assertively investigating the truth, the implications need to be unpacked carefully. The TRC was accused by the National Party, the IFP and other opponents, of a pro-ANC bias (Jeffery 1999). Specific truth-related allegations include that it failed to adequately investigate certain ANC human rights abuses (refusing, for example, to hold specific public hearings on abuses in the ANC camps in Angola), and was partisan in some of its findings. To the extent that these allegations are true, the TRC as a state inquiry sacrificed truth for party political or governmental legitimacy, with its activities serving as little more than an attempt to entrench the ANC's power (reconciling the ANC with power).

A further charge of truth-timidity is that the TRC failed to assertively use its powers of subpoena, search and seizure. Although there were some politically sensitive uses of these powers – the subpoena of former President P. W. Botha, for example – a reluctance to rock the political boat in this arena applied across the political spectrum. Most strikingly, the TRC did not subpoena Chief Buthelezi, leader of the IFP but also serving Minister of Home Affairs, despite the fact that his party was soaked in apartheid-era blood; and did not fully use its search and seizure powers to access documents from parties ranging from the former South African Defence Force (SADF) to the ANC (Cherry *et al.* 2002: 25–27, 30). As a result, diverse actors were protected by partial truths and managed delegitimisation. This second strategy coincided with ANC priorities to the extent that a broader-based reconciliation mandate protected those constituencies considered important to securing a peaceful transition to democracy and the consolidation of the new post-apartheid state. But the outcomes for the ANC could be ambiguous, as when, much to its chagrin Richard Wilson (2001: 62–73) argues, the TRC in its 1998 report condemned it more categorically than the apartheid state and IFP for the political violence between 1990 and 1994, ironically in part because it was more cooperative and open in the search for the truth.

Complex truths are inevitable because commission objectives extend well beyond truth-gathering, and may include strengthening the government of the day, fostering democracy and state institutions more broadly, and various accommodations and sleights of hand seen as necessary to keep the peace. A major arena of political contention for the TRC was in deciding when to compromise an aspect of its own legitimacy (truth as objectivity) for its broader mandate of legitimising the new South Africa, narrowly or broadly defined, by massaging truth for other objectives such as reconciliation. Where the TRC rubbed against the grain of expectation, however, was in breaking down this latter legitimacy mandate. While commentators such as R. Wilson (2001) argue that the TRC's role encompassed a wide-ranging legitimacy agenda – key state institutions such as the criminal justice system, human rights, the ANC, the state, reconciliation and nation-building – this chapter argues that the TRC found that these objectives could not all always be pursued successfully or simultaneously. On occasion, for example, the ANC was criticised and delegitimised, and arguably national unity and reconciliation were promoted at its expense. It is also important to note that the ANC's ownership of the speaking truth to reconciliation paradigm changed over time, diminishing after the Government of National Unity collapsed in 1996 and more particularly when Mandela passed the presidential baton on to Mbeki in 1999 (Krog 1998: 109–13). A similar argument can be made for the ANC's ownership of the TRC, which came to be despised by many within the party's ranks.[9]

The use of a state inquiry for the purpose of reconciliation is noteworthy, both for its idealism and for its 'unintended effects': the manner in which that idealism at times, and over time, unravelled. Thus a difficult balancing act between truth, reconciliation and politics was the interpretive repertoire of the TRC as state inquiry.

Human rights report

> The human rights movement has given us a new vocabulary, new standards, new mechanisms and a new literary form: the human rights report … [T]his type of publication has now quietly established itself as a genre of its own. Not a journalistic report, not a peer-reviewed academic piece, different from a legal brief, not quite a non-fiction documentary, and aiming at being something other than the old-fashioned political pamphlet: it is a whole new kind of publication, with its own rules of style and presentation.
>
> (Dudai 2006: 783)

The TRC was tasked with writing a human rights report in the sense that gross human rights violations were the lens through which it viewed and represented the past. Its report has been described as 'one of the most important human rights documents of our time' (Dudai 2009: 252). Given their status as state inquiries, commissions such as the TRC can also have, or appear to have, the ear of the state. A role for human rights forged through an alliance between truth and power is understandably an intoxicating prospect for those in the human rights community.

Human rights organisations or institutions, like state inquiries, are deeply dependent on the manufacturing of legitimacy. Organisation- and institution-specific factors such as reputation and mandate are important in this regard. But more important for this analysis are the features common to all human rights actors. While one cross-cutting source of legitimacy – objectivity – allies their work with that of state inquiries, another marks a departure: human rights activists seek both to legitimise their own activities and to legitimise or delegitimise state practice with reference to international human rights law. This marks a parting of the ways with state inquiries as, rather than speaking truth with power, it often demands the more strident function of speaking truth to power, specifically state power. In short, human rights organisations and institutions work with a similar methodological legitimacy regime to state inquiries, but in this case truth as objectivity usually serves a different interpretive function. In this section two questions are posed to assess the TRC's contribution to the genre of human rights reports. First, to what extent did the TRC secure legitimacy *and* enhanced impacts beyond report 'fetishisation'? Second, how did it negotiate the challenge of speaking truth both with and to power?

Legitimacy and impacts beyond report 'fetishisation'

Interests, ideologies and judgements, including those of the author, are always part of the human rights report-writing process. In an attempt to distance itself from this reality 'the whole enterprise of reporting has generated its own styles of talking and working' (Cohen 1995: 9), with objectivity sought via established methodologies of data collection, corroboration techniques, references to legal standards and report-writing formats. Dudai (2006) memorably describes the interpretive repertoire of fact-finding with legal analysis as 'advocacy with footnotes'.

The methodological scaffolding of the state inquiry and human rights report makes use of a virtually identical set of sources and strategies. Information-gathering is based on interviews/testimony, on-site visits and written documentation – and data can come from such sources as victims and survivors, witnesses and their families, government or security force officials, and NGOs, as well as laws, legal judgments and court or medical records.[10] Reliability and corroboration are secured through the use and evaluation of direct testimony, careful questioning and cross-checking (with other sources, identifiable injuries, location descriptions). The TRC used a system of 'corroborative pointers', and the balance of probabilities as its standard of proof (TRC 1998, Vol. 1: 91–92, 139, 142–43, 164; Vol. 5: 208). There are also similarities of presentation and rhetorical style in the reports themselves. These include the use of collaborative, impersonal authorship; an emphasis on facts ('speaking for themselves') over interpretation; measured language and a transparent acknowledgement of sources; a lack of reflection on methodology, researcher subject position and research context; a legal discourse that deliberately speaks the language of the state and of power; and standardised report structures. But these elaborate forms of truth-gathering and presentation do not necessarily translate into impact.

Reporting is the main activity of many human rights organisations, and it is often seen as an end in itself and a route to human rights implementation and compliance. Cohen (1995), however, critiques a 'fetishisation' of the report by human rights NGOs as an end in itself, a focus on the report-writing process accompanied by a comparative neglect of the report's wider impacts. NGOs give too little attention to dissemination and how their information is communicated to and received by the public beyond the human rights community. Resulting problems, which resonate clearly with the TRC and truth commissions or state inquiries more generally, include an excessive faith in the power of transforming ignorance into knowledge rather than examining how knowledge is acknowledged and acted upon, and poor or non-existent evaluation.

There is a very strong element of report 'fetishisation' in the work of truth commissions and accompanying academic analysis. 'The document becomes an end in itself, an absolute value, a magical notion indeed. What is the magical role assigned here to public memory as a guarantee that what we remember will never again occur?' (Taylor 1994: 196). To provide just one example of report 'fetishisation', the Sierra Leone TRC spent 'considerably more time' writing up its report than on the operational phase of its activities. This was in part due to over-ambition. Schabas (2006: 27) continues:

> It was decided that the report should be several volumes in length, perhaps so as to match that of the South African Commission. A shorter and more succinct report would have been far more accessible to Sierra Leoneans, and yet could have covered all of the essentials.

Beyond challenges such as widespread illiteracy, such practices beg the question: who reads truth commission reports?

The short answer is that we do not know. The TRC report consists of five weighty volumes (TRC 1998) complemented by two equally voluminous stragglers, one to mark the completion of the amnesty process ('the codicil' – 2003) while the final member of the family contained the comprehensive list of victims (2002). A scattergun approach to the publishing, over a five-year period, is hardly ideal in terms of optimising impact, neither is the high price charged for the hardback editions. Allocation of the publishing contract to a private publisher meant that the report is expensive and the full text was initially only available on the internet for a limited period.[11] It has not been widely read, beyond a small set of transitional justice groupies like me.[12]

Truth commission reports have been best-sellers – for example, a shorter version of the report of Argentina's National Commission on the Disappeared (CONADEP), *Nunca Más (Never Again)*[13] – when, following a research process behind closed doors, they represent a dramatic act of first disclosure. And truth commissions have disseminated and adapted their often very long reports (12 volumes in Guatemala, nine in Peru) for different audiences and to be more media-friendly. Moderate pricing; publication of a summary of some kind (for the general public; for children and schools); translation of certain products into relevant languages; press supplements or serialisation; accompanying television broadcasts; internet access; a CD ROM or video version; an accompanying photographic record; free distribution of relevant products to libraries, schools and universities; and copies sent to each named victim's family – these are among the strategies that have been used. Dissemination of the TRC report has been inadequate. Successes (press supplements and coverage at the time of the report's publication) are outweighed by the failures (a popular summary and school version of the summary, both in all 11 official languages, have yet to see the light of day).[14] Nevertheless, a broader claim remains valid: truth commissions, while often investing heavily in a report, have also explored a range of representational forms and are at the forefront of efforts to combine such diversity with objectivity and legitimacy in human rights work.[15]

At this juncture it is important to cite two important differences between conventional human rights reports and state inquiries. First, while human rights reports generally have a short life-cycle – they make an impact immediately or not at all – state inquiries and official truth commission reports, and indeed the archives they generate, as state-sanctioned enterprises have greater potential to enter into a dialogue with history. They can feed into memorial practice, educational curricula, cultural production and ongoing academic debate. Second, public hearings are rarely used in human rights investigations but are a common feature of state inquiries, and increasingly constitute a key component of truth commission activities. Hearings, particularly those featuring victims, were central to the impacts of the TRC.

> The reality is that the testimony of a single victim relayed to the country by the media will ultimately have had more of an impact upon the national consciousness than any number of volumes of the report. The enduring memory of the Commission will be the images of pain, grief and regret conveyed relentlessly, week after week, month after month, to a public that generally remained spellbound by what it was witnessing. For other truth commissions, their final reports may have represented the crowning achievement of their work. We feel that our report takes its place humbly in

a wider range of achievements, and should not be the only or final measure of the Commission's success.

(Cherry *et al.* 2002: 35)

The TRC was one of the first truth commissions to hold public hearings. Security concerns can render such hearings impractical, but the TRC experience informed the mainstreaming of public hearings in truth commission work worldwide. These two features of the state inquiry have the potential to increase the impacts of human rights practice: hearings constituting a media and public awareness 'bit hit' in the short term, while the report is able to secure influence in the longer term.

Before getting too carried away, it is necessary to juxtapose this potential with the need to be aware of the uncomfortable historical truth that human rights and state inquiry reports, although they may spur debate, shine a spotlight on priorities for advocacy, provide a reference point for public mobilisation and have unanticipated longer-term impacts, often change less than we might hope. For example, in 2002 Hayner wrote '[t]o date, there has been no thorough review of how many of the hundreds of recommendations by truth commissions have been put in place'; less surprisingly: 'It is clear, however, that the record of implementation of truth commission recommendations has been among the weakest aspects of these commissions' (168–69). Little has changed.[16]

However, a prognosis of unread reports and unimplemented recommendations is too bleak. As we have seen, channels of dissemination have broken out of these conventional confines. The TRC's most interesting contribution to the legitimacy beyond report 'fetishisation' debate is the fourfold truth classification it provides (TRC 1998, Vol. 1: 110–14). The four foes of 'fetishisation' are factual or forensic truth (objective, corroborated evidence with regard to individuals, patterns, contexts and causes), personal and narrative truth (subjective, experiential story-telling to restore dignity), social or 'dialogue' truth (affirmative processes of inclusive participation, transparency and public debate), and healing and restorative truth (emphasising the context of human relationships and acknowledgement). After this reflective moment, the TRC's report itself largely proceeds in conventional factual truth mode, but the truth – gloriously! – was already out of the bag; or perhaps one should say liberated from the report.

Critiques of the truth categorisation have been scathing (e.g. Chapman and Ball 2001: 9–12, 34, 42; Foster *et al.* 2005: 22–24; Jeffery 1999; Posel 2002: 154–57; R. Wilson 2001: 36–38). Posel writes: 'This is a very wobbly, poorly constructed conceptual grid' (2002: 155). Many of the critiques are valid: it represents a post-hoc rationalisation for the TRC's work, both the grounds for prioritisation and the nature of interrelationships are unclear, and it arguably attempts to make sense of a broad and contradictory mandate that makes no sense. While inadequate as it stands, there is the outline here of a truth framework that goes beyond the 'fetishisation' of reports to explore the intersection of processes, products and potential impacts, short- and long-term time horizons, and qualitative and quantitative methodologies. Human rights organisations are crying out for new tools that will enhance both the impacts *and* legitimacy of their work; and for imaginative ways of revisiting classic impact-related debates (pitting strategies used for education against those for fundraising and mobilisation, contextual understanding against emotive spectacle). This analysis of the TRC and other truth commissions suggests some ways forward. For example, process (how we work) matters as much as product (what we write). Crucially, if the TRC's experience is anything to go by, the established sources of legitimacy (fact-finding, legal analysis, the report) can withstand the competition from processes and products that are more in tune with the media age (public hearings, more accessible versions of reports).

Speaking truth with and to power

The second human rights-related question requires an unpacking of official truth commissions' complex balancing act, speaking truth both with and to power, and the magnificent prospect that they may be able to do both. Initially, an analysis is needed of the fact-finding and legal analysis rubric of conventional civil–political reporting and the way in which it sidelines individual subjectivity and broader political context. Through such acts of inclusion and exclusion the parameters of truth and power and the relationship between the two are defined. Next, it is necessary to address the fact that the law and human rights are not necessarily pro-poor (consider the right to property, or who can most easily access their rights). They are Janus-faced, of power and yet a means of countering power. The TRC, by embracing the human rights paradigm, also embraced its ambivalent relationship to power. Throughout, the truth–power equation was informed by decisions beyond the TRC's control (its legislative underpinnings), the political context of transition, the potential and limitations of the discourses used (human rights), and choices made by the TRC itself (see, for example, TRC 1998, Vol. 1: 60–65).

Wilson (1997) argues that the realist and legalistic language of human rights reports serves to decontextualise and depoliticise events. A universal human rights template strips events of their individual subjective and local meanings. '[L]ife becomes text becomes genre' (146), in a way that may speak truth to power, but also privileges a liberal, universal, legal agenda over personal and local politics. More specifically, Buur (2001, 2002) and R. Wilson (2001: 33–61) critique the triumph of a particular kind of human rights discourse that colonised the work of the TRC. The legalistic, positivist and statistical methodology of the TRC led to the report's focus on forensic truth without an integrative conceptual framework or explanatory historical narrative.

In a complementary critique, Mamdani (1996, 1998, 2000) accused the TRC of establishing a narrow, diminished truth, focusing on a tiny, elite minority (individualised perpetrators and victims, state agents and political activists) rather than the majority (beneficiaries and a broader category of victims). By drawing on the analogy of Latin America, and using the prism of brutal dictatorship and gross human rights abuses, the TRC obscured what was distinctive about apartheid – violence directed at communities and population groups more than individuals, systemic socio-economic as well as political abuse, 'the colonial nature of the South African context: the link between conquest and dispossession, between racialised power and racialised privilege, between perpetrator and beneficiary' (1998: 40). While Mamdani is incorrect to categorise the TRC's constituency as an elite (political activists often kept away), he is correct that majority beneficiaries and victims were excluded.

Further truth impoverishment fostered by human rights came via the focus on political violence and motivation as opposed to criminal acts, and the tendency to see much racist violence as outside the TRC's mandate (as not linked to political organisations and conflicts but rather a matter of private belief). Victims and perpetrators often found such distinctions puzzling and irrelevant to their understandings of the conflict. The political–criminal distinction undermined the TRC's capacity to penetrate patterns of violence which merged politics and crime (examples from the 1980s and early 1990s include the state's involvement in the 'third force' and 'black on black violence'; and local Self Defence Units [SDUs], to varying degrees aligned to and controlled by the ANC) and trajectories of continuity and change in violence pre- and post-1994 (see Chapter 4). The TRC's reluctance to conceive of racism as political *per se*, and its conception of the political in largely party or organisational terms, particularly affected rural areas and resulted in the exclusion of a swathe of violent history from the TRC's narrative. Racism was largely excluded as a relevant motive in the amnesty process, with similar results.[17] The outcome of this blinkered perspective was a profoundly thin description of politics and racism (Foster *et al.* 2005: 6; Fullard 2004; Simpson 2002; R. Wilson 2001: 79–93; also see TRC 1998, Vol. 1: 84–85).

At an institutional level, the influence of this particular form of human rights came to the fore with a shift in the TRC's focus and working methods in mid-1997, from its first year's prioritisation of victim hearings and narratives, to the making of victim and, in particular, perpetrator findings and amnesty hearings. It is true to say that the whole identity and legacy of the TRC turned on this axis, which distilled its truth tensions to an essential core: 'its own dual role as a fact-finding, quasi-judicial enterprise obsessed with forensic truth and verifiable information on the one hand, and a psychologically sensitive mechanism for victim storytelling and "healing" on the other' (Simpson 2002: 237). The change encompassed a variety of interlinked and incomplete transitions: from a victim to a perpetrator focus; from hearings to findings; from public, onstage to backstage and invisible activities (Buur 2001, 2002); from testimony to text; from qualitative to quantitative methods; from the listening state to the bureaucratic state.

At the level of an individual's testimony, decontextualisation took the following route. Individual narratives were progressively dissected as data, deconstructed and reconstructed into the 'higher' grammar of human rights. The statement form or 'protocol' became 'a highly structured questionnaire' (R. Wilson 2001: 44), restructured to privilege facts over narrative; during data processing statements were broken down into discrete human rights violations (acts) and categories of persons (victims, perpetrators, witnesses); while the report, organised using broad parameters – chronology, spatial coordinates and geography, political actors, human rights abuses (du Toit 1999: 20–22) – similarly fragmented individual stories, as well as local histories, to different sections and volumes. Buur remarks: 'the memories of victims materialised first as narratives, and then, through a chain of translations, became *signs* of gross human rights violations under apartheid' (2002: 80). What is lost in such analysis is the integrity, framing and subjectivity of individual narratives, instructive ambiguity and instabilities of meaning, and local, social and political context. The flattening of context is accompanied by the flattening of language, into a 'cold', neutral, institutional prose (Cherry *et al.* 2002: 22).[18]

The weakness of human rights, narrowly construed, as an analytical tool and some of the ways in which it constructs a one-dimensional truth and past, is clear.[19] Decontextualised human rights truths remake conflicts and histories in a single image. This is a feature of human rights discourse, which under-emphasises broad political questions (apartheid *per se*) and thereby 'distort(s) a total system of domination' by looking only at certain brutal manifestations that the said system shares with many other oppressive regimes, e.g. torture (Dudai 2009: 257). Within the TRC, human rights discourses diminished individual subjectivities and political contexts, and as a result a decontextualised truth was spoken to an analytically impoverished and incomplete notion of (political) power. This truth–power nexus is problematic not only because it smothers the individual and the local and warps history within a universal register, but also because it highlights apartheid's symptoms (torture, killings) rather than its structural violence and enduring legacies (racism, inequality, violent crime). It also frames narrow understandings of accountability and responsibility.

Nevertheless, this human rights lens is not without its merits. One strength of the exclusion of context from human rights reports is that no amount of contextual thickness should be used to justify the commission of human rights abuses. But beyond defensive responses, what are the alternatives? First, not all human rights research and reporting is, or has to be, like this. There are research methodologies that provide a thicker description of violence.[20] Second, human rights reports are more diverse, complex and contested documents than many critics suggest and therefore need to be read with greater subtlety (see Phelps 2004). Dudai's (2006: 789–91) argument that human rights reports include first-person testimony to say the otherwise unsayable – 'rain and cold enter the otherwise bare forensic tone' – and to complement the rational (required to secure legitimacy) with the emotional (necessary to generate empathy for victims) is one place to start. On these terms, the TRC reports went beyond purely forensic truths. Third, an alternative reality could be uncovered by operationalising the human rights mantra that economic, social and cultural rights matter in their own right, and that different categories of rights are indivisible and interdependent. By focusing on key building blocks of apartheid or its legislative foundations (pass laws restricting freedom of movement, forced removals entrenching segregation), and linking specific events to structural contexts (the Soweto uprisings in 1976 to dissatisfaction with education), a broader picture of South Africa could have been both acknowledged and contained. At the same time the critique of power would have been deeper and the net of responsibility thrown wider. The first truth–power interface within the TRC constituted as much an act of colonisation within human rights (elevating certain kinds of research methodologies and understandings of rights) as it did an act of colonisation by human rights.

The Janus-faced nature of law, and human rights, constitutes the second truth–power interface. The TRC regularly made use of international legal standards, such as when using international human rights and humanitarian law to interpret its mandate (TRC 1998, Vol. 1: 48–102). On this basis, its criticism of, and ultimate unpopularity with, all political parties, although all parties could have come off a great deal worse, can be seen as a kind of human rights vindication.[21] Importantly, when the TRC sidelined legitimising the new government (state inquiry) in favour of legitimising the law (human rights), it critiqued not only past political power (the National Party and its allies) but also current power (the ANC), albeit for past actions.

Prior to the TRC, the ANC, uniquely for an armed opposition group, had created two commissions of inquiry, the Skweyiya (1992) and Motsuenyane (1993) Commissions, to investigate allegations of its own abuses. Partly as a result, it initiated the idea of, and was subsequently instrumental in establishing, the TRC, to comprehensively investigate abuses from the apartheid past. However, the relationship between the ANC and TRC during the operational period of the Commission was not without differences of opinion. Notable hiccups included the October 1996 statement by Mathews Phosa, then premier of Mpumalanga province and legal advisor to the ANC, that ANC members would not apply for amnesty as they had fought a just war, a position that was withdrawn after Archbishop Tutu threatened to resign as TRC Chairperson; and a collective application for amnesty by 37 ANC members and leaders which was first granted by the Amnesty Committee in November 1997, and then successfully challenged in the courts by the TRC itself. Commissioners testified to a sense that 'trouble was brewing' (Orr, interview 19/4/2005; Sooka, interview 20/4/2005). The report redefined the relationship, irreparably, for the worse. Du Toit (1999) argues that ongoing debate and occasional friction between the ANC and TRC over even-handedness and moral equivalence, concerning those who fought to uphold and those who fought to overthrow apartheid, was transformed into outright confrontation with the critical perpetrator findings made against the ANC in the TRC's report. They were perceived by some as delegitimising the liberation struggle.

The politics of comparison is a familiar source of contention within human rights work.[22] The TRC carefully staked out a position of even-handedness and legal equality, without forgoing moral judgement. Thus, it found that apartheid was a crime against humanity and made its 'primary finding' against the apartheid state (TRC 1998, Vol. 5: 212). But the TRC also, legally and morally correctly, made the distinction between a 'just war' and 'just means'. While recognising that the liberation struggle was a just war, a just war can be unjustly executed, and individual human rights violations were regarded as equivalent regardless of who perpetrated them. Tutu in his foreword to the report echoes this position of legal equivalence – 'A gross violation is a gross violation, whoever commits it and for whatever reason' (TRC 1998, Vol. 1: 12) – and moral difference: 'I cannot, however, be asked to be neutral about apartheid. It is an intrinsically evil system' (13). As with the need for both victims/survivors and perpetrators to have rights in naming or criminal procedures, human rights in this context is required to weigh issues and address both sides in ways that resist an uneasy slide into moral equivalence.

As a result of this stance, there were times, including poignantly in its findings, when the TRC criticised the ANC. In its codicil report, the TRC notes candidly that there was 'a great deal of acrimony between the Commission and the ANC about the findings made' (2003: 643). The ANC National Executive Committee, like former State President de Klerk, after receiving notification of the adverse findings to be made, sought to block the report's publication in the courts. While the High Court ruled against the ANC, the TRC withdrew its findings against de Klerk – blacking them out (TRC 1998, Vol. 5: 225–26) – rather than jeopardise the publication of its report.[23] As has already been noted, after 1998 the ANC's, and then President Mbeki's, anger found further outlets, as the government has been at best ambivalent towards the TRC's reparation regime and recommendations. In part, what is noteworthy about this episode is the rather narrow and partisan role the ANC, or at least constituencies within the ANC, in the end appears to have expected the TRC to play, and the TRC's refusal to fully toe the line. Human rights, one might argue, enabled the state inquiry to rub against the grain of expectation. However, there was a price to pay: when truth spoke to power, power barked back.

To this point, the TRC constitutes a fairly conventional human rights project. Coverage of abuses committed by all sides in a conflict, for example, is now an important, and mainstream, device in establishing legitimacy. There are further legal challenges that both took on a particular form within the TRC and are of more general relevance. These relate to another subset of interpretative questions, and to uneven access to human rights protections.

The interpretive questions concern the relevance and reach of international human rights law. First, violations of human rights were equated with violations of apartheid law. By focusing on acts that were illegal under apartheid and not on violations of international human rights law the TRC contravened a central premise of human rights (that international law trumps national law) and, again, considerably narrowed its remit by overlooking a structural foundation of apartheid (because institutionalised racism was legally sanctioned). Strong legal counter-arguments were thereby side-stepped, such as charges of retroactive justice and the fact that when particular acts became illegal under international law is an evolving story. But this partiality nevertheless leaves an unpleasant taste in the mouth.

The second question concerns the legality or otherwise of the amnesty provision. The issue of amnesty was predetermined by political negotiation – in the 'postamble' of the interim Constitution (Act 200 of 1993) which contained a commitment to some form of amnesty, and the Promotion of National Unity and Reconciliation Act (No. 34 of 1995), the TRC's founding Act, which specified the relevant criteria and procedures for a policy of conditional amnesty. External validation came via a legal challenge to the constitutionality of the amnesty provision, *Azanian People's Organisation (AZAPO) and Others v. the President of the Republic of South Africa and Others (CCT 17/96)*, on the grounds that the interim Constitution guaranteed access to a court of law or other appropriate fora for the settlement of justiciable disputes. The case resulted in a July 1996 Constitutional Court judgment arguing that the 'postamble' trumped this particular provision.

But, in doing so, the Court failed to adequately address the international legal dimension of the amnesty question. The judgment restricts itself to a consideration of the 1949 Geneva Conventions and their Protocols, and even here inadequately interrogates the nature of the conflict – international or internal? – precipitated by apartheid. It offers a cursory and distorted overview of international amnesty experience, highlighting examples more sympathetic to its conclusions (Chile, Argentina, El Salvador) but overlooking less conducive examples (Rwanda, former Yugoslavia). In short, difficult legal and human rights issues are simply avoided, parliamentary will is privileged over fundamental legal protections, and national over international law. It is hard to avoid the conclusion that the rather florid judgment, written by Justice D. P. Mahomed, is another example of transition-induced genre confusion with the judge turned poet producing a poorly argued hybrid text. From a human rights and international law perspective it is now generally agreed that amnesties should not be entertained for serious 'international crimes' (war crimes, crimes against humanity, genocide), and even the broader category of gross violations of human rights – in fairness, this claim has sharpened considerably in the post-TRC era.[24] While a fuller discussion of state obligations may at the time have yielded a similar outcome, the resulting judgment would have had greater weight, informing debates and jurisprudence in a less parochial and muddled fashion.

A final set of challenges concerned access to human rights protections. The law and the protections provided by human rights were not divorced from considerations of power; they never are. 'Ultimately, it was those who had most to hide who astutely sought constitutional protection, almost crippling the TRC by wrapping it up in costly and time-consuming litigation' (Simpson 2002: 237;

also Sarkin 1996, 2004: 92–97). In short, the law was used more effectively to protect perpetrators than victims, as noted above in connection with the naming names dimension of truth-telling. A further irritant for victims was the discrepancy in the legal assistance provided to perpetrators and victims. Amnesty hearings were influenced by the absence/presence and unequal quality of legal representation for different amnesty applicants, and for applicants and victims. The state generously covered the costs of applicants who were present and former state employees and, in theory at least, members of liberation movements, in contrast to a very meagre legal assistance scheme made available for other amnesty applicants and victims (TRC 2003, Vol. 6: 87–88, 377). Similar, inequitable patterns in the practice of law have been observed in other transitional justice settings (see Hegarty 2003, on public inquiries in Northern Ireland). Finally, decisions in which amnesty was denied have been, and will in all likelihood continue to be, taken to review at the High Court, as applicants attempt to halt possible and actual prosecutions.[25] So, the question of who can access and use the law remains crucial.

So where does this leave us in terms of human rights speaking truth with and to power? The impacts of human rights law on the TRC were varied and mixed. A narrow human rights discourse marginalised individual subjectivity and political context, and overlooked structural violence and broader notions of accountability. Law spoke truth to specific powers but power also mobilised the law to contain the agendas of truth and justice. In this particular guise, human rights can be critiqued for speaking partial truths to similarly selective constructs of power. Part of the reason for this is down to inherent weaknesses in human rights discourse itself, while part is attributable to the fact that the TRC was informed, and compromised, by the fact that it was both a political and a human rights institution, and in this context certain choices were made and others foregone (both for the Commission, and by the Commission). Human rights law runs the risk of being made to look an ass in transitional settings if its perceived net effect is to endorse amnesties (*de jure* or *de facto*), entrench impunity, invoke invidious comparisons or equivalences, overlook structural violence and protect perpetrators. If this is the net effect of speaking truth with and to power, it represents a whimper in the direction of power at best.

But this is not the whole picture. While the genre of state inquiry had to balance the regime of speaking truth to reconciliation with the need for truth as objectivity, to the extent that it produced a human rights report the TRC refracted a similar imperative for objectivity and reconciliation through a more assertive, if specific and partial, critique of power. While on occasion the TRC sacrificed truth to reconciliation, it also told unpopular truths to all parties, asserting its own truth as objectivity legitimacy over the legitimisation of the ANC and parties across the political spectrum, and a specific discourse of nation-building (legal equality) over the more partisan valorisation of the ANC or the protection of parties deemed necessary to democratic consolidation. This is more than a whimper by any fair estimation.

This discussion of the TRC report within the generic possibilities of human rights has sought to explore the potential for legitimacy and impacts beyond report 'fetishisation' and to unpack the linkages forged between truth and power. What is its legacy for human rights? The TRC made a contribution to long-standing human rights debates: to rely on the power of critique and/or constructive engagement with the state (a variant of speaking truth to and with power)? To produce objective knowledge to educate and/or manipulate emotions to engage and mobilise? In both cases the TRC was at the cutting edge of human rights work in suggesting ways of combining the two activities. Realising human rights in contemporary South Africa will require assertive strategies to expand its challenge to power, including using human rights not only to identify what has changed most since apartheid's demise but also to highlight what has changed least. This, then, was a second interpretive repertoire of the TRC.

Official history

There is no agreement among commentators as to whether the TRC report is an official history. Among those who present and analyse it as a historical text, Bundy (2000: 13) states that '[i]t goes without saying that the TRC was charged with writing an official history'. The TRC and its staff were generally more cautious (see TRC 1998, Vol. 5: 257). The Director of Research at the TRC, Villa-Vicencio, states, 'I think [Bundy] is wrong in suggesting that the Commission was charged with "writing an official history"' (2000: 22), preferring the phraseology of a 'historical comment' (22) and 'the first stages of historical narrative' (25). In part, this difference of opinion arises because, as we have seen, the TRC was mandated to go beyond lists of facts and catalogues of abuses to address what are interpretive and historical questions – to establish 'as complete a picture as possible' *and* to address issues such as antecedents, causes, context, motives and perspectives in relation to gross violations of human rights – without specifically being asked to write 'a history'.

In generic terms, the first point to note is that the ambition of this mandate took the TRC well beyond the scope of the average human rights report. An engagement with the discipline of history, and indeed with the social sciences, pushes human rights beyond an investigative repertoire to interpretive concerns. These are truths of a different order. An exhumation can lead to a forensic examination which proves that the deceased was executed by being shot in the back of the head at point-blank range, rather than killed by state forces acting in self-defence during an exchange of fire. The debate about the causes of so-called 'black on black' violence and the role of the 'third force' in South Africa cannot be brought to a close in the same fashion. A commission can take a view on such a debate, but it will remain one view, albeit perhaps an authoritative one, among many. Certain conceptualisations of truth unhelpfully muddy the waters. The TRC itself defined factual or forensic truth as objective, corroborated evidence with regards to individuals and patterns, but also contexts and causes.

Truths relating to individual cases and patterns of abuse (who? what? when?) can be delivered as fact, but the other truths, notably those relating to the causation and motives (why? how?), are more complex. That said, facts and interpretations are to some extent interdependent, as the accumulation of facts shapes the limits of plausible interpretation. But truth commission mandates invariably go further than this modest remit. As such, truth commissions raise interesting questions about the truth ambition of human rights reports.

A second genre-related point is that it is important to distinguish between official history and other forms of history. An official history is a state-sanctioned history. Such histories, like state inquiries, are officially legitimised and also have a legitimising function, in the TRC's case sanctioning the discourse of speaking truth to reconciliation. Leman-Langlois and Shearing (2004: 228–31, 239) talk of '[a] history that is at once not a history – it repairs rather than establishes a past'. Official histories in transitional contexts can take a variety of forms, from truth commission hearings and reports, to memorials and state education curricula.

Why, beyond the need for legitimation, is an official history needed during periods of political transition? The writing of such a history is in itself righting a past wrong, 'setting the record straight', by writing a revised official history to replace its distorted and divisive counterparts from, in this case, the apartheid era. An official history can also serve the related function of 'drawing a line under the past', establishing the essential difference between the past and present. Du Toit (2000) contrasts historians' concerns with the past with the objective of truth commissions to establish a new moral and political order: 'If truth commissions are backward-looking, they are so precisely as historical founding projects; they deal with the past not for its own sake but in order to clear the way for a new beginning' (125). Addressing civil–political abuses that could be consigned to the past rather than economic and social issues that could not, is a clear example of this function. Finally, constructing a more inclusive, consensual narrative history is seen as a means of furthering national unity. Rewriting the past is predicted on inclusion of the previously voiceless, and new kinds of relationships with the benign state. This is part of a trend in history-writing, in which the victorious and elite have made way for the marginalised: 'Over the last two generations the writing of history has shifted focus from the history of perpetrators to the history of victims' (Barkan 2000: xxxiv). Official histories, in short, rewrite the past, draw a line under the past, create a moral community/nation, and provide a foundation for the future.

Official histories in South Africa have often been part of the state's speaking truth to reconciliation paradigm – a tendency documented for memorials, museums and monuments (Coombes 2003; Rassool *et al.* 2000), and in education (Dieltiens 2005) – and, in general, can easily become 'victors' history' (Garton Ash 2000: 300). But there has also been vigorous contestation over interpretations and ownership of the past. To reflect this scenario, what follows examines the relationship between the TRC *and* history (detailing pre-existing revisionist history, the post-1994 decline in history in the academy and schools, and the rise of heritage and public history); the TRC *as* history (through the prisms of methodology, meta-narrative and context); and finally, the TRC as archive.

The TRC and history

A first entry-point into the TRC–history intersection is that from as early as the 1960s a revisionist, social history developed and ultimately flourished in the academy, closely aligned to and involved in political struggles. This meant that South African history, come 1994, had to a significant degree already been rewritten. So the TRC, carrying official history within the complex demands of its genre tributaries, was destined to occupy a complex position within the multiple versions and rewritings of the past. It potentially challenged not only residual official apartheid history and its allies on the right, but also the revisionist history that by 1994 had a significant hold within history departments and beyond at universities.

Perhaps as a result of the history of history an uneasy relationship developed between the TRC and academic historians. Few historians worked in, contributed to and, at least initially, studied the TRC and its work, despite several attempts to generate dialogue. Attempts included the 'Historians, Social Scientists and the TRC' workshop in March 1995 and 'The Future of the Past' conference in July 1996 (Lalu and Harris 1996: 33–35; Verwoerd 1996). Tellingly, TRC research staff, including Villa-Vicencio (2000) and Verwoerd (1996), expressed frustration at what they perceived to be the unwillingness of the academic community, and specifically historians, to engage with the TRC and muddy themselves with the compromises of political practice.

Second, rather than the anticipated move to centre-stage in the new dispensation and its nation-building agendas, formal history suffered what was often termed a 'crisis'. In the academy, the discipline was portrayed as under siege from within, from the challenge of the post-modern and post-colonial turn, and from without, from an altered economic and political landscape. Features of the siege included a fall in the number of students studying history at university, for reasons ranging from the political discomfort generated by the past (guilt, anger) to the discipline's perceived irrelevance to employment prospects and the marketplace; history departments in decline, shedding staff; and challenges posed by white dominance of the discipline. Schools fared little better. The establishment of the TRC coincided with the marginalisation of history teaching in schools. The first major stab at school curriculum reform, Curriculum 2005 (introduced in 1997), merged history and geography into Human and Social Sciences. In 2002, under the tenure of Kader Asmal as Minister of Education, history was restored as a subject in its own right in response to the aforementioned 'crisis'. Critics argue that the TRC's impact on the 'crisis' in history has been slight, because it was seen by the government as a way of closing off debate about the past rather than opening it up, and as nation-building in education has been linked to economic development needs rather than history (Harries 2004; Nuttall and Wright 2000).

The disjuncture between the TRC and education/history was in part induced by the state, academia and external factors, but it was also in part self-inflicted. The Commission's own historical inquiry did not address the role of education under apartheid, or 'Bantu Education', and more specifically did not hold a sector hearing on education. Unsurprisingly, in this context, it provided few resources for educational transformation. To cite one example, some education-related recommendations are vague and added little to what was already taking place – the call for the government to give 'even more urgent attention to the transformation of education', for example (TRC 1998, Vol. 5: 308; Dieltiens 2005: 13). Other recommendations have not been implemented, e.g. there is not as yet a version of the report suitable for use in schools (TRC 2003, Vol. 6: 732). In contrast, the Sierra Leone TRC swiftly produced versions of its report for young children (2004) and for senior secondary school students (2005). But commentators also point to some more positive trends. The TRC features in school educational materials as a subject of study, for example, and provides valuable resources for teachers (such as personal testimonies). Assessing the impacts of the TRC on education transformation, Dieltiens (2005) asserts that reforms over time increasingly mirrored the nation-building values of the Constitution, and the TRC (restorative justice, reconciliation, human rights), with history teaching serving as one of the main conduits for these values. That said, priorities change over time – Kader Asmal, who had a keen interest in the TRC (Asmal *et al.* 1997) and drove the return of history as a distinct subject of study at school level, is no longer Minister of Education – and the TRC remains something of a 'footnote' in history; further, history education in the schools and the academy remains in a perilous state.

Such educational dynamics need to be placed in a wider context. From the East Asian 'textbook wars', as disputes rage between Japan and its neighbours over the teaching of history, to the protracted hiatus in history teaching in post-genocide Rwanda, the role of education in both producing and potentially overcoming societal divisions and the difficulties of teaching history in the aftermath of violent conflict are well documented. The challenges can be immense, ranging from the need to rebuild schools and train teachers from a virtual ground zero, to reforming entrenched structures of inequality and discrimination, developing new curricula, altering modes of classroom instruction, and the related revolution required in teacher training. Much of the literature sets the bar very high, stressing the need to foster debate, critical thinking and engagement with plurality, as opposed to rote learning, singular narratives of history and hermetically sealed understandings of culture and identity.

Two additional points are worth mentioning with regard to the place of history in transitional politics and justice. First, the issue of timing, or sequencing, is important, and helps to explain the disjuncture outlined above in South Africa between the TRC and education. Truth commissions are designed as up-front measures to generate greater consensus about history; educational reform is slower, usually reflecting rather than pioneering change (Cole and Barsalou 2006: 5, 9). Second, transitional justice mechanisms, in South Africa and elsewhere, invariably give scant attention to education and the teaching of history (the Chilean, Peruvian and Sierra Leone truth commissions are partial exceptions), thereby accentuating this temporal or sequential divide, rather than seeing this domain as absolutely central to their work and legacy. Cole and Barsalou (2006: 15) rightly state:

> Local and international scholars, policymakers, and practitioners inadequately understand and exploit the connections between teaching history and transitional justice processes. More research is needed on the design and impact of educational initiatives growing out of truth commissions. Moreover, transitional justice experts should address how future interventions might be designed to mesh more effectively with educations systems.

A final development in the TRC *and* history remit is that the decline in academic history has been accompanied by a TRC-influenced flourishing of heritage, public history and societal debate about the past. Truth commission work, more generally, can be situated within debates about the global decline of formal history and the rise of public history in a multi-media age (the internet, memorials, theatre, film, novels, etc.) – commissions are, therefore, at the forefront of a new kind of democratised and multi-form history, mirroring their similarly radical position in transforming human rights reporting.

The trend towards public history in South Africa is both officially sponsored and rooted in civil society (see Chapters 2 and 5). Although the ANC government is criticised by historians for its disregard for, and instrumentalisation of, history, it has invested energetically in heritage as history. Where such heritage is state-funded it has become part of the broader nation-building drive, initially within the speaking truth to reconciliation paradigm and thereafter within a more African nationalist narrative in the Mbeki era. These settings are new, and uncomfortable, territory for many historians, in part because of the overt links to the market and new solidarity-agendas:

> Deliberately and cleverly vague notions of 'African Renaissance' offer a vehicle for combining the market-based development strategies of GEAR [Growth, Employment and Redistribution], the advancement of the black middle class, and the cultural and geopolitical redefinition of South Africa as part of the African continent.
> (Nuttall and Wright 2000: 32)

Some historians have tended to flinch at heritage and other similarly packaged forms of official history as history-lite, both depoliticised and highly political, and fatally infected with commercialism, sentimentality and nostalgia. It is arguably preferable to see the rise of public histories, including but going beyond the official, as democratising history and providing new opportunities for the practice, production and contestation of history. Public histories for the historian, like public hearings for the human rights activist, are places where generic purity and control are sacrificed, or simply appropriated, for greater inclusion and wider impacts. A raft of new courses in South Africa dedicated to the study of heritage, museums, tourism, etc., suggest that universities are moving with the times.

Many of the challenges facing the discipline of history are not unique to post-apartheid South Africa. But they arrived collectively and suddenly, underwritten by the arrival of democracy and greater interaction with a globalised world. They suggest the need for histories linking local and global concerns, plotting the origins of contemporary human rights issues (HIV/AIDS, land, poverty), attempting to balance critique with constructive engagement (as with human rights), and flexibly navigating the waters between academic, official and popular histories. These are some of the debates which inform the discussion of the TRC as history.

The TRC as history

Despite the ambivalent relationship between the TRC and historians, the Commission was obliged to engage with history and, more specifically, with the challenges of telling a form of history. Much the same can be said for truth commissions elsewhere. Here we return to the question of whether truth commissions should have an interpretive as well as an investigative truth remit. The TRC *as* history raises questions about methodology, meta-narrative and context; each will be considered in turn.

In the South African setting, the difficulties of writing an official history have been explored most fully by Posel (2002). She identifies three mandate-related tensions linked to different kinds of historical knowledge and writing (150–53): objectivity versus acknowledging contending voices and experiences; a comprehensive record versus a representative and politically strategic account (balancing memory and forgetting, truth and forms of reconciliation); and focusing on apartheid as mere backdrop to a descriptive account of gross violations of human rights versus a fuller engagement with apartheid as source and explanation.

Truth commissions and history share a great deal in the methodological realm (multiple sources, strategies for corroboration, a focus on both individuals and patterns). Where methodological differences emerged in South Africa – such as the TRC's shift over time to the use of quantitative methods and making findings – these linked particular understandings of truth and reconciliation to particular objectives in the mandate. Arguably, the TRC's research process came to represent not just the marginalisation of testimony, but also the marginalisation of history, if history is understood as contested, contextual, interpretive and explanatory, exploring patterns of social relations and institutional dynamics. The sidelining of a historical regime of truth occurred for a variety of reasons.

Apart from the absence of historians, these included: (1) an overwhelmed research capacity – the TRC employed very few researchers (12–14) in comparison to data analysts and investigators (about 60); (2) the legalisation of the TRC process (issuing prior-warning notices, making findings, amnesty functions); (3) an increasingly reactive research agenda; (4) limited engagement with secondary sources and archival material; (5) and a report-editing process that sacrificed detailed case studies, local histories, analysis, context, causality and explanation (Cherry *et al.* 2002).[26] These developments taken together amounted to a shift from historical analysis to the investigative repertoires of the state inquiry and human rights report, and from academic history to the nation-building and legitimising functions of official history.

Second, truth commission reports undertake the conventional historians' task of providing a containing meta-narrative, or interpretive framework, for the past. Posel (2002) problematises the TRC's failure to link individual cases to more general causative patterns in a coherent analytical synthesis, and an absence of serious engagement with apartheid in preference for a moral narrative about wrongdoing across the political spectrum, rooted in the over-riding evil of the apartheid system. R. Wilson concurs that in the service of national building and reconciliation, more easily modified and unifying notions of morality and values were often preferred to political confrontation and challenging analysis: '[m]orality ventured where analysis feared to tread' (2001: 93).[27]

This moral parable is all that binds together a report otherwise characterised by description, fragmentation, repetition and multiple messages. Various examples could illustrate this point. Suffice to note the failure to integrate testimonies and statistical analysis; the need to relate things treated separately (time periods, regional profiles, categories of abuse, parts of individual stories); and the treatment of sector hearings and related structural issues in a separate volume (TRC 1998, Vol. 4). Consideration of 'causes, motives and perspectives of perpetrators' takes place in a very insightful separate chapter in the 1998 report (TRC 1998, Vol. 5: Chapter 7), and is then treated somewhat superficially in the long consideration of the truths emerging from the amnesty process (TRC 2003, Vol. 6: 181–501; also Foster *et al.* 2005 13–24). To this list should be added the decision to begin, and therefore frame, the whole report with a chairperson's foreword (genre: sermon). This is followed by a first volume of the report consisting largely of a manual of methods and bureaucratic arrangements, when it should be grabbing the reader with a strong statement of core findings. The absence of an index is similarly 'symptomatic of the lack of an intellectual map' (Posel, interview 14/8/2002). All these qualities detracted from the TRC's capacity to provide historical analysis and an interpretive framework.

From interviews with former commissioners and commission staff (for example: Fullard, interview 21/4/2005; Orr, interview 19/4/2005; Sooka, interview 20/4/2005), it is clear that there was no agreement about the meta-narrative of the TRC report, even among those closely associated with its production: 'In 1998, I don't think anyone writing had a major sense of the uber-points we were trying to make' (Fullard, interview 21/4/2005). The meta-narrative of the codicil report (TRC 2003), a document drafted by a smaller group of writers, is clearer: accountability and reparations. The codicil is characterised by a strong legal justification for its meta-themes, a focus on 'unfinished business', and certain elements of self-critique (a clearer meta-narrative; modest rewritings of earlier findings and recommendations). As weaknesses of the TRC were acknowledged, new material emerged within the Commission, old material was better analysed, and the outlines of a government response, or lack thereof, became clearer, this process of reflection was perhaps inevitable; but it is nonetheless intriguing, and the (re)writing process deserves further study.

Some argue that the weakness of the report's meta-narrative may be a strength, inviting rather than curtailing further debate (Posel 2002: 168–69; Posel and Simpson 2002: 12–13). Certain analyses map ways in which commissions combine meta-narrative and multiple voices. In the reading of truth commission work and their reports provided by Phelps (2004), Bakhtin's carnival serves as a template, allowing story-telling within the polyphonic TRC hearings to be conceived as liberating victims and survivors by disrupting existing social structures, equalising social relationships and temporarily inverting the established official order. The inclusion of such stories in the master narratives of truth commission reports 'allows for the *carnivalisation* of history, an entirely new kind of history telling and nation making' (Phelps 2004: 69). With reference to such reports, and exemplified in the Argentine report, *Nunca Más*, Phelps (2004: 74–128) invites a reading that recognises a blend of victim/survivor and authorial/commission voices: 'and the two together manifest a unique sharing of power reflecting the promise of democracy' (81). Beyond providing evidence, testimonies become explanatory, exemplary and disruptive partners in a conversation, thereby preventing an appropriative master narrative from becoming too dominant, or too focused on perpetrators. If the TRC victim hearings represented a rare example of the carnivalesque in contemporary political life, the TRC report was an exercise in order and control, an effort to 'contain the uncontainable' (115), in which residues of the carnival perhaps remain. The report's three typefaces provide an initial mapping of its voices: regular for the master narrative, italics for the first-person victim and perpetrator stories, and bold for the TRC's findings. The master narrative, according to Phelps, is one of forgiveness and reconciliation.

A third area where history and historians ask important questions of the truth commission enterprise – context – revisits the discussion of human rights and its tendency to decontextualise. Human rights abuses, in truth, are a narrow and idiosyncratic prism through which to attempt a rewriting of history. Posel writes that the:

> inability to grapple with the complexities of social causation is compounded by the TRC's having to tie its account of apartheid to the story of gross human rights violations. Having to focus a narration of the past around the

clash between 'victims' and 'perpetrators' provides very blunt tools for the craft of history-writing.

(Posel 2002: 166)

Bundy reiterates the point that the narrow focus on gross human rights violations served to diminish the full iniquity of the apartheid past (2000: 16–19). As we have seen, the decontextualisation critique applies at various levels, encompassing individual testimony, community histories and macro- or meta-narratives.

Historians and social scientists have begun to critique the community analyses and impacts of the TRC in relation to often complex local dynamics of power and violence.[28] Van der Merwe's work on Duduza, a township in the Greater Nigel Area on the East Rand (2002, also 2001; 2003; and in TRC 1998, Vol. 5: 423–29), argues that the TRC privileged top-down, national reconciliation – between racial groups and political parties, involving moral and institutional change – over, and even at the expense of, community reconciliation, locally understood as the reconstruction of local social networks and political relationships. Between April 1996 and May 1997 around 80 community hearings were held, lasting between one and three days. The TRC held a one-day hearing in Duduza in February 1997, which combined Duduza with neighbouring communities.

Following a common pattern, statements were collected and a selection of deponents, chosen for their representivity but otherwise lacking cohesion or local priority, were granted a platform at the public hearing. The TRC liaised mainly with political leaders and structures, with inadequate broader consultation, in a community alienated from its political leadership and structures. This strategy fed local perceptions that leaders were being protected, perceptions which existed alongside the view that the hearing and investigations privileged prominent over ordinary people. In this community, a long history of political conflict had severely undermined community cohesion. The main community truth priorities concerned local patterns of black intra-communal conflict ('black on black' violence) key local incidents, divisions between and within political parties, and the identity of local collaborators and perpetrators. Community reconciliation, as understood by residents, required a deeper, longer-term engagement with the complexities of local conflicts. Van der Merwe argues that community reconciliation is poorly served by the imposition of external agendas – national reconciliation, a narrow focus on gross human rights abuses, a concentration on political offences.

Such contextual analysis provides insights into the different kinds of truths desired by particular constituencies, but also divergent perspectives on whether truth is desired at all. Van der Merwe's argument is that it is, even for sensitive issues such as informing and collaboration, where the fact that perpetrators may be neighbours and mistrust and division lingers, gives a potency to the falsehoods and truths concerned. The work of Cherry (2000), focusing on the Eastern Cape, paints a different picture. She indicates a more circumspect attitude to truth in such contexts, in which close-knit communities have to learn to live together. Dynamics such as these have been observed elsewhere, whether in the form of 'social forgetting' (Sierra Leone: Shaw 2005) or 'chosen amnesia' (Rwanda: Buckley-Zistel 2006). In sum, local histories and contextualised truths require a sensitivity to the consequences of truth not always demonstrated by the human rights fraternity.

Local histories of these kinds lack the clear lines and unified, crisp agendas of official histories. Before signing off on this subject, a cautionary comment is required with reference to historical and other academic analyses. History as context, while rectifying the decontextualisation of legal discourse and human rights reporting, can simply provide another, broader narrative and set of external agendas with similarly expansive truth claims into which testimonies and communities are appropriated as sources of evidence and facts. The interpretive context is still imposed from above, filtering voices from below. If truth commissions and social historians are to fulfil their claims to give voice to the voiceless, and to democratise history, they need to incorporate insights into power relations in narrative construction, understandings of oral testimony and memory beyond their use as evidence, and interpretive worlds as well as voices from below (du Pisani and Kim 2004; Lalu and Harris 1996; Minkley and Rassool 1998). The TRC's record as history has rightly been subject to rigorous critique by academics across the concerns addressed here – methodology, meta-narrative, context – but both truth commissions and the academy have lessons to learn from transition, notably from the rise of public history.

The TRC as archive

A final facet of the truth commission as history is its relationship to the archive. Archives have become a sufficiently important aspect of truth commission work and legacies to generate their own 'how to' guides (Peterson 2005). The official memory of the past in times of political transition is fought over by the shredder and the archivist. In South Africa, the shredders were at work during the whole apartheid era, but particularly systematically between 1990 and 1994 (TRC 1998, Vol. 1: 201–43). In the wake of this documentary carnage the TRC 'engaged archive, rescued archive, created archive, refigured archive' (Harris 2006: 53). Its own archive is now largely located at the National Archives of South Africa. It is part of the TRC's contribution to truth-seeking as ongoing history lesson, but the archive is also central to the ANC government's attempts to regain control over the past and its narration, and the as yet unresolved tension between openness and secrecy in the emerging democratic space. As such, the struggle over archival memory is ongoing, and the TRC's archive has become a source of contestation between public, academic and official history.

Some recent South African commentary on archives has been influenced by Derrida's *Archive Fever* (1996), and the notion of the 'violence' of the archive as a form of exclusion, silencing/forgetting, closure and fixing (Hamilton *et al.* 2002) – another institutionalised matrix of truth and power. It is indeed important, and in fact somewhat uncontroversial, to see archives, like truth commission reports, as partial and contested, and as both constructed and constructing forms of knowledge. That said, there is no doubt that the TRC's archive contains more information than was previously in the public domain, more information than the TRC could digest in its report – Villa-Vicencio describes the report as 'an annotated road map into the archive' (2000: 24; also see Tutu in TRC 1998, Vol. 1: 2) – and that the material in the public sphere and the report can be revisited as new information comes to light.

However, at present the TRC's archive is 'only partially processed, largely unaccessible, and little used' (Harris 2006: 58). The Commission's archive-related recommendations (TRC 1998, Vol. 5: 343–47; 2003, Vol. 6: 729–30) remain largely unimplemented (Harris 2006; SAHA 2003 voices some criticisms of the recommendations). Any determination of 'violence' will ultimately be made on the interlinked grounds of accessibility and coverage. Will the archive span administrative, programme and investigative records (Peterson 2005: 4–6)? To what kinds of material will access be denied citing privacy or security concerns? Will the National Archive be able to access apartheid military and intelligence materials concealed from the TRC (SAHA 2003)?

As these questions are answered, the archive has the potential to serve a variety of functions. Archive as 'memorial site' (Burton 2000: 112), for example, or as the TRC's dialogue with history, 'a means for interpreting events from perspectives other than that of an immediate reference for action' (Ashforth 1990: 10). Beyond offering the potential for reflection, in various forms, the archive has become a site of contestation, the subject of legal action and political struggle. The South African History Archive (SAHA), an NGO based at the University of the Witwatersrand in Johannesburg, has used the Promotion of Access to Information Act (No. 2 of 2000) in an attempt to extend the parameters of freedom of information, maintain the integrity of the official archive, and strategically access material. Pigou (2009: 52) concludes:

> SAHA's efforts in trying to access TRC records have had some positive results, but have too often resulted in unnecessarily lengthy, hostile and litigious engagements. In all such instances, SAHA has secured favourable settlements, forcing DOJ [the Department of Justice] and DAC [the Department of Arts and Culture] to provide records that they had previously refused to disclose. Despite this, last minute out-of-court settlements have ensured that no legal precedents have been set, enabling continued employment of the blocking tactics.

Through such advocacy, SAHA is using the TRC and its legacy to define the boundaries of the democratic state and build up its own archive of TRC-related material. The archive, like the human rights report, can also be reinvented through technological innovation – see, for example, SAHA's digitalised archive, *Traces of Truth*, at truth.wwl.wits.ac.za – probing the traditional constraints of form and access, while hopefully remaining sensitive to the fact that technology creates its own fault-lines of exclusion and inclusion. If TRC-related archives foster reflection, activism and innovation, they will serve their most important function:

> The archive is an invitation to do better; indeed, in understanding the flaws of any particular hearing, one gets a sense of how to continue the work of elaborating the archive. One can opt to treat the trauma of the past, and the problems in retelling it, as a promise.
> (Dyzenhaus 1998: 179)

The interpretive repertoire of history places truth commissions at the intersection between the state, the academy and the public, posing questions about ownership and control of the past: to repair, establish or democratise the past? Truth commissions perform this interpretive role in a way that is at once uniquely authoritative and often highly contested, in part because of the close affiliation between official histories and the nation-building agendas of new governments. Furthermore, commissions, informed more by the methods of human rights (investigation) than of history (interpretation), can deal with certain forms of knowledge (individual case histories, patterns of abuse, the policy and institutional environment) more easily than others (causation, motives). It is extremely unlikely that they will provide a meta-narrative to eclipse all other meta-narratives, although greater consensus may be forged around certain core truths (apartheid was a crime against humanity; both the apartheid state and its opponents committed abuses [Gibson 2004]). Ignatieff (1996) helpfully suggests an interpretive goal for truth commissions, arguing that they can change the frame of public discourse and memory – 'The past is an argument and the function of truth commissions, like the function of honest historians, is simply to purify the argument, to narrow the range of permissible lies' (113) – thereby providing the parameters, but altered parameters, for future discussion and argument. The often cited joke in post-apartheid South Africa, that it soon became impossible to find anyone who supported apartheid, may well be one way in which the facts (or lies) uncovered by the TRC helped to shape interpretive outcomes. While it is necessary for commissions to take on interpretive questions – how will preventive recommendations be framed without insights into causes and motives? – two questions remain unresolved: (1) How can investigative and interpretive functions be better aligned? and (2) What blend of methodologies and academic disciplines is required? (The answer is likely to be a variant of human rights hybridity, informed but not monopolised by human rights.)

The TRC as official history had to balance an official regime of speaking truth to reconciliation with a disciplinary regime and methodology of speaking truth to, and debates about, contexts and meta-narratives. The failure of the TRC to speak truth to context at micro and macro levels, and to provide an explanatory narrative about the apartheid era, can be attributed in large part to its retreat from historical to investigative repertoires, and from the contested arena of academic history to the political, legitimising agendas of official history. As has been suggested above, and in subsequent truth commission practice, this is not an inevitable outcome.

Conclusion

The TRC was a human rights and a political institution, with the capacity to speak truth to power and with power. Juggling these inherent tensions, the Commission worked within the generic confines of the state inquiry, the human rights report and the official history. A basket of generic methodologies seeking objectivity were linked respectively to an impulse towards speaking truth to reconciliation, to power, and to context and meta-narrative. Such priorities map different routes through which the TRC sought legitimacy, diverse truth profiles, a spectrum of objectives, and the Commission's deepest struggles over power and ideology. As such, its report, and work more generally, represents a 'genre colony', but a colony which failed to achieve a hybrid or synthetic coherence. Rather, genre status and the kinds of truth prioritised changed over time and through different sections of the organisation and report. An initial focus, at least within sections of the TRC, on narrative and history was overtaken midstream by quantitative methodology and a focus on making findings. This was an act of colonisation by human rights, narrowly construed. But it was also an internal coup within human rights, elevating to power a particular set of civil–political rights and quantitative research methodologies.

The methodological and conceptual challenge, especially for truth commissions with broad truth mandates, is how to render the multiple genres, truths and methodologies productive rather than fragmentary and mutually undermining. Less ambition is one option, through perhaps choosing to privilege one genre tributary or form of truth. Another is to acknowledge the different emphases in various facets of commission work, while seeking on occasion at least to integrate the parts into a coherent whole. The TRC's four truths provide a framework with which to begin the discussion. What the TRC did achieve was a unique repertoire of ways of engaging with a national and international public, including the report, but also the dissemination revolution forged through public hearings and media coverage. The TRC's impact on social truth deserves special attention and as such it is analysed further in the next chapter.

Notes

1 'Truth trials', designed to identify perpetrators, establish responsibility and uncover the fate of the 'disappeared', circumvented wide-ranging amnesty laws in Chile

and Argentina. Such trials are based on the idea that there is a right to truth, derived from the right to 'seek, receive and impart information' (Article 19 of the Universal Declaration of Human Rights), and international legal obligations to investigate gross violations of human rights and crimes against humanity. Truth trials have been categorised as a hybrid of trials and truth commissions, and such trials can also provide information to inform future prosecutions. The right to truth, which has an individual and a collective dimension, features in normative contributions to the transitional justice field, e.g. the Updated Set of Principles for the Protection and Promotion of Human Rights through Action to Combat Impunity, UN Doc. E/CN.4/2005/102/Add.1, February 2005, Principles 2–5; and has become an important component of victims' rights discourse. An emerging right to truth has implications beyond investigative trials and is of considerable relevance to truth commissions, not least as such a right carries the potential to increase their standing and to alter the criteria for the design and evaluation of transitional justice interventions (for example, amnesty for truth mechanisms might be viewed more positively in human rights terms).

2 One of the role ambiguities facing truth commissions is that they are, in part at least, human rights institutions, but they are not courts of law. This can lead to tensions between reporting and adjudicating functions. Du Toit (1999) argues that truth commissions as investigative bodies rather than courts of law should not make perpetrator findings – they lack legal due process protections, such findings have questionable legal standing and coherence, and, in the TRC's case, it already had a concurrent amnesty process.

3 In October 1996, just before the initial cut-off date for amnesty applications (this date was later extended), two seminal trials came to their conclusion. Colonel Eugene de Kock, a Vlakplaas hit squad commander, was convicted, and through his evidence in mitigation of sentence, agreement to testify in other criminal cases and amnesty applications, subsequently flushed out a number of amnesty applications from within the security police. The acquittal of former Minister of Defence, Magnus Malan, and others, also for hit squad related activities, had the opposite effect within the South African Defence Force (SADF). A few amnesty applications were motivated by civil claims. The timing of amnesty hearings and the release of decisions were on occasion managed to encourage further applications, e.g. the release of a positive decision as an application deadline approached (Sarkin 2004: 152–55; TRC 1998, Vol. 5: 112–13).

4 See Cherry (2000); Fullard and Rousseau (2003); Sarkin (2004: 259–75); TRC (1998, Vol. 1: 120–22); and in particular, on the truth dividend of amnesty, see TRC (2003, Vol. 6: 181–511) – for an analysis of this latter account, usefully summarising its contribution and remaining gaps, see Foster *et al.* (2005: 13–24).

5 The discussion that follows draws on Chapman and Ball (2008: 156–58, 162); Cherry (2000); Foster *et al.* (2005); Fullard and Rousseau (2003); Jeffery (1999); Krog (1998: 82–89); Pigou (2002, 2003); Sarkin (2004); Slye (2000); TRC (2003, Vol. 6: 1–91, 181–511) – also see Abrahamsen and van der Merwe (2005) on views of the amnesty process held by applicants from the liberation movements; and Phakathi and van der Merwe (2008) on victim/survivor views of the amnesty process.

6 Internationally, truth commissions have often been established by presidential decree (Chile, Argentina) or as part of peace agreements (El Salvador, Guatemala, Sierra Leone).

7 The commissions discussed by Ashforth do not include some of the immediate precursors to the TRC, such as the Commission of Inquiry Regarding the Prevention of Public Violence and Intimidation (the Goldstone Commission). A list of commissions of inquiry held between 1960 and 1995 can be found in TRC (1998, Vol. 1: 498–508).

8 The commissioners for truth commissions have been appointed using a variety of strategies to advance objectivity. The National Commission for Truth and

Reconciliation in Chile had eight commissioners evenly distributed across the political spectrum (Pinochet supporters and opponents). In some cases foreign participation is seen as a means of securing objectivity, modulating threats and criticism, and/or providing specialist expertise: in El Salvador all the commissioners were selected from outside the country, while in the cases of Haiti, Guatemala and Sierra Leone a combination of internal and external commissioners was preferred. The South African TRC's 17 commissioners were chosen on the grounds of political, racial and gender representivity; that said, representivity did not encompass the full political spectrum. A possible tension between representivity and effectiveness is an important issue for truth commissions to resolve when considering staff composition.

9 In a revealing passage in his biography of Mbeki, William Gumede (2005: 64) claims that Mbeki, on hearing that the TRC's report condemned ANC abuses in its camps in Angola, denounced the report without reading it and instigated a court action to prevent publication. Gumede writes that Mandela, in contrast, welcomed the report and several ANC National Executive Committee members contacted TRC commissioners to register their support. Further, it is clear from this account (e.g. 295), and elsewhere, that Tutu and Mbeki's relationship, and in all likelihood the impacts and legacy of the TRC, suffered as the two men disagreed over not just the TRC's recommendations but also a host of other political issues (economic policy, HIV/AIDS, foreign policy towards Zimbabwe).

10 Drawing on the experience of the Documentation Affinity Group (DAG), an NGO network, to outline best practice for documentation projects designed to combat impunity, establish truth, and build democratic and just societies, Bickford *et al.* (2009: 5–6) state that 'telling the story' requires four components: the testimony and voice of victims, witnesses and others; official records; unofficial records and physical materials (videos, human bones and clothing); and analysis and other created documents (*habeas corpus* briefs, databases).

11 All seven volumes of the report can now be accessed via the website of the Department of Justice and Constitutional Development: www.doj.gov.za.

12 Based on January 2008 figures obtained from the South African publishers of the report, Juta and Company Ltd. Publishers, domestic sales figures were as follows: +2,400 copies of Volumes 1–5 as a set; +37 copies of Volumes 1–7 as a set; +800 copies of Volume 6; and +281 copies of Volume 7. The very small sales figures for Volume 7 are particularly striking given its potential role in acknowledging victims and survivors. As a point of comparison, Random House, the publisher of Antjie Krog's *Country of My Skull*, perhaps the best-known book about the TRC, reported that, by the end of 2007, 17,000 copies of the book had been sold, with the bulk of these sales having been within South Africa. Both sets of sales figures were obtained via personal communications with the publishers.

13 Hayner writes:

> A shorter, book-length version was published by a private publishing house in cooperation with the government. The report was an immediate best-seller: 40,000 copies were sold on the first day of its release, 150,000 copies in the first eight weeks. It has now been reprinted over twenty times, has sold almost 300,000 copies, and is one of the best-selling books ever in Argentina's history. Over fifteen years after it was released, the report can still be found for sale at many sidewalk kiosks throughout Buenos Aires.
>
> (Hayner 2002: 34)

The contrast between these figures and those cited in note 12 is striking.

14 An Executive Summary (Summary and Guide to Contents) of Volumes 1–5 is available at www.doj.gov.za. Electronic versions (CD ROMs) of the TRC's reports have sold more than 1,000 copies.

15 Clearly, gaps remain – for example, interactive media, which have been so successful in memorialisation, remain an under-explored mode of dissemination and engagement in truth commission and human rights work. The National Vision project of the Sierra Leone TRC is one example of an interactive intervention, providing as it did a platform for Sierra Leoneans to express their expectations and aspirations.

16 The poor record on implementing recommendations even extends to those few cases (El Salvador, Sierra Leone) where commission recommendations were formally binding (see the initial evaluation of the Sierra Leone TRC by the Sierra Leone Working Group on Truth and Reconciliation [2006]). The South African government's response to the TRC's recommendations has been poorly coordinated, lacklustre and insufficiently consultative. In 2005, a TRC Unit was established within the Department of Justice and Constitutional Development to coordinate the implementation of the four categories of recommendations approved by parliament. These are: financial reparations to victims; tracing missing persons and exhumations; symbols and monuments; and medical and other forms of social assistance. The Unit will work alongside the President's Fund, a pre-existing body set up to administer funds for individual and community reparations (Seekoe 2006).

17 Fullard's (2004) nuanced discussion of the TRC's engagement with race and racism reveals that it was 'partial, unsystematic and even contradictory' (46), – but also that race rubbed against the grain of its exclusion. As one indicator of unevenness, while race was relegated to the margins in both victim statements/testimony and amnesty applications, in the TRC's sector hearings racism was acknowledged as profoundly political. Such mixed messages led to some alarming disjunctures. Truth-telling and findings of responsibility took place primarily around a political axis while the national project of reconciliation mainly focused on race. Framed in this way, it is hard to see how the truth leads to reconciliation.

18 A particular quantitative research methodology is increasingly dominating the work of truth commissions. Much less work is being done on how to imaginatively use qualitative methods in large-scale human rights projects or how to integrate a range of methodologies. The quantitative agenda was driven by the American Association for the Advancement of Science (AAAS), which helped to design information management and database systems for a number of commissions, including those in El Salvador, Haiti, South Africa, Guatemala, Peru, Sierra Leone and Timor Leste (Ball *et al.* 2000; Chapman and Ball 2001; Landman 2006: 107–25; TRC 1998, Vol. 1: 140–45, 158–64, 322–25). This 'who did what to whom' methodology has its strengths, particularly when multiple data sources can be cross-referenced to overcome the limitation of unrepresentative, convenience samples. It can identify sometimes hitherto unknown patterns of violence and challenge prevailing myths about past violence. But it is complex and resource intensive, essentially descriptive, and thin on context and as an interpretive and explanatory tool. It also constitutes report 'fetishisation' writ large. In South Africa, there were criticisms from advocates of the information management system that the TRC, including its research staff, did not use the database effectively and to the full, while commission staff criticised the accessibility and utility of the methodology and database. In fairness, it should also be noted that truth commissions have led the way in managing large data sets in human rights research.

19 It should also be noted that other processes within the TRC also served to winnow out context. Z. Bock *et al.* (2004) suggest that four kinds of information were 'lost' in the translations/interpretations and transcriptions of testimony from human rights

violation hearings: cultural meaning, emotional content, factual truths and paralinguistic information (gesture, intonation, facial expression). For related observations on translation and interpretation, see Krog *et al.* (2009). How various processes of decontextualisation intersect is a subject deserving further research.
20 See for example the action research approach used by Penal Reform International (PRI) in its monitoring of the *gacaca* courts in Rwanda. This longitudinal research goes beyond a narrow monitoring remit to mine the perceptions and behaviours of a range of actors in order to understand the *gacaca* process and the broader context in which it unfolded; www.penalreform.org.
21 On criticisms of and from all sides of the political spectrum, see, for example, TRC (1998, Vol. 1): the chairperson's foreword (8–17), and legal challenges to the TRC (174–200); TRC (1998, Vol. 5): findings (196–249); TRC (2003, Vol. 6): legal challenges (54–82, 678–701) and findings (614–725); also see Boraine (2000: 145–71, 187–257, 300–339) and Tutu (1999: 165–70, 187, 196–203).
22 In transitional justice settings the ugly face of comparison is revealed by the 'doctrine of two demons' in the Southern Cone, and the equally problematic 'double genocide' thesis in Rwanda.
23 Various report-related legal challenges, specifically this one from de Klerk and others from the IFP, were settled in the period between 1998 and the publication of the TRC's codicil in 2003. In both these cases the findings were modified (TRC 2003, Vol. 6: 54–65, 678–701).
24 Seminal contributions to the amnesty debate include Orentlicher (1991, 2007); on South Africa, see Dugard (1997, 1997a); and van Zyl (1999, 2000). As noted in the main text, the debate on amnesty has moved on since the South African TRC and has given rise to various normative clarifications. We will return to these debates in Chapter 3.
25 Any relevant party may seek a review of an amnesty decision which considers whether a decision is justifiable rather than correct, in short determining whether there is a rational connection between the facts and the finding rather than re-examining the evidence.
26 Fullard (2004: 23) provides some background to the writing of the 'historical context' chapter in the TRC report (TRC 1998, Vol. 1: Chapter 2). A lengthy, detailed history chapter written by academic historians was deemed to be 'too academic' and ultimately unsuitable; it was replaced at the last minute by a shorter chapter written by a TRC researcher. For further, rather exasperated, reflections on the writing and editing process, from an academic involved in the drafting of the TRC report's chapter on the business sector (TRC 1998, Vol. 4: Chapter 2), see Nattrass (1999: 374, 386).
27 Writing about early truth commissions in Latin America, Grandin (2005: 3) comments:

> In most truth commissions, history was not presented as a network of causal social and cultural relations but rather as a dark backdrop on which to contrast the light of tolerance and self-restraint. In other words, truth commissions, by presenting an interpretation of history as parable rather than as politics, largely denied the conditions that brought them into being.

Again, as in various other academic analyses, the Guatemalan commission is presented as an exception to this trend.
28 See, for example, Bonner and Nieftagodien (2002) and R. Wilson (2001) – community and victim/survivor histories are discussed in Chapter 2.

Chapter 2

From social truth to rights-based participation

If part of the function of truth commissions, and transitional justice measures in general, is to engage the public and generate debate, and these criteria constitute one means of evaluation, then the South African TRC was a significant, if qualified, success. In detailing its four categories of truth, the TRC stated, 'it was in its search for social truth that the closest connection between the Commission's process and its goal was to be found' (1998, Vol. 1: 113). The process of the TRC was important in its own right:

> because it was through this process that the essential norms of social relations between people were reflected. It was, furthermore, through dialogue and respect that a means of promoting transparency, democracy and participation in society was suggested as a basis for affirming human dignity and integrity.
>
> (114)

This form of truth fosters means of accommodating and weighing different pasts and views. Emphasis is placed on process as well as products, on deliberation as well as adjudication. Civil–political rights and legal and political procedures which seek to embrace diversity and mediate disputes are central to what I call liberal proceduralism.

In the previous chapter, I argued with regards to 'truth as content' that the TRC challenged power to an extent, but could have gone further. In this chapter I make a similar argument about 'truth as process'. The case made here is that the TRC had an important discursive effect, but that certain debilitating features of the new democratic dispensation in South Africa – elite-pacting, authoritarian actors or attitudes (discussed in a less confrontational vocabulary below as decision-making 'blind spots'), deliberative and material inequalities – were largely untouched by its work. Many will argue that such problems are not the business of truth commissions, and that to make them so is an act of hubris. My point is that while commissions cannot solve such problems alone, they also cannot afford to ignore them when they constitute important and enduring legacies from the past and, as such, threaten to undermine other truth commission achievements.

The chapter develops this argument, first by examining the relationship between the TRC and civil society, finding it to be characterised by commendable transparency and high levels of civic engagement but also notable exceptions to this rule. It continues by exploring the TRC's influence on the South African public sphere (a broader realm than civil society), and the extent to which it shaped the values and discourse of democratic debate. In conclusion, a tale of the mixed potential of social truth, exemplified by the power *and* vulnerability of testimony in a globalised public sphere, cements the case that for voice to really matter requires (1) control over voice, and its representation, interpretation and dissemination (a subaltern method to complement the subaltern voice), and (2) rights-based participation, to further increase the likelihood that the such voices will be twice and three times heard.

In building my case on the merits of participation, I am aware that the literature on participation is voluminous and characterised by both high hopes and frequent disappointments (Cooke and Kothari 2001; Hickey and Mohan 2004). The evidence, notably from the development literature, suggests that participation in official consultative forums, when civil society actors are invited to the decision-making table, fails to challenge prevailing power dynamics, and in particular fails to remedy the exclusion of the poorest and most marginalised. In a South African context, Friedman (2006), for example, argues that while formal participatory forums and participation in policy processes abound, they have not offered citizens an effective say in policy-making. In short, 'participatory mechanisms do not enhance participatory governance', as they are biased towards better-resourced groups with a capacity to organise who would be heard anyway (3). Participation by the poor is actually impeded by such mechanisms (owing to the languages used, technical expertise required, etc.). What, then, is the alternative? Friedman goes on to claim that the most effective example of citizen participation in post-apartheid governance, the change in government policy towards dispensing anti-retroviral medication to people living with AIDS, was the outcome not of formal mechanisms of participation but of activists using constitutional rights to make demands on government.

> Instead of viewing [participatory governance] as the product of government willingness to create formal channels for citizen participation, we need to see it as a process in which citizens use rights, employing methods and channels of their choice (within the constraints imposed by democratic order) to compel governments to deal with them on their terms, not those convenient to power-holders.
>
> (Ibid.)

Other analyses illuminate the task at hand. Friedman's analysis has clear links to a distinction made recently in the participation literature, between 'invited' and 'popular' spaces of governance (Cornwall 2004). Invited spaces are provided by governments and official agencies, whether in response to popular demands, donor pressure or shifts in policy, and define the contours of sanctioned public deliberation. Popular spaces are unsanctioned arenas, where people come together at their own instigation to protest against government policy, to produce their own services, or for solidarity and mutual aid. Boundaries between the two spaces are not fixed and actors may seek to work both to their advantage.

Another useful participation framework starts from the premise that different forms of participation are often placed on a continuum: information-sharing (knowledge transfer but limited decision-making powers); consultation (people can express views, but these are not necessarily incorporated); joint decision-making (gives participants the right to negotiate the content of a strategy or project); and initiation and control by stakeholders (implies a high degree of citizen control over decision-making) (Stewart and Wang 2005: 452). There is disagreement about whether such forms of participation should be seen as a ladder or hierarchy, implying some are better than others, or as spokes on a wheel, suggesting that they are all useful in particular contexts. Using this framework might assist stakeholders in truth commission processes address difficult questions, such as what level of influence victims and survivors should have over interventions and whether influence may legitimately vary over time or in different aspects of truth commission work.

Finally, both transitional justice interventions and academic commentary increasingly register a distinction between official, top-down mechanisms and unofficial, local, community or grassroots initiatives (Bickford 2007; McEvoy and McGregor 2008). One challenge facing this emerging typology is participation related, in that the former fail to resonate with the local while the latter often cannot find significant national purchase and therefore are difficult to 'scale up'.

By rethinking participation, truth commissions with some degree of both state and societal support can help to bridge these divides (official–unofficial, invited–popular, state responsiveness and rights-based mobilisations) and more effectively engage with relevant publics. The TRC had a unique opportunity in this regard. It stood to gain from a rich heritage of civic action and cultures of resistance, some of which was profoundly democratic and rights-based. That it did not fulfil its potential owes something to its frayed relationship with the ANC government, but also reflects the TRC's own chosen focus and ways of working. This chapter suggests that rights-based participation offers a way to link the local to the national and global, truth commissions and processes of democratisation, and powerful articulatory moments with more enduring forms of public decision-making.

Before embarking on the substance of the chapter, a brief definitional digression is necessary. By civil society, I mean the associational realm between family and state, including the media. A strong public sphere is required for such associations to flourish, through interaction, debate and contestation that is both horizontal (with each other) and vertical (with the state). Finally, deliberative and participatory democracy are often considered to be compatible if not synonymous. But participatory democracy and political activism are most likely among like-minded people, in whose company confronting difference is either unnecessary or unsettling. In contrast, deliberation among people of diverse perspectives may foster tolerance and respect for differences of opinion, but it is unlikely to generate political passion and participation (Mutz 2006). The processes of truth commissions tend to privilege deliberation over participation, and official, invited participation over bottom-up, popular, rights-based participation. This chapter argues that a rebalancing is necessary if such interventions are to optimise their impacts.

The TRC and civil society

While civil society engagement with truth commissions is to varying degrees a feature of their contested origins, operations and aftermaths, the South African TRC, particularly at the outset, was a strikingly public, participatory enterprise.[1] Engagement with TRC structures over time, and with the government in its aftermath, proved uneven and more problematic. This section adopts a 'before', 'during' and 'after' framework to discuss TRC–civil society interactions. Themes that punctuate the discussion include the role of truth commissions in deepening participation and reconfiguring civil society–state relations in times of transition; the difficult balance between 'access points' and 'blind spots' in commission work; and the often 'double-edged' role of the media in processes of dissemination.[2]

Before the TRC came into being, NGOs and civil society played an important role in the conceptualisation of the TRC and, in particular, the lobbying process around the drafting of its founding legislation – the Promotion of National Unity and Reconciliation Act (No. 34 of 1995) – despite its technical and resource-intensive nature. The NGO, Justice in Transition, was set up by Alex Boraine, who developed a close working relationship with the new Minister of Justice, Dullah Omar, and later became Deputy Chairperson of the TRC. Justice in Transition served as a facilitator of early debates and a conduit between civil society and the government and legislative process. Discussion coalesced at two conferences: the first, 'Dealing with the Past' in February 1994, drew on international experiences from Eastern Europe and Latin America (Boraine *et al.* 1994); the second, 'Truth and Reconciliation' in July 1994, turned to South African participation and local debates (Boraine and Levy 1995).

Because of political tensions within the Government of National Unity, it was convenient for Dullah Omar to build coherence around and momentum for the idea of the TRC outside mainstream government structures. An informal committee, including political and civil society constituencies, was established to draft the legislation, which was then submitted to the parliamentary Portfolio Committee on Justice and Constitutional Development for further debate. This Committee conducted extensive public hearings – 150 hours in total – on the legislation. A range of civil society actors, NGOs and networks, including human rights, religious and mental health groups, made representations during the drafting process. Jurists and legal NGOs were also instrumental in these discussions (Rombouts 2002). One often cited example of impact is the opposition to an ANC and National Party compromise that amnesty hearings should be held behind closed doors. This was contested and the principle of public hearings was secured, other than where *in camera* hearings were necessary due to a likelihood of harm to any person or in the interests of justice.

Similarly, NGOs and others influenced the process of commissioner selection, preventing a narrow political deal. Although President Mandela could have simply appointed the commissioners, a selection process drafted by the NGO Coalition on the TRC (Johannesburg) was adopted with only minor changes. A committee, appointed by President Mandela, which included both political party and NGO representatives, called for nominations. In all, 299 people were nominated. Interviews for a shortlist of around 50 prospective candidates took place in public hearings. A range of constituencies nominated candidates, and participated in and monitored the hearings. Thereafter, a list of 25 names was submitted by the committee to President Mandela. The President chose 15 commissioners from this list in consultation with the Cabinet of National Unity, and appointed two others who were not on the list – supposedly to make the commission more representative, but in violation of the otherwise transparent and accountable process. South Africa spent 18 months designing its truth commission, in large part because of the degree of consultation.

During the TRC's tenure, NGOs and civil society had to engage with a completely new structure. The relationship took essentially three forms: support and capacity-enhancing, information-sharing and policy formulation, and lobbying and critique. In the first category, the designated statement-taker programme utilised faith-based, non-governmental and community organisations to increasing the TRC's statement-taking capacity (TRC 1998, Vol. 1: 140–41), while the provision of victim support, and psychological and counselling services, relied heavily on outside assistance. The Khulumani Support Group, the main victim–survivor support group, for example, facilitated participation in the TRC through education and outreach, assisting people to submit statements and providing support before and after hearings.

The Reparation and Rehabilitation Committee was particularly dependent on civil society engagement, for example in the realms of policy development and subsequent monitoring of, and advocacy for, recommendation implementation (TRC 1998, Vol. 1: 287–89, Vol. 5: 170–95, 312–13; also see TRC 2003, Vol. 6: 92–180, 726–32). With support came expectations, and the perhaps inevitable disappointments, for example on reparations, saw support shade into more aggressive TRC- and government-directed lobbying and critique. Also at an information and policy level, the Centre for Applied Legal Studies (CALS) at the University of the Witwatersrand led an initiative that modified the TRC's policies on women's experiences and the gendering of human rights abuses

(Goldblatt and Meintjes 1998; Ross 2003, 2003a; TRC 1998, Vol. 4: 282–316). The TRC's sector and theme hearings, in general, sought out NGO and civil society submissions and participation with the aim of accessing a broader picture of apartheid. Such engagement was often important, if unevenly so, in framing the content of the hearings, and subsequent report entries and findings.[3]

It is also worth charting some of the difficulties that hindered civil society–TRC interaction. Relations were hampered by factors including (1) the *ad hoc* and uneven nature of relationships with the TRC (by region, urban/rural setting and issue coverage), that failed to make the most of complementary capacities (NGO databases and networks were one under-used resource); (2) poor coordination among NGOs; (3) a lack of funding for NGOs, and loss of staff to the TRC; (4) the complex organisational and management structure of the TRC; (5) a desire to maintain independence on both sides, and sensitivities within the TRC to accusations of bias arising from alliances with previously anti-apartheid organisations; and (6) a tendency for the TRC to prioritise and bring to the fore formal structures and specialised organisations rather than a broader-based community involvement. The TRC's lack of engagement with local justice structures, for example, was a notable omission (R. Wilson 2001). The TRC, in essence, prioritised well-resourced, organisational forms (NGOs) over less formal mobilisations, and invited over popular spaces of participation. Further, while there was information-sharing, consultation and some joint decision-making, participation rarely extended to initiation and control by stakeholders.

That said, it is important to acknowledge that reconfiguring state–civil society relations is a major challenge in transitional contexts in general, and for transitional justice interventions in particular (Backer 2003; Bell and Keenan 2004; Crocker 2000; ICHRP 2003). Civil society itself can be weak: virtually non-existent, internally divided, mired in clientship relationships with power-holders and service delivery functions, dependent on the state or international donors, partisan, undemocratic and uncivil. Even for robust civil society actors, moving beyond an oppositional stance towards a previously repressive state requires not only macro-political change but also political processes and institutional arrangements through which new relationships can be negotiated. However fleetingly, official truth commissions potentially provide such processes and arrangements, that while emblematic in their imperfection, help to shift mainstream civil society into new terrain. Civil society actors can learn to balance and shift between collaboration and capacity-building to make the most of the legal and political opportunities within the new dispensation on the one hand, and monitoring, lobbying, critique and outright confrontation on the other. Negotiating roles, relationships and spheres of influence represents a foundational lesson in democracy for both civil society and the state; and it is not always an easy set of lessons to learn:

> As with civil society's general relationship to the new government, there were inherent tensions involved in NGOs' multiple roles as critic, supporter,

watchdog and partner. It was particularly this 'watchdog' function that was not well received by the TRC.

(van der Merwe et al. 1999: 66)

The final dimension of TRC–civil society relations was media coverage. A policy of 'maximum publicity' (TRC 1998, Vol. 1: 352, see 352–63) enabled the TRC to have an extraordinary reach, both within South Africa and internationally. As with many African countries the most widely accessible medium in South Africa is radio, and the South African Broadcasting Corporation (SABC) radio service appointed a pool of journalists to cover the work of the TRC in all South Africa's 11 languages. Comprehensive news and current affairs coverage was supplemented by a weekly 'wrap up' of TRC activities on all language stations and live coverage of hearings on Radio 2000 between April 1996 (when hearings commenced) and September 1996, and from June 1997. The cessation of the latter forms of coverage due to financial constraints was reversed when the TRC secured a grant for recommencement from the Norwegian government. Also important in shaping public perceptions of the TRC was the often extensive television news coverage, and SABC-TV's weekly programme, *TRC Special Report*, hosted by the high-profile journalist Max du Preez, on Sunday evenings. This landmark programme secured audiences of over a million each week. Finally, the TRC's work was widely covered in the print media, with many newspapers appointing specialist correspondents. Its website carried news, written submissions, hearing transcripts, amnesty decisions, policy documents and more. Such coverage and information dissemination remains without precedent in the relatively short history of truth commissions.

Nevertheless, for the TRC, as for other commissions, a core problematic was the need to achieve 'maximum publicity' *and* balanced publicity. There was a perception, shared by high-level staff within the TRC, that media coverage was a 'double-edged sword' (Boraine 2000: 54; Verwoerd 1996: 70–73; Villa-Vicencio 2000: 25–27; Villa-Vicencio and Verwoerd 2000: 283–85; also TRC 1998, Vol. 1: 104–5). Media-informed perceptions of the TRC increased its reach and accessibility but also mediated its impact, rendering it vulnerable to political criticism and caricatured modes of representation. An often hostile Afrikaans media led the criticism ('talk shop', 'witch hunt'); simplified messages and stereotyped images (the weeping black woman, the Afrikaans white male perpetrator) were illustrative of the prevailing caricatures.

> The televisuality of the TRC encourages the simplistic dichotomy of perpetrator/victim. The unattractive physical appearance of perpetrators from the security apparatus ... are ideal for the villain role. When we see – literally – characters like these, we find it easier to dismiss the more ambiguous and difficult questions of culpability and complicity ... The televisual

medium makes it difficult to get beyond the mass media cult of personality into structural issues.

(Krabill 2001: 582)[4]

Such depictions can alienate as well as engage, and were a process impact that it was difficult for other facets of the TRC's work to remedy. Criticisms have been directed at the TRC's decision to opt for advertising and communications agencies, and thereby media profile, over a public education programme involving a broad range of NGO, community and media actors (public education still took place but on a much reduced scale and often without TRC support: van der Merwe *et al.* 1999: 72). A predictable outcome was the triumph of symbolism and value change over substance and structural change, as national impacts and agendas, and often misplaced and media-driven public perceptions of justice delivery and reconciliation, trumped a more genuine victim or community focus (van der Merwe 2003).

The media, therefore, was the most important arena in which the TRC took on a public form, and through which societal knowledge was acquired of its work and ethos. Krabill (2001) speaks of a symbiotic relationship, and a profound synergy of working methods and interests linked the two, not least in speaking truth to reconciliation and because the media was among those societal institutions tainted by the past and seeking rebirth in the new South Africa.[5] If the TRC appropriated the media to nation-building agendas such as unity in diversity, democratic inclusion and reconciliation, and to educate and inform the public; the media also performed the TRC, constructing and mediating it through its own agendas, discourses and constraints. Testimony, in particular, fed the media's processes of selection, and its use of sound-bites, narrativisation and personalisation, dramatic moments and images of emotion and suffering, as the media served to broker the public event (McEachern 2002).

Truth commission–media relations, in conclusion, bequeath a range of possibilities and limitations. Outcomes can be problematic, characterised by layers of formula and standardisation; spectacle, distance and selection producing impoverished understandings of truth; and commodification of suffering, cultures of victimhood and 'compassion fatigue'. A conspiracy of top-down discourses is a seductive explanation of TRC outcomes. The media, human rights and religion shared a tendency to individualise (the spectacular), and universalise (in shared paradigms of violence, suffering, remorse, redemption and reconciliation), thereby overlooking more nuanced engagements with context, complexity and complicity (Posel and Simpson 2002: 7–9).[6] Yet the universalising impulse can have positive as well as negative repercussions. McEachern (2002: 48–56) argues that in South Africa the universalising tendencies of the media coverage of the TRC, stressing sameness rather than difference, served to unsettle apartheid's rationale and legacies. In addition, beyond mimicry, the media also appropriated the TRC to serve a variety of ends, by debating and contesting its work and ethos, and by enabling others to do the same.

Finally, and in contrast to its access points and avenues for participation, the TRC was also characterised by forms of closure and exclusion. Among the latter were (1) policies on amnesty provisions and prosecutions which throughout have largely been decided by political actors behind closed doors; (2) choices that the TRC itself made that fit into this category (for example, with regard to its participation agenda); and (3) sites of closure in the aftermath of the Commission (decisions on reparations and the TRC's recommendations in general; archival access; plus a continuation of policies identified in point (1)).[7] Thanks to a failure to engage with civil society on these issues, it is largely around such blind spots that civil society activism has been mobilised.

Ultimately, the legacy of the TRC has been informed by transparency and engagement with civil society, but also blind spots and a 'double-edged' relationship with the media. It has also been informed by the transition from the relatively open TRC process to its decidedly more closed aftermath, overseen by a sometimes hostile, sometimes simply otherwise preoccupied, ANC government. Participation through the before, during and after phases outlined above follows a familiar transitional pattern: a window of participatory opportunity, part adjustment to the new order and a lack of capacity, part genuine openness to new ideas and ways of doing things, is soon diminished by formulaic participatory processes and government reassertions of control. For these reasons, the 'after' phase in South Africa has at one level been the most difficult one for civil society engagement, and many actors have upped their criticism of both the TRC and the government in pursuit of the 'unfinished business' agenda. But arguably it has also been the most liberating, allowing NGOs and others to appropriate and refashion the TRC's legacy more freely. Nevertheless, as a democratic learning process the lessons have been chastening. They are emblematic of the fact that it is difficult to move participation beyond formal structures and official venues, call-and-response patterns, points of access and closure patrolled by governments or truth commissions, and from invitation-based to rights-based paradigms.

The TRC and the public sphere

Alongside the TRC–civil society partnership, the TRC also played a role in reshaping the public sphere, as illustrated by the discussion of the media above. This chapter continues with an examination of the ways in which the TRC informed the values and discourse of democratic debate as key components of social truth. The TRC sought to make a contribution to cementing the shift from conflict to politics and civic discourse. It did; but the TRC's chosen investment in procedural and political liberalism also limited its challenge to power and structural inequality.

Values

As noted in Chapter 1, it may be easier to reach consensus on values than on history or structural change. According to this line of argument, truth commission truths can be understood to be as much about creating conditions for dialogue and civil disagreement in the future as about documenting or fundamentally challenging the past or present. What might this value-base look like?

In his empirical analysis of South African public opinion, conducted in 2000–1, Gibson (2004) argues that the homestead of reconciliation has four rooms: interracial reconciliation, political tolerance, the creation of a culture of human rights, and the legitimacy of political institutions. The picture that emerges from this survey as to whether the TRC, and more specifically its conception of truth, contributed to reconciliation is one of at best modest success (Gibson himself puts a more positive slant on his findings). Interestingly, interracial reconciliation between the black majority and racial minorities, taken to mean trust, rejection of stereotypes and respect for those of other races, is more advanced than the very weak levels of political tolerance, understood as the minimalist coexistence required for political disputation and debate (117–75, 213–57). A culture of human rights and political institutions are both defined in the narrow terms of traditional liberalism, as captured by support for the rule of law or legal universalism and for parliament and the Constitutional Court respectively. Neither the principles nor the institutions of liberal democracy enjoy widespread support (176–212, 289–327). In general, black South Africans are the least reconciled group in the country. The TRC's impact on these attitudes has been uneven. Gibson's analysis suggests that the truth and reconciliation process impacted positively on interracial reconciliation (except for black attitudes towards whites, where it seems not to have had a negative impact). Acceptance of the TRC's truth has not played a dominant role in enhancing political tolerance but is related to a stronger acceptance of the need for legal universalism. Solace can be found in the fact that a young democracy is unlikely to overcome a fractured past overnight, but equally it would be unwise from these findings to see the TRC as any kind of panacea.

Snapshots of evidence for shifting values can be found elsewhere. Stavrou (interview 17/8/1998), speaking about KwaZulu-Natal, argues that the TRC, through notions such as reconciliation, can be understood as an attempt to inculcate the foundations of democracy and a political culture that goes beyond the absolute contrast between victory and defeat, winner annihilating loser. In a similar vein, Buur (2003: 159) notes that victim/survivor groups in South Africa have followed democratic rules, actively engaging in a 'democratic learning process', while registering their discontent with the TRC. Respect for democratic rules can be seen as one definition, or component, of reconciliation (Hayner 2002: 159; also Gibson 2004). In this sense, truth commissions can be an instrument of procedural liberalism, nurturing political processes and discourses through which to manage difference. The TRC's activities, through its public hearings and access points, and due to the fact that it both listened to and criticised all sides, support this thesis.

More troubling implications of this emphasis on procedural liberalism were brought to the fore by truth-related arguments put forward by the literary and cultural studies fraternity. Many in this camp remained wary of replacing one historical master-narrative (that of the apartheid state) with another (that of the new, ANC-dominated dispensation; of reconciliation and nation-building). Although, as we have seen in Chapter 1, the TRC did not articulate a clear master-narrative in its report, arguably it did communicate a meta-message in its public, discursive platforms (speaking truth to reconciliation). The Commission never resolved the tension between facilitating closure and encouraging ongoing debate. Voices from literature and cultural studies provoked heated controversy around the time of the publication of the TRC's report by calling for the debate in relation to the past to remain open and encompass the full spectrum of viewpoints and opinions.

Their lexicon was one of fragments, necessary incompleteness and multiple versions. The novelist André Brink's (1998, 1998a) vision, for example, is of the writer providing a tapestry of narratives, versions and voices, with the challenge of moral choice left to the reader. For poet and journalist Antjie Krog (1998), truth is primarily personal, experiential, multiple, linked to identity, the crucible for the restoration of the humanity of all South Africans:

> Will a Commission be sensitive to the word 'truth'? If its interest in truth is linked only to amnesty and compensation, then it will have chosen not truth, but justice. If it sees truth as the widest possible compilation of people's perceptions, stories, myths and experiences, it will have chosen to restore memory and to foster a new humanity, and perhaps that is justice in its deepest sense.
>
> (16; also see Nuttall and Coetzee 1998)

Factual or forensic truth is not prioritised, and is even potentially undermined, in these deliberations. Values such as inclusion are privileged over a human rights grammar of facts, corroboration and adjudication. In their closest institutional approximation, these are the truths of the TRC's various public hearings. More tellingly, they are the truths of the novel. But, returning to the tension between hearings and reports, a truth commission report is not generically a novel, and while being multi-vocal it cannot embrace the same degree of open-endedness, ambiguity and non-resolution. Crucially, the tenacity with which multiple, divergent truths are held by their disciples as the only truth poses a major obstacle to reconciliation. Simply mapping contradictory truths potentially entrenches difference.

While a core argument of this book is that human rights in practice often needs to balance, if not morally equate, different rights and constituency interests, this does not mean that there is no role for judgement. Far from it, in shaping truth some adjudication is required. An unsettling family resemblance exists between cultural problematisations of truth and the political stance of rationalisers and deniers. Former President F. W. De Klerk, in the first National Party submission to the TRC (1996), stated:

> The Commission should also consider the elusive nature of 'truth' in an historical or political context. Perceptions of what is true vary from time to time, from place to place and from party to party according to the affiliations and convictions of those involved. The Commission should bear this in mind when considering the motives and actions of those involved in the conflict of the past.

Looking for a response one need stray no further than the observations of the sociologist Stan Cohen (2001: 286–87), who writes that 'as a citizen of South Africa, Ethiopia, Cambodia or Zaire, I would prefer not to have a deconstructionist appointed to be chairperson of our Truth and Justice Commission. The resulting text would be interesting, but not in my interests.' To provide a concrete illustration, where perpetrators applied for amnesty in South Africa they often gave synchronised accounts, but when they provided different accounts of events – involving, for example, 'sanitised' or more brutal versions of a killing, or whether an activist was an informer for the state or a security policeman was an informer for the ANC – who should the families of the victims believe? (Cherry 2000). Such determinations could bequeath the status of hero or villain; they were life-defining and life-changing.

Of course, we each have our own interpretation of the past, truth is distilled through relations of power and experiences of history, and the past is infected with the agendas and priorities of the present. Of course, different interpretations of and beliefs about the past will remain within the public sphere. But, as argued in the previous chapter, facts and interpretations are interdependent; the accumulation of facts shapes the limits of interpretation. Certain claims can transmute into verifiable fact. Victims and survivors demand truths the hand can touch:

> Somewhere there is an elusive vantage-point that is not on the side of either side, but just a little beyond both sides. From here, routine exaggeration and manipulation of the facts can be observed; cover-ups can be photographed (secret graves, destruction of evidence, cleaning up a previously photographed burial site), and the voices of Karadic-equivalents recorded on tape ('So-called massacre'; 'no order to kill them'; 'atrocity stories part of an international conspiracy ... '; 'the bodies were Muslim soldiers killed in legitimate fighting').
>
> (Cohen 2001: 283)

Through their truth processes, truth commissions aspire to shift, not simply reproduce, the national truth profile, and increase and relocate the core of shared truths. Gibson's (2004: 68–116, 156–66) empirical research suggests that the TRC did just this, and helped create a more shared collective memory of apartheid by increasing the consensus that apartheid was a crime against humanity *and* that abuses were committed by both sides. Such an outcome suggests that the TRC went beyond facts to make an interpretive contribution, and indicates a shift in public perception to a middle ground. Gibson notes that it is difficult to achieve reconciliation between absolute good and evil; but the journey is made easier if the hard edges of each encampment are compromised somewhat. In short: 'Moral relativism, I hypothesize, contributes to reconciliation' (76). But such a moderating and moderated truth is not uncontroversial, in part because it raises the danger of perceived equivalence (see Chapter 1), but also because the balm of moderation appears to include a scenario in which *all* South Africans are surprisingly uncritical of apartheid (or aspects thereof, e.g. racial segregation). If a portion of the TRC's gift to collective memory is 'a moderate view of apartheid' (99) (apartheid as ideology), despite rallying people behind the view that apartheid was a crime against humanity (apartheid as implemented), this is surely an ambiguous outcome. As such, shaping understandings of truth alone is also not enough, attention needs to focus on how truth, especially interpretive truth, is refracted through other priorities and agendas.

It is imperative that truth commissions go beyond the most banal post-modern truths (all are victims; all voices should be heard and equally valued). Plurality and difference are not necessarily good regardless of content and context. There are narratives, versions and voices that need to be confronted and refuted. Writers and critics should be wary of providing the ammunition to undermine the quest for empirical evidence and objective knowledge that many of apartheid's victims still so desperately need, and for revisionists and relativists congregating at the gateway of disinformation. These are key challenges for truth commissions and nascent democracies. How to combine acknowledgement of the experiential validity of testimonies from all sides with the ability to identify facts and adjudicate between competing claims? How to balance two prevailing dynamics of transition – inclusion and compromise versus principle and adjudication – as played out in the realm of public truth? How to make a benchmark contribution to documenting and understanding the past without closing off debate? Truth commissions are tasked with collaborative, democratic history-making, but situated in a transformative process, in which history is an act of reparation and vindication for the oppressed and voiceless. Truth, in this process, must take sides and make enemies.

The TRC, in conclusion, articulated the values of procedural liberalism through its working methods and public engagements. It provoked diverse reactions and sometimes acrimonious responses. It can also claim to have shifted the terms of the debate about the past and the moral standing of participants in the discussion, and to have provided some support for the value-base necessary to manage difference in the future. This is a positive contribution to political transition and human rights, as long as deliberation does not preclude the ability to adjudicate and make moral judgements.

Discourse

The TRC also shaped the discourse of democratic debate (as in Chapter 1, Bhatia's definition of discourse is employed: 'language use in institutional, professional or more general social contexts'). Within the official discourse of apartheid, violence was done to, and through, language. The definitions of terms such as 'communism' and 'terrorism' were rewritten to the extent that they became a nonsense. The government denied that it sanctioned detention without trial, that torture or custodial deaths due to torture took place, and that there were any political trials or political prisoners. Meaning itself was rewritten, resulting in what Taussig (1987: 4) calls the magical realism of state discourse. Official lies, secrecy, denial and misinformation were challenged by the TRC in ways that helped to restore meaning and integrity to official discourse. The TRC's findings on the language and policy of eliminations, the real meaning of terms such as 'take out', 'wipe out', 'eradicate' and 'eliminate', provide an illustrative example (TRC 1998, Vol. 5: 214–18, also 294–99). A 'gray zone of deniability' (Gobodo-Madikizela 2003: 65) can begin to be replaced by the sharper, clearer light of transparency and accountability.

Language, therefore, has to be rescued from its own history of abuse, reclaimed by state and citizen. Phelps (2004: 50) uses the analogy of pollution and cleansing, Feitlowitz (1998: 62) that of a scarred body needing to be healed.[8] Victims/survivors at the TRC hearings were reduced to silence, without language, struggled for words but also, remarkably and poignantly, found words and language, often in their mother tongue.

> [A]cademics say pain destroys language ... And to get that memory, to fix it in words, to capture it with the precise image, is to be present at the birth of language itself ... So maybe this is what the Commission is all about – finding words.
>
> (Krog 1998: 42–43)

On a broader canvas, the TRC, and media coverage of its proceedings, gave South Africans a shared vocabulary – truth, justice, reconciliation, reparations, forgiveness, accountability, apology – with which to discuss the past and present.[9]

Finding words, forging language in new democracies, can be an exercise in the reallocation of power. Helping to navigate this terrain, Anthonissen (2006) suggests, is critical discourse analysis and more specifically discourse sociolinguistics. This approach posits discourse as a social practice embedded in context and relations of power, whereby language reflects and constructs society and societal change. As such, the TRC victim hearings (in Anthonissen's analysis the focus is on the theme hearing for what became known as the Trojan Horse ambush killings), reflected a range of powers, but in the process demystified old power and communicative strategies and actively sought to bring about a redistribution of power:

> The selected excerpts from the Trojan Horse texts show an interesting shift in power: in 1985 Mr V was in a position to use live ammunition in the pursuit of apprehending teenage 'ringleaders'; in the court case that followed he was protected by the position he held in relation to the government and armed forces. Such positions afforded him a degree of security that those traumatised by the shootings did not experience. At the TRC hearing the tables appear to be turned. Mr V finds himself in a considerably less powerful position, which is textually marked: he does not testify freely; he reads from a carefully prepared text. His testimony starts with a request for permission to continue.
>
> (Anthonissen 2006)

The reframing of testimony by commissioners at the hearings, constructing victims and witnesses in a more positive light and perpetrators in a more negative light than they themselves had done in their own self-reporting, is a further example of the TRC's role in the discursive redistribution of power. 'The hearings became a new kind of public discourse', Anthonissen argues, as the mediation of the past and relations of power helped to forge new discursive and democratic practices. Such reversals were a feature of the TRC's hearings, but need to be put into context. Reversals reflected a pre-existing transitional redistribution of power as well as acting as generators of change. Empowering moments are not necessarily indicative of empowered lives.

This discussion of the values and discourse of the TRC illustrates that the two are interconnected, and one strength of the Commission was that it helped to locate a subset of principles and words to foster debate and the managing of difference. Nevertheless, the chosen vernacular and procedures of liberalism are somewhat modest agents of change. Particularly in societies marked by stark inequalities, notably in relation to education and access to the public sphere, an obvious shortcoming is that this approach is likely to leave deep-rooted power dynamics and structural fault-lines relatively untouched. In fact it may just provide a more acceptable veneer for the maintenance of elite privilege. Where the TRC was weak was in creating links between democratic principles and the legacies and contingencies of power in such a way that the former became an enduring challenge to the latter. In short, it was weak on linking deliberation and participation so that both facets of democracy, including the necessary preconditions for their realisation, came to be routinely framed as an entitlement. To have created such links would have required a different repertoire of values and discourses (stressing values such as redistribution and social justice, and a rights-based approach to process as well as content issues).

The two preceding sections have explored the interface between the TRC and the society in which it operated, identifying openings and opportunities as well as barriers and challenges in a relationship in which each influenced the other. The chapter concludes by exploring a case study of the interaction between the TRC, civil society and the public sphere. What happens when testimony, often initially embedded in relationships of immediacy and even intimacy, enters an increasingly global and media-dominated public sphere?

Testimony in the public sphere

Self-narration offers what Hofmeyr calls 'transitory forms of power' (1988: 4): it allows the narrator to relive, control, transform, (re)imagine events, to reclaim and construct chosen identities and social interactions. Enormous expectations are placed on testimony, both oral and written, in the contexts of political resistance and transition. From truth commissions, to the court room, to trauma counselling, to collaborative narratives such as *testimonio*, these potentials are often seen as empowering, cathartic, as heralding the arrival of a new 'regime of truth' (Foucault 1991: 73). The purpose of the final section of the chapter is to ask some questions about the politics and ethics of this process when it takes place in public fora and an increasingly globalised public sphere. The argument presented is that the marginalised and subaltern increasingly have a voice, but little or no control over representation, interpretation and dissemination.[10] To speak is not a one-off event but a process spanning various narrations, interpretations and reinterpretations, the telling and the representation and reception of the telling.

Testimony is spoken, written, translated into visual images by the media; moves between the private and the public, memory and history, the personal and the political; between different expectations of the genre of testimony, between South and North, between cultures; between an original context of performance and subsequent (re)performances. In this movement across and between, testimony retains the highly suggestive capacity to be in both places at once.

> 'Testimony' as a concept has a special double connotation: it contains objective, judicial, public and political aspects as well as subjective, spiritual, cathartic and private aspects. Testimony thus contains the quality of uniting within its structure the private and the political levels.
> (Agger, cited in Ross 2003b: 331)

From the 1990s onwards there was the interconnected rise of globalisation, human rights and testimony or personal narrative, and specifically such narratives as a potent vehicle for advancing global human rights claims (Schaffer and Smith 2004). There was an enabling proliferation of narrative sites, and unprecedented access to platforms from which the subaltern voice could be heard and disseminated. Such sites and platforms were provided by UN mechanisms and a series of global conferences (on human rights, women, etc.), new human rights-related institutions (national human rights institutions, truth commissions), an explosion in the number and reach of NGOs and social movements, the World Social Forum and anti- or alternative-globalisation movements, 24-hour news broadcasts, the web, and a growing market for subaltern autobiographies, collaborative narratives and *testimonio*.

Where the shared language, experience and values necessary for democratic debate are absent, testimony, it is claimed, can help forge understandings across difference and create the conditions for argument and debate to begin (Young 2002: 70–77). Mapping on agenda that goes beyond procedural liberalism, testimony assumed power not only in the here and now, but in the elsewhere and tomorrow, to humanise the hitherto abstract, transcend cultural and political difference, and cement the solidarity of strangers.

But a schism can arise between the right to voice and the right to frame its meaning and control its subsequent use – a tension that Schaffer and Smith (2004: 5–9) ascribe to the transformations of stories across the processes of production, circulation and reception. A central concern in the discussion that follows, therefore, is who owns and controls testimony within the increasingly globalised public sphere. Any number of snapshots illustrate the tensions between the global and the local in the circulations and use of testimony. While there are several high-profile illustrations of these patterns – such as the Menchú–Stoll controversy (Arias 2001; Menchú 1984, 2001; Stoll 1999)[11] or the Video Archive for Holocaust Testimonies at Yale University (Hartman 2000) – the following example is perhaps more closely linked to the work of truth commissions. Keck and Sikkink (1998: 19), in the context of the work of transnational advocacy networks and the mobilising potential of testimony, write:

> activists interpret facts and testimony, usually framing issues simply, in terms of right and wrong, because their purpose is to persuade people and stimulate them to act ... however, we have to recognize the mediations involved ... [t]here is frequently a huge gap between the story's original telling and the retellings – in its sociocultural context, its instrumental meaning, and even its language. Local people, in other words, sometimes lose control over their stories in a transnational campaign.

Persuasive arguments suggest that the global is reshaping the local in the testimonial realm. To cite one example: 'Cultural responses to the traumatic effects of political violence often transform the local idioms of victims into universal professional languages of complaint and restitution – and thereby remake both representations and experiences of suffering' (Kleinman *et al.* 1997: x). Global or universal discourses engendering and framing testimonial truth-telling include the already mentioned discourses of human rights, the media and religion, but also those pervading the economic marketplace, memorial practice and tourism, academia (current fashions for memory, memorialisation, witnessing, trauma and so on), and interventions addressing health and post-traumatic stress. A trend to reframe suffering as individual and universal chimes with the demands of many of these discourses, as well as with the perceived requirements of advocacy and activism. Through such processes, expectations about how suffering should be addressed are also remade. A lack of control over reception, and often unmet expectations regarding response, can rebound to diminish the future potential for radical voicing.

The implications of increasingly globalised patterns of self-narration and reception are wide-ranging, however, and include more democratic access to international attention and mechanisms of redress. Deeper insights can be gained by viewing the various discourses traversing the global and local as sites of struggle and debate, simultaneously appropriated, adapted and mobilised from above and below (McEvoy 2008: 33–37; McEvoy and McGregor 2008: 7–9). For example, testimonial truth-telling can engage with human rights in ways that assert both universality and difference, holding the two in dialogue across diverse sites of narration and reception:

> [T]he invocation of universal principles paradoxically makes certain local particularities visible. Simultaneously, the local inflections of universal principles attached to the concept of universal human rights generate implicit and explicit critiques of the exclusionary terms of the universal.
> (Schaffer and Smith 2004: 227)

Such dynamics play out quite explicitly in the work and aftermaths of truth commissions. Ross (2003: 100–1), discussing the work of the TRC, states that local discourses 'reflect and refract' larger processes, as seen in the framing of certain, but not all, encounters in terms of 'reconciliation'. Therefore, the effects of testimonial truth-telling, and the local-global interface, need to be plotted with care.

That said, it is clear how easily trust, painstakingly constructed and forged in the intimacy of safe spaces, including some official spaces, can be violated within an ever expanding public sphere, as the distance between narration and reception grows in time and space. With voice comes power; the lack of control over representation in truth commission or human rights reports, the court room, the media or elsewhere, can mark a return to powerlessness. The issues of ownership and control of testimony in a globalised public sphere raise important political and ethical questions that need to be addressed by academics and activists alike. What is our duty of care to those with whom we work and to their stories? What expectations can realistically be attached to public voicing? How do we react when the subaltern speaks and then regrets having spoken?

Such questions suggest that for truth commissions not to tackle structural concerns, and specifically issues of control and participation, is likely to imperil their symbolic impacts. What follows looks at the work of and research on the TRC as an example of the challenges posed by the public life of testimony. An examination of problematic aspects of institutional practice and narrative circulation is followed by an exploration of bottom-up research strategies developed by victim/survivor groups and NGOs which are reclaiming control and ownership over their life stories, and supplementing the subaltern voice with a subaltern method. What this discussion confirms is that 'restoration of dignity is not simply a function of restored voice, but of a voice in control – that is, a voice with a signature' (Ross 2003b: 336).

The TRC and testimony[12]

Alex Boraine, deputy chairperson of the TRC, has described the public victims' hearings of the South African TRC as a 'liberated zone' (2000: 99). Although not an uncontested framing of the hearings, it provides a useful way of distinguishing between the locations of testimonial delivery and subsequent circulation. Several challenges are discussed briefly below in order to map the determinants of whether and how testimony circulated. These include: hearability or narrative inequality; the reification of victimhood; and circulation in communities and beyond.

One problem arose from what Blommaert et al. (2000) describe as 'narrative inequality and the problem of hearability' with regard to the public victim hearings. Echoing Boraine, these authors depict the hearings as spaces of intended equality, 'a format of power and prestige [was] offered to the powerless' (5), while acknowledging that '[p]eople don't enter the public forum as equals' (2–3). Inherited, structural inequalities percolated into the hearings. Some stories made it more easily than others into the public sphere and history. Certain narratives and individuals attained considerable prominence while others were reduced to facts and data. Impacting on the 'who, what and how' of hearability were factors such as the testifier's communicative skills, understandings of and ability to adapt to the requirements of the hearings (logical consistency, linearity), and awareness of the immediate and more distant audiences. Blommaert et al. provide three commentaries on these inequalities: (1) commissioner elicitation and co-authorship to bridge the communicative divide and improve the discursive 'fit'; (2) the clash of discourses in the testimony of one individual, Colin de Souza, which, despite commissioner interventions, stressed resistance rather than suffering;[13] and (3) shortcomings of poorly recorded transcripts (stripped of the performative aspects of delivery, differences in coherence and structure impact on hearability).[14]

The issue of hearability echoes concerns about whether the subaltern has a voice and control over his/her voice, and about the propensity for human rights discourse to erase, decontextualise and appropriate individual stories within its higher grammar of victims/perpetrators, violations, etc. The reification of victimhood as almost a condition of hearability, and a dominant characteristic of testimonial reception, illustrates the dangers. In the second of the three Blommaert et al. (2000) commentaries, de Souza, having resisted the imposition of victimhood at the hearing, is reinscribed as victim as the authors read for the 'deeply hidden transcript' of suffering and victimhood, arguing that this is his testimony's 'real' meaning. While de Souza clearly suffered, and the reading provided is subtle, de Souza himself sought to frame his life as one forged in struggle and resistance. Surely the possibility for such self-framing was the very essence of the TRC's potential? If he did not see himself as a victim, should others seek to so label him?

Other, related examples are not hard to find. Ross (2003, 2003a) details how the TRC constructed women as victims. In particular, she argues that the emergence of 'women' as a category in the Commission's work carried with it assumptions about the nature and severity of particular harms, notably privileging sexual violence while silencing other kinds of experience:

> diverse identities, activities and experiences were obscured through the emphasis on sexual difference and harm. The result is an overemphasis on the similarity of bodily experience at the expense of an understanding of the subjectivities produced through apartheid and resistance to it.
> (Ross 2003a: 175)

The fixing of identity serves to reinscribe gender roles, reify the concept of 'victim', limit acknowledgement of harm, and narrow the range of identities projected onto the past and into the future. A familiar pattern re-emerges in which lives are retold into the narrow human rights frame of violation, unilaterally de/recontextualised.[15]

Yvonne Khutwane's experience exemplifies these patterns (Ross 2003: 80–93).[16] Khutwane was the first woman to include a description of sexual violation in her public testimony. During her testimony at the victim hearings in Worcester in the Western Cape during June 1996 she spoke about her experience of abuse, including solitary confinement, torture, sexual molestation, and the petrol bombing of her house and alienation from her political community due to rumours that she was an informer. Sexual violation in the form narrated at the hearing was not part of Khutwane's written statement (in which a threat of rape was mentioned, not actual sexual molestation). Despite her reticence at the hearing, the new revelations were both solicited and returned to by the persistent interventions of HRV Committee member and psychologist Pumla Gobodo-Madikizela (also see Gobodo-Madikizela 2003: 90–94). In the end, one third of the testimony time was taken up by questions and answers about an event of sexual violation that Khutwane seemingly had not intended to narrate. In this collaborative narration, subsequent media coverage, the TRC report (in four separate entries) and academic studies, sexual violence is represented as the primary violation. The narrative Khutwane seemingly wanted to tell was displaced; certain kinds of violence and her political activism were downplayed as she was reduced to a victim of sexual abuse.[17]

TRC testimony also inserted itself into, and became the subject of debate and contestation within, national and community politics. Truth claims accepted in one site can be questioned elsewhere. The concerns of the TRC were not necessarily those of other constituencies, as illustrated by the reception of Khutwane's testimony in her home community, Zwelethemba. This reception included public responses to her account of sexual violation – 'I didn't know it would be like this' she comments (Ross 2003: 86) – but also discussion and disputes about the political strand of her narrative, specifically allegations of betrayal and the arson attack on her home, as issues germane to local politics (93–102). Within the community the story, locally embedded and interpreted, provides a commentary on a complex intersection of personal and political concerns: late 1980s political repression and the deep damage done by real and rumoured informing; political cleavages and fragility within the community, fuelled by Khutwane's affair with the ex-boyfriend of a powerful female comrade; and intergenerational tensions with activist youths. The politics of the past continues to shape the present, resulting in the reassertion of a broader political agenda in relation to testimonial interpretation in communities. As Ross suggests (100–2), reassessments of testimony in different locations and over time, 'the contingency of interpretation and the unevenness of reception', matter in relation to claims that truth produces healing and reconciliation. While the community impacts of the TRC may have been superficial overall, studies such as this indicate that testimonies did circulate locally, with some unexpected effects.

Finally, testimonies circulated beyond communities in the broader public sphere. Again, there is a need to revisit the question of who gets heard and why. 'The betrayer' was perhaps even more compelling than 'the victim' as a subject. Yazir Henri's experience with the TRC provides a final set of insights into testimonial circulation.[18] He has stated that the opportunity to testify before the TRC provided a previously lacking space to speak out in his own voice and to confront his past and reclaim his dignity. Henri sought to reassert his solidarity with the struggle, contest an existing narrative of betrayal, and contextualise his story within layers of compromise and complicity: 'I have a question: where does culpability rest? ... I wish to be recognised for who and what I am so that the falsification of my history be rectified.'[19] To speak, while not uncomplicated, was on balance a positive experience.

Beyond the public hearing, and in a manner that can be said to be characteristic of the TRC's charismatic narrators, Henri's story ceased to be his, took on a life of its own as it was variously appropriated, edited, (re)interpreted, retold, sold by others – the media, individual commentators (Krog 1998: 50–55), the TRC report (TRC 1998, Vol. 3: 458–59) – in a way that impacted profoundly on his life.

> Since testifying ... I have been called many names, placed within several stories, given several histories and the most harmful of narratives ... have now become a part of my public face ... the agonised confessor ... the betrayer.
>
> (Henri 2003: 266)

Henri has written: 'At the time of my testimony I had no idea what the consequences of "public" could have meant in the context of public hearings' (266). His attempt to reclaim and recontextualise himself, his voice and his past were undermined, in the short term at least, by public processes of dissemination and commentary.

For those who testify, a violation of their testimony can be felt as a violation of the self. Ross asks: 'If selfhood and "story" come to be experienced as congruent ... then what happens to the sense of self when "experience" is traced through the processes of entextualisation in which "testimony" becomes "text" and is re-embedded in diverse products?' (2003b: 333). While, of course, outcomes of such processes can be positive (fresh perspectives, deeper understandings) as well as negative (disempowerment, distortion), they are often disorientating for the testifier. It should also be noted that Henri is unusual in that he both testified before the TRC and subsequently produced commentary on his testimony and its public life.[20]

In circulations and appropriations expanding outwards into the global public sphere, TRC testimonies were de/recontextualised in arenas ranging from the media to community politics. Human rights discourse was clearly not the only perpetrator of such crimes. Dominant, if not always consistent, patterns emerge: testimonies were selectively and unequally heard, homogenised into stories of suffering and victimhood, and received differently in multiple sites of reception. Testimonial reception can easily create new contexts of vulnerability and violation. Initial sites of delivery ('liberated zones'), alongside their objectives and benefits, run the danger of being erased. This matters because such processes undermine the envisaged link between truth-telling and reconciliation. Facilitating this link requires greater control for the testifier in the realms of representation, interpretation and dissemination; and such control depends on more genuine forms of participation and accountability.

Subaltern research methods

One outcome of these fault-lines between narration and reception is that some victims and survivors reinhabit a narrative space all too reminiscent of the past, characterised by a sense of disempowerment, a loss of agency, retraumatisation, a distrust of research relationships lacking reciprocity, and a reluctance to retell stories that appear to benefit others while their lives remain unchanged. Unsurprisingly, part of a more critical grassroots, bottom-up response to the TRC has been a critique of prevailing research methods. Individuals and organisations have attempted to develop subaltern research methods to complement the subaltern voice. The struggle for ownership, control and participation in relation to narrated lives continues, but elsewhere.

Arguably, the methodologies of official institutions contain the seed of alternative approaches, in part because truth-telling can be linked, albeit often implicitly, to human rights consciousness-raising within truth commission research processes.

This connection is not always made in mainstream human rights research methods. In the case of the Peruvian TRC, it has been argued that an officially sanctioned form of truth-telling, and a process that linked truth-telling with human rights consciousness-raising, was the first step in breaking down entrenched habits of fear, silence and distrust, and empowering victims and survivors to participate in grassroots movements pursuing truth and justice. Laplante (2007: 435) writes: 'Victims–survivors are beginning to reject passive telling to third-party authors, and instead are appropriating their own agency in disseminating memory'. As such, it is 'the change in personal and political status as truth-tellers, and not just the content of this truth' that makes truth-telling important. Such conscientised citizens could, with time and support, act as keepers of memory, watchdogs against repression and as the midwives of democracy.

Other truth mechanisms, operating at the official–unofficial interface, also suggest that large-scale human rights projects have the potential to mobilise and conscientise. The unofficial Recovery of Historical Memory Project (REMHI) in Guatemala, initiated by the Human Rights Office of the Archbishop of Guatemala in 1995, through its more qualitative research methods is a suggestive example, in part because it sought to feed into, and augment, the official Commission for Historical Clarification (CEH). In all, 6,500 interviews were conducted. Training local people, many of whom were indigenous and spoke indigenous languages, facilitated a community statement-taking process that reached into rural areas. Questions went beyond the act of violence and the facts about a particular violation to address the personal characteristics of the victim, and experiential accounts of causes, context, impacts and responses from interviewees and communities. Emotional and psychological support was provided. In a context of widespread illiteracy, diverse media were used to disseminate REMHI's work and report (*Guatemala: Nunca Más*, published in 1998) – theatre, radio, videos, public workshops, educational materials, rituals and ceremonies. Teams, based on the network of interviewers, worked on popularising the report. Reflecting a research process driven by civil society, and concerned with participation, consultation and accessibility, Beristain, a member of the REMHI project team, describes it as a social movement seeking 'social reconstruction' and the return of memory to the communities (Beristain 1998, 1998a). This unofficial intervention, therefore, both fed its official counterpart and developed local capacities for history-making.

Mobilisations such as those in Peru and Guatemala are an indication of the potential of deeper forms of participation, and rights-based participation, as each positions victims and survivors of human rights abuses as agents rather than subjects of research, and gestures to ongoing processes of inquiry and activism beyond particular interventions. Important work has, therefore, been done within both official and unofficial truth projects. That said, the relationship between the two can be conceived in a variety of ways. Some commentators use the official as the main point of reference, with the unofficial essentially mimicking or gap-filling – see, for example, Bickford's (2007) discussion of 'unofficial truth projects', which conceives of three kinds of relationship: replacement, precursor and complementarity. This chapter adds a fourth component to the mix, a more conflictual relationship, and argues that official mechanisms need to take on board various lessons from below (as such, it echoes the call of McEvoy and McGregor (2008) for transitional justice from below as a form of grassroots activism). Again we see the tension between collaboration and critique in civil society–state relations, as both parties grapple with the challenges of transition. Despite some more radical official outlyers, it is largely due to unofficial projects that it is now possible to say that a subaltern voice is forging a subaltern methodology. A South Africa initiative helps clarify the nature of a subaltern method with greater precision: the ethics and research work of the Human Rights Media Centre (HRMC), based in Cape Town.

Shirley Gunn, a former member of Umkhonto we Sizwe (MK), the armed wing of the ANC, and now Director of the HRMC, uses the terms 'plundering' and 'rape' to describe the testimonial research attention and processes surrounding the TRC in South Africa – she testified before the TRC and her story acquired a high public profile.[21] As a result, HRMC's work entails an explicit rejection of mainstream academic and human rights research methodologies. The HRMC uses forms such as books of collected interviews, exhibitions and films. Projects have included the film, *We Never Give Up* (2002), made with the Western Cape branch of the Khulumani Support Group, as part of the post-TRC reparations campaign. This was followed by an exhibition of memory and healing work entitled 'Breaking the Silence: *A luta continua*' (2004), again involving Khulumani members and featuring scrap books and body maps as autobiographical forms. The HRMC publishes books of life stories on issues such as the experience of refugees from war-torn African countries in Cape Town, and the impact of political activism on mothers and their daughters (Gunn and Tal 2003; Gunn and Krwala 2008). Such books are complemented and rendered more accessible by other outputs, such as radio programmes.

The Trojan Horse history project is an ambitious and illustrative intervention combining life stories, education and memorialisation. Its goals include providing victims with dignified tombstones, engaging victims and perpetrators, and working with and across communities. As such, it includes participatory and deliberative objectives. Its focus is two apartheid-era shooting incidents in Athlone (a coloured community) and Crossroads (a black, African community), Cape Town, in October 1985 (Gunn 2007). These incidents were part of a pattern in which ambush tactics were used by the security forces concealed in a moving vehicle or at the scene to shoot at protesters and bystanders. There is 'unfinished business' here because the TRC focused on Athlone and neglected Crossroads and made no attempt to bring together the security force members and victims (ibid. 116–17; also see TRC 1998, Vol. 3: 435–37). Bringing together perpetrators and victims, and communities that remain racially distinct and divided, has proved difficult. But the HRMC's attempt to combine participation with working across societal divides and its commitment to rich, multi-form personal and community stories is exemplary.

The Centre also offers oral history and media training. The former includes the development of skills in areas such as oral history interviewing and the rights of subjects, research methods and ethics, and computing, while media training encompasses radio, film and print dissemination. A guide for practitioners on how to do oral history projects tellingly covers three phases: pre-production, production and post-production. The guide outlines a highly inclusive research process, including, for example, a series of consultative workshops with narrators. It is clear that the narrators or story-tellers should be encouraged to discuss ethical concerns; read and comment on interview transcripts and to-be-published life stories; shape interpretation, formats and media strategy as well as provide narratives; sign a publication consent form; and be supported in the post-publication phase.[22]

A recent publication, *The Story is Yours, the Choice is Yours: Media Ethics for Storytellers* (HRMC 2006), goes further, outlining a rights-based ethical code for story-tellers, in the following terms:

1 *Know your rights*. The reader is told: you have the right to decide whether or not you want to tell your story; you have the right to be treated with respect and to refuse to answer questions; you have the right to stop the interview at any point; you have the right not to have anything published about you that is not true, and that shows you to be a bad person.
2 *Ask questions*. Again, the reader is given concrete advice on what to ask a would-be interviewer: what is your name, who do you work for, and how can I contact you? Why do you want to interview me? Where will the interview material be used, and who will read, see or hear it? Will I be identified by name or in another way? Will I be able to check the story/photos/recordings before it is made public? May I refuse to let you use my story if I do not like the way it is written or shown?
3 *Decide on your terms*. Terms of agreement move towards a clear position on issues such as how the interview will be used and whether the narrator wants to be identified by name or photograph, to see the story before it is published and to have the opportunity to refuse to let their story be published.
4 *Have a written agreement*. This codifies relevant terms in writing and, if signed by relevant parties, has standing in legal disputes.
5 *Think before you talk*. Features a series of more reflective points about concerns such as the story-teller's feelings relating to the relevant experience (of anger, sadness, fear) and how these feelings may be affected by telling the story; and also how the perceptions or plight of others many be altered by hearing the narrator's story.
6 *Protect children*. Many of the above points apply, alongside measures such as the requirement that permission be obtained from parents or guardians for

interviews or photographs, and that interviews with children take place in the presence of a parent or trusted adult.
7 *Work through an organisation.* Indicates that organisations can provide the necessary support.

In the work of the HRMC, which seeks to apply these stipulations, the norm of unequal power relations within research is explicitly critiqued, and an attempt is made to give control within collaborative life-story narration and dissemination to the narrator/testifier. The ideal scenario is that through skills training and the loaning out of equipment (tape recorders, etc.), oral history work will be handed back to communities. Outputs realise an extraordinary, and necessary, creativity in the forms and media utilised, and the imperative to respect the integrity of life stories. In short, the HRMC seeks to enable people and organisations to take ownership of their stories – Gunn states, 'there is a lot of power in that, it is often all people have got' – in an attempt to free them from the agendas of outsiders. This is a very different research process to that of the TRC, advocating a distinctive politics, ethics and methodology. It is also an example of a human rights organisation seeking to secure legitimacy *and* enhanced impacts by not 'fetishising' conventional reports or methods.

An interesting, alternative route to and interpretation of ownership and control is provided by other activities of the Western Cape branch of the Khulumani Support Group. They have sought to control access to members and to manage the transit of stories into the public sphere themselves (through educational outreach initiatives, for example), and have treated testimony as an object or commodity to be sold (Colvin 2000: 24–31). The latter helps to overcome a tension between story-telling in a range of sites (the TRC, applications to government for welfare and social services, counselling, support groups), and socio-economic change, and frustration at the inability of the former to secure the latter. It self-consciously transforms narrative and research relationships into a means of redress.

> [T]he 'story' became not only an 'object' vested with a kind of moral force that could be exchanged within networks of social and moral obligation (i.e. traded to perpetrators, bystanders, government officials, likeminded victims, etc.); the story also became a commodity, something that could be literally sold outside of these close, personalised and historically grounded networks, into the impersonal networks of international academic production, development and humanitarian agencies, heritage industries and the global media.
>
> (Colvin 2000: 28)

Financially-based transactions both facilitate and undermine a sense of ownership and control, and a narrative marketplace can in turn shape and discipline the stories themselves. Tomaselli (2003) found a similar practice of commodification among the San Bushmen in the Kalahari Desert ('stories to tell, stories to sell'). Commodification breeds standardisation (the 'anthro-tourist text'). Among marginalised communities, identities inscribed in notions such as 'primitiveness' or 'victimhood' may be a given constituency's only developmental resource.

To conclude, those who testified before the TRC, alongside other marginalised groups such as those who did not have access to the Commission at all, have entered the debate about research methods and ethics, and indeed about what constitutes human rights research. Theirs is a subaltern method to complement the subaltern voice, and at its core is a radically transformed notion of participation which clearly does extend to the level of initiation and control by stakeholders. Its components can be summarised as follows:

1 The identification and development of local capacities, specifically capacities for interviewing and documentation, as the subjects of research become active agents in conducting research.
2 Human rights are embedded in the research process, and interviewees experiencing rights in this process is key to them claiming rights beyond.
3 Identity transformation, like alterations in state-civil society relations, requires facilitative processes, and such research processes hold the potential for victims (potentially passive) to acquire new identities (survivor, empowered agent, rights-holder).
4 Testimonies and their representation are creative in form and subversive in intent (hierarchies of research, knowledge and power are challenged).
5 Testimonies are handled with sensitivity – with life stories often represented in their entirety, or at least more fully – as is their passage between the private and public spheres.
6 One-off voicing is replaced by sites and skills that facilitate cycles of telling, as local people conduct their own research and activism in a more sustainable way (e.g. victims engage in research projects and memorialisation work).
7 Sustainable truth-telling and rights-based research processes create active citizens who will continue to champion justice and contest their marginalisation. Victim groups develop a 'civic competence' among their members (Madlingozi 2010: 220 – see Madlingozi for a powerful call for transitional justice to move beyond experts speaking about and for victims, to a position where victims speaking for themselves).[23]

It is clear that voice articulated on a public platform or in a statement-taking process can no longer be considered, if it ever really could, a simplistic form of power. The struggle now is both for the articulation of the marginalised and subaltern voice and for greater control over voice, representation, interpretation and dissemination. This in turn requires greater control of research processes and rights-based participation in such processes. Voice without control may be worse than silence; voice with these enabling features has the capacity to become a less perishable form of power. Such power could provide a more enduring challenge to the power relations of research, the public sphere, activism, the state and globalisation.

Conclusion

This chapter is a case study in ambiguous power. It has outlined an understanding of social truth, carried on the engines of the media and globalisation, as a complex, yet indispensable, weapon in the service of change within transitional politics. Several important lessons emerge from the analysis. The interfaces between truth commissions and civil society/the public sphere are characterised by opportunities and challenges. They have the potential to invigorate state–civil society relations and the values and discourse of democratic debate. A less optimal outcome is one of more blind spots than access points, indulgence of difference at the expense of necessary judgement, and appropriation of life stories by actors other than the narrator. The media in this setting is a 'double-edged sword'. Spectacle and iconic moments have the power to engage and distance, persuade and misrepresent. The need for maximum publicity and balanced publicity make the media a difficult partner in the quest for truth, justice and reconciliation. The key question is this: should the priority be symbolism, procedures and values or transforming power relations and structural change? It is argued here that both are important, and that neglect of the latter undermines genuine progress in the former. While clearly a truth commission cannot do everything, it equally should not be the nod towards justice that legitimises other forms of injustice, nor is there any point in having certain positive impacts (the catharsis of truth-telling, for example) undone by entirely predictable counter-impacts (the fact that lives are otherwise unchanged).

To contribute to the more ambitious goal of structural change in the context of remaking the public sphere, truth commissions need to facilitate participation as well as deliberation, and bottom-up, popular, rights-based participation as well as official, invited participation. Such participation, and the preconditions for it to flourish, should be framed as rights in both truth commission activities and their recommendations. Rights-based participation, linked to the radicalisation of truth-recovery as ongoing process, will help to maximise the legacy of commissions and ensure that the once articulated voice will in fact be twice and three times heard. Returning to one of the core arguments of the book, the goal of truth commission should be public description alongside constituency-building. Participatory, rights-based research methodologies are one way of building capacities so that marginalised voices can be heard in a more sustainable way.

This approach is not without its difficulties. To those already mentioned, we might add: why would any government and other official bodies provide the necessary responsiveness to such invasive citizen participation? Apart from the usual arguments – the instrumental need for citizen buy-in, the moral case for deepening democracy – there is an effectiveness justification. Friedman (2006) makes the point that social policy in South Africa is hampered because of a consistent gap between anti-poverty policy and the preferences of the poor. Listening to the poor would help to close this gap. Second, there is the danger that in post-conflict situations local, participatory histories will entrench inter-community divides. Commissions will need to ensure that they maintain the tradition of working across community divides, developing methodologies that combine deliberation *and* participation.

And finally, with specific reference to research, not all human rights research can be participatory. Those familiar with human rights missions will know that visits to prisons and police stations are often infrequent and brief; certain events, such as reports of torture or news of an imminent execution, require urgent action. Truth commissions can have the advantage of official and civil society support, focus predominantly on past events, and as a result have the potential to break new ground in participatory thinking. Even here, it is important not to make the perfect the enemy of the good: practitioners need to think in terms of a participation spectrum, a flexible set of methodologies to adapt to given contexts, aligned with the goal of aiming to secure the maximum participation possible in a given context (in short, seeing participatory options as spokes on a wheel rather than a hierarchy).

Let me conclude with a final conceptualisation of participation: the distinction between 'performed' and 'lived' participation (Pells 2009). Performed participation is extraordinary to everyday lives, often a one-off event, takes the form of consultation and involves the language of listening and being heard. Lived participation is rooted in the structures, activities and contexts of daily life, and as such is part of ongoing supportive relationships, for example in communities, and is seen as a right and a means of accessing other rights. Truth commissions typically practise the former form of participation. Performed participation has its place, but the ultimate goal is lived participation, and to achieve this goal official interventions have much to learn from unofficial, grassroots projects (see chapter 6). Participation of this kind could itself help to (re)define the keywords of transitional work, and it is a second core concept, justice, that is our next port of call.

Notes

1 The 'essential relationship' between non-governmental organisations (NGOs) and truth commissions has also spawned a 'how to' guide, structured to examine the relationship before, during and after the commission's period of operation, and containing useful country-based illustrations (International Centre for Transitional Justice and CDD-Ghana 2004; also see Backer 2003). There are broader questions relating to the legitimacy and constituency of NGOs that also need to be addressed. Who do NGOs represent? On whose behalf can they legitimately claim to speak?
2 This discussion draws on Boraine (2000: 11–75); Krog (1998: 1–25); Ross (2003: 134–35); and van der Merwe *et al.* (1999); also see the TRC report (TRC 1998) for further discussion of these issues: for example, a discussion of interactions with civil society is contained in the regional reports in Vol. 1: Chapter 12.
3 In addition to the sources cited above on the women's hearings, see, for example, Dyzenhaus (1998), Rombouts (2002) and Rombouts and Parmentier (2002) on the legal sector; Baldwin-Ragaven *et al.* (1999) on the health sector; Lyons (1999) and

Nattrass (1999) on business and labour; Cochrane *et al.* (1999) on the faith community; Chubb and van Dijk (2001) on the children and youth hearings; and, in general, TRC (1998, Vol. 4). See Chapman (2008) on the extent to which these hearings were able to provide a broader, or macro-, truth about apartheid.

4 On media representations of perpetrators, see Foster *et al.* (2005: 27–54). In response to a question about the TRC's impacts, Madeleine Fullard (interview, 21/4/2005) stated that the TRC delegitimised apartheid through 'iconic moments' in its public hearings. She cited a relative as someone who was not particularly interested in politics or the TRC, but who was reached by certain horror images – the example given was the brutal murder and braaing (barbecuing) of the bodies of four anti-apartheid activists – through which the past came to be understood and condemned. While this outcome may be positive, it was achieved through a misconception, as in this corner of the public imagination the unrepresentative, 'iconic moment' came to represent the true nature of apartheid violence.

5 A certain schizophrenia in relation to the first point can be seen by comparing the mainstream media's coverage of the TRC to its reporting on, for example, crime (see Chapter 4). On the second point, the TRC's media hearings were instructive (Garman 1997; Krabill 2001; TRC 1998, Vol. 4: 165–98).

6 R. Wilson (2001), in a wide-ranging critique of the influence of religion on the TRC process, states that it provided 'the main societal infrastructure' (131) and strong value support for the Commission:

> The TRC's organisational structure was intertwined with a number of societal institutions, but none like the church sector. The use of the same networks of personnel by both institutions led to an overlapping of structures and the joint (or parallel) transmission of the idea of national reconciliation to individual victims. The TRC relied more on the churches than NGOs ... as it saw the former as more authentic representatives of 'the community'.
>
> (132; see 130–42)

7 Colvin (2006) plots civil society input into the reparations debate before, during and after the TRC process. On the latter phase he writes:

> Part of the difficulty in understanding the deeper reasons and motivations behind the government's (frequently haphazard) position on reparations is that it has failed to engage victims, NGOs, and other groups in the kind of ongoing dialogue that might better illuminate their perspective. Government and civil society interactions have generally taken the form of an offhand 'call and response' where government officials make a brief comment on one aspect of reparations, civil society responds with its counterarguments and pleas for consultation, and the government remains silent. The next round only begins when some other government official makes another, usually unrelated, comment and the cycle begins anew.
>
> (201)

8 The scars left by repression on language are not static. As transitional violence becomes more criminal than political in nature, appropriations of language, at once creative and perverse, can take place. In their study of *amagents* (members of township gangs), Segal *et al.* (2001: 99) note the use of the term 'house arrest' for burglaries: '[t]he political meaning of the word has clearly been converted in the post-apartheid era'.

9 Again, not all the outcomes were particularly inspiring. Mbembe (2006: 3) has written about contemporary South Africa: 'A culture of corruption, impunity and non-accountability is fast becoming the norm. In the aftermath of the Truth and

Reconciliation Commission (TRC), public and private lives are conducted as if forgiveness was an inalienable right'.
10 On the subaltern voice, see Spivak (1988). By using the term 'subaltern' I mean to prioritise the agency of the oppressed and marginalised, notably as makers and recorders of history.
11 Writing about the *testimonio* at the heart of this particular controversy, *I, Rigoberta Menchú*, Beverley (2001: 233) states:

> It would be yet another version of the 'native informant' to grant a narrator such as Rigoberta Menchú only the possibility of being a witness, but not the power to create his or her own narrative authority and negotiate its conditions of truth and representativity. This would amount to saying that the subaltern can, of course, speak, but only through *us*, through our institutionally sanctioned authority and pretend objectivity as journalists or social scientists, which gives us the power to decide what counts as relevant and true in the narrator's 'raw material'. What *I, Rigoberta Menchú* forces us to confront is ... someone ... who assumes the right to tell the story in the way she feels will be most effective in molding both national and international public opinion in support of the ideas and values she favors.

12 The discussion that follows under the subheadings 'The TRC and testimony' and 'Subaltern research methods' owes a debt to the work of Fiona Ross (2003, 2003a, 2003b, 2005).
13 De Souza was a member of Umkhonto we Sizwe, the military wing of the ANC, and the Bonteheuwel Military Wing, a group from an area north of Cape Town with unclear and contested links to more formal oppositional groups such as the ANC.
14 For a further meditation on the hearability of testimony, see Krog *et al.* (2009).
15 It is interesting to note that while NGO advocacy was largely responsible for the Peru Truth and Reconciliation Commission integrating gender issues throughout its work – 'in training and communication strategies, guidelines for interviewers and statement takers, workshops, and public education, and as a cross-cutting theme throughout the Final Report' – an approach attempting to mainstream gender *and* address it as a specific focus area, as opposed to a strategy leaning towards parallelism or even ghettoisation, still led to an emphasis in the report on sexual abuse and rape (International Center for Transitional Justice and CDD-Ghana 2004: 13, 19).
16 Khutwane is a veteran political activist for the ANC.
17 This is a far from unique example of the way public testimony in official arenas can (re)violate women through processes of selection, representation, interpretation and dissemination over which they have little control: see Mertus (2003) on the landmark Foca rape trail at the International Criminal Tribunal for the Former Yugoslavia.
18 Henri was a member of Umkhonto we Sizwe, and is now Director of the Direct Action Centre for Peace and Memory in Cape Town.
19 This reference is from the testimony of Yazir Henri to the TRC's HRV Committee, on 6 August 1996. The testimony is available on the TRC's website, now housed on the Department of Justice and Constitutional Development website: www.doj.gov.za/trc.
20 For Henri, writing has become an important way to reclaim voice and agency, to take back his right to comment on and explain his life and experience of the TRC: 'the right to claim memory with honour, to live with it in dignity on one's own terms' (2003: 270, see 2000, 2003).
21 This discussion draws on a series of interviews conducted by the author with Shirley Gunn in Cape Town, especially those on 27 August 2002, 5 April 2005, 21 February 2006 and 26 August 2009.

22 'Three Phases of a Life History Project: A Model Developed by the Human Rights Media Centre', November 2004 (unpublished document on file with the author). Thembi Mgonjeni (telephone interview: 29/4/2005), formerly of the Treatment Action Campaign (TAC: an HIV/AIDS-focused social movement), who participated in a HRMC training programme, credited the training with increasing the use of oral histories in the TAC newsletter and more ethically sensitive practice.
23 This methodological template clearly resonates with certain established research methodologies, such as participatory action research, and the methodologies of others working 'from below' in the transitional justice field (see McEvoy and McGregor 2008; Gready 2008).

Chapter 3

Justice past

The central argument of the two justice-focused chapters is that newly democratic governments need a more integrated, coordinated strategy informing the meanings ascribed to, and policy interventions undertaken in the name of, justice. Ordinarily, in both the policy arena and academic commentary, there are distinct, mutually exclusive narratives rather than a synthesised plot. The first narrative concerns what is conventionally known as transitional justice. It is essentially backward-looking (how to reckon with a legacy of human rights abuses). To the extent that it projects into the future it does so through the prism of the past, seeking to prevent the past returning in the future. The second narrative is essentially forward-looking, and speaks of the criminal justice system and its reform, and the challenges caused by increases in criminal and social violence that often accompany the transition towards liberal, market democracy.

To begin to engage with such complex dynamics entails bringing the various narratives of violence and justice into dialogue. Political transition can provide a rare political opening, allowing meanings and policies in the justice field to be revisited, publicly debated and potentially revised. At present, the outcome is invariably a story of opportunities lost. This chapter focuses on the first justice narrative, justice past, while Chapter 4 addresses the second narrative, justice present.

The first narrative (1): the TRC and justice

The TRC's impact on the workings and reform of the criminal justice system and on prevailing conceptualisations of justice has been multi-layered. This chapter explores the relationship between amnesty and (in)justice both theoretically and in practice, and examines day-to-day cooperation, competition and mutual scrutiny and critique at the interface between the TRC and the criminal justice system (first narrative [1]). It concludes with an analysis of the TRC's conceptualisations of justice, specifically restorative and social justice (first narrative [2]).

Amnesty and justice: the theory

In the wake of an era characterised by violence and oppression, the central justice-related dilemma is the very basic one that comprehensive prosecutions are usually impossible, yet sweeping amnesty provisions are unjust. The more nuanced position is that some amnesties are more unjust than others, and the quest to reclaim as much justice as possible from any given amnesty provision. There are legitimate grounds for non-prosecution. Concerns such as threats, sometimes violent threats, to forestall or undermine transitions to democracy, judicial corruption and incapacity, and the huge cost of often complex and potentially endless human rights trials, can be very real. To insist on the impossible can itself undermine human rights and the rule of law. That said, amnesty can subvert the ideal that gross violations of human rights should be punished, that victims have fundamental rights in this regard, and the seminal notion of equality before the law. Yet again, it is invariably the powerful who get off and the powerless whose interests, and often strong desires for justice, are comprimised. Justice delivery, in contrast, would indicate that the new dispensation is different from the old and that impunity will not reign unchallenged. The issue, therefore, relates to more than narrow questions of legality, although these are important; it also concerns a broader potential for justice to remake the values and power relations of a new democracy (see Matear 2004, on post-Pinochet Chile). How, then, can justice be reclaimed from necessary and inevitable compromise?

There are commentators, including the TRC itself, who have argued that the conditional amnesty provision in South Africa was a form of justice. To make this case entails expanding understandings of justice well beyond prosecutions. For Slye (2000a) the argument rests on three basic premises: (1) that amnesty reflects the sovereign will of the people in making difficult choices, (2) that it contributes to truth and acknowledgement, and (3) that it contains a measure of accountability (procedurally through process requirements, and substantively in terms of the criteria to be met, such as full disclosure and political objective). The fundamental question here is whether these premises are best or widely understood as components of a holistic form of justice, and, if so, how much – democratic ownership, truth, accountability and so on – is enough to cross the justice threshold?

The record on each of Slye's premises is decidedly mixed (see Chapter 1 for the amnesty provision's record on truth and acknowledgement). Democratic ownership was diminished from the start by the fact that the issue of amnesty was not subjected to the otherwise rigorous levels of democratic debate during the political negotiations process and the drafting of the 1993 interim Constitution (No. 200 of 1993). Rather, the 'postamble' was a last minute deal between the ANC and the National Party. Similarly, while the precise details of the amnesty provision in the TRC's founding legislation did benefit from political debate and civil society input (leading to public hearings, for example), the TRC's Amnesty Committee members, unlike its commissioners, were appointed without a transparent or participatory process. As noted in Chapter 2, amnesty provisions overall constitute a democratic 'blind spot' in South Africa, in which elite pacting and behind-closed-doors decisions have prevailed. For long-term democratic ownership it is vital that pragmatism keeps a foothold in principle, and builds a supportive constituency for acceptable injustice, especially among victims and survivors. There is evidence that a broad public can engage constructively with difficult transitional policy decisions and compromises.[1]

Questions such as those cited above can also be asked of arguments put forward by the TRC (1998, Vol. 1: 121–22), and its staff (Verwoerd 1996: 76–80), that amnesty contributed to conventional justice in various ways. Crucially, amnesty, it is claimed, facilitated the transition to peace and democracy. It also provided insights into the causes of, and agencies responsible for, past abuse and, as a result, enabled the TRC to make preventive recommendations. This is what Dyzenhaus (1998: 6) describes as 'reconstructive' justice, 'a mode of justice which seeks institutional transformation through an examination of the wrongs of the past'.[2] Finally, those who were denied or failed to apply for amnesty could be prosecuted.

The TRC has given rise to what can be summarised as the 'no justice', 'as justice' and 'more justice' approaches. Similar terrain is covered by Verwoerd's (1996: 73–80; 1997) distinction between 'justice vs the TRC' and 'justice and the TRC'. The 'justice vs the TRC' approach (combining the 'no justice' and 'more justice' positions), distinguishes between justice and morality, arguing that criminal justice is but one string to the bow of morality. Criminal justice is not the only social goal, nor always the ultimate value, and there are contexts, such as fragile transitions to democracy, where the political compromise of amnesty may be morally justified for the sake of the common good, stability and peace. One should also note that if the promises made in justifying injustice prove to be false, it is entirely possible for so-called morality to be less than justice too. The 'justice and the TRC' approach (combining 'as justice' and 'more justice') identifies the ways in which the TRC tried to hold on to and contribute to due process requirements and forms of retribution, but more particularly championed restorative and social justice.

Kiss (2000: 69) notes that supporters of the TRC and the TRC's own report argue simultaneously that it was compelled by political necessity to do something unjust and that it promoted a more ambitious vision of justice. It was in this context that top-down conceptions of restorative justice were presented as both a 'necessary compromise – a way to make up for the lack of retributive justice – and an ideal form of justice for a transitional political context. It is thus a combination (or confusion) of pragmatic and idealized notions of justice' (van der Merwe 2001: 198). It is clear that it may suit truth commissions to privilege different understandings of justice, just as they may privilege different truth genres, to different audiences, in difference facets of their work and reporting, and over time. It is also clear how strong the desire was within the TRC to lay claim to the 'more justice' justification for its work, and hence to legitimise, and in a sense 'own', the political compromise of amnesty.

Amnesty, therefore, sits at the heart of broader debates about the nature of justice in transitional contexts. These debates are played out in the theoretical ether, but are sometimes troubled, as we have already seen, by the reality of practice.

Amnesty and justice: the practice

The justice of the TRC's amnesty provision ultimately does not rest solely on abstract claims or on its conceptual coherence or incoherence. Its justice claims also rest on practical application and delivery, on such issues as (1) its relationship with other related provisions governing indemnities, immunities, releases and pardons; (2) its legal standing as decided in relevant court cases; and (3) its governing social contract, which combined the promise of amnesty with the threat of prosecution.

The TRC entered an arena already occupied by a series of amnesty provisions – the highest profile of which was its own, the conditional amnesty developed though the 1993 interim Constitution (No. 200 of 1993) and the TRC's founding legislation, the 1995 Promotion of National Unity and Reconciliation Act (No. 34 of 1995) – and departed leaving a landscape darkened by the shadow of further possible amnesties. In the complex net of indemnities, immunities, releases, and pardons leading up to the 1994 elections, of particular importance were the Indemnity Act (No. 35 of 1990) and the Further Indemnity Act (No. 151 of 1992) (Berat 1995; Keightley 1993; Parker 1996; Sarkin 2004: 25–28, 36–49, 194–99). The former was designed to facilitate the negotiations process by granting temporary immunity or permanent indemnity against prosecutions for exiles returning to South Africa while also securing the release of political prisoners. The latter was passed unilaterally by the National Party government, extending indemnity to state offenders and providing for secrecy regarding the actions for which indemnity was granted.

In a portent of what was to come, the administrative and political procedures for indemnity lacked transparency and accountability, particularly in relation to the 1992 Act, and the definition of what constituted a political offence was contested. The 1992 Act, in contrast to the TRC's amnesty provision, was a self-amnesty of the blanket and quick-fire-forgetting variety. Almost 3,500 members of the security forces and National Party cabinet members were secretly indemnified in the lead-up to the 1994 elections. Although the legality of these particular indemnities is disputed, indemnities granted in terms of these Acts have been respected in the democratic era. A further category of measures, whereby indemnities are granted to persons to secure their cooperation during investigations and trials (often as state witnesses) in the prosecution of others, constitute an accepted part of the criminal prosecution system in South Africa. Apartheid-era deals were again negotiated behind closed doors, in several cases while the TRC was ongoing. For example, a number of people navigated this route to indemnity during and after the de Kock trial (see Chapter 1, note 3).

The most important points to distil from this complex and evolving picture are the following (see Sarkin 2004). First, far more people received indemnity under the 1990 and 1992 Acts – between 13,000 and 21,000 – than received amnesty under the TRC's conditional amnesty provision (1,167 were granted amnesty, and 145 partial amnesty). Second, these earlier processes were marred by a lack of clarity and transparency around the numbers affected, their names and offences, as well as the processes, if any, employed with regard to individual cases. Finally, their impacts on the TRC's amnesty process warrant further exploration, in part because individually and together these provisions were not well understood, notably by the perpetrators and political parties themselves. Further, while there were reasons why an individual previously indemnified might have applied for amnesty – for offences not previously covered, for example, and as indemnity and immunity release an individual from criminal and civil liability but amnesty has a wider scope as the criminal record is expunged (released prisoners in addition retained civil liability) – almost none did so. The TRC also does not seem to have examined the information from indemnity and other applications and processes, or to have questioned its beneficiaries. These troubling insights, and the fact that a discordant family of measures folded into the TRC and post-TRC eras, have serious implications for the TRC amnesty provision's claims to have provided either truth or justice. The lesson for elsewhere is the need to keep an eye on the linkages between all amnesty-related measures.

A second component of the amnesty–justice interaction, in practice, concerned the relationship between the amnesty provision, the interim Constitution (No. 200 of 1993) and international law. Whatever the criticisms of the amnesty provision, its conditionality makes it both legally and morally more legitimate than a blanket amnesty. A challenge to the constitutionality of the amnesty provision (the AZAPO case) failed. The Constitutional Court justified its constitutionality on the grounds that amnesty facilitated the transition to democracy, truth recovery and reparations:

> The result, at all levels, is a difficult, sensitive, perhaps even agonising, balancing act between the need for justice to victims of past abuse and the need for reconciliation and rapid transition to a new future, between encouragement to wrongdoers to help in the discovery of the truth and the need for reparations for the victims of that truth; between a correction in the old and the creation of the new.[3]

But, as already mentioned in Chapter 1, the amnesty provision's compatibility with international law was not adequately addressed. At the time of the TRC there was no unanimity in South Africa, or elsewhere, about whether and how amnesty provisions could be made compatible with human rights standards. To cite one example, van Zyl (1999, 2000) claimed that newly established democracies had four basic obligations under international law: to establish the truth, to reform state institutions, to provide victim reparation and to punish perpetrators. In the rather optimistic view of the author, South Africa satisfied three of the four obligations. An interesting claim is that the amnesty provision and failure to prosecute was tempered by being structured in such a way as to further the other three objectives (1999: 622; 2000: 53). While the reality of this assertion can be contested in the South African case, van Zyl's framework, like Gibson's (2004) notion of compensatory forms of justice, provides a useful way of going beyond bland holistic definitions of justice to open up a strategic debate about interactions between component parts of justice, and ways in which amnesty provisions could be designed to maximise the justice dividend.

That said, there is now a stronger consensus behind the call for prosecutions for serious 'international crimes' (war crimes, crimes against humanity and genocide), and even the broader category of gross violations of human rights.[4] By this measure the South African amnesty provision would now be unacceptable. Orentlicher (2007) notes that the development of international norms against impunity for serious crimes has been accompanied by the affirmation of the central importance of victim and citizen participation in the design and implementation of transitional justice measures. These norms may be mutually reinforcing or create tension, as when victim and survivor groups express a preference, at least in the short term, for peace over justice. Here we see the challenge posed by rights-based participation for human rights practitioners, as genuine participation sits uneasily with predetermined outcomes.

A third, and final, practical interface between amnesty and justice hinged on the social contract at the heart of both the amnesty provision and broader TRC legitimacy, which stated that those who did not apply for or who were refused amnesty would be prosecuted. As the TRC's report was submitted it became clear that the problems associated with justice had to a large degree merely been deferred, with renewed debate about amnesties and prosecutions and the criteria to be followed in each case. A taste of some early contributions to the debate is provided below:

- Bulelani Ngcuka, at this time the National Director of Public Prosecutions, stated that there would be no automatic prosecution of perpetrators named in the report and that some offences would be dropped for the sake of reconciliation (October 1998).
- Archbishop Desmond Tutu, Chair of the TRC, proposed a cut-off date beyond which prosecutions would stop, and suggested a two-year period after the termination of the amnesty process (October 1998).
- A coalition of national and international NGOs and civil society groups called for vigorous prosecution of human rights perpetrators identified by the TRC, rejecting suggestions of blanket amnesties, selective non-prosecution or time limits on prosecutions (November 1998).
- In July 1999, Barney Pityana, then Chairperson of the South African Human Rights Commission, called for an end to apartheid-era prosecutions on the grounds that they are costly and deflect resources from tackling crime in the

present, and for the sake of reconciliation. This position was also contested by an NGO and civil society coalition.

In relation to prosecutions, the TRC could only make recommendations and then pass on the baton to the government and judiciary. Responsibility for general policy frameworks and specific prosecutions lies here, not with the TRC. The breaking of the TRC's amnesty-related contract is both predictable and problematic. It is predictable because the amnesty provision was in many respects an act of faith. Faith that perpetrators, and in particular leadership, would apply for amnesty in significant numbers. Faith that a largely unreconstructed judiciary and a new political and human rights institution (the TRC) would work together symbiotically to facilitate this outcome. Faith that the circumstances which precluded thoroughgoing prosecutions initially – a fragile democracy, lack of political will, a politicised judiciary, cost – would have been transformed enough, in part through the activities of the TRC, to enable partial prosecutions, if necessary, at a later date. It is problematic because these things did not happen, and as a result prosecutions have not taken place on any scale and will not do so in the future. The cost is too high; political priorities have moved on.[5] Those who thought they could avoid, and even derided, the accountability regimes of both the court room and the truth commission have been proved right.

The investigation of apartheid-era crimes continues in the present under the remit of the National Prosecuting Authority (NPA), created in 1998, and coordinated by a specialised unit created in 1999 and restructured in 2003 as the Priority Crimes Litigation Unit (PCLU). PCLU is responsible for prosecutions and missing persons from the TRC's 'unfinished business' agenda, but its brief extends to a range of other concerns including treason and matters relating to the International Criminal Court. It has done important work, for example in relation to the exhumation, identification and reburial of previously missing persons, but its activities have been hindered by political interference and a lack of resources (Fullard, interview 21/4/2005).

In a protracted phase of indecision without coherent polices for prosecutions, or the future of amnesty provisions, goalposts shifted and secret discussions leaked provocatively into the public domain. As with reparations, the ANC government seriously underestimated the damage that can be caused by delay, confusion, a lack of consultation and the perception of unfairness. There were persistent rumours of further amnesties, whether in the form of specific provisions for the province of KwaZulu-Natal, a 'general's amnesty', a general amnesty, presidential pardons – such as President Mbeki's pardoning of 33 prisoners in May 2002, mainly from the ANC and PAC, most of whom had been denied amnesty by the TRC[6] – or further amnesty/indemnity for truth measures. There was no doubt awareness among the powers that be that any new government policy directives or legislation would be vulnerable to constitutional challenge (Sarkin 2004: 381–89).

Prosecutions were put on hold in late 2004 pending the formalisation of prosecution guidelines and in December 2005 the guidelines, framed without consultation with the broader public or victims/survivors, finally emerged into the light of day.[7] It should be remembered that in 1998 the TRC handed a list of more than 300 names to the National Prosecuting Authority (NPA), requesting further investigations with a view to initiating prosecutions. The guidelines in effect provided a second chance for perpetrators who failed to apply for, or were denied, amnesty by the TRC, this time under the guise of prosecutorial discretion, rather than by passing new legislation. Indemnity from prosecution could be exchanged for full disclosure (immunity from civil claims would not be granted) and the process was to be 'normalised' using processes by which people become state witnesses and engage in guilty plea and sentencing agreements. Criteria for indemnity were extended beyond those of the TRC process (full disclosure, political objective) to include other, rather nebulous, considerations (e.g. personal circumstances of the alleged offender, including ill health, their degree of remorse and attitude to reconciliation, and the degree of indoctrination to which they were subjected). Further weaknesses were that deliberations would take place behind closed doors; the indemnities granted and reasons given were to be made public, but not any truth disclosed; and efforts to obtain the views of victims were circumscribed ('as far as is reasonably possible'). A legal challenge was launched by victims/survivors and NGOs, and in December 2008 the prosecution guidelines were judged unconstitutional and invalid by the Pretoria High Court, on the grounds that the measure amounted to a 'copy-cat' of the TRC's amnesty process – the Court found that where there is evidence to prosecute, the NPA should do so. In May 2009 a request for permission to appeal the decision was dismissed.[8]

Policies relating to presidential pardons are cut from the same cloth. Following extended delays and a lack of transparency in the processing of applications for presidential pardons, in November 2007 then President Mbeki established a procedure to consider applications from individuals convicted of politically motivated offences before 16 June 1999 (extending the TRC's amnesty cut-off date of 10 May 1994 to include political violence during the early democratic period). A three-month window in early 2008 was set aside for applications to be made. A reference group, comprising political party representatives, assessed the applications against similar criteria to those used by the TRC's Amnesty Committee (full disclosure, political motivation) and made recommendations to the President (those denied amnesty by the TRC cannot apply for a pardon under this provision). The reference group reportedly received over 2,000 applications; in the region of 120 were recommended for pardons. The pardon procedure is less robust than its TRC amnesty predecessor, on the grounds of transparency (the reference group met behind closed doors), victim/survivor participation and consultation (there was none), and public truth disclosure (no truth disclosure was required). After lobbying to modify these procedures failed, in April 2009 an NGO coalition secured an interim order from the North Gateng High Court stating that it was unconstitutional for pardons to be issued without victims being granted the right to be heard. In February 2010, the Constitutional Court, in a unanimous appeals judgement, sanctioned the right of victims to be heard within this particular process (*Albutt v. Centre for the Study of Violence and Reconciliation and Others* [CCT 54/09]).

These developments only partially help to build confidence in justice and the rule of law. Interventions need to be considered in their own right, and for the ways in which they recast the past, including now the work of the TRC. Sarkin wrote, prior to the publication of the new prosecution guidelines and pardons procedure: 'A new amnesty, by whatever means … would be a monumental admission that the South African model has failed' (2004: 389). Public debate and victim/survivor involvement could have helped to render any further amnesty-related measures more palatable, and to some extent value-driven, rather than narrowly political in motivation. Sadly, this has not been the path chosen by a political leadership who, across the board, are now facing the consequences of not having applied for amnesty before the TRC. Equally disappointing is the fact that NGOs have failed to lead the debate by saying what actually should realistically happen rather than what should not – this would require adopting a stance that is both principled and really engages with the challenges posed by competing priorities, a compromised judiciary, the need for selection criteria, etc.[9] As things stand, the government's prosecution/amnesty strategy is in disarray.

Yet comparative analysis reveals that decision-making in this area is not a singular or irreversible undertaking. Recent experience in countries like Chile and Argentina (Matear 2004; Roht-Arriaza 2006; Sikkink and Booth Walling 2006: 313–21) and Sierra Leone (Schabas 2006) suggests that amnesties, unlike diamonds, are not forever. Amnesty provisions remain divisive, and provide the engine for ongoing local and international human rights activism. Thus the decision about whether/who to prosecute is contested as the balance of power changes within a given society.[10]

In general terms, some authors suggest a potential for greater assertiveness over time. Pankhurst (1999), for example, outlines a possible shift from a minimalist version of the rule of law (the 'best' peace) in the short term to a maximalist conception, including human rights, democracy and good governance, which may only be possible in the longer term. Fletcher *et al.* (2009) employ the analogy of the tortoise and the hare. They argue that stronger, self-reliant states, such as South Africa and Northern Ireland (the tortoises), initially adopt modest transitional justice measures and benefit from a gradualist, home-grown approach. Weaker, internationally reliant countries, such as Sierra Leone or Timor Leste (the hares), in contrast, are pressurised by the international community into early, ambitious, formulaic interventions – trials and truth commissions – with mixed results. There are certain ironies here, such as that countries with the strongest courts use them the least. In virtually all cases, transitional justice policies change, with more done to address the needs of victims over time (six to eight years), often through reparations. This may in part be because victim mobilisation itself takes time to gather momentum. These findings suggest that an evolutionary approach to transitional justice, highly attuned to local context, is likely to be more productive in the long term than universal prescriptions.

Yet factors influencing whether the window of opportunity for prosecutions opens or closes over time remain poorly understood. As we have seen, South Africa's gradualist approach has not taken it very far in this regard. The challenge is how to keep the window to greater justice open in the face of forces advocating stasis, moving on and even regression. In South Africa, factors ranging from new international norms prohibiting amnesties for gross violations of human rights, a strong after-taste of injustice, and gradual shifts in the political and judicial landscape, suggest that attempts will continue to be made to challenge existing and any potential new amnesty provisions. South Africa can anticipate moments when the past bursts into the present, otherwise marginal victim/survivor groups engage with broader constituencies, the balance of power within society decisively shifts, and aggressive political and judicial registers chime. The prosecutorial agenda will return.

The TRC and the criminal justice system

While a positive relationship between the TRC and the criminal justice system was important for both partners, and crucial to the success of the amnesty process, the relationship was perhaps inevitably a complex one both in terms of day-to-day working arrangements and as each sought to monitor and evaluate the other.

There were a number of fault-lines in day-to-day cooperation. A Special Investigations Unit, established prior to the TRC, under Dr Jan D'Oliviera, Attorney-General of Gauteng, was at the hub of prosecutorial initiatives at the time (prior to the creation of the National Prosecuting Authority in 1998), necessitating communication between it and the TRC's Investigation Unit. The TRC cites tensions with regard to perceived interference with investigative work, a lack of cooperation in information flows and perceived slow progress in investigations, with problems mainly occurring where the parties were conducting concurrent investigations (TRC 1998, Vol. 1: 343). But actual and potential prosecution did in some cases flush out amnesty applications, notably in the aftermath of the successful de Kock prosecution. This was an illustration of the way the collaborative relationship was supposed to work. But from the perspective of the criminal justice system it is easy to see how this arrangement could be demoralising, with investigations taken over by the TRC in the short term and a complex and reconfigured prosecutorial agenda handed back to it in the post-amnesty era. Because evidence in amnesty applications and obtained during the amnesty process could not be used in criminal proceedings against the applicant, even in cases where the application was rejected, the amnesty provision was seen as hampering prosecutions.

In these circumstances, interactions between the TRC and all the offices of the Attorneys-General were characterised by the full gamut of cooperation, competition, and sometimes public criticism, and underscored by territorial battles as each sought to solve high-profile cases. The positive truth–justice momentum sought by the TRC, engineered through information-sharing, their own inquiries, criminal prosecutions and amnesty applications, was sporadic. In short, the lack of a complementary criminal prosecution process can be seen to have undermined the amnesty process (Pigou 2002: 54–56; Sarkin 2004: 127–34). The task that truth commissions are still grappling with is now to institutionally design such complementarity, as it impacts on both truth commission effectiveness and reform and performance of the criminal justice system.[11]

There were also legal challenges to the TRC's constitutionality (amnesty provision), procedures and impartiality, and to decisions of the Amnesty Committee. The first three grounds for legal challenge have already been discussed in some detail. Klaaren (1998: 198) describes the Constitutional Court's AZAPO ruling as 'the high water mark of the judiciary's respect for the TRC'. But it was accompanied by more critical interventions, as the lower courts, for example, complicated the TRC's work, and particularly its deliberately less rule-bound victim hearings, with procedural regulations. In addition, amnesty decisions have been and will in all likelihood continue to be reviewed by the High Court, given accusations of bias; the lack of consistency and absence of a system of precedent in decisions; the poor quality of written decisions and reasoning; and the question of whether there should have been an entitlement to more due process protections (Sarkin 2004; TRC 1998, Vol. 1: 192–94, 2003, Vol. 6: 66–82).[12] Applicants, victims and other interested parties can request a review, and there is a clear danger that as soon as prosecutions are instigated those charged, if they have been denied amnesty, will seek a review of their amnesty cases. Victims may seek to review the granting of amnesty with the aim of instigating civil proceedings or to push for a criminal trial. Thus the courts endorsed the contract on which the TRC was based while also monitoring, and on occasions unhelpfully obstructing, its day-to-day operations and decision-making (in post-TRC rulings the courts have so far continued to uphold the amnesty-related contract, which in current circumstances has more radical implications for both truth-seeking and prosecutions: see above).

Not only did the courts ask hard questions of the TRC, but the TRC also asked hard questions of the judiciary. It did so in three main ways: first, by subjecting the legal sector to scrutiny for its role under apartheid and, perhaps most controversially, calling on judges to testify before the TRC; second, by making findings on and recommendations for referring the judiciary and legal sector; and third, by taking on the mantle of a 'higher court' in re-examining past judicial rulings.

From 27 to 29 October 1997, the TRC held a hearing on the legal sector, as part of its attempt to provide a broader, structural insight into the apartheid past (Chapman 2008; Dyzenhaus 1998; Klaaren 1998; Rombouts 2002; Rombouts and Parmentier 2002; TRC 1998, Vol. 4: 93–108). Because apartheid was built upon, implemented through and defended against opposition via the edifice of the law, these hearings had the potential to shed light on the connections and continuities between the ordinary and extraordinary violence of apartheid (Dyzenhaus 1998). Furthermore, such core dilemmas as whether to work with or against such a legal system, or the optimal relationship between the legislature, executive and judiciary, raised concerns about the role of the judiciary in the past and present as matters of public debate.

The level of truth-telling and acknowledgement at these hearings, however, was generally disappointing, as past political differences were largely replayed rather than reformulated. While the sector was otherwise reasonably well represented, judges refused to come before the TRC in person, nor were they subpoenaed to do so, submitting only written representations chiefly on the grounds that to appear in person would compromise their independence. The irony of this stance is hard to overstate as they were called to testify precisely because their conduct in the past raised serious questions about their independence. While evidence on the compromised role of judges in enforcing discriminatory and oppressive laws was heard at the hearing, by placing themselves above this seminal and one-off process of public accounting and acknowledgement the judges undermined, rather than strengthened, respect for the judiciary and the rule of law. They also lost an opportunity to help clarify their role in the new dispensation, at the interface of the law and politics, needing to be both independent and accountable (Klaaren 1998). That said, it is worth noting in mitigation the claim that the non-participation of judges in the legal sector hearings could be justified on the grounds of building trust and reconciliation between new- and old-order judges. The almost total lack of participation by magistrates, either through written submissions or in person at the hearing, was also significant as these legal practitioners were the front-line implementers of apartheid's oppressive legal order. Magisterial reticence, like that of the judges, can be interpreted as an unwillingness to face up to their actions in the past and truly engage with the challenges of transformation in the present (Gready and Kgalema 2003). Ongoing dissention about racism and a lack of transformation in the judiciary and magistracy merely highlight the cost of this lost opportunity.

Relationships within the legal profession merit further attention. As an example of the complex machinations played out under the umbrella of the TRC process, two power dynamics are identified by Rombouts (2002; also see Rombouts and Parmentier 2002) when comparing the role of the legal sector in the legislative process (leading to the enactment of the Promotion of National Unity and Reconciliation Act, No. 34 of 1995), the legal sector hearing and various court cases. The first is that in the legislative enactment and TRC sector hearings the participation of legal NGOs (such as Lawyers for Human Rights and the National Association for Democratic Lawyers) was more widespread and willing, progressive and self-critical, and less legal in substance and tone, than that of the organised profession (for example insisting on public amnesty hearings and advocating that judges participate in the sector hearing). Judges and magistrates played little direct role in either process. The second dynamic is that while NGOs wielded some influence in the legislative process, it was the judges who framed the agenda in, and adopted a narrowly legalistic attitude towards, the sector hearing and certain, particularly procedurally focused, court cases. At the former the judges were a pervasive absent presence, shaping proceedings and the subsequent TRC report entry on the sector, with a consequent focus on issues such as independence, parliamentary sovereignty and the margin of judicial discretion. That said, it was the NGO critique of the organised profession, including judges, which was affirmed in the analysis and findings of the TRC report. Unfortunately, despite this input and a potential for structural analysis, the legal hearing failed to prioritise the everyday manifestations of apartheid. Such dynamics provide important insights into linkages between transitional keywords. For example, Rombouts states: 'It is unlikely that the [TRC] Report generated a consensus about the past and smoothed away the differences between the organised profession and the NGOs' (2002: 27).

The TRC made findings arising out of the legal sector hearings, criticising both non-participation in the hearings and past conduct (TRC 1998, Vol. 4: 101–8; Vol. 5: 253–54), and provided a set of recommendations across concerns such as access to justice for victims and accused persons, training and education, representivity, and indigenous, informal and alternative court structures (1998, Vol. 5: 322–28).

While the TRC's legal sector hearing was explicitly not about establishing individual responsibility or retrying particular cases, the TRC has been criticised for attempting to undertake precisely these functions in aspects of its work. Jeffery (1999) is particularly critical of the TRC for repudiating, ignoring and misrepresenting apartheid-era judicial rulings, and for failing to provide persuasive, or indeed any, evidence or reasons for its own contrary findings (albeit that the TRC operated under a lower burden of proof, the balance of probabilities rather than beyond reasonable doubt). The net effect, she argues, is that the judiciary is painted in an unnecessarily and unfairly negative light. While there were clearly flaws in the TRC's research and findings, Jeffery's arguments are undermined by her uncritical faith in the integrity of apartheid judicial rulings, and by her research errors (Sarkin 2004: 259–61). Amnesty decisions also contradicted earlier judicial rulings (on the Malan case, see Sarkin 2004: 264–69).

The central question addressed by the first narrative (1) is the overall coherence of the complex relationship between the TRC and the legal system, and its implications for the perception and practice of justice. Outcomes were predicated on knitting together the amnesty provision, forms of collaboration and mutual critique, and an overarching attempt to support, strengthen and transform institutions central to the rule of law. On the plus side, the TRC demonstrated the effects of a corrupt and politicised legal framework under apartheid, extracted a measure of accountability from perpetrators, provided an unequivocal moral condemnation of apartheid itself, and helped to popularise a particular, narrow understanding, and even acceptance, of human rights. Such outcomes have contributed, if modestly, to a greater acceptance of the values of constitutionalism and human rights (Gibson 2004). Furthermore, the South African amnesty experiment also deserves credit, for envisaging a twin-track policy of amnesty for truth alongside a process of residual criminal prosecutions, and for moving the debate about amnesty provisions into territory where it seeks to retain a toe-hold in justice rather than accepting a completely oppositional relationship.

Negative outcomes include the breaking of the social contract used to justify amnesty and the inability of the TRC to decisively impact on reform of the criminal justice system, through either its day-to-day workings or recommendations. In analyses of the criminal justice sector, the TRC often does not even get a mention as an engine of reform (see, for example, AfriMAP and the Open Society Foundation for South Africa 2005). Nagging doubts remain over whether confidence in the rule of law and human rights can be generated through a form of human rights so thoroughly modified by politics and by unfamiliar forms of justice and depressingly familiar injustice. The potential of transition to provide the necessary space to reimagine justice requires debate, and a conceptual framework that informs decision-making about the past and present, and balances principle and pragmatism, in such a way that an inner core of coherence is not overwhelmed by contradiction.

The first narrative (2): the TRC's conceptualisations of justice

The first narrative (1) illustrates that justice, like truth, is a multi-layered concept. This is clear in the TRC's attempts to lay claim to the legitimising aura of justice despite, and even through, an amnesty provision. So what is justice, and whose justice should prevail? Recent empirical research on perceptions of justice has uncovered three important trends in public and victim/survivor understandings of the term.[13]

First, understandings of justice are personal, and hence extremely diverse. Weinstein and Stover (2004: 4) suggest that '[j]ustice, like beauty, is in the eye of the beholder and can be interpreted in a variety of ways'. By way of illustration they continue:

> For many of our informants, justice meant having a job and an income; for others, it was returning to the home they had lost; still others saw justice as the ability to forget the past and move on with their lives. For some, justice was testifying at a trial against the soldiers and paramilitaries who had murdered their families and destroyed their homes. For others, justice had to be exacted by revenge. Some said justice could only take place once their neighbors looked them directly in the eye and apologised for betraying them. Still others said it was finally learning the truth about their missing relatives and receiving their bodies for proper burial.
>
> (4; also see 323–24)

Second, understandings of justice tend to be reactive and locally informed. The Iraq study (ICTJ and Human Rights Center 2004: ii) found that '[r]espondents viewed the concept of justice as the inverse of the previous regime and a just society as everything that the old system was not'. While this valuable body of empirical research always now calls for greater consultation in the design of justice-based interventions, it is important to note that popular perceptions that a life of dignity and security implies a reversal of the past echo those of many transitional justice advocates in assuming that the main challenge of transition is to prevent the return of the past in its original guise. A core argument of this book is that this is often not the most helpful way of anticipating the future; problems from the past do invariably return, but frequently in an altered form.

Third, research structured around understandings of keywords (human rights, justice, reconciliation, etc.) and attitudes towards an established repertoire of interventions (trials, truth commissions, local justice mechanisms, reparations, vetting, institutional reform, etc.) seems predetermined to support the prevailing holistic approaches to keywords and transitional justice as a whole. A related shortcoming is that the research often underplays socio-economic concerns. There is limited scope, I would argue, for radically different local models to emerge from such methodologies. Local ownership is both called for and constrained. More use of open questions about, for example, needs, interests, hopes and possible solutions might partly alleviate this shortcoming. Research is also required as transitional justice interventions are rolled out (moving from the 'What would you like?' to the 'What did you receive or gain?' agenda). Instructive examples from South Africa include van der Merwe's work (2001), which spans both agendas on the clash between top-down and bottom-up understandings of restorative justice at community level;[14] and his later research on what victims and survivors said about justice at the TRC's victim hearings (van der Merwe 2008).[15]

The TRC's contribution to the conceptualisation of justice lies largely with social justice and restorative justice (first narrative [2]). Both of these conceptualisations need to be seen in the light of its attempts to retain a foot in the camp of justice, against the backdrop of the amnesty provision. While commentaries by the TRC itself, and its staff and supporters, provide useful conceptual insights, they are hindered by being essentially post-hoc rationalisations for the TRC's mandate, notably in relation to amnesty, which as we have seen was a political compromise rather than a tool to further justice. Again, the weak conceptual foundations and thinking of the TRC reduced its coherence and impact.

Social justice

Social justice addressed the links between the TRC's amnesty provision and (1) reconciliation, reconstruction and development, and (2) facilitating and consolidating democracy (TRC 1998, Vol. 1: 124–25). In relation to (1), the granting of amnesty extinguished civil liability for both the perpetrator and the state, with the latter defended on the grounds that it contributed to reconciliation and reconstruction by avoiding prolonged and divisive litigation and giving the state discretion to deploy limited resources to benefit the majority of South Africans. In the difficult decisions about resource allocation, the nation of victims, and broad-based social and economic concerns, were privileged over individual victims of gross human rights abuses. The TRC report (1998, Vol. 1: 124) cites the then Minister of Justice, Dullah Omar:

> We have a nation of victims, and if we are unable to provide complete justice on an individual basis … it is possible for us … to ensure that there is historical and collective justice for the people of our country. If we achieve that, if we achieve social justice … then those who today feel aggrieved that individual justice has not been done will at least be able to say that our society has achieved what the victims fought for during their lifetimes. And that therefore at that level, one will be able to say that justice has been done.
> (Omar 1996: xii)

For this to happen, a second dimension of social justice (2) was necessary. Amnesty, in this context, is framed as a necessary requirement for the political transition to democracy, which in turn was a precondition for the developmental transition. This posits a two-phase political–economic transition process.

A gesture was made via the reparations granted through the TRC process (see Chapter 6); the substantive contribution to social justice, however, was to be made through longer-term efforts to secure economic development for all. The logic of favouring a wider, over a more narrow, conception of 'reparations' (and victimhood) was sanctioned by the Constitutional Court in the AZAPO case. The disjuncture between a truth-telling regime focusing on gross violations of civil and political rights and this 'reparations' regime purportedly targeting the alleviation of economic deprivations for the majority of South Africans is, however, problematic for the TRC's justice claims.

Care is also needed when framing the promises made in the name of (in)justice. It can easily appear that something seemingly tangible, immediate and personal (prosecutions, individual reparations) is being sacrificed in the name of generalities, imponderables and unlikelihoods (social justice, development). Can what many would consider to be simply good governance and service delivery legitimately be reframed as justice, or 'reparations'? Further, the prevailing global dominance of neo-liberal economic policies, including in South Africa, make the wager of (in)justice underpinning political compromise but also economic gain for the majority precarious, at best.

Restorative justice

The TRC itself acknowledged that if justice was seen in narrow retributive terms, then it was difficult to make connections between amnesty and justice.

While arguing that the conditional amnesty provision provided elements of justice, and contributed to restoring the rule of law and to future prosecutions, it proposed restorative justice as an alternative, arguing that '[t]his means that amnesty in return for public and full disclosure ... suggests a restorative understanding of justice, focusing on the healing of victims and perpetrators and on communal restoration' (TRC 1998, Vol. 1: 118).[16] For victims, this form of justice was to be made possible through the trinity of voice, recognition and dignity, backed up by amnesty's truths and wide-ranging reparation recommendations. For perpetrators, restorative justice meant taking responsibility, accountability, and the making of a contribution to the restoration of the well-being of their victims. Further bonuses were a greater understanding of perpetrator motives and perspectives, and the facilitation of rehabilitation and reintegration. Restorative justice was sourced in the constitutional and TRC mandate commitments to restore human dignity and *ubuntu* ('humaneness'), and the restorative dimensions of a number of religious and cultural traditions in South Africa (see TRC 1998, Vol. 1: 125–31). While contributions were made with respect to the agenda sketched above, these ideal type descriptions were imperfectly realised within the TRC process.

Restorative justice as a dimension of the TRC's self-presentation has received considerable positive attention in the transitional justice literature. Two examples will suffice, one from within the Commission itself, and one from outside. From within, Villa-Vicencio (2000a, 2003), who argues that truth commissions are essentially instruments of restorative justice, identifies three phases in a viable theory of restorative justice in transitional societies. Acknowledgement respects legitimate resentment and anger, and requires that perpetrators and beneficiaries take responsibility and apologise. Reparation fans outwards from counselling for victims and rehabilitation for perpetrators, to tackle material needs, inequality, and participation in, and a sense of ownership of, development, democracy and human rights. Reconciliation entails the restoration of relationships, forged through democracy and the rules and language of democratic debate, as an accepted means of problem-solving. In essence, restorative justice requires the restoration of relationships as a basis for preventing a reoccurrence of human rights abuses, and the reparation of damage to the personal dignity and material well-being of victims.

For Kiss (2000), an external commentator on the TRC, an effort to affirm and restore the dignity of victims/survivors, and the overlapping remits of truth-telling, healing, acknowledgement and/as justice, are key. Also, perpetrators must be held accountable, if in new and creative ways. The distinctive nature of restorative justice comes into sharpest focus, Kiss argues, with its final component: reconciliation, alongside forgiveness, is privileged over retribution. Reconciliation requires that the first two components of restorative justice be fulfilled. The transformation and reconstruction sought is ultimately moral, social, material and institutional. Restorative justice's over-riding goal is to create the conditions in which people are treated with respect.

Through conceptualisations such as these an outline of restorative justice as a moral foundation for the TRC, and for other truth commissions, becomes apparent. This approach has supporters and detractors. As an indication of hurdles the restorative model faces, the TRC's venture into the field has been critiqued on a number of grounds – late conversion; weak conceptualisation; clashes between restorative justice and other approaches; inappropriate transferral of an intervention from minor criminal offences to gross violations of human rights; its use as a metaphor rather than an applied tool; limited capacity and limiting institutional design;[17] top-down delivery; instrumental cultural and religions readings; pressure placed on victims to forgive and engage in gestures of reconciliation; a narrow definition of victims and perpetrators; and excessive ambition. Often such critiques culminate in accusations of partial delivery and missed opportunities (Maepa 2005; van der Merwe 2001; S. Wilson 2001; Zehr 1997). Five main criticisms are considered in more detail below.

Reluctant perpetrators

It is clear that the TRC, through its founding Act and mandate, was not coherently designed to deliver restorative justice. For example, perpetrators were not required as a condition for amnesty to apologise – over 65 per cent of amnesty applicants provided no, or only a superficial, expression of remorse at their hearings (Phakathi and van der Merwe 2008: 137) – or contribute to redressing the damage done and restoring the lives of their victims. The TRC report (1998, Vol. 1: 131) criticises the amnesty process with regard to the latter issue. The link between violation and responsibility to repair the violation was absent.

Restorative justice assumes participation in good faith by all parties. Many perpetrators consistently undermined this assumption, not only by failing to voluntarily apologise or contribute to restoring the lives of their victims, but also by seeking to only minimally and begrudgingly meet some of the stipulated requirements for amnesty, such as full disclosure. When victims contested amnesty claims because they felt perpetrators did not exhibit good faith, and perpetrators were still granted amnesty by the TRC, restorative justice became a very distant goal indeed. In fact, Sarkin (2004: 158–63, 199–232) details the major role victims' support, or lack of support, had in influencing amnesty decisions, but also makes the point that not enough effort was made to find victims or to acknowledge them and their interests in the amnesty hearings, to the detriment of truth, justice and reconciliation.

Parallelism or genuine encounters

As parallel streams, neither the victim nor amnesty hearings were set up to generate appropriate interpersonal encounters. Arguably, truth commissions as an institutional form, are ill equipped to facilitate such encounters (Chapman 2008b). The terms of perpetrator participation in Human Rights Violations hearings were contested and ultimately determined by the courts. On occasion perpetrators were subpoenaed to attend. Within these hearings the sanctity of victim testimony was protected from perpetrator questioning or cross-examination. The amnesty hearings allowed more engagement between the parties, with some victims questioning perpetrators and making statements, but these interactions took place in an adversarial, court-like environment. Hearings were often the first such victim–perpetrator (re-)encounters. Despite these arrangements, there were some public and private encounters of a more restorative kind, but the TRC at no point institutionalised a restorative agenda. The Commission approved a programme of survivor–offender mediation offered by a group of NGOs, which failed to take off due to a lack of TRC referrals and the reluctance of the lawyers of amnesty applicants to allow their clients to participate (Phakathi and van der Merwe 2008: 138–39; Stauffer and Hamber 1996; Zehr 1997). Post-TRC work by NGOs revealed significant demand for dialogue and restorative justice interventions, notably from black perpetrators and survivors living in the same communities, and restorative justice interventions have been set up to try and meet these demands (Abrahamsen and van der Merwe 2005; Ramírez-Barat and van der Merwe 2005).

Amnesty trumps reparations

The coherence of a restorative justice approach has been significantly undermined by the TRC's capacity to grant amnesty but only recommend reparations, and by the delayed delivery of reparation payments significantly below the amount recommended by the TRC alongside ongoing initiatives to extend access to amnesty. Llewellyn (2004) – defining restorative justice as relationships reconfigured on the basis of social equality, inclusive in process and outcomes, and as extending before and after an 'encounter' stage – argues that understanding the TRC as a process informed by an ethos of restorative justice clarifies the role and objectives of reparations. Various forms of reparation become part of the plan for the future emerging from the 'encounter' stage. This conceptualisation is chiefly used to critique the ANC government's position on reparations. The author argues that '[t]he TRC process, while not perfect, was restorative in its orientation and approach, and its reparation recommendations were born out of this process and thus reflect a commitment to restorative justice' (180). But consultative and participatory processes are not restorative *per se*. Further, the identification of the relationships restored is problematic given that the state bore the responsibility for delivering reparations. This smacks of an attempt to recast a policy (reparations) in conceptually coherent clothing that it does not fully merit.

Instrumental cultural and religions readings

A frequently cited criticism of the TRC's approach to restorative justice is that pressure was exerted on victims to forgive and engage in public acts of reconciliation, and that the cultural and religious wrapping for these encounters (an underlying Christian ethos, *ubuntu*) was both vague and oppressive. Based largely on an analysis of victim hearing transcripts, Chapman (2008a: 51–53; 2008b: 76–80) in fact argues that there were few overt attempts to impose reconciliation or forgiveness. More generally, the marshalling of sympathetic strands within relevant religions and local culture was a way of trying to gain public, especially black, support for the often contentious mandate of the TRC. But it needs to be acknowledged that these are selective, instrumental readings. While there are those who argue, for example, that restorative justice resonates with indigenous concepts of justice and *ubuntu* (Tutu 1999), other commentators point out the salience of retribution and revenge within local justice (R. Wilson 1996, 2001). It is a banal truism that all cultures and religions are multi-dimensional, but the truism reminds us of the imperative to question who gets to speak on their behalf, and to what ends.

Restorative justice versus human rights

Combining these two discourses within transitional justice is not straightforward as they traditionally have different emphases. Set against human rights, restorative justice provides a focus on:

- people and relationships rather than legal norms – the latter relate to both perpetrator rights (fair trial guarantees, such as the right to remain silent) and victim rights (raising issues such as coercion to participate), which can be compromised in restorative justice (Ashworth 2002; McEvoy and Eriksson 2007);
- horizontal relationships (victim/survivor, perpetrator, family, community) rather than the conventional human rights axis between the individual and the state;
- needs and interests rather than rights; responsibilities rather than rights;
- the common good and majoritarian concerns that can appear utilitarian and precisely the threat to individual victim and minority interests that human rights conventionally contest (social justice and restorative justice share this emphasis). As a result, restorative justice has been criticised for sanctioning *de facto* impunity.

Despite these apparent tensions, accommodations between the two approaches are possible. Viewing human rights as a way of balancing interests and weighing values, of dealing with but not morally equating all sides, identifies some common ground. Based on the experience of community restorative justice initiatives designed to lower the levels of punishment beatings by Republican and Loyalist paramilitaries in Northern Ireland, McEvoy and Eriksson (2007) argue that restorative justice can constitute a form of 'bottom-up' human rights, embedding relevant legal norms in local contexts. The familiar challenge appears to be how to link official, top-down mechanisms and unofficial, bottom-up initiatives, so that interventions can potentially be 'scaled-up' while remaining locally grounded (on the South African TRC, see van der Merwe 2001; more generally on restorative justice in South Africa, see Maepa 2005a; Skelton and Batley 2006; also see Chapters 4 and 6 of this book).

Conclusion

The brief tenure of the TRC represented an opportunity, at a critical junction in South Africa's history, to ask questions about what justice is and whose justice should prevail. The initial window of opportunity for rethinking justice, past and present, closed fairly rapidly, barely lasting beyond the life-span of the TRC itself. This opportunity was lost for a variety of reasons. As an outcome of its own conceptual and impact-related shortcomings, the TRC failed to direct a national conversation, to build a broad constituency for progressive change among policy-makers and the general public, or to integrate the justice-based narratives that it inherited and created. But here, as elsewhere, many of the reasons for failure lay beyond the control of the TRC. The transitional moment brought together a unique constellation of justice-related projects, including the negotiation processes for the interim Constitution (No. 200 of 1993) and final Constitution (No. 108 of 1996), attempts to realign the justice system with the new constitutional dispensation, shifting patterns of crime and violence, and the impacts of market-led economic policies. In this context, the window of opportunity for rethinking justice, like the prosecutorial window, closed but was not definitively slammed shut – reformers need to continue to anticipate moments when the balance of power within society decisively shifts, and progressive political and judicial registers chime. Restorative justice, as we will see in the next chapter, has made progress during such moments. While attribution in general, and direct causal links to the TRC, are hard to pin down when assigning credit for policy changes, the TRC appears to have been a bit-part player in progressive reforms. Returning to a key argument of this book, the TRC did too little to insert itself into the agendas and priorities of the present, in this case debates about reform of the criminal justice system and the issue of violent crime. It is to these issues that we now turn.

Notes

1 Despite democratic shortcomings, and the fact that the overall picture is uneven, both over time and between different sectors in society, evidence suggests that there was substantial public support for the amnesty provision in South Africa. Gibson (2004: 258–88) gauged public attitudes to amnesty, finding that the majority (57.3 per cent) approved of amnesty to at least some degree. Black South Africans were far more likely to approve of amnesty (71.6 per cent), thereby making up for the disapproval of a majority of other race groups. Nevertheless, the amnesty provision was also considered to be unfair. Gibson pushes the analysis further to assess whether

other forms of justice can make up for the unfairness of amnesty (the justice deficit), specifically distributive justice (compensation), procedural justice (giving voice to victims and their families), restorative justice (perpetrator apologies) and retributive justice (through regimes of punishment such as shame and stigmatisation). Responses to imaginary scenarios suggest that even when all four components of compensatory justice are present, most respondents think the outcome is unfair. That said, these justice outriders, with the exception of diluted retribution, make a contribution to enhancing perceptions of fairness. On views about amnesty/justice at community level, see van der Merwe (2001: 196–204); and on the impact of the amnesty process from the perspective of victims/survivors, see Phakathi and van der Merwe (2008). It is clear that such support as there was for amnesty among victims and survivors was usually contingent upon, and ultimately undermined by, delivery on other concerns such as truth and reparations.
2 A potentially sweeping means of institutional transformation is through vetting, which excludes people from public office, often on human rights grounds, and is a form of individualised punishment *and* institutional reform. Vetting can be seen as a kind of administrative justice as it involves the application of administrative law and, as such, should be distinguished from purges (in which people are targeted for group membership or affiliation rather that individual responsibility for human rights violations, e.g. de-Nazification in Germany and de-Baathification in Iraq). Lustration processes in the former communist countries of Eastern and Central Europe also fall into this family of measures (Mayer-Rieckh and de Greiff 2007). Such measures were not widely employed in South Africa, either in the public service or in related professional arenas such as the judiciary. A political compromise forged in the negotiations process to ensure employment stability was endorsed by the TRC in its report. Other modes of institutional transformation have taken precedence, such as affirmative action (TRC 1998, Vol. 5: 310–11; see Klaaren 2007). Human rights concerns, therefore, can be seen as one among a range of often competing agendas, some urging institutional continuity or stability, others calling for transformation, within transitional societies.
3 *Azanian People's Organisation (AZAPO) and Others* v. *the President of the Republic of South Africa and Others* (CCT 17/96), Judgment, Justice D. P. Mahomed, 17–18.
4 See, for example, The Rule of Law and Transitional Justice in Conflict and Post-Conflict Societies, Report of the Secretary General, UN Doc. S/2004/616, August 2004, para. 64 (c); the Updated Set of Principles for the Protection and Promotion of Human Rights through Action to Combat Impunity, UN Doc. E/CN.4/2005/102/Add. 1, February 2005, Principles 19, 24 and 28 (in the latter case noting that disclosure should not exempt a person from criminal responsibility, but can be considered in mitigation of sentence); and the Basic Principles and Guidelines on the Right to a Remedy and Reparation for Victims of Gross Violations of International Human Rights Law and Serious Violations of International Humanitarian Law, adopted and proclaimed by UN General Assembly resolution 60/147 of 16 December 2005, UN Doc. A/RES/60/147, Articles 4, 6 and 12.
5 The time taken, and resources and personnel required, for complex political trials should not be underestimated. The TRC (1998, Vol. 1: 123) notes that it took over 18 months to secure the conviction of Eugene de Kock. A specialised investigative unit, consisting of over 30 detectives and six civilian analysts, spent over nine months investigating and preparing the indictment for the trial of former Defence Minister, Magnus Malan and others, which lasted a further nine months. Where the accused are former state employees the state is obliged to pay the legal costs for their defence. These amounted to over R5m and R12m respectively in the above trials (excluding the costs of investigators, prosecutors, and supporting and protecting witnesses).

The net outcome of the above trials was a single successful prosecution. In the post-apartheid era some prosecutions resulted in guilty verdicts (notably, convictions of de Kock and of three people for the 'Motherwell 4' bombing, carried out at Motherwell, Port Elizabeth, in 1989) but others culminated in acquittals (such as the trials of Malan *et al.* and Dr Wouter Basson, the head of the apartheid-era chemical and biological warfare programme) (see Ernest 2007: 10–11, 13–15; Sarkin 2004: 373–79).
6 The President of South Africa has the power to pardon or reprieve offenders under Section 84(2)(j) of the Constitution (No. 108 of 1996).
7 Prosecution Policy and Directives Relating to the Prosecution of Offences Emanating from Conflicts of the Past and Which Were Committed on or before 11 May 1994, promulgated 1 December 2005.
8 For commentary on the 2005 prosecution guidelines, see Ernest (2007: 15–21) (containing analysis based on the points raised in the legal challenge) and Sooka (2006). The first prosecutions under the new guidelines fuelled the fears of victim/survivor groups and critics. In August 2007, former apartheid-era Law and Order Minister Adriaan Vlok, former Police Commissioner Johan van der Merwe and other lesser luminaries all pleaded guilty to the attempted murder of Reverend Frank Chikane (formerly Secretary General of the South African Council of Churches; then Director General of President Mbeki's Office). They received suspended sentences of various lengths under the terms of a plea bargain. No new information (truth) came to light, but information from those concerned may be used in prosecuting other apartheid-era crimes.
9 Panizza (1995: 175), writing about Latin America, is instructive in this regard:

> And while the justice of the demands for the punishment of human rights crimes can hardly be disputed, those demanding justice never seem to have a coherent political strategy to achieve their aims. In some cases, in their radical rejection of any kind of compromise, human rights' groups showed a contempt for politics which was not radically different from that of the former military rulers and became equally isolated from society.

In fairness, it is no easy matter deciding who to prosecute. 'Evidence-led' prosecutions can seem random while others will claim that 'strategic' prosecutions seeking, for example, 'balance', compromise prosecutorial independence and can be criticised as implying moral equivalence. A focus on leaders and intellectual authors may not satisfy victims wanting their day in court with their personal perpetrators. The only sensible way out is to suggest an open debate, led by those most affected by the violence, in an attempt to reconcile local priorities with international norms on issues such as amnesty.
10 The impact of the seemingly increasingly precarious nature of amnesties on future peace negotiations and peace processes also needs to be part of the international debate on this question.
11 The precise texture of the relationship between a truth commission and the criminal justice system in any particular country is context-specific, but often seems to be an area of policy that is given insufficient consideration. In essence, both often require access to the same evidence, information and witnesses. For example, Yasmin Sooka (interview 20/4/2005), a commissioner on both the South African and Sierra Leonean Truth and Reconciliation Commissions, reported that the debate about how the Sierra Leone Special Court and TRC would work together took place after the institutions were up and running, and turned on the issues of confidentiality and access to testimony and detainees (also see Schabas 2006: 33–40).
12 To recap, a review considers whether a decision is justifiable rather than correct, in short determining whether there is a rational connection between the facts and the finding rather than re-examining the evidence.

13 This analysis is based on research by the International Center for Transitional Justice (ICTJ), often in collaboration with the Human Rights Center at the University of California, Berkeley: see their reports on Iraq 2004; Northern Uganda 2005 and 2007; Aceh, Indonesia 2008; Nepal 2008; and Eastern Democratic Republic of Congo 2008. The resulting publications are available on its website: www.ictj.org. Also see the Afghanistan Independent Human Rights Commission 2005; Office of the United Nations High Commissioner of Human Rights (OHCHR) 2007, on Northern Uganda; and Stover and Weinstein 2004, on Rwanda and the former Yugoslavia. These research reports also feature insights into public attitudes towards amnesty.

14 Van der Merwe argues that the TRC nurtured broad initial acceptance and a deeper understanding of restorative justice as the basis for reconciliation at community level, among leaders and victims/survivors (in Duduza and Katorus on the East Rand). Support for restorative justice was withdrawn, however, because of the different meanings ascribed to the concept (top-down, national-level concerns and bottom-up community and interpersonal priorities) and resulting divergent – and in the communities largely negative – views on whether the TRC delivered on its promises, such as truth and reparations. In essence, a victim/survivor sense of injustice relating to the TRC mainly focused on a failure to provide restorative, not retributive, justice.

15 Several findings from this research are of note. Justice was *a* key concern but far from *the* key concern: 20 per cent of victims and survivors mentioned justice at the hearings, while 58 per cent mentioned reparations, 49 per cent truth and 23 per cent interaction with the perpetrator. Further, more victims/survivors articulated a retributive than a broadly restorative understanding of justice. Finally, commissioner responses at the hearings and the TRC generally tended to sideline this emphasis, preferring to push a restorative ethos as the Commission's main justice paradigm.

16 Restorative justice is generally understood as a form of justice that prioritises the involvement of, and attention to, all parties with a stake in an offence, emphasising restoring social relationships, process as well as outcomes, and harms done and needs arising rather than rules broken. It seeks to reaffirm the dignity of victims (through reparations of various kinds, for example), and the rehabilitation, rather than the prosecution, of offenders.

17 An example of a transitional justice procedure designed to facilitate restorative justice is the Community Reconciliation Process of the Commission for Reception, Truth and Reconciliation (CAVR) in Timor Leste (see Burgess 2006).

Chapter 4

Justice present

The second narrative (1): criminal violence

A coherent response to the challenges of transitional justice and criminal justice reform will only emerge once divisions between past and present, political and criminal violence, and restorative and retributive responses, are questioned and interventions provide integrated responses to complex, evolving problems. At present the transitional era is characterised by hopelessly mixed messages. The apartheid assassin is granted amnesty, while the car hijacker is portrayed as the new nation's nemesis. Amnesty measures and prosecutions in relation to apartheid-era abuses appear self-interested or arbitrary. Similarly, the balance between hard-line and more progressive measures addressing present-day crime often seems to lack coherence.

Violence in myriad forms is now widely acknowledged to be a characteristic of transitional societies. Violent crime is endemic in a number of Central American states – writing about Guatemala, for example, Snodgrass Godoy (2005) refers to the 'razor's edge' between crime and human rights, and the transition from the 'public' violence of state-sponsored genocide to a massive wave of 'private' postwar criminality. Based on a survey of social science studies of internal conflict and civil wars, Thoms and Ron (2007) argue that processes such as democratisation and regime change are themselves dangerous, in essence that regime transition is a major conflict risk factor. 'Democracy, it seems, is good for peace if you have it, but efforts to achieve democracy, such as elections-promotion, may plunge a country into conflict' (702). Explanations for such violence include the ruptures in dominant political and economic arrangements caused by 'conflicts over liberalisation' (the rapid adoption of democratic norms and liberal economic policies in countries where patrimonialism or clientism reign: Lund 2006: 48–49); related conflicts over the terms of accumulation and the distribution of wealth, the scramble for position before the rules of the game become fixed, leading to a continuum of violence in late capitalist transitions (Cramer 2006); enduring structural violence (poverty, inequality, discrimination); and weak states, whether in terms of modest institutional reach and legitimacy or an inability to secure a monopoly over the means of violence. Many of these explanations are both globally informed and locally textured.

In South Africa the evidence points to significant and often rising levels of crime in the transitional era, both pre- and post-1994 (ICHRP 2003: 85; Shaw 2002). There were divergent patterns within such broad generalisations: black South Africans were more likely to be victimised than whites; for reported crime over the period from 1994 to 2000, incidents of murder fell, while the number of murder attempts, serious assaults and rapes rose slightly, and all violent interpersonal crime displayed significant seasonal patterns; property crime remained largely stable (Shaw 2002: 42–58). Nevertheless, eye-catching quotes around the turn of the century painted a bleak picture: 'South Africa is said to have the highest incidence of murder of any country in the world not at war' (Ellis 1999: 49). Overall, reported crime in the post-apartheid era peaked in 2002–3, with subsequent improvements troubled by 'spikes' and some more enduring exceptions affecting particular crimes and locations (e.g. certain forms of aggravated robbery remain problematic, such as residential robberies).[1]

In this context, Simpson (2001, 2002, 2004) has argued that the evaluation of transitional justice mechanisms, such as the TRC, must be placed in the context of the linked challenges posed by justice in transition and violence in transition. In such evaluations the stress should arguably fall on the forward-looking task of assessing how truth commissions contribute to institutional transformation and resurrecting the rule of law, in contexts where the entire administration of justice is often in crisis. Simpson argues that patterns of violence and social conflict are reconfigured and redescribed during political transition rather than brought to an end. Truth commissions need to anticipate both that social conflict will play itself out in different ways in the future and that violent crime that may appear new is often both historically informed and rooted in ongoing experiences of social marginalisation, political exclusion and economic exploitation. In essence, the past returns in the future, but in forms that transitional justice mechanisms such as truth commissions often fail to anticipate, and criminal justice responses often fail to place within a historical context.

The TRC, as we have seen, adopted a narrow political focus, on a limited set of gross abuses of human rights. The HRV Committee held hearings that exposed the role of criminal gangs in political assassinations, as well as more broadly focused sector hearings, but it was in the work of the Amnesty Committee, given the fact that political motive was one of the main conditions for amnesty, that the political–criminal tension mainly came to the fore. Over half the total number of amnesty applications were turned down, invariably in chambers, due to a lack of political motive. Among those contesting the political–criminal divide were amnesty applicants serving prison terms who sought retrospectively to redefine their offences as political. But others emerged from even murkier ground. Simpson (2004: 11–14; also TRC 2003, Vol. 6: 39–47) analyses three categories of particularly problematic cases: witchcraft killings; the activities of Self-Defence Units (SDUs, to varying degrees allied to and controlled by the

ANC); and operations, especially robberies, undertaken by members of the Azanian People's Liberation Army (APLA, the armed wing of the Africanist organisation, the Pan African Congress [PAC]). The arbitrariness of decision-making on this issue spoke to conceptual confusion and inconsistency, but also to genuine definitional challenges.

The amnesty process was problematic, therefore, because it focused on political violence and defined political motive in terms of party or organisational association. As detailed in Chapter 1, this stance impoverished understandings of violence. It also cleansed the past, on both sides of the political divide, of anti-social elements and criminal pathologies, and overlooked the criminalisation of politics and the politicisation of crime under apartheid. The outcome was the creation of an artificial divide between past and present, and political and criminal violence, which reduced the TRC's potential impact on the present and ongoing patterns of violence.

Various commentators have begun to plot the complex histories of violence and social conflict in South Africa, and their reconfiguration during political transition. The work of Simpson, Kynoch, Steinberg and Ellis sets the scene (as, it is worth noting in passing, does the best post-apartheid crime fiction: see Meyer 2000, 2007).

Simpson (2001), applying his own argument about transitional dynamics to youth violence and gangs, illustrates that the blurred line and gravitation between politics and crime, between 'socially functional resistance' and 'anti-social banditry', in counter-culture youth organisations has a considerable history (from late nineteenth-century embryonic bandit gangs of marginalised black migrants drawn to the industrial cities, to the contemporary gang culture on the Cape Flats over a century later). Experiences of marginalisation, impoverishment and alienation, alongside the nurturing of alternative resilient identities and belonging, have shaped these responses *and* young men's engagement with political organisations and the violence of liberation struggles in the apartheid era. These circumstances remain largely unchanged and underpin the sustained involvement of such men in criminal gangs in the post-1994 period. Over a similar historical range, Kynoch (2005) asserts that understanding transitional violence and crime requires a historical approach which highlights the persistence of often locally specific urban violence in South Africa throughout the twentieth century. Arguing that criminal violence folded into politics under apartheid before political violence folded into crime in its wake, the author stresses the criminal dimension to the political violence of the 1980s and 1990s (also see Bonner and Nieftagodien 2002).

Further insights into this world are provided by Jonny Steinberg. *The Number* (Steinberg 2004) is a portrait of Magadien Wentzel, documenting a lifetime spent in prison gangs and his attempts to escape their clutches. It suggests that those embroiled in crime and prison gangs throughout the twentieth century perceived themselves as political actors (anti-colonial and anti-apartheid; true revolutionaries fighting the system). In 1994, there was a nationwide prison rebellion, caused in part by the fact that the criminal fraternity, contrary to their expectations, were not granted an amnesty and released alongside political prisoners from the left and right (272–73). They had anticipated political recognition at the democratic dawn. This sheds a different light on a previously noted facet of the TRC's work: the rejection of the majority of amnesty applications which came from criminals in prison trying to depict their crimes as political. *Midlands* (2002), Steinberg's investigation into the murder of a white farmer in KwaZulu-Natal, shines a spotlight on the fact that youth without work or prospects, transgressing the borders between politics and crime and using violence to escape from youth into manhood, have increasingly roamed between urban and rural areas refashioning relationships and geographical frontiers as they go.[2]

Ellis (1999) comes at the same issue from a different angle, arguing that during apartheid both state and opposition fought to secure control over communities – arming diverse groups as state-sanctioned vigilantes within a counter-revolutionary strategy on the one hand (criminal gangs, former prisoners, rural migrants, IFP militias), and comrades in the battle to render the country 'ungovernable' on the other. It is here that the recent roots of recasting crime as politics lie. Ellis's work on the 'third force' (1998) and law-enforcement (1999) details how the borders between politics and crime were blurred from the perspective of the apartheid state and its security forces, through a potent mix of subcontracting policing functions; covert operations; front companies; destabilisation within and beyond South Africa's borders; the growth of informal economies; disregard for the rule of law; and the loss of centralised control, or privatisation, of violence.

Across the political fence, the United Democratic Front (UDF), an umbrella movement of anti-apartheid groups founded in 1983, and its ally the ANC, he contends, successfully transformed local and particular grievances into a national and generalised struggle against apartheid, but without ever fully controlling their constituency. Political violence, in essence, fed on, politicised, amplified yet masked, exploited yet never fully controlled, already existing social divides (generational, gender, ethnic, migrant–resident), and cultures of crime and violence. These problems cannot simply be wished away by macro political change and vague notions of reconciliation. The demise of political violence at a national level unleashed these local, social struggles involving often well-armed and battle-worn participants. Relocalised and depoliticised, such violence was labelled 'criminal'.

In a sense, both the ANC government and the security forces reaped what they sowed in the last decade of apartheid. The incomplete divide between security and gangsterism, politics and crime, was well illustrated during the transitional phase by the armed groups, sometimes in the guise of Self-Defence or Self-Protection Units (SDUs, SPUs) claiming allegiance to the ANC or Inkatha Freedom Party (IFP) respectively, who effectively controlled sections of some black townships. Such groups were evocatively called 'com-tsotsis' or 'comrade-gangsters'. To draw a line between politics and crime is the task at hand, not an automatic outcome of political transition. It entails, as Ellis stresses, creating an environment in which social struggles can be played out in civil society, political expression and legal institutions.

Continuity *and* change characterise the relationships between past and present, politics and crime, and patterns of violence and responses to violence, and, therefore, the very essence of what ought to constitute the deliberations of any truth commission. The remainder of this section analyses a series of case studies of the shift from political to criminal and social violence as one manifestation of the dynamic of continuity and change;[3] the section that follows examines the same dynamic in relation to responses to violent crime.[4] The former discussion draws on a series of outstanding reports in the Centre for the Study of Violence and Reconciliation's (CSVR's) 'Violence and Transition' series (Simpson served as Executive Director of CSVR until 2005, and the reports reflect his vision of violence in transition). Covering violence from 1980 to 2000, the reports addressed here focus on vigilantism, taxi violence, ex-combatants, warlords and organised crime.[5]

The 'razor's edge' between political and criminal violence

In Harris's (2001) report on vigilante violence, vigilantism is defined as 'a blanket term for activities that occur beyond the parameters of the legal system, purportedly to achieve justice' (6), variously defined. It potentially nets a range of actors from organised groups – such as Mapogo a Mathamaga and People against Gangsterism and Drugs (PAGAD) (see below) – to private security companies, people's courts, instruments of customary law, taxi associations, citizen and commando groups in rural areas, and spontaneous, local incidents of 'mob' justice. Vigilantism has always been a method used by the most marginalised, but also by those with political and economic interests to defend. Although characterised by a long and varied history, from the 1980s until 1994 'vigilantism' was generally used to refer to violence that was politically conservative, often sanctioned by the apartheid state to prop up sympathetic black allies (homeland leaders, Black Local Authorities), and serving as a decentralised form of social control. The TRC predominantly adopted this narrow (political, conservative) interpretation (see, for example, TRC 1998, Vol. 2: 302–12, 383–86, 684–85).

However, the conventional wisdom, focusing on motive rather than actions, concealed a range of motives (including crime) and the fact that actors resisting apartheid often employed similar methods (corporal punishment; necklace killings using a car tyre filled with petrol and set on fire). By the early 1990s the public perceptions of vigilantism had become very muddy terrain indeed, and often included various forms of community or informal justice. Some retrospective commentary about the pre-1994 era has expanded the definition to more consistently focus on illegitimate actions, labelling certain acts committed by groups opposed to apartheid (such as SDUs) as vigilantism, e.g. violent internal policing practices which intruded into what were seen as 'non-political' arenas, such as crime and domestic disputes. Harris notes that this definitional expansion is contested terrain as the definition 'slips along dimensions that include political–criminal activities, political–criminal motives, and political–domestic divisions' (2001: 14).

Post-1994, vigilantism became associated with rising crime, the failings of the criminal justice system and a lack of public security – primarily in public perception a positive and legitimate form of crime-fighting, but also a cause of crime and criminal violence. Both motivations and actions became diverse, but while in the past crime was concealed under the guise of politics, now crime and politics were masked by claims to be fighting crime. The adoption of a crime-fighting mantle created problems, notably of popular resentment when the criminal justice system sought to tackle vigilantism. That violence and vigilantism have been shaped by apartheid *and* the transition itself is illustrated by often paradoxical patterns of continuity and change – on the one hand the legitimacy of violence as a means of resolving problems, and the violent methods themselves; on the other, the definitions of and justifications for vigilantism, and the targeting of mainly criminal rather than political victims. The only partially enhanced legitimacy of the state and criminal justice system exhibits qualities of both continuity and change.

As a second case study, a series of 'taxi wars' scarred the largely black-owned and operated minibus taxi industry after its deregulation in 1987 (Dugard 2001, 2001a). In a not dissimilar way to, and often as a form of, vigilantism, in the apartheid era taxi violence was linked to the mainstream of political violence, driven by political alliances and orchestrated by the state to exploit the contours of political division and conflict (urban/rural, IFP/ANC). These conflicts were relatively few in number, if protracted, but rapid deregulation in the context of political destabilisation and community fragmentation laid the foundations for the upsurge in violence that was to ravage the new democracy. Deregulation was designed to create a constituency of black South Africans with a stake in the market, and the stakes were high as within 15 years it became a R10bn industry. The taxi industry developed rapidly and unchecked into highly contested and divisive economic as well as political terrain, characterised by intense competition over routes. This context could be manipulated by the state to destabilise pro-ANC communities and the negotiations process. That said, state control was generally weak and taxi associations emerged as informal agents of regulation, protection and extortion, and as formidable agents of violence.

Taxi violence escalated in the post-1994 era: 'if one form of violence has characterised the post-apartheid period it has been the taxi wars' (Dugard 2001: 13). Taxi-related conflicts became more widespread, localised, informal and criminal in nature, feeding on more generalised transitional social and economic tensions and inequalities (such as coloured/African divisions and gangsterism in the Cape). Rooted in the dynamics of deregulation and destabilisation, and long-standing cycles of revenge, the violence took on a life of its own, more clearly linked to income generation rather than politics and more difficult to control. Trends included the role of 'mother bodies' or large umbrella associations targeting violence to extract funds, secure compliance and protect spheres of interest (rather than simply to protect routes). Second, government attempts to reregulate and restructure the industry challenged vested interests and unsettled established power relations, resulting in a violent response from some quarters. Finally, official complicity was no longer political and linked to destabilisation, but rather took the form of ownership of taxis by police and other government personnel. The predictable result was that state interventions in taxi conflicts were often partisan and self-interested.

Related patterns emerge in CSVR's work on former combatants from Umkhonto we Sizwe (MK, the armed wing of the ANC), SDUs, SPUs and APLA, who remain outside the new South African police and army (Gear 2002). Many ex-combatants have also undergone an incomplete realignment over time between politics and crime; crime fighting and criminal activity; and publicly oriented and private, domestic violence. In the transition process they ceded ground in the crime fighting and legitimacy stakes not only to the criminal justice system but also to vigilantism, while their own activities overlapped on occasion with these two camps. In a striking irony, crime fighting was both formal and informal, as some former MK and SDU personnel were incorporated into the South African Police Service (SAPS) and South African National Defence Force (SANDF); and yet ex-combatants were also harassed and targeted by criminals, the police and army, sometimes working in alliance, seeking revenge for past and present activities. Informing these ex-combatant experiences of violence was a nest of negativity: ongoing unemployment; marginalisation and a sense of betrayal (by communities and leadership); brutalisation and traumatisation; stigmatisation, and their articulation in public discourse as a problem (crime, etc.) rather than a resource; and the lack of new, positive identities.

The TRC process engaged inadequately with these challenges and even exacerbated certain problems, such as the perception of leadership betrayal and the prevalence of partial and negative histories. The experience of ex-combatants also clearly illustrates the need, at another level of response, for coherent policies of force demobilisation, disarmament and reintegration. These have been reasonably effective, but not untroubled, arenas in South Africa. The ability of such processes, if poorly handled, to generate perceptions of unfair exclusion, resentment and impoverishment can easily rebound into crime, as criminal activity represents one of the areas for which military training provides transferable skills. Further, integration processes can include training for personnel, with very varied claims to former combatant status and chequered pasts, who are subsequently demobilised, discharged or resign from formal agencies and carry into public life a potent blend of bitterness, insider knowledge and military skills.

Moving on, in one of the many available windows onto the violence in KwaZulu-Natal, Taylor (2002) maps the systemic continuities in pre- and post-1994 political violence in the province, through studies of Shobashobane,

Richmond and Nongoma. This is an example of political reconciliation between the ANC and IFP at provincial and national levels not translating into the resolution of local conflicts. The failure to adequately comprehend or confront this violence, through local political interventions or the TRC, alongside impunity and official policies characterised by denial and the disowning of responsibility, generated violence spiralling beyond the original protagonists to intra-organisational conflict and organised criminal networks. Taylor identified an integrated set of problems, drawing together the roles and complicities of paramilitary forces (MK, Inkatha hit squads, SDUs, SPUs and covert state agents), the security forces (police and military), and the criminal justice system (investigations and prosecutions). Local strongmen or warlords implicated in the violence were assassinated rather than being dealt with by the rule of law.

> In KwaZulu-Natal there has been no determined or integrated attempt to promote smooth demilitarisation, unbiased policing, and effective prosecutions. Blocking the way forward has been the weight of wartime divisions and the way in which this relates to how political power is passed into the hands of the two main protagonists – Inkatha and the ANC. For, with KZN now being governed through a divided system of (IFP) provincial and (ANC) national authority, and with both sides claiming, and having, the right to deploy security forces and set up investigations and commissions, the rule of law has remained politically contaminated. In fact, the way in which Inkatha–ANC differences feed through into the authority structures tasked with resolving political violence has come to drive ineluctably a political pragmatism that rests more on a politics of denial than on the pursuit of justice.
> (Taylor 2002: 504)[6]

Nowhere is it more apparent that the past, and a failure to address its full legacy, has systematically informed the present and the complex networks of complicity linking crime and politics, than in the geographically informed rise of organised crime:

> It is not by coincidence that those areas of the country which experienced the highest levels of political conflict – KwaZulu-Natal and the townships to the east of Johannesburg – now have one of the highest levels of syndicated criminal activity. These places are characterised by established networks to smuggle contraband; few opportunities for legitimate economic activity; the presence of former combatants with military training; control by strongmen of distinct geographical areas; and a disrespect for the rule of law generated through ongoing conflict and harsh state actions.
> (Shaw 2002: 72)

The normalisation of South Africa's place in the international community opened it up to various facets of globalisation, including organised crime

(Ellis 1998, 1999; Shaw 2002: 63–82). New forms of organised crime were introduced, and older patterns that had often been officially condoned under apartheid were rendered more visible. Defining and more locally informed features of organised crime in South Africa were a complex, evolving network structure often built around past allegiances and relationships, and the already mentioned correlation between areas that had experienced violent conflict and the emergence of criminal groups. Organised crime, in short, fed on local, regional and global dynamics.

Within southern Africa, a set of factors inherited from a bloody past rendered the region vulnerable to organised crime. Among the regional catalysts were a history of wars; weak states and fragile criminal justice infrastructures; large informal economies; poverty; a corruption of the relationship between politics, business and crime; and rudimentary regional cooperation. The result was a flourishing business in cross-border smuggling and crime, with South Africa at its epicentre acting as a major regional exporter of organised crime (Gastrow 2001, 2003). Adding to the problems, Ellis (1998, 1999) argues that the South African police force was ill prepared for the new dawn, as on the one hand it had been cut off from changing patterns in the regional and international political economy of crime, and on the other it had become thoroughly corrupted by security force complicity in crime both at home and in its regional campaign of destabilisation. The police had engaged in criminal activity and formed alliances with criminal syndicates in the fight against political opposition, to fund vigilante groups and militias, to break sanctions and in pursuit of personal enrichment. Strong links to the past are evident at every turn.

Local and regional dimensions were augmented by the globalisation of organised crime in the 1990s. Countries undergoing transition have been particularly hard hit by this uncivil component of globalisation. Criminal justice systems are transformed and thereby, at least initially, often weakened, and countries integrated into the international community are ill equipped to police porous borders and the growth in flows of people and goods. Writing in 1999, Ellis stated that South Africa 'has become Africa's capital of organised crime', with international criminals and syndicates, mainly dealing in drugs, money laundering and business fraud, attracted by its 'first-class transport infrastructure and banking system and the world's tenth largest stock exchange, which make it an ideal base' (50–51). The Russian mafia, Chinese triads and Nigerian organised crime groups expanded their operations in the country. As international operations increasingly used the country as a destination and trans-shipment point, local criminal actors became more sophisticated, operating as competitors and partners (for example, as suppliers of stolen goods and as agents of violence). Organised crime directly contributed to the growth in certain kinds of criminal activity, such as vehicle hijackings, bank and cash-in-transit robberies and taxi industry crime.

This discussion hints at broader concerns for transitional justice and politics, such as the ambiguity of its encounter with globalisation. Furthermore, some authors have questioned the sharp division between organised crime (as predatory, anti-social) on the one hand and the state and mainstream business (as respectable guarantors of a good society) on the other. Making a point of general relevance to transitional countries, while drawing specifically on organised crime in the Cape Flats, Standing (2004) argues that the relationship between organised crime and the state, as well as business, is more complex and compromised than this, shading into the realms of partnership and complementarity. The argument is not only that state actors collude with organised crime for mutual gain, a point with which Steinberg (2001: 12) concurs: 'No underworld survives without official corruption ... Organised crime is only as strong as a state is weak'. It goes further, to claim that in the absence of an effective state organised crime can provide not so much a threat to the state but a crude alternative, taking on a social aspect and providing a form of criminal governance. This generates a layered set of relationships between criminals and local communities beyond the solely exploitative, and between crime and the state as the former cushions the latter's political and economic shortcomings. Again, crime can be seen as socially functional as well as anti-social.

Similarly, organised crime, rather than being solely antithetical to and undermining of the market and economic progress, is arguably an extreme variant of capitalism, motivated by many of the same principles (innovative as well as deviant, entrepreneurial as well as violent and illegal). If such capitalism is based on extraordinary wealth for a few and abject poverty for the exploited majority, one need only lift one's eyes to the rest of South Africa and the global economy to see these outcomes mirrored in the mainstream marketplace. Standing's analysis suggests a continuum, rather than a fissure, in which organised crime can be understood as a form of 'predatory capitalism' and, furthermore, potentially a functional component of, rather than dysfunctional to, the capitalist system. Those with formal or informal power are best situated to secure illicit economic gains, and many of those in power in the past, although they may have shifted camp (formal/informal sector, politics/business/crime), are still in power today.

The aim here is not to idealise organised crime. If unchecked, it will deter foreign investment, undermine service delivery, infect governance with corruption and violence, marginalise civil society and pervert the rule of law. In the end, as Ellis (1998: 229, 1999: 68) notes, the question is whether organised crime will so penetrate and dominate South Africa as to undermine the state and democracy on the one hand, and the formal economy on the other, or whether it can be contained enough so that mainstream politics and economics can still coexist with it, and even flourish. Extending the argument, a series of parallel powers – organised crime, vigilantes, etc. – will coexist with the state, but must not overwhelm it.

To conclude, what is to be done about crime and politics? Cohen (1996), in his article 'Crime and Politics: Spot the Difference', plots the multiple linkages between crime and politics, spanning the necessary politicisation of criminological discourse *and* crime assuming a prominent position in contemporary political life.

Cohen argues that changes in today's political conflicts (nationalist and ethnic wars, civil conflicts), notably their criminalisation, highlight that while the two domains must not be considered separately, they must also not be indistinguishable. Echoing Ellis, he writes: 'For these countries, the remote prospect of democracy lies in a radical *separation* between crime and politics. This is one way of expressing the ideal of civil society' (19).

It is worth reiterating that the marriage of crime and politics, in South Africa as elsewhere, is not new to the transitional era (Snodgrass Godoy 2005, on Guatemala). The danger, prior to and during the transitional moment, is that a human rights prism segregates and prioritises the political, while subsuming and overlooking other forms of violence. As violent crime becomes rooted in the intersections between the past and the contradictions of the transitional present, there is a shift from political violence obscuring criminal violence to criminal violence obscuring its political implications. Criminal violence in this latter setting is inextricably linked to politics: reworking responses to political legacies; drawing on familiar methods and actors; rooted in enduring 'identities of exclusion' (Harris 2005); confident of political connections, protection and impunity; and, increasingly, an expression of dissatisfaction with the new order. Violence must be understood as a threat to democracy *and* a symptom of the process of democratisation itself (Harris 2005: 7).

To help prevent future violence, truth commissions will have to engage with these dynamics of continuity and change. They will also have to help create a division between politics and crime, where often no such division exists. This is a difficult mandate in the context of fragile democracies and rising levels of violent crime. It has been further complicated by the post-11 September 2001 tendency for both perpetrators of violence and government responses to manipulate the border between politics and crime, social justice and social banditry, between opposition to the prevailing order and opposition to any order, in their own interests. The TRC largely assumed that there was a divide between crime and politics and that political violence could be consigned to the past, rather than seeking to bring such transformations about. Segregating crime and politics requires the ability, beyond crime and violence, to secure influence, access status, derive subsistence and resolve disputes. In short, it requires rights-based participation and economic justice.

The remainder of the chapter argues that truth commissions, if they seek to prevent violence and contribute to the rule of law, will have to engage with responses to crime as well as shifts from political to criminal violence, with justice in transition as well as violence in transition.

The second narrative (2): responses to criminal violence

> Criminal justice institutions are more than reflections of the state; they are emanations of its basic character.
>
> (Gordon 2006: 4)

Response strategies to violent transitional crime sit on a continuum from hard-line, more repressive measures to efforts to develop means of democratic social control. The work of Panizza (1995) and the International Council on Human Rights Policy (ICHRP) (2003) provide a framework for looking at how and why new democracies combine these different approaches, and changes over time. Panizza draws on the experience of Latin America to identify three strategies that governments are likely to employ: 'instrumental authoritarianism', 'legal fetishism' and 'paralegality' (Panizza 1995: 182–86). The ICHRP (2003: 26–33) place official responses to rising levels of transitional crime in two broad categories. One category of responses, coinciding in particular with Panizza's instrumental authoritarianism, are non-consultative, more hard-line responses to crime. These include severe punishments, mandatory sentences, attacks on rights defence and defenders, policies that foster police brutality, and political manipulation of public security issues. The second category is a set of often more liberal measures developed in collaboration with human rights NGOs and civil society actors. These include community policing programmes, police training, witness and victim protection initiatives, external oversight mechanisms and restorative justice initiatives. It is not unusual to find elements of the two approaches employed simultaneously. As with the explanations for violence, responses to violence are both globally informed and locally textured.

One driving force behind such responses is public opinion. Important differences exist between reality on the one hand, and public concerns and perceptions on the other, in relation to crime and insecurity (ICHRP 2003). Fear about crime is certainly not new to the transitional present, but a more democratic environment increases the visibility of crime and creates conditions in which new forms of crime emerge. Under-reporting and a focus on political violence is often replaced by more accurate collation and reporting of crime statistics, extensive media coverage and a focus on criminal violence. Changes in the profile of victims and the displacement of crime also have an impact – for example, an increased targeting of whites and white areas in South Africa since the removal of apartheid's political and spatial strait-jacket. A predominantly white-owned business sector and media in South Africa have amplified white victimisation, fears and priorities. Public perceptions of crime and policing are not homogenous, and are susceptible to manipulation by politicians for political gain as well as by media coverage characterised by sensationalism and oversimplification. As Shaw notes: 'Perception in fighting crime is all' (2002: 36, also see 83–95). Damage done at the level of public perceptions can be difficult to rectify; figures indicating a decline in serious crime can be combined with an increase in public fears about crime (du Plessis and Louw 2005). Predictably, the accuracy of official crime figures and determining levels of crime constitute contested political terrain in new democracies.

The triangulation between (1) the incidence, severity and risk of criminal victimisation, (2) public perceptions about the seriousness of crime, and (3) rhetorical manipulation of these two factors by the media and politicians, has established crime as a high political priority not only in transitional contexts, but internationally (Cohen 1996: 8). In another trend that is at once global and takes on a local hue, populism informs a set of conservative responses – for example, politicians and the media marshal xenophobic discourses and negative stereotypes to blame foreigners and illegal immigrants for social ills such as crime (Harris 2001a).

Perceptions about crime are also symbolic, providing a form of metaphorical societal commentary. Such metaphors are another way in which the past is reborn in the present in transitional contexts. Crime, and debate about crime, rearticulates concerns about change, societal divisions and notions of 'otherness' in the post-oppression or post-conflict era. It provides a language for the otherwise and variously unspeakable. In South Africa, crime – and reporting, public debate and private discussions about crime – can take the form of racism disguised and revisited; the new, acceptable face of talking about 'us' and 'them', where race and class now pit whites and middle-class blacks against the marginalised and still impoverished majority. Caldeira, in *City of Walls: Crime, Segregation, and Citizenship in São Paulo* (2000: 19–53), argues that 'the talk of crime' as a discursive act simplifies, encloses and seeks to symbolically reorder an unfamiliar, threatening world. As such it is both expressive and productive.

Simplification, enclosure and reordering can take material as well as symbolic forms. For example, public responses to crime are writ large on the urban and rural landscape of the new South Africa, in its inherited but slowly changing patterns of segregation: gated communities, shifting frontiers of land ownership, 'First World glamour alongside Third World despondency' (van der Spuy, interview 8/4/2005). Ivan Vladislavić's suggestively titled account, *Portrait With Keys: The City of Johannesburg Unlocked* (2006), is a sympathetic, yet stark, portrait of a frontier city of contested, shifting boundaries – 'The township is written in longhand across the printed page of the white city' (60) – and of the everyday life of inhabiting both insecurity and responses to insecurity: 'The first principle of key management is to separate working groups on interlocking rings' (111). In urban and rural areas there is a new frontier; it is simultaneously criminal, economic, political, racial and even military (Steinberg 2002). Its message adds up to a deeper threat.

Stories about multiple break-ins or gratuitous violence, and stories about such stories, are a powerful narrative of generalised, imagined and anticipated insecurity that could scarcely be more at odds with the TRC's narrative of speaking truth to reconciliation. Crime and perceptions of crime, in combination, have implications for the democratic project as 'a code for political unease' (Cohen 1996: 8). Crucially, this unease speaks to the various faces of vulnerability and uncertainty inspired by political transition: it affects blacks whose expectations have not been fulfilled as well as whites who feel that their fears have been proved justified. It also speaks to what Caldeira (2000) calls disjunctive democracy (also see Holston and Caldeira 1998), and the way in which crime, violence, inequality and segregation intersect to undermine the promise of the new democratic era. Human rights have gained a secure purchase in certain areas (political rights) but simultaneously barely feature in others. Such disjunctures indicate that human rights and democracy remain contested terrain. Crime and politics again merge in various ways. Among the outcomes of the public visibility of security concerns in South Africa is that crime has become a high-profile political and electoral issue, often ranked first or second, behind employment, as public priorities.

Therefore, in the context of rising levels of violent crime, hard-line law and order measures, and a backlash against human rights, can attract widespread public support. This is a profound challenge for human rights and transitional justice practitioners. The shift from political to criminal violence is accompanied by other forms of displacement that run the risk of marginalising human rights. Violence is carried out by private actors in the interests of power and wealth as well as the state at the bequest of politics. Priorities veer from an embrace of human rights and the rule of law to muscular crackdowns, from hatred of authoritarian responses to a certain nostalgia for the past (on 'apartheid nostalgia', see Kynoch 2003), from human rights being seen as part of the solution (on the side of the victim/people) to its reframing as part of the problem (on the side of the criminal/enemy).[7] Human rights organisations themselves struggle with transition from a familiar discourse of critique to an unfamiliar one of constructive engagement.[8] A human rights disconnect seems commonplace:

> it could be argued, that the stubborn adherence to these categories [political/criminal] has become the Achilles heel of the human rights movement in Latin America, producing a dangerous disconnect between the concerns that most citizens consider paramount and the issues traditionally advocated by rights groups. Populist politicians have stepped into the breach – many of them with individual and institutional ties to past atrocities – promising a platform of *mano dura* ['rule by an iron fist'] that has paved the way for the rollback of many hard-won democratic rights.
>
> (Snodgrass Godoy 2005: 600)

With this backdrop, the case studies that follow illustrate official responses to crime, spanning hard-line (public, private) and more collaborative approaches. Instrumental authoritarianism, legal fetishism, paralegality and restorative justice are considered briefly in turn. Again, continuities as well as change mark the transitional present; and the coverage, as for the emerging forms of violence, concentrates on the early democratic years.

Instrumental authoritarianism

Instrumental authoritarianism, for Panizza (1995), means that while new regimes generate the kind of human rights discourse characteristic of liberal constitutionalism, authoritarianism remains grounded in political practice and institutional memory, a template readily reactivated in 'extreme' or 'exceptional' circumstances. Measures may include the excessive use of force by the police, suspension of constitutional guarantees, or the deployment of armed forces to certain regions of the country. These are hard-line, generally non-consultative policies. As noted above, a nostalgia for authoritarian responses may also develop among the general public.

The ICHRP (2003: 4, 21–25) identify a 'dismantling mentality' among emerging democracies, which seek to disband oppressive apparatuses and end abuses without the necessary investment or capacity in democratic means of crime control. In short, existing institutional arrangements either break down or are dismantled more quickly than it is possible to institutionalise new arrangements. This is one component of a broader process of change management, and the challenge of addressing situations without precedent, that is conducive to a rise in criminal activity. A disjuncture develops, to use Simpson's terms, between justice in transition and crime in transition. This disjuncture creates the reality and perception of a security vacuum, and the context within which authoritarian responses make a comeback.

In South Africa, the ANC's first term in office under President Mandela (1994–99) was an era of dismantling, reform and often ambitious, innovative policy formulation. The second term in office (post-1999, under President Mbeki) unapologetically accentuated the existing authoritarian impulse. Already, prior to 1999:

> The government developed new 'tough' policies. These included minimum sentencing, which effectively removed the court's discretion in the sentencing process; amendments to the Criminal Procedure Act that provided courts [with] more power to refuse bail [and] to consider vague criteria such as the sense of 'community outrage' in deciding on bail and imprisonment; and closed prisons, modeled closely on the maximum security prisons of the United States, which provided for effective solitary confinement.
> (ICHRP 2003: 88)

From 1999 the authoritarian impulse was in the ascendancy. Shaw (2002: 38, for example) cites a decisive shift in focus from human rights and issues of accountability to fighting crime through effective law enforcement. Such a tough strategy entailed risks, of raising expectations without delivery, of targeting socially disadvantaged groups (illegal migrants) and of seeming to sanction impunity (87–88). It also massively increased prison overcrowding. The TRC and the crackdown emphasis within criminal justice policy can be seen as two different facets of the new South Africa's embrace of symbolic politics (Gordon 2006).[9]

More recently, there are signs of a third era of responses which seek to combine aspects of the previous two eras (the 'policy pendulum', swinging between conservative and more progressive measures, finding middle ground: see, for example,

Gordon 2006: 268–70, 281–85). While all of the post-1994 eras have combined different approaches in pursuit of an effective response to transitional crime, the three phases identified here – dismantling/reform, authoritarian impulses and a more balanced approach – provide a useful schema, the utility of which will be illustrated in the following case study focusing on the police.

The police and the 'policy pendulum'

The dilemma in relation to policing is summarised by Neild (2003: 283): 'In much of the developing world, states are Janus-faced: as instruments of coercion and control they are supremely powerful; as agents of protection and development they are profoundly weak'. Gordon (2006), in the South African context, points out that an apparatus that had been constructed to protect the state under apartheid had to be redirected to protect the state's citizens (also see Leggett 2005; Shaw 2002: 22–41, 119–40; Rauch 2004). The task of turning an instrument of oppression and occupation into a democratic public service was vast, skewed as it was towards violence (including extra-legal measures, but also within the law, for example, prosecutions could be gained by forced confessions), and towards certain sectors of the population. In 1994, 74 per cent of police stations were situated in white suburbs or business districts. To move from confessions-based to evidence-based prosecutions entails a revolution of the mind as well as in skills. Not surprisingly, the police force was not trusted and lacked legitimacy in black communities. Characteristically, old systems were dismantled before new ones were established to replace them, problems without precedent were faced and often not anticipated.

The South African Police (SAP) became the South African Police Service (SAPS), incorporating the South African and former homeland police forces (11 agencies in all). The Department for Safety and Security was reformed to include the SAPS and a civilian Secretariat for Safety and Security (intended to provide civilian input into strategic policy, reform and monitoring). Envisaged civil society input, therefore, went beyond investigation and monitoring to a more substantive contribution to decision-making, through civilian secretariats at national and provincial levels and community police forums in each police station. However, the prospects for democratic policing were not aided by the fact that apartheid-era police were guaranteed security of tenure as part of the political compromise emerging from the negotiations process, and by the inclusion in the SAPS of significant numbers of poorly skilled and often illiterate *kitskonstabels* ('instant constables', with little training), municipal police and members from SDUs and SPUs, as it became a 'dumping ground for unwanted men with guns' (Leggett 2005: 158). Understandably, emphasis in the new era was placed on transformation, accountability and oversight, and more specifically on human rights compliance, civilian oversight, community involvement and local accountability, demilitarising police ranks and increasing the profile of black police.

A coordinated response to crime and criminal justice reform, entitled the National Crime Prevention Strategy (NCPS) and driven by the Secretariat for Safety and Security, was not developed until 1996. The NCPS characterised crime as a social, structural issue, which would have suggested, at least in part, developmental preventive remedies. But its proposed responses and actual implementation have been dismissed by critics such as Dixon (2004) as 'cosmetic', subverted by the dominant paradigms of reactive crime control and neo-liberal economics. Nevertheless, this era of police policy was strong on 'visioning', idealism and standards imported from established democracies. But if it was strong on the 'ought to be', it was weak on the 'what actually is': how such an approach could be adapted to a context characterised by high crime, a lack of resources, and entrenched institutional, and increasingly popular, resistance. The buzzwords of this period of more liberal, consultative measures, in rough chronological order, were accountability, human rights, social crime prevention, agency coordination and managerial 'efficiency' approaches.

The relative failure of these measures to contain crime, and high-profile incidents such as a series of bomb attacks in the Western Cape between 1998 and 2000 (see below), produced a fresh range of responses from the second post-democracy government. There was an accentuation of existing policies prioritising the most serious forms of crime and high crime areas, and the increased use of measures reminiscent of an earlier era. Initially tied to what became known as 'Operation Crackdown', its overarching policy framework was the non-consultative National Crime Combating Strategy (NCCS) launched in April 2000. 'The NCCS differs from the NCPS by one word and an ocean of ideology' (Leggett 2005: 164). Tackling both realities and perceptions, with a fixation on crime statistics on which a brief moratorium was placed in June 2000, was seen as a key determinant of government legitimacy. The self-conscious irony of Leggett's commentary does not mask the serious message:

> the SAPS has resorted to traditional, albeit targeted, authoritarian policing. The police and the military show up in force. They make themselves visible. They wake everyone up at three a.m. and search their sugar bowls, without specific probable cause ... They seize lots of undocumented people and guns, as well as drugs and suspected stolen property. They add any incidental arrests to their statistics. They throw up roadblocks and cordon-and-search operations to accomplish the same thing on the roads and sidewalks. What year is it again? This return to militaristic policing should surprise no one. To a man with a hammer, everything looks like a nail. Organisations do what they know how to do, and they cannot do otherwise when they have not been trained to do otherwise.
> (Leggett 2005: 165)[10]

The highest-profile actor in this new era was the Directorate of Special Operations, usually known by a predictably muscular shorthand, the Scorpions, launched by the newly incumbent President Mbeki to tackle organised crime (Redpath 2004).[11] The shift away from institutional transformation and prevention to fighting crime coincided with the promotion of ANC insiders to key positions (National Director of Public Prosecutions; National Commissioner of Police; Minister for Safety and Security), which was designed to reduce tensions between politicians and the criminal justice system and speed up delivery. It also coincided with a downgrading of civilian oversight and the consultative paradigm of policing, as the role of the Secretariat for Safety and Security, NGOs, research institutes and community policing was diluted.

Transformation, enforcement and prevention are difficult bedfellows to manage simultaneously. The outcome can be one of role confusion, excessive ambition (many aspects of prevention lie outside the remit and expertise of the police), insufficient capacity and contradictory impacts. As an example of the challenges faced when attempting to juggle transformation and effective responses to violent crime, Dixon and Johns (2001: 43) document one state official's interpretation of the public order policing of the death of gang leader Rashaad Staggie, lynched following a People against Gangsterism and Drugs (PAGAD) march in August 1996. The respondent felt the police had been disabled, in part as a result of their 're-training and re-acculturisation' – they knew 'what not to do so as not to repeat the mistakes of the past', but 'they didn't know what to do in the new democratic order'. From another angle, enforcement and crime fighting can impede necessary reform. While there were various enduring systemic problems, such as the very low number of violent crimes that lead to a conviction, nowhere was the systemic legacy of the past more apparent than in the striking levels of police corruption, criminality, brutality, torture and deaths in custody. Two video recordings, one screened in April 1999 by the BBC showing police officers assaulting car hijack suspects in Johannesburg, the second shown on South African TV in November 2000 revealing police officers setting their dogs on illegal immigrants from Mozambique, illustrated how much work still remained to be done.

Rauch (2004) is one of the few authors to reflect specifically on the impact of the TRC on institutional transformation and reform within the police. She argues that victim hearings had a significant impact on public perceptions of the police, and on some police perceptions about themselves and the organisation for which they had worked, but notes that very few former police officials applied for amnesty (see Chapter 1). Dominant legacies from these processes for police personnel included a sense of being abandoned by past leadership and stigmatised in the eyes of the public. An important limitation on its impact was the TRC's neglect of the ordinary practices of policing as a result of its focus on gross violations of human rights, and on those gross violations that were politically motivated. Rauch also details ways in which the TRC's recommendations on policing were misdirected – 'weak and inarticulate' (Rauch 2004: 9) – and thus largely irrelevant and ignored. Among the reasons for this were the haste with which recommendations were formulated (failing to make the most of the available evidence), and an ignorance of policy initiatives in the transitional present (for example, in relation to public order policing):

> most of the TRC's recommendations concerning policing covered ground which had already been covered elsewhere ... The TRC did not come up with any recommendations which challenged or added to the model of transformation that had already been adopted ... This was particularly disappointing given the rich data on the history of policing in South Africa which the Commission had been able to gather through the victim and amnesty hearings. At best, the TRC merely endorsed some of the elements of the new government's reform programme; a harsher judgement would be that it missed the opportunity to make an appropriate contribution to the process of reform.
>
> (47; for the TRC's recommendations on policing, see TRC 1998, Vol. 5: 330–34)

Rauch concludes that the TRC made little impact on the process of police reform, although there may be longer-term intangible effects relating to police accountability and the moral climate within the police. This example illustrates that truth commissions operate in the context of changing profiles of crime and violence and equally fluid policy responses and institutional reform. Commissions need to address both sides of the equation if their recommendations are to deserve serious attention.

Throughout the transitional era there has been a combination of approaches to crime and the policing of crime, but the emphasis shifted in around 1999 towards a more authoritarian approach. Having said this, in the more recent past there has been a move back to the rhetoric of social crime prevention and community policing (as a component of sector policing). While it may be easier to revert to law enforcement solutions regardless of transformation and prevention, effective and sustainable policing ultimately requires prevention and punishment, long-term structural ambitions and short-term visible results. Achieving the right balance is also work in progress in other areas (central powers versus decentralisation; specialist units versus policing the everyday). Balance, finding an equilibrium for the 'policy pendulum', has to be sought in the context of new links between crime and politics which often drive the authoritarian impulse: crime as a high-profile electoral issue; contests over statistics and whether crime rates are increasing or decreasing; crime as the source of various public mobilisations; the retargeting of the marginalised; and pressure to shift from the socialisation of crime and crime prevention to the criminalisation of social policy and the political (Dixon 2004, 2004a).

Legal fetishism

Legal fetishism (returning to Panizza 1995), or 'virtual legality' (DePalma in Cohen 1996: 9), refers to an excessive legalism in public debate. Legal provisions comprehensively regulating social life are undermined by an enforcement vacuum. The danger is that the rule of law, in practice, will be disregarded and irrelevant. Legal fetishism can include a range of practices, from the relegalisation of political repression to the ratification of international and regional human rights instruments and the setting up of human rights bureaucracies.

Although apartheid made use of the extra-legal, particularly in its death throes, it was predominantly a legal and legalised system of oppression. But apartheid was also contested through the law. As oppositional lawyers stormed the new South Africa's citadels of power – notably the negotiations process, the new government and the Constitutional Court – it was in part because of this latter tradition that the rule of law figured so prominently as an agent and ultimate objective of transition. But it was privileged within the constraints of the transitional era, as law became the site on and through which political compromises (such as the amnesty provision) were made. It was subject to its own dynamic of continuity (of procedure, personnel and more) and change. As such, the law became an arena of struggle over power and values, and a means of adjudicating political and cultural disputes, contesting social and economic realities, as well as crafting the meaning of the rule of law itself.

The argument made below resonates with Klug's (2000) thesis that the local adoption of a globally pervasive notion of democratic constitutionalism with bounded possibilities (civil and political human rights, market economics) enables political transition to proceed while providing and testing the institutional capacity to manage local political demands and conflicts. The outcome, Klug argues, is a hybridisation and reshaping of universal principles through their reflection in and appropriation by local histories, cultures and struggles. Both the potential and limitations of law as an agent of transformation during political transition are explored in more detail below.

A range of positive legal measures were introduced in the new South Africa. It has a strong, independent Constitutional Court and a progressive Constitution (the interim Constitution, No. 200 of 1993, and the final Constitution, No. 108 of 1996), as well as a host of state institutions, called the Chapter 9 institutions after their constitutional location, designed to support the new democratic order (such as the South African Human Rights Commission, the Public Protector, the Commission for Gender Equality, and the Commission for the Promotion and Protection of the Rights of Cultural, Religious and Linguistic Communities). Various legislative measures also sought progressive outcomes: a new Correctional Services Act (No. 111 of 1998) aimed to align the penal system and the conditions of detention with international standards; amendments of the Criminal Procedure Act modified practice with regards to arrest and the use of force; while several inherited laws were struck down by the Constitutional Court, abolishing the death penalty, corporal punishment and various presumptions that undermined the presumption of innocence (ICHRP 2003: 82).

Both the 'dismantling' and the legal fetishism paradigms are evident in these developments, and in the fact that 534 new laws were enacted during the tenure of the first democratically elected parliament (1994–99), many of which replaced apartheid-era legislation (McGreal 1999).[12]

But new laws do not automatically translate into changed, progressive realities. This is, in part, because legal fetishism is not always progressive. But even progressive laws depend upon effective implementation to have an impact. Ndebele (2000: 155) summarises the challenge as one of bridging the gap between law-making as an act of freedom and law-making as regulation. Well-meaning interventions such as the Firearms Control Act (No. 60 of 2000) and the Domestic Violence Act (No. 116 of 1998) encountered difficulties ranging from the poor research and knowledge base for policy interventions, to over-extended police capacity (resources and skills), and deep challenges relating to the need for attitudinal and political change (Altbeker 2004; Smythe and Parenzee 2004). The government has sometimes failed to comply with court rulings and new laws. Its response to certain Constitutional Court rulings, such as the 2001 Grootboom case (right to housing) and 2002 Treatment Action Campaign case (seeking access to the anti-retroviral drug nevirapine in public hospitals, to reduce the risk of mother-to-child transmission of HIV), indicates that judgments from the highest court in the land will not necessarily be implemented smoothly or in full.[13]

Three further issues merit brief consideration: (1) the limits of the law and human rights as agents of transformation; (2) whether South Africa has the capacity or constituency for liberal constitutionalism; and (3) the challenge of legal pluralism.

First, the limits of law and human rights as agents of transformation have already been discussed (Chapter 1). Post-apartheid South Africa occupies a particular place in this narrative of ambition. Mutua (1997: 63–64, 68) states: 'Never has the recreation of a state been so singularly the product of such focused and relentless advocacy of human rights norms' and notes the 'virtually exclusive reliance on rights discourse as the engine of change'. By way of caution, the author stresses the double-edged nature of the rights regime which, particularly in contexts of stark inequality, can serve to preserve power and economic privilege, notably through entrenching private property rights. Such a scenario formed part of the political compromise that emerged from the South African negotiations process (other compromises included the already mentioned security of tenure guarantees for civil servants, judges and magistrates, and police and army personnel). In short, human rights law both produced and placed limits upon change (the partial human rights focus of the TRC being an exemplary example), suggesting again that there are chastening as well as laudable outcomes from the human rights balancing act. To facilitate transition, human rights law provided a space in which different priorities and interests could be recognised. To facilitate transformation is an altogether different and more difficult task, and one in which human rights law will need to deliver progressively framed economic, social and cultural rights as well as their civil–political counterparts, confront rather than side-step questions of politics and power, and find ways to render abstract claims real. To do this requires a move beyond legal fetishism, with social action informing legal action and other agents of change complementing human rights (hybrid approaches).[14]

A second set of concerns hone in on the question of whether South Africa, as a developing country emerging from the shadow of apartheid, has the material and institutional capacity for liberal constitutionalism. Realising the promise of human rights requires a strong and well-developed state apparatus, and the new South Africa inherited weak institutions and a crisis of state legitimacy. In reality, 'legal reach' is very limited in rural areas and many black communities, not only in terms of material capacity but also in terms of value resonance. Alternative legal norms and forms of adjudication often prevail (R. Wilson 2001). One crisis of legitimacy (the illegitimacy of the apartheid state) can easily be replaced by another (the promise of human rights undone by deflated expectations and value dissonance).

The explosion in constitutionalism since the end of the Cold War (1989), notably in transitional contexts, expresses a faith in civic nationalism as opposed to, and as a remedy for, ethnic nationalism. Nations were to be constituted not on the basis of race or ethnicity but founded instead as 'a community of equal, rights-bearing citizens, united in patriotic attachment to a shared set of political practices and values' (Ignatieff 1994: 3–4). Constitutionalism and human rights provide both an alternative to nationalism and a form of nation-building, seeking a civic national identity forged through claiming basic rights and an inclusive, democratic experience of citizenship. Yet for many, such constitutional patriotism, and the idea of a nation united by and in law, is a dry, distant and alien form of belonging. South Africa has witnessed both an attempt to use human rights law as the raw material of nation-building, and the use of other vernaculars. The TRC and the Constitutional Court, the latter most famously in its decision to strike down the death penalty, have attempted to marshal public support for human rights outcomes by drawing on local concepts such as *ubuntu* (R. Wilson 1996, 2001).[15] These strategies reveal certain dangers associated with legal fetishism, notably the fallacy of seeing law as too effective an instrument of social cohesion or too absolute a defence against politics and culture. But they also indicate that further forms of hybridity need to be more fully explored and assessed (see Klug, above).

This leads logically into a third issue: while constitutionalism and human rights have a high profile in the official discourse of the new South Africa, legal pluralism characterises many everyday lives (see, for example, R. Wilson 2001). One stark way of demonstrating the legal fetishism–legal pluralism conundrum is to say that while one concern addressed in this chapter is the difficult task of drawing a line between crime and politics, there is an equally difficult line to be drawn between crime and culture.

John and Jean Comaroff (2004, 2004a), writing of the dramatic rise in witchcraft killings in post-apartheid South Africa in the northern provinces, interpret the 'epidemic' in occult-related violence, and the various forms of 'cultural policing' accompanying it, as a product of a structural contradiction in the new South Africa. The contradiction arises from the ideal of a unitary, modern state both embracing and undercut by the reality of difference. Reflecting and hoping to manage this contradiction is a constitution that gives primacy to universal rights but also protects cultural relativism. It by implication, therefore, sanctions both the state infrastructure of justice and at least certain forms of cultural policing. In its own act of magic, a fetishised faith in law is expected to conjure a functioning, coherent nation-state.

Neither the problem nor the response is unique to South Africa. But the situation in South Africa takes a particular shape, informed by local and global inflexions: intergenerational hostilities and inequalities, and a marginalised youth confronted by, yet excluded from, local and global economies of desire; economic impoverishment accentuated by neo-liberalism; identity politics, often with an ethnic tinge, driven by market forces and globalisation. The occult, like crime, becomes an expanding mode of violence and of producing and redistributing value – a commentary on the contradictions and disenchantments of transition. While the criminal justice system is tentatively articulating new modes of response, including creative and mutually reconstituting normative intersections, the pervasiveness of cultural policing remains an indictment of the state's inability to deliver security and prosperity for its citizens.

And yet, for all these shortcomings, legal fetishism is pervasive in South Africa. It has informed the responses of human rights NGOs in the transitional present (ICHRP 2003: 87–88), the TRC's approach to the past, and channelled civil society and NGO frustration with the TRC and its aftermaths, e.g. legal challenges relating to amnesty/prosecutions and other matters. South Africa has not fully embraced the potential of an encompassing human rights vision of legal action and social action; economic, social and cultural rights and civil–political rights; and human rights combined with other agents of change. It faces problems emblematic of the shortcomings of legal fetishism. The relationships between law, morality and legitimacy are highly contested terrain, laws often remain acts of freedom rather than channels of regulation, enforcement and delivery, while South Africa has enjoyed (political) transition without sufficient (socio-economic) transformation. The analysis above indicates the necessity of the rule of law for political transition but also questions law's capacity to fulfil the excessive hopes – management of cultural difference, diffusion of political disagreement, forging of national unity, securing economic transformation – invested in it.

Paralegality

Paralegal forms of social control, according to Panizza (1995), create a new kind of human rights violator, emerging from the privatisation of policing and the erosion of state monopolies over the use of legitimate force, and as faith erodes in the capacity of the state to provide security and law and order. They represent the emergence of parallel powers imposing their own forms of social regulation.

The apartheid state was reasonably effective at guaranteeing the security of white people. But it did so mainly through repressive regulation, as residential segregation and restrictions on freedom of movement (pass laws), for example, sought to keep black people out of white areas, not through established procedures of criminal justice (such as police investigations). Crime control was indistinguishable from political control, while crime levels were high but often unseen and unrecorded due to crime's concentration in poor black communities (Shaw 2002: xi, 1). In apartheid's twilight years, as political control unravelled, crime became more visible, reworking relationships between race and class, and redrawing geographies of security and crime control. One outcome was an increase in private- and self-policing measures – from private security firms to *makgotlas* (a revival of customary courts with an ethnic base), street committees, people's courts, vigilantism, instruments of customary law, and more *ad hoc* arrangements. Localised policing was part of the violence *and* response legacy inherited by the new dispensation.

While the distribution of security services remained directly correlated to wealth and inversely correlated to levels of insecurity and violence, non-state responses to state failure have occurred in all communities:

> It is true that vigilantism and commercial security firms, to take both ends of the non-state policing spectrum, have significant differences ... but they have similar origins. First, they are continuations of an established culture of self-reliance; for the white community, what might be loosely termed a 'frontier' culture; and for the black community, the traditional forms of village and clan protection and popular justice. Second, they both arise from communal dissatisfaction with the state policing services as experienced under apartheid and under the current democratic regime.
> (Baker 2002: 30)

Located in between the extremes of private security firms and vigilantism are a host of local citizen responses – such as neighbourhood watch schemes (Schärf *et al.* 2001) – that often seek to collaborate with the SAPS and work within the law. The degree of local support such non-state policing groups enjoy, their relationship to formal policing structures, the legality of their activities, and the effectiveness with which they are officially regulated, varies considerably.[16] This chapter analyses private security firms and vigilantism, as two extremes of the non-state policing spectrum.

Private security firms

> The presence of private security companies is everywhere, much more so than the public police. They patrol city blocks, guard shopping malls, respond to home alarms and 'panic signals', act as gatekeepers in fenced-off neighbourhoods, investigate criminal cases and install a variety of electronic

security measures. They dress in a multitude of uniforms, many resembling the light blue of the SAPS itself, and compete vigorously among themselves for market share.

(Shaw 2002: 102)

The growth in private policing is an international phenomenon. In South Africa the take-off was a dramatic accompaniment to political transition. At the turn of the century there were over 5,000 active registered security businesses in South Africa, 166,000 registered security guards, and private security guards outnumbered uniformed members of the SAPS engaged in visible patrol work by a ratio of 4:1 (Shaw 2002: 102). While the benefits of private policing may be an increase in public security for some, these forms of security are by definition exclusionary.

Heritage Park in the Western Cape is a gated town, partnered by a former squatter camp now upgraded into a township that will serve as the out-of-sight labour pool. While this is presented by the developers as a 'win–win situation', the echoes from the past are clear (Johnston and Shearing 2003: 142–43). Accentuating such trends, increased private commercial influence over the management and control of urban public space, through initiatives such as public–private partnership based city improvement districts (CIDs), can improve services, restrict access and increase input into policy-making, for a fee (Dixon 2004). Security remains a tool used by white against black, rich against poor, a service for clients who can pay (a commodity) rather than an entitlement for all citizens (a public good). Shaw (2002: 115) describes private security companies as 'guardians of societal divisions'. If South Africa is resegregated by class as well as race, notably in city developments such as gated communities and even gated towns, democracy will have reworked, rather than transformed, apartheid's fundamentally unequal geography of crime and protection. Such divisions also undermine public engagement with and pressure on the state to deliver security from some of its most vocal and articulate constituencies.

Again, it should be noted that the volatile mix of staggering inequalities, private security and forms of segregation is a global urban phenomenon, cause and effect of violence in many of the world's big cities, as well as a prism on the shortcomings of political transition. Patterns of segregation, epitomised by the 'fortified enclave' (Caldeira 2000: 256–96), illustrate ways in which inequality and crime, the two Trojan Horses of transition, reshape the urban landscape. The result is what Caldeira calls 'the implosion of modern public life' (297–335): the public is replaced by the private, heterogeneity and the accommodation of difference by homogeneity, openness and accessibility by separation and closure, circulation by stasis.[17]

One final point of note is that the security industry in South Africa absorbed many former employees of the apartheid-era security forces, and to a lesser degree the opposition armed groups. On the one hand this was a constructive redeployment of personnel with particular, largely non-transferable, skills; on the other hand these skills could easily be misused in a way that infringes people's human rights. This is a telling example of the ways in which the absence of transformation is potentially reworked back into civil and political rights abuses. All in all, private security weakens the democratic project.

Vigilantism

More often than not, the poor are fighting the poor in the violence that scars many of the world's cities, as the effects of violent crime, poverty and segregation are tragically turned inward. Vigilantism is one illustration of this trend, and a typically ambiguous one. Two of the better-known South African vigilante groups – People against Gangsterism and Drugs (PAGAD) (Dixon and Johns 2001; Gottschalk 2005; Shaw 2002: 96–99) and Mapogo a Mathamaga (Oomen 2004; Sekhonyane and Louw 2002; von Schnitzler et al. 2001) – provide exemplary insights into two interlinked themes that will be explored in more detail below: (1) the ways the past folds into the transitional present to mould violent crime and responses to such crime; and (2) vigilantism as a form of violence that challenges the authority of the state, while also negotiating and constructing its responsibilities (Buur and Jensen 2004). Vigilantism retains its ambivalent position as both a cause of crime and violence and a response to crime and violence: a potential partner for, target of and challenge to the state.

PAGAD's changing nature over time, while contested, is a useful place to start. Dixon and Johns (2001) claim that for the state PAGAD metamorphosed from popular movement to vigilante group to urban terror organisation. For Shaw (2002), PAGAD in time became less a vigilante, self-protection group than an organisation that combined crime, terrorism and political opposition. Formed in 1995, PAGAD offered a response to the local nexus of gangsterism, drug dealing and violence on the Cape Flats, and the perceived lack of state response to post-apartheid crime and lawlessness. It quickly mobilised significant public support around an ethos of community empowerment. The most cited initial strategy was to march in numbers on drug dealers' houses to deliver a stark message: stop or face the consequences. This landscape was altered by a number of violent transformative moments, including the widely reported lynching of Rashaad Staggie, a leading member of the Hard Livings gang, in August 1996. Violence spiralled: PAGAD members carried firearms and wore masks at public rallies; further gang leaders were killed; and urban terror attacks between 1998 and 2000 relocated the violence from the city margins to its centre. Targets included restaurants and night spots in Cape Town's tourist areas and affluent suburbs, and its international airport. The response from gangs to PAGAD's unwanted attention was equally violent, while the state by 2000 increasingly employed enforcement measures (for example, significant numbers of PAGAD members were arrested, charged and, in time, convicted). State responses to

PAGAD occupy a particularly prominent place in crackdown rhetoric and policy.

Several historical arteries, beyond the stock apartheid legacies of segregation, discrimination, dislocation and marginalisation, carried the life blood of this violence and the responses to the violence. Divisions within the Muslim community in the Western Cape, between a conservative, apolitical leadership and young radicals involved in the fight against apartheid and/or the global politics of radical Islam, continued to be replayed and reworked. The increased influence within PAGAD of more politicised, militarised and organisationally experienced elements associated with Qibla and other radical Islamic groups also draws on the past – Qibla allied itself to the Pan African Congress's armed wing in the anti-apartheid struggle – as does PAGAD's deployment of a military wing (G-force). Struggle slogans were adopted and modified: 'one settler, one bullet' became 'one [drug] merchant' or 'one gangster', 'one bullet'. A reputation for militancy, useful to the liberation movements in the past, was used to discredit Qibla, and therefore PAGAD, in the transitional period. Media and government pronouncements were quick to blame PAGAD, and PAGAD alone, for the upsurge in violence, with the result that the organisation came to see itself as the target of media misrepresentation and state repression. Also influencing response agendas was the fact that in the pre-1994 era, gangs forged links with state officials (as informers, hit men) and the liberation movements, which endured as police– and political–gangland connections. Thus, the criminalisation of politics and the politicisation of crime spanned the transitional divide.

As PAGAD came to be seen as a threat to constitutional democracy, the focus of the state's response changed from constructive engagement, itself often a case study in mutual incomprehension (Dixon and Johns 2001), to demonisation (for example by association with global Islamic fundamentalism), rigorous enforcement and repression. Instrumental authoritarianism and legal fetishism kicked in, as the state resorted to security strategies from the past – convictions under the doctrine of common purpose; terrorism charges under the old Internal Security Act (No. 74 of 1982); and proposed new terrorism provisions.[18] But there were other response motives, reflecting challenges to, and the construction of the responsibilities of, the new democratic state. Value dissonance between PAGAD and the state included mainstream political issues – the latter's intolerance of political dissent and the high profile of crime as a political issue – but it also drew on a desire by the state to defend a range of other values. PAGAD increasingly targeted state buildings, such as police stations and magistrates' courts, prominent tourist sites and targets with symbolic connotations (gay venues, synagogues). Further, PAGAD sought to excise drug dealers and gang leaders from communities, expressing indifference to their deaths and a willingness to take action outside the law while claiming opposition to attacks on civilians and terrorism. The prevailing doctrine of the time – tolerance, dialogue, reconciliation, reintegration – was considered only after those targeted had changed their ways. Different views about the market and international capitalism, the rule of law, and social and religious pluralism, placed PAGAD and the state on a collision course. The charge against PAGAD that informs this set of accusations and responses is that crime, and crime fighting, became a cover for a political agenda that sought to undermine both the ANC government and the values of the democratic state.

While acknowledging an interplay of internal and external factors influencing the evolution of PAGAD, Dixon and Johns (2001) argue that it was state repression that primarily succeeded in transforming PAGAD – from a popular mass movement, a loose-knit network extending beyond the bounds of Islam, to a smaller, tighter, better-organised outfit, restructured along 'struggle' lines, but more isolated, homogenous, intolerant, defensive and oppositional. The irony of a liberation movement in government potentially creating opposition in its own past image is striking (see Gottschalk 2005 for a much more anti-PAGAD and pro-state account). A further irony, in an increasingly retributive environment, is that PAGAD was contained by legal enforcement measures while the gangs proved to be more resilient. The ultimate in non-state enforcement responses failed as assassinating gang leaders led to a process of decentralisation, factionalisation and regrouping, with leadership struggles and turf battles fuelling increased levels of gang violence.

Launched in 1996 by a group of businessmen in the Northern Province (now Limpopo), Mapogo a Mathamaga (from the Sotho proverb, 'If you [the criminal] conduct yourself like a leopard, remember the victim can change into a tiger') was just as controversial as PAGAD. Emerging first in the rural setting of one of South Africa's poorest provinces to promote business interests and fight crime, it became both a vigilante group and a private security company (Mapogo a Mathamaga Security Services), boasting a membership in the tens of thousands and a presence in several provinces. The organisation, like PAGAD, was over time restricted and contained by internal differences, conflicts and splits – due in this case to disagreements over its violent methods, allegations of internal corruption, and the dictatorial style and oppositional politics of its president, John Magolego – and by a combination of state enforcement measures and co-option (the latter tactic was utilised for Mapogo much more than it was with PAGAD).

Mapogo bears the past into the present in large measure as the past seeking to reassert itself and discipline the present. As was starkly apparent at its margins, apartheid had decentralised and privatised oppression, creating a conservative constituency – a political and administrative elite in the form of local chiefs and homeland administrators, and a small economic elite with monopoly market control – with a stake in defending the status quo. In the 1980s in the Northern Province, the youth mobilised in a revolt that was political, social and intergenerational; against elders and parents as well as apartheid, and against apartheid's agents and beneficiaries in the homelands (local elites, apartheid-era vigilante groups). During the early post-1994 years, reported crime and police resource allocation in the Northern Province were both the lowest in

South Africa, but crime was clearly perceived to be a problem. In this context, the blame for crime directed at the youth drew, at least partly, on apartheid-era antagonisms. The businessmen who founded Mapogo felt both that they were being targeted by criminals and that the criminal justice system was failing to protect them. Given the collapse of the local state and social order, the institutions that have emerged to try and fill the void are often strongly rooted in the past.

One central characteristic of Mapogo can perhaps be captured by suggesting that it attracted apartheid beneficiaries (including white businesses, farmers and right-wingers), who, under siege in various ways in the new dispensation, resorted to crime fighting and vigilantism in an attempt to retain and regain their social status, wealth, power and security. Revealingly, members pay joining and membership fees, albeit with price flexibility, and the organisation focuses on property-related crimes (von Schnitzler *et al.* 2001). A related interpretation of Mapogo is that it was a moral community conveying an alternative post-apartheid citizenship, rallying constituencies within elite, conservative, rural society (parents, chiefs, business and church leaders) who sought to use a discourse of patriarchy, privilege and custom to reassert their status and authority, notably over the youth (Oomen 2004). Conversely, it has been argued that Mapogo is uniquely integrated, across race, class and urban–rural areas (Sekhonyane and Louw 2002). Whether vigilantism entrenches or reconfigures past divisions, therefore, remains disputed.

With reference to challenging the authority of the state, and helping to define its limits responsibilities, Mapogo administered a very particular brand of instant justice. Its methods were illegal and violated due process rights: members who became victims of crime called Mapogo, recounted the incident and named suspects; Mapogo tracked down the suspects, demanded the stolen goods and, in a strategy reminiscent of the apartheid regime, administered beatings to extract a confession, most commonly using a *sjambok* (beating with a leather whip). Such beatings led to serious injuries and deaths. Magolego talked allegorically of extracting all the necessary water from a sponge (Sekhonyane and Louw 2002: 39; von Schnitzler *et al.* 2001: 15). The appeal of Mapogo lay in a blend of charismatic leadership, high visibility, populist rhetoric and symbolism, a climate of fear and intimidation, as well as a perception that Mapogo's methods effectively combated crime. References to 'African justice' and 'African medicine' were both retributive and restorative (in the latter case, there was a focus on victims and the promise to repair the damage done, usually by returning stolen goods). While obviously another selective reading of tradition and culture (often seemingly reducing African justice to corporal punishment), this case provides an example of value dissonance that contrasts 'African' and 'Western' justice rather than, as in the case of the TRC, trying to integrate the two. Such vigilante action was antithetical to constitutional human rights and democracy, in its methods but also in its values (patriarchy, hierarchy, privilege).

The challenge of Mapogo also assumed party political dimensions, especially through Magolego, who has a chequered political history and clear political ambition. Believed to have been a supporter of the National Party in the 1980s in the Lebowa homeland, in the 1990s he also flirted with the IFP and other opposition parties. Magolego's personal political history, alongside support for Mapogo from opposition political parties, the white right-wing and apartheid beneficiaries, and a disciplining function generally used against blacks rather than whites, and by employers and farmers against workers, suggested a politics that shifted uneasily between legitimate questioning of the ANC and threatening the very foundations and principles of the democratic state (von Schnitzler *et al.* 2001). Others argued that it was Mapogo's unique diversity that posed such a threat to the new democracy (Sekhonyane and Louw 2002: 28). In contrast to PAGAD, ANC supporters constituted a significant proportion of Mapogo's members, which perhaps accounts for its different, less severe treatment within the early narrative and practices of crackdown. Mapogo's challenge was depoliticised when Magolego joined the ANC in 2003 and as a result of its own transformation from the bearer of an alternative mode of citizenship into a private security company (Oomen 2004).

Vigilantism remains a partially understood phenomenon in South Africa. Why is it prevalent in some parts of the country and not others? To the extent that it carries a political message and moral agenda, is vigilantism a legitimate expression of political opposition, cultural difference and alternative conceptions of justice, or an illegitimate threat to the democratic order? It is not a singular phenomenon, often manifesting a context-specific complexity. The voice of the past is loudly heard and the limits of the state are both negatively established (lack of capacity, complicity in violence, political intolerance, stark value dissonance) and positively extended (pushing an agenda informed by social justice, equality and non-discrimination). Policing, in all its forms, remains on a knife-edge between reactionary and progressive elements, between repeating the past and remaking the future. An article by Lynnette Johns in the *Weekend Argus* of 22 August 2009, entitled 'Pagad Mobilises against Drugs and Gangs', indicates that these tensions remain relevant. On the one hand, PAGAD was reported to be reforming on the Cape Flats, voicing a preparedness to meet 'force with force' and 'violence with violence' in the fight against drug lords, gangs and the state; on the other hand, neighbourhood watch and street committees were rallying behind the police and the use of lawful methods of crime control.

Part of the solution to crime in South Africa has to be forms of parallel or partnership policing, linking rather than segregating communities, the various forms of policing on offer, and civil society and the state. The ambition should be to provide security in ways that are more equitable and accountable, and to supply constructive and legal routes for public participation in tackling the problem of crime. Despite problems experienced with community policing, a number of initiatives have attracted positive publicity, including Sector 4 in Alexandra and peace committees originating in Zwelethemba near Cape Town (Johnston and Shearing 2003: 151–60; also see Schärf *et al.* 2001). The latter is a case study of perhaps the most sophisticated model reflecting the diversity of actors engaged in policing and security. Johnston and Shearing's (2003: 138–60) notion of networked nodal, rather than state-centred, governance, in which no set of nodes is given conceptual priority, provides one possible way of challenging ineffectiveness due to a lack of coordination, and injustice due to inequalities in provision. In criminal justice, as in transitional justice, participation is central to the deepening of the democratic project.

Restorative justice

Restorative justice is the one case study of the four that usually falls in the realm of more consultative and liberal criminal justice measures. It is a useful study for our purposes because it often comes with an assumed division of labour between state and civil society, a combination of top-down and bottom-up energies and expertise.[19] While there are a range of restorative justice initiatives in contemporary South Africa, many of which are deeply informed by a collaborative, consultative ethos and practice (Skelton and Batley 2006; Maepa 2005), the story of the Child Justice Bill (later Act) sits centre-stage as a parable of justice in the transitional moment. If restorative justice were to take off anywhere within the criminal justice system, surely it would be in relation to child and juvenile justice?[20]

Under apartheid, children were routinely detained without trial, arrested and held on politically related charges, and tortured. There was no separate, coherent juvenile justice system. The non-governmental sector rallied to provide assistance and, as the transitional era dawned, intensified and coordinated calls for reform. Experimentation began with restorative justice initiatives such as diversion and family conferencing. When the new Minister of Justice, Dullah Omar, appointed the Juvenile Justice Project Committee under the auspices of the South African Law Commission (now the South African Law Reform Commission) to draft new legislation on juvenile justice, this constituency moved decisively into the policy-making fold. The Juvenile Justice Project Committee began work in 1997 and, after a highly consultative process (including children), in 2000 produced '[o]ne of the most radical pieces of draft legislation to emerge from the South African Law Reform Commission in recent years' (Skelton 2004: 215).

The draft Child Justice Bill contained significant restorative justice provisions, beyond the fact that restorative justice and *ubuntu* were built into the objectives clause. These included the potential for diversion from the mainstream criminal justice system before, during or after a trial (in the latter case as part of the sentencing process); referral to family group conferencing, victim–offender mediation and other non-conventional restorative justice processes; and comprehensive sentencing alternatives. Infused with the idealism and 'visioning' of this period, van Zyl Smit (1999: 205) writes that '[juvenile justice] probably attracted more debate and development resources than any other criminal justice issue and therefore the ideas of how society should ideally be organised in the future were articulated most fully in this context'. In the beginning, therefore, enabled by the ethos of the TRC (reconciliation, *ubuntu*), and aided by the international movements for restorative justice and child rights and certain strands of indigenous and alternative conflict resolution, transition provided 'a window of opportunity for legal reformism' (Skelton 2002: 500). This was the era of seemingly limitless possibilities, of government consultation with academics and NGOs evincing a striking coincidence of objectives. Heady days.

The Child Justice Bill (No. 49 of 2002) was approved by the Cabinet for introduction to parliament in 2002. As with the Promotion of National Unity and Reconciliation Act (No. 34 of 1995), the Bill was debated by the parliamentary Portfolio Committee on Justice and Constitutional Development. The process provided a further platform for public participation through hearings and submissions. At this point public and political concerns about crime, already registered in the early drafting process, became more evident in a tussle between restorative and retributive responses. The passing of the Child Justice Bill was held up by the 2004 elections, the appointment of a new Minister of Justice and internal departmental wrangling. In an interview in April 2005, Skelton (28 April 2005) expressed disappointment at the extent to which the Portfolio Committee had rewritten the Bill within a retributive, crime-fighting rubric and concerns that the end product would be schizophrenic. In essence, while measures such as diversion and alternative sentencing were retained, certain children were excluded on the grounds of age or the seriousness of their alleged offences.

An NGO coalition, called the Child Justice Alliance, formed to support the Bill through parliament and beyond (see: www.childjustice.org.za/, for the various versions of the Bill, public submissions on the Bill, and more). On the one hand a civil society constituency remained vigilant and innovative practice continued unabated, sometimes involving branches of the state. On the other hand a restorative justice agenda remained vulnerable to the marginalisation of the consultative paradigm, and wavering political and public support for more progressive strategies. After an extended hiatus the Bill re-emerged, having been redrafted by both the Portfolio Committee and Cabinet, to be debated again by the Portfolio Committee on Justice and Constitutional Development, with a new chairperson, in February 2008. The new version of the Bill reflected the shift in emphasis outlined above, and was significantly different from its 2002 iteration. Civil society actors made a fresh set of written submissions and the battle between retributive and restorative justice was rejoined.

Many of the losses from the previous round of redrafting were reversed at this point. That said, there is a strong sense in the Bill of a search for 'balance'. Certain features of the resulting Bill – renamed the Child Justice Act (No. 75, 2008) – are worth highlighting. These include attempts to balance the rights of the child and the rights of the victims of crime and restorative justice measures and procedural rights for children; the return of a unified restorative justice ethos to be applied to all children irrespective of age or offence, if with somewhat tighter regulation (e.g. diversion in Chapter 8 of the Act);

positive support for state–civil society cooperation; and attempts to address capacity concerns across the threshold of implementation (for example, through a national policy framework). This parable, therefore, ends with a further example of the 'policy pendulum' finding middle ground (and perhaps government becoming more receptive to civil society input), providing a positive example not only of progressive policy formulation but also of civil society advocacy. NGOs and others initiated, monitored and ultimately crucially shaped reform and adapted to a shifting public and political mood. They also combined principles and pragmatism, informed advocacy with research, and helped address (enduring) concerns about resources and implementation (Skelton and Gallinetti 2008 – interestingly, this historical overview, by two veteran participants in the advocacy campaign, contains no mention of the TRC as an inspiration or influence). This is not to say that heaven has arrived on earth. The pendulum is unlikely to stop swinging as the Bill is implemented, but invaluable lessons have been learnt about transitional advocacy, and progressive legal and policy reform.

Influencing transitional law and policy involves hitting a moving target. Strategic or pragmatic as well as principled arguments will be required for those seeking to render judicial interventions more creative and progressive: in this case, highlighting that restorative justice focuses on victims, its capacity to ease certain institutional and resource constraints (such as prison overcrowding) and its potential to facilitate ex-combatant reintegration. Diminished space for restorative justice in high politics can coincide with greater opportunities at an institutional or departmental level (Batley, interview 28/4/2005). Formal participation on the government's terms (call-and-response patterns, access patrolled by governmental or parliamentary bodies) was productively exploited at times in the child justice story. The main lessons from this case study are reasonably positive. But if top-down and more bottom-up energies have married successfully on occasion in policy-making, the challenge remains for them to deliver with regard to implementation, and scaling-up their delivery potential.

Conclusion

Let me start by stating clearly what I am not arguing in this chapter on justice present. I am not arguing that all crime and violence during political transitions is rooted in the past. Nor am I arguing that truth commissions can or should do everything to curb crime and violence. I am arguing (1) that the past is a significant influence on transitional patterns of crime and violence, and on policy responses to these problems; (2) that the past and its legacy take shape in reformulated and often unanticipated ways; and (3) that transition and transitional politics themselves currently produce structural contradictions that feed crime and violence.

Continuities and change in the realms of crime, and also poverty, are locally and globally informed. Global patterns include neo-liberal economics and the growth of social movements contesting such policies; organised crime, punitive criminal justice responses, the growth in vigilantism and private security firms, patterns of urban segregation, and a backlash against human rights; as well as liberal constitutionalism and a focus on civil and political rights. Transition provides a particular inflexion to such global trends, and the local renders global imposition to varying degrees hybrid. While truth commissions, themselves now a form of political globalisation, cannot do everything, they can anticipate these realities. They can also anticipate the fact that justice past (in this case amnesty, in theory and in practice; the TRC and its interactions with the criminal justice system; and the TRC's own conceptualisations of justice) coexists with justice present (the shift from political to criminal and social violence, engendering responses ranging from the authoritarian to the participatory). Cogent understandings of violence and appropriately designed responses will aid the coherence of recommendations and increase the coherence of public debate about justice.

This chapter on justice present suggests several ways in which truth commissions could engage more effectively with the challenges of justice in transition and violence in transition.

- Strong, positive identities and anchors of social belonging, especially for the youth, are required, beyond the templates of victims and perpetrators peddled by the TRC, and the transitional era's alternative of criminal as hero or nemesis. 'Identities of exclusion' (Harris 2005) need to be replaced by identities of inclusion. This may well require a narrative of the past that is not so relentlessly negative. Stories about the 'righteous', rescuers and cosmopolitans working across societal divides would provide a set of role models. More ambiguous identities also need to be acknowledged, for example for those who were both victims *and* perpetrators, or political activists *and* criminals. Vigilantes, for example, may be victims, perpetrators and protectors. A youth rebellion, that appears to have been passed from one generation to another, is a common threat in the evolving patterns of violence described above. Without various forms of inclusion, in which routes to employment, status and dignity are paramount, this problem runs the danger of becoming an almost irresolvable cleavage in South African society. The lessons for other countries with intergenerational divisions, very young populations often marginalised from the mainstream, and child soldiers and youth ex-combatants, are clear.
- The TRC emphasised high politics and the state, and party political reconciliation, at precisely the moment when violence was becoming delinked from formal politics and political actors were losing control of increasingly globalised and privatised, local and fragmented forms of violence. Transition, as noted above, produces its own violence and social ruptures. Of far more relevance to people's lives and experiences of violence during transition, and indeed before, were local contexts that in some cases remained 'ungovernable' ('governed' in the new era by overlapping networks of gangs, vigilantes, organised crime and warlords). The TRC did little to further understandings

of, or constructive interventions in these conflicts. Similarly, violent crime and inequality ensured that people's lived experience of human rights and democracy was determined at least as much by the rewriting of urban and rural geographies of segregation as by the rewriting of laws.

State-level political change may gain the keys to the political kingdom, but it is macro- and micro-political change that is needed to secure its future and sustainability. In moving away from state-centrism, truth commissions could benefit from criminological insights, among others, into the way in which the state's control over violence, policing and security is now routinely diminished, shared with actors operating 'above and beyond', 'alongside' and 'below' (McEvoy 2008: 37–43; also see Johnston and Shearing (2003: 138–60) on networked nodal governance). Violence *and* response templates share these features, and would benefit from layered vision.

- There is an urgent need to strengthen criminal justice systems. Dispute resolution by hit squads and assassination cannot prevail, nor can endemic impunity. This assumes a broad-ranging effort to build state capacity and integrity that is often claimed as truth commission territory, but where actual delivery has been disappointing. It also assumes that the state is willing to receive support, and criticism, from such commissions and civil society. It is now possible to anticipate some of the challenges associated with this agenda. It means engaging with the state, even as the pendulum swings between more liberal and more hard-line measures, and between 'no' control (private security, vigilantism) and 'full' control (instrumental authoritarianism, legal fetishism). As a target for advocacy, such pendulum swings offer a realistic hope of inserting more progressive agendas (see the discussion of the Child Justice Act above). Achieving progressive goals, in a context often characterised by the politicisation of crime and a backlash against human rights, will require strategic thinking: a human rights as effectiveness agenda (for example, addressing concerns about security), a balanced perspective (a focus on victims as well as perpetrators), attempts to bridge the gap between the law and public moralities, and rights-based participation. Links could be forged between the two victim/survivor lobbies, past and present, which are invariably separate entities. An overarching challenge is the threat posed by crime to democratic consolidation, which has to be addressed at various levels: the reality of crime, perceptions about crime, and crime as symbolism/metaphor. Many facets of contemporary South Africa, from private security and vigilantism to residential segregation, are commentaries on the weakness of the criminal justice system, and the state in general. In the end, strengthening the criminal justice system, understood as a partnership of state and non-state interventions, is the only way to secure greater access to justice for all, and thereby legitimise democracy.
- Truth commissions should describe violence as a currency of the past and present in the broadest possible terms. In the absence of alternatives, violence seeps into all spheres of life and becomes a means of gaining power, resolving

conflicts, protecting interests, making money and achieving status. In the resulting culture of violence, violence is seen as a legitimate, normal way of solving problems and conducting social relations. Most damagingly, it can assume a social and political utility, carving out a parallel state. An engagement with structural violence is a necessary rejoinder. While commissions often seek to draw a line between the past and present, perhaps the most effective way to address structural concerns with regards to everyday experiences of violence and justice is to help draw a further set of lines – between politics and crime, and culture and crime. This involves nurturing ways through which influence, status, subsistence and dispute resolution can be sought in the public sphere and civil society, as well as legal institutions and political expression. Rights-based participation and economic justice would be good places to start.

Responses to all four challenges outlined above can be informed, but not monopolised, by human rights – hybrid solutions are required. Through such interventions truth commissions could alter the terms of the debate on, and the possibilities for, justice, past and present, rather than simply deferring difficult decisions and leaving prevailing, often repressive orthodoxies unchallenged. As these two justice-focused chapters reveal, in a variety of ways the TRC's record on this agenda was disappointing. Again the argument is that a re-conceptualisation of the work of truth commissions would increase their impacts, and specifically that a more coherent approach to justice, past and present, is needed to maximise impacts. The two sets of narratives cannot be neatly separated either in terms of their forms of violence or their response reflexes. To alter the possibilities for justice involves acknowledging this fact and devising measures, such as those outlined above, that will render a continuum more of a rupture. On that note, it is time to move onto our third keyword: reconciliation.

Notes

1 Crime statistics for South Africa can be accessed via the South African Police Service (SAPS) website: www.saps.gov.za/. Crime statistics have been rigorously critiqued as a measure of actual crime, the basis for policy interventions or as a performance indictor for the criminal justice system. Reported crime, for example, may go up because people feel more faith in the police and criminal justice system or because crime has shifted into areas where reporting levels are higher. Further, official statistics need to be complemented by victim surveys which indicate what percentage of crime is reported to the police.
2 Of course, marginalisation and impoverishment are not the only, or even necessarily a major, cause of all (youth) crime. Steinberg (2001) opens his edited volume *Crime Wave: The South African Underworld and its Foes* by asking:

> How, for instance, does one explain the fact that the poorest of our provinces are also the least crime-prone … ? How does one account for the fact that so many

of the hijackers and armed robbers whose stories are told in this book are comfortable professionals or pupils at good suburban schools?

(Steinberg 2001: 1)

Steinberg and others (Segal *et al.* 2001; Gear 2002) have noted the power and cult of the materialist youth culture, where crime is inextricably intertwined with particular values, style, status, respect and identity. This raises the spectre of crime as lifestyle, as brand, for poor and wealthy alike and presents different, if no less difficult, challenges for remedial interventions.

3 Echoing note 2 above, this argument is not intended to suggest that all transitional crime and violence is solely rooted in past politics – there are obviously multiple causes, as well as new targets and forms of violence (see Harris 2001a, for example, on violence directed at foreigners, linked to xenophobia, which was a problem in post-apartheid South Africa before the well-publicised violence targeting foreigners in 2008). But it is the intention to highlight the fact that politics and the past are often overlooked in discussions about crime, and that these are relationships that transitional justice mechanisms cannot ignore.

4 For a discussion of crime, violence and various responses in transitional democracies in Latin America, which illustrates the broader relevance of the concerns discussed below, see Neild (2003).

5 The analysis that follows is not a comprehensive overview of this project, but draws on the reports from the first phase of the research (1999–2002). For a consolidated review of the research project (phase 1: 1999–2002, and phase 2: 2003–5), see Harris (2005). The analysis in this chapter is a snapshot of violence across the cusp of transition. It does not attempt to update all findings and case studies to the present day.

6 At the time of writing both the national and KwaZulu-Natal provincial governments are controlled by the ANC. The ANC and IFP remain the dominant political players in this province of the country.

7 Victim-related initiatives in South Africa have gradually become more influential in government policy and NGO work seeking to influence government policy, often informed by a desire to further human rights and restorative justice. The Constitution and Bill of Rights have been criticised for their silence on victims' rights, and an organised and vocal victims' lobby, responding to crime concerns, has campaigned for victim voices to have a more central role in policy-making and for policy to be more responsive to their needs. A central objective of victim-related initiatives is to include victims, and their interests, in the criminal justice process. Important achievements, supported by human rights groups, include *The Service Charter for Victims of Crime in South Africa* and *Minimum Standards on Services for Victims of Crime* targeting the criminal justice system (available at www.doj.gov.za); and the more broadly framed Victim Empowerment Programme (VEP) (see Frank 2007).

8 Balancing critique and collaboration in the criminal justice sector echoes the reconfiguration of civil society–state relations outlined with regard to transitional justice in Chapter 2. It entails a shift in focus from a violations approach to an emphasis on effectiveness (conviction rates, policing competence) and prevention. Difficult questions are raised by these realignments. Can NGOs overcome their ingrained hostility towards the state and security institutions? Can they work with the state and yet avoid co-option? How should perpetrators' and victims' rights, human rights and public security, be balanced? Organisations are frequently inadequately equipped for the transition from a focus on political to criminal violence, and may take time to develop the skills necessary for a more partnership-oriented role. The ICHRP (2003: 84–89) argues that the human rights community in South Africa was poorly prepared for, and slow to adapt to, the challenges of the post-apartheid era.

9 The ICHRP (2003) states that this era heralded conservative policy initiatives and diminished access to parliament and parliamentary committees, which marginalised NGO input into policy and law-making processes. They continue that NGOs were forced to rethink their strategies and relationships with government:

> It is slowly but gradually being realised that a complex relationship with the state is possible – one that enables NGOs to support reform programmes while remaining independent and able to critique abuse. This nuanced understanding reflects a growing maturity among many NGOs.
> (ICHRP 2003: 89)

10 As already indicated, the authoritarian reflex frequently targets marginalised and vulnerable groups, such as foreigners, and particularly those deemed illegal immigrants, who were criminalised and made scapegoats for crime during 'Operation Crackdown' (Harris 2001a).

11 After a slow start, the fight against organised crime has been assisted by a range of new initiatives at legislative, policy and operational levels (Schönteich 1999). These included the Prevention of Organised Crime Act (No. 121 of 1998), which allows for the prosecution of an individual for being a member of a criminal organisation and for civil forfeiture of the proceeds of crime (without first obtaining a criminal conviction). Important successes were achieved by the Scorpions and the Asset Forfeiture Unit in fighting organised crime and corruption. Interestingly, the Scorpions unit was located outside the SAPS and the Department of Safety and Security, in the Department of Justice and Constitutional Development, and more specifically under the National Prosecuting Authority. The success of the Scorpions illustrated the advantages of having investigators and prosecutors within a specialist unit. It tackled high-profile cases, showed considerable media savvy and recognised the importance of managing public perceptions. As a result it garnered public support. More critical assessments raised concerns about allegations of politically motivated prosecutions and remarked on tense relations with the SAPS over turf. The Scorpions unit was disbanded after they targeted high-profile public figures on corruption charges – Jackie Selebi, the National Commissioner of Police (an Mbeki ally), Jacob Zuma (an adversary of Mbeki, and from May 2009 the South African President) – and became embroiled in intra-ANC divisions and the Mbeki succession controversy. Their replacement, the Directorate for Priority Crimes Investigations (DPCI), dubbed the Hawks, was launched in July 2009 with a remit to address organised crime, commercial crime and corruption. Unlike its predecessor, it is located within the South African Police Service (SAPS).

12 AfriMAP and the Open Society Foundation for South Africa (2005: 10) note: 'However, to date, there has been no systematic repeal of colonial or apartheid laws that conflict with the Constitution, and the Law Reform Commission has drafted papers mostly as a result of lobbying efforts by civil society'. At an international level, the new government has also been prolific. For example, before the turn of the century it had ratified the African Charter on Human and People's Rights, the Convention on the Rights of the Child (CRC), the Convention on the Elimination of All forms of Discrimination against Women (CEDAW), the International Convention on the Elimination of all forms of Racial Discrimination (CERD), the International Covenant on Civil and Political Rights (ICCPR), and the Convention against Torture and other Cruel, Inhuman or Degrading Treatment or Punishment.

13 *Government of the Republic of South Africa and Others* v. *Grootboom and Others* 2001 (1) SA 46 (CC); *Minster of Health and Others* v. *Treatment Action Campaign and Others* (No. 2) 2002 (5) SA 721 (CC). On executive compliance with the law, see AfriMAP and the Open Society Foundation for South Africa (2005: 13–15, 27–32). Indicating that

international law has perhaps been fetishised rather than embraced in its entirety, the report by AfriMAP and the Open Society Foundation for South Africa (2005: 3–6) identifies weaknesses in the domestication of international human rights treaties, and inconsistency in monitoring and reporting for treaties that have been ratified.
14 The role human rights assumed in the national transformation agenda and within the TRC exemplifies Kennedy's (2002: 108–9) critique that human rights 'occupies the field of emancipatory possibility', crowding out and delegitimising alternatives that may potentially be more effective. That said, a few other agents of transformation were operative in South Africa, such as affirmative action.
15 *The State* v. *T. Makwanyane and M. Mchunu*, Case No. CCT/3/94.
16 Private security firms are regulated by the Private Security Industry Regulation Act (No. 56 of 2001) and the Private Security Industry Regulatory Authority.
17 'The implosion of modern public life' is not uncontested. The anti-gun lobby group, Gun Free South Africa (GFSA), has done important work to 'resocialise' one challenge facing the country, rearticulating security as a public and not just a private issue:

> This is evident in the increasing numbers of private and public buildings such as schools, churches, NGO offices, government buildings, clinics and taverns, that have declared themselves 'gun-free zones'. This is a space in which firearms are not welcome and is denoted by a no-gun sign (similar to the no-smoking sign).
> (Cock 2006: 345, 347)

18 The Internal Security Act was repealed by the Protection of Constitutional Democracy Against Terrorist Activities Act (No. 33 of 2004), which although less draconian than similar legislation elsewhere nonetheless caused considerable disquiet because of its broad and vague definition of terrorist activity.
19 In the South African context, Skelton and Batley (2006: 125) write: 'it is our contention that the cause of restorative justice would be best served by civil society's playing an active role in direct service delivery, with the State fulfilling the roles of enabler, resourcer, and guarantor of quality practice'. Among the potential advantages of civil society organisation involvement is their proximity to local, community concerns and ability to implement flexible, innovative responses. A 'values base', the authors claim, will ensure that civil society moves beyond service delivery to 'involvement in advocacy and public education. They are in a position to agitate for structural change'.
20 This section draws on Gallinetti (2006); Gallinetti *et al.* (2006); Skelton (2002, 2004, 2005, 2006); Skelton and Gallinetti (2008); and Stout and Wood (2004).

Chapter 5

Speaking truth to reconciliation

> Reconciliation initiatives are appealing because they can respond to the multifarious needs of each nation as it transitions from one dispensation to another. They can simultaneously be legal and political; they can be national or international; they can respond both to public and private needs; they can be moral and pragmatic; they can be transformative, while maintaining connection to the past. Their appeal is broad because their promise is virtually infinite.
>
> (Sarkin and Daly 2004: 688)

More than the other keywords of transition, reconciliation is the canvas onto which contemporary post-conflict societies project their ideals and ambition. In the introduction to *Remaking a World: Violence, Social Suffering, and Recovery*, Das and Kleinman (2002: 3–4) argue that reconciliation, or what they describe as 'the recovery of the everyday', engages survivors of collective tragedy in, on the one hand, the 'creation of alternate public spheres for articulating and recounting experience silenced by officially sanctioned narratives', which folds into the broader demand for political recognition and a renegotiated citizenship from previously marginalised voices. On the other hand, it requires 'repair of relationships in the deep recesses of family, neighborhood, and community'. This chapter addresses the creation of alternative public spheres; the chapter that follows situates relationships at the heart of reconciliation praxis. The best place to begin is by outlining the manner in which the TRC itself understood and sought to facilitate reconciliation.

The TRC and reconciliation

> Defining exactly what was meant by reconciliation remained one of the great incomplete tasks of the TRC.
>
> (R. Wilson 2001: 101)

The TRC conceptualised reconciliation as both a process and a goal or outcome, required at various, interlinked levels. The latter archaeology spanned the individual or person (individual closure around truth, victims reconciling with their pain and perpetrators with guilt and shame), the interpersonal (between victims and perpetrators), community, nation and the redistributive. At times these levels were cast in relational terms, as when the TRC report talks of:

> the vital importance of the multi-layered healing of human relationships in post-apartheid South Africa: relationships of individuals with themselves; relationships between victims; relationships between survivors and perpetrators; relationships within families, between neighbours and within and between communities; relationships within different institutions, between different generations, between racial and ethnic groups, between workers and management and, above all, between the beneficiaries of apartheid and those who have been disadvantaged by it.
> (TRC 1998, Vol. 5: 350–51)

The TRC is usually understood to have privileged individual or interpersonal and national reconciliation. Borer (2004; also see R. Wilson 2001: 97–122) notes that the former, thick, reconciliation applied primarily a religious or medical/therapeutic rubric and the language of healing, apology, forgiveness, confession and remorse. The latter, thin, reconciliation worked through a secular sociopolitical lens, utilising a political ethos and the language of peaceful coexistence, the rule of law, democracy, a human rights culture and public debate. Thin reconciliation is sometimes framed as civic nationalism or liberal constitutionalism (see Chapter 4); or deliberative democracy (Chapter 2). Potential contradictions between the two approaches – thick reconciliation seeks to overcome disagreement and division; thin reconciliation embraces, while seeking to manage, such cleavages – were not adequately addressed.

Confusion originated in the absence of a clear definition for, and the low profile of, reconciliation in the TRC's founding documents: the 'postamble' of the interim Constitution (No. 200 of 1993) stated that amnesty was necessary to advance reconciliation, and the Promotion of National Unity and Reconciliation Act (No. 34 of 1995) provided the TRC's primarily investigatorial and amnesty-based mandate, while reiterating the 'postamble's' overarching objective of promoting national unity and reconciliation. As such, reconciliation stood as 'an inarticulate premise' (Lax 2004: 225) at the core of the TRC's ambition.

Unsurprisingly, given this starting point, definitional debates were a feature of the TRC's operational phase. Richard Wilson (2001: 104–21) talks of three internal narratives: legal–procedural, religious–redemptive and mandarin–intellectual (the latter prioritised the national rather than the individual/interpersonal paradigm, specifically the need for the nation to reconcile with its past). Chapman (2008a), drawing on an analysis of the TRC's report and especially transcripts from the HRV hearings, documents the lack of a clear conception of reconciliation from the Commission and commissioner interventions. As a final example, Borer (2004) describes the way that different perspectives found textual manifestation in the TRC's final report. Discussion of reconciliation is concentrated in three main locations: the 'Concepts and Principles' chapter (TRC 1998, Vol. 1: 106–10, 115–17, 125–34) covers the process/goal and levels thesis outlined above, and features aspects of both of the main reconciliation paradigms; the 'Recommendations' chapter (Vol. 5: 304–7, 349) focuses almost exclusively on promoting national unity and reconciliation; while the very next chapter on 'Reconciliation' (Vol. 5: 350–435) is similarly one-sided, this time foregrounding individual and interpersonal reconciliation. Thus, the multi-dimensional nature of reconciliation was acknowledged by the TRC, but the challenge of coherence was restated rather than resolved (also see Boraine 2000: 340–78).

It is to say the least surprising, given the centrality of reconciliation to the work and rhetoric of the TRC, that it did not achieve a clear conceptualisation or working definition of the term. Over time the Commission toned down its reconciliation-related claims, emphasising national rather than individual and interpersonal reconciliation (with the exception of the HRV hearings and Tutu's personal statements), and asserting that it made a contribution to the process of reconciliation while calling on others – state and society – to complete the task. It resorted, in essence, to trickle-down reconciliation. For all the weaknesses of this approach, the TRC did initiate a national debate about reconciliation.

Hamber and van der Merwe (1998) neatly summarise five prevailing societal discourses on reconciliation: non-racialism, intercommunalism, religious, human rights and the rule of law, and community- and relationship-building. While different approaches can coexist – the TRC both prioritised non-racial nation-building and shuffled the cards in its pack – there are more troubling, conflictual aspects to the debate, such as different political party and racial understandings of reconciliation. A dominant view among whites, for example, is that reconciliation entails unity, racial integration, cooperation and also pluralism. At the thin edge of the reconciliation wedge, this coexistence-based model bypasses apology and material benefit, thereby severing links between reconciliation and responsibility and certain forms of much-needed transformation (Nagy 2004: 721–22). While the TRC launched a debate about reconciliation, and such a debate is clearly part of any reconciliation process, a lack of conceptual clarity in the Commission's work rears its head again. The TRC's aftermath has been plagued by disagreement about what reconciliation is, what its preconditions are, how much has been achieved, who is committed to it and who is not, and so on.

Speaking truth to reconciliation

The argument of the current chapter is that as a component of the reconciliation debate and the openness of the TRC process, modes of truth-telling from the TRC's HRV hearings seeped into South African society and its public sphere (see Chapter 2). The result was a 'public culture of telling' (Kayser 1999: 2; see Boraine 2000: 356; McEachern 2002: xii, 135). The chapter analyses truth-telling in post-TRC South Africa, and the ways in which the proliferation of testimony engaged with and critiqued the Commission's most hallowed premise: that the truth reconciles.

How does the truth lead to reconciliation? This relationship was also not coherently conceptualised by the TRC. The TRC did not argue that truth automatically and always leads to reconciliation, but did aver that reconciliation is impossible without truth, i.e. truth is a necessary, but perhaps not a sufficient precondition of reconciliation. The relationship was conceived as operating on essentially three levels, reflecting the TRC's focus on individual/interpersonal and national reconciliation. It was in the HRV hearings that truth-telling was claimed to be most obviously linked to reconciliation through an enabling relationship between voice, acknowledgement, the restoration of dignity and healing (the individual level). The TRC also placed great importance on assertions that people would or could forgive if they knew what had happened and why, whom to forgive and if perpetrators confessed/apologised (the level of relationships, potentially incorporating the amnesty process), and stressed the provision of a more inclusive, consensual narrative history as a vehicle for establishing national unity (the national level). TRC banners, posters and slogans proclaimed its philosophy: 'Reconciliation through Truth', 'Truth: The Road to Reconciliation' and 'Healing is Revealing' (TRC 1998, Vol. 1: 115–17; Vol. 5: 306, 351–56, 371–82; also see Tutu 1999). It is beyond dispute that some victims found testifying before public hearings a powerful and positive experience (see Irene Mxinwa's claim to this effect in Chapter 1; also TRC 1998, Vol. 5: 351–56), but it is equally important to register that others did not – few victims mentioned reconciliation in victim hearings, while of those who did many were negative about its prospects or attached conditions, often truth-related, to its promotion (Chapman 2008a: 53–62; 2008b: 80–82).

Speaking truth to reconciliation is my phrase, not the TRC's, and by proposing it as a new 'regime of truth' in post-apartheid South Africa I mean that the TRC provided an officially sanctioned testimonial space, predominantly for victims of human rights violations, which was framed, largely from above, in a discourse of forgiveness, catharsis and healing and linked to a broader nation-building project.[1] The idea that victim-led reconciliation could be achieved through truth-telling derived from the already-mentioned coming together of religious, particularly Christian, and psychological/psychotherapeutic discourses. It is largely from these sources that the TRC borrowed its vocabulary of forgiveness, catharsis, healing, closure and reconciliation, and its emphasis on confession, testimony and truth-telling (Botman and Petersen 1996; Cochrane et al. 1999; Herman 2001; Tutu 1999: 71–73). Various important critiques have been levelled at this approach.[2]

First, the assumption that narratives of pain and suffering are accessible, expressible and somehow whole is widely questioned. Rather, such hurt struggles for and through language, seeks supportive modes of communication, emerges through fragments, repetition and translation/mediation. Second, there are a number of institutional constraints, relating to both suitability and capacity (also see Chapter 2). As an example, the TRC platform was selective and restricted, and lacked the necessary support infrastructures. Only those who had suffered gross violations of civil and political human rights were recognised as victims; around 2,000 of the over 21,000 victims who submitted statements were selected to testify at public hearings; victims narrated their stories in one short sitting; and there was often valuable, if rather uneven briefing/debriefing, and very limited longer-term support, referral and follow-up. Progressive counselling discourses stress the importance of supportive relationships, security, and holistic, community-rooted interventions. Given the absence of these conditions at the TRC, and in many everyday lives, the sustainability of 'therapeutic moments' (Minow 2000: 245) is open to question; as Shaw (2005) notes, '[a] truth commission is not therapy'.

Third, some causal assumptions have been queried. It is clear that truth-telling by victims as well as perpetrators can, and often did, breed anger and alienation rather then reconciliation, and that truth can be sidelined in, and become a casualty of processes of reconciliation (see Chapter 1). Others provide reminders that space is needed for, and indeed that closure/healing can be secured through, anger, retribution and revenge (Hamber and Wilson 2002; R. Wilson 2001). A fourth point is that such definitions of reconciliation, which often relegate accountability, justice and reparation to a secondary position, ask a great deal of the victims/survivors and very little of the perpetrators and beneficiaries. Fifth, the transferability of the paradigm from the individual to the nation – 'psychologising the nation' (Hamber and Wilson 2002: 35) – and the efficacy and morality of harnessing the individual and individual narratives as the raw material on and through which to achieve national unity and reconciliation, has been the subject of debate and dispute (among others, Boraine 2000: 360–78; Ignatieff 1996; Minow 2000; Shriver 1995).[3] A final and sixth critique is that this mode of public truth-telling and confession is alien to many non-Western cultures, and risks becoming another externally imposed but supposedly universal discourse.[4]

Despite these drawbacks, speaking truth to reconciliation was the TRC's prevailing reconciliation paradigm, and a powerful legacy left within South Africa and beyond. To assess the impact of this paradigm requires a more concrete conceptual framework: the truth-telling template.

Truth-telling template

South Africa had a rich testimonial heritage on which to build. Archbishop Tutu and the TRC report stressed the central role of 'story-telling' in (South) African 'oral tradition' (Tutu 1996: 7, TRC 1998, Vol. 1: 112). Further, story-telling was a familiar part of NGO practice (for example, in conflict resolution and therapeutic processes: van der Merwe *et al.* 1999: 73); in academic circles, oral history flourished; and there was a rich autobiographical corpus, notably around human rights abuses such as detention, political imprisonment and exile (Gready 2003).

Any claim to a new testimonial era or framework raises a number of more specific questions.

The TRC's HRV hearings were a landmark in the historiography of South African testimony, but the dynamics of continuity and change need to be identified with care. Commentators have plotted the influence of oral tradition on certain forms of narration in the HRV hearings (Krog et al. 2009; Ross 2003: 34–47), and categorised the TRC as a hybrid institution incorporating aspects of traditional and popular justice and politics (Scheper-Hughes 1999: 163–68; R. Wilson 2001: 116). Thus, the first question is: what was new and different about this testimony? Analysts stress narrative structure and objectives, its public nature and wide dissemination, and the fact that it was officially sanctioned, and therefore both legitimised and legitimising:

> much was already known about apartheid, told in diverse genres – in stories, songs, political rhetoric, magisterial orders, court cases, newspapers, scholarly work, parliamentary debates, at funerals and rallies and so on. What the Commission's human rights violations hearings offered was a new structure for narrating experiences of violence and suffering to a broad public. The hearings also offered an alternative means to attend to harm – the opening of a public space that reached far beyond the Commission personnel and audiences present at the hearings.
>
> (Ross 2003b: 327)

A second question probes this distinctiveness further: what was the narrative arc of the testimonies? Of the HRV hearings, Richard Wilson (2001: 111) writes that 'a universal redemptive template' was applied 'across individual victims' testimonies, with predictable chronological stages', moving from the individual to the collective and the nation, and back to the individual to facilitate reconciliation and forgiveness. Contextualisation and broader meaning were provided by bridging concepts, such as the seemingly contradictory notions of shared and morally equivalent suffering on the one hand, alongside the heroism/martyrdom of sacrifice for liberation on the other (ibid.: 109–21). This arc is not universally agreed – some identify a contrary tendency to frame testimony at the beginning and end with broader community and contextual concerns.

HRV hearings and testimonies quickly became standardised and somewhat formulaic. The above-mentioned narrative arc is one explanation; another is the often noted assertion that certain responses, essentially those congruent with the speaking truth to reconciliation paradigm, were solicited and embraced by commissioners, whereas contributions that rejected this paradigm were less sympathetically received. In essence, institutionalised truth-telling is prone to formalism, welding individual testimonies on to broader political agendas. While it is useful to think in terms of formulas in the plural, e.g. the tendency for women to testify to the experience of (male) others, a third question surfaces.

What are the implications of testimonial standardisation or formalisation for the speaking truth to reconciliation paradigm?

Despite dominant paradigms, the TRC's truth preferences were contested by victims/survivor agency, and 'non-fitting testimonies' (Krog *et al.* 2009: 43, discussing the testimony of Notrose Nobomvu Konile; Colin de Souza's testimony, discussed in Chapter 2, is another example of a 'non-fitting testimony'). Hence, alongside certain patterns, a diversity of truth-telling forms, strategies and outcomes emerged (Ross 2003). The result was part individual emphasis, part testifier–commissioner collaboration, part local narrative style and cultural inflection, part institutional formula, part layered political agendas. The outcome(s) could reinforce or contest both the TRC's priorities and pre-existing community and political narratives (Bozzoli 1998). More open ways of interpreting testimony and the hearings are suggested by a number of authors. Phelps's (2004: 67–69, 104, 113) account of the TRC hearings as carnival is helpful (see Chapter 1), as is Blommaert *et al.*'s (2000) discussion of discourses of power and authority (media and legal forms) mixed with subaltern discourses, and public and hidden transcripts (drawing on Scott 1990). Du Toit (2000) depicts the contested framing of narratives as indicative of the TRC's democratic credentials. In short, the truth-telling template was contested and multi-vocal, inviting the question: in what ways did individuals attempt to testify against the grain of the dominant truth paradigms, and were such narrations 'heard'?

A final point in effect summarises the above-mentioned questions. Victim/survivor truth-telling shifted from its long-established position of contesting the official and the mainstream under apartheid, to a new scenario where it helped to construct the new nation; from an instrument of resistance to a passport to acknowledgement and recognition. This represents a shift to a new truth paradigm, truth's own transition, from speaking truth to power to speaking truth to reconciliation. Mamdani (2000: 177–78) notes the distinction between individual truth, which speaks truth to power, and institutional truth, which links truth to power. The TRC was most obviously positioned in the latter camp. While the distinction is too absolute – the TRC also spoke truth to power, as its unpopularity with all political parties indicates, and individuals within the TRC hearings challenged old and new power – it can shed light on processes that attempted to co-opt the individual to institutional/national agendas. This argument, alongside its predecessor, begs the question as to the relationship between speaking truth to reconciliation and to power.

This chapter argues, in partial response to the questions raised above, that a truth template shaped the reconciliation-related debates launched by the TRC, and consisted of five interrelated strands:

1 The arc of life stories hinged on instances of, and responses to, violence, but with diverging definitions and understandings of violence and violation (gross human rights abuse or structural violence, focusing on the apartheid era or a longer history of colonisation and dispossession).

2 Past and present coexisted in testimonial narratives.
3 The private, secret and censored and the public, similarly, were characterised by a troubled coexistence rather than the new sweeping away the old.
4 The new order's speaking truth to reconciliation cohabited with a more contestual paradigm of speaking truth to power. Both voices are intrinsic to longer-term demands for political recognition and citizenship from the marginalised.
5 Contests emerged over post-apartheid and post-TRC identities and self-identification (victim or survivor; singular or multiple identities; the direction and dynamics of identity transformation).[5]

The TRC-fuelled rebirth of life story narratives speaks to the challenge of situating the self in changing political and social circumstances. That life stories should be mobilised as transitory forms of control, to negotiate uncertainties, is not new. But the template speaks to a new conflagration of apartheid and post-apartheid concerns. Before discussing a number of truth-telling sites in post-TRC South Africa, the chapter will analyse in more detail the privileging of the victim within truth-telling, and the rise of cultures of victimhood in transitional settings, as an example of a truth template debate.

The culture of victimhood

> You see times are different. When I was told that I was a victim, it was at the time I was not working. I thought I would get help so that I can change my life. Now, to me now, it's not so important to be given the status of being a victim. To me it's some kind of a suppression. Today I don't want to be identified as a victim. I am a survivor, I can do more than the status of being a victim.
>
> (Kumalo, interview 17/8/2002)

Into the transitional fray in South Africa stepped the TRC to both define and disseminate a central component of the new nation's identity: victimhood. The TRC report acknowledged 'some discomfort' with the use of the term 'victim' due to its associations of passivity, suffering and lack of agency. It conceded that 'survivor' has positive connotations 'implying an ability to overcome adversity and even to be strengthened by it', and that many described as victims might be better described, and prefer to be described, as survivors. Further, beyond the notion of survivor, many saw themselves as having participated in, and emerged victorious from, a political struggle. Nevertheless, seeking refuge in the wording used by its founding Act and a narrow legal fetishism, the TRC resolved the terminological difficulty thus:

> However, when dealing with gross human rights violations committed by perpetrators, the person against whom that violation is committed can only

be described as a victim, regardless of whether he or she emerged a survivor. In this sense, the state of mind and survival of the person is irrelevant; it is the intention and action of the perpetrator that creates the condition of being a victim.

(TRC 1998, Vol. 1: 59; also 2003, Vol. 7: 2–3)

While in narrow human rights terms this is arguably correct, it is nonetheless an extraordinary statement. It is hard to see how, for a commission dedicated to making links between voice, dignity and healing, linking truth to reconciliation, 'the state of mind and survival of the person' can possibly be 'irrelevant', or how 'the intention and action of the perpetrator' can so totally set the agenda.[6]

This terminological snapshot already begins to indicate why the victim typology can be problematic. However, it is important to make clear at the outset that a focus on victims and the victims' movement, like many cultures of truth-telling, can empower the previously marginalised in important ways. Internationally in recent years the victim's voice, whether from a victim of crime or human rights abuse, has contested its marginalisation within processes of justice and what are often seen as excessive defendant's rights (a fair trial having traditionally been gauged in terms of treatment of the defendant rather than the victim). Certain important victim's rights – improving the position of victims with respect to criminal investigations and trials, compensation and restitution, and access to support services – have been fought for and are now reflected in national and international law.[7] 'Asking the victim question', and placing the victim first, provides an important corrective lens on crime and human rights abuse (Marks and Clapham 2005). The human rights and transitional justice movements now champion the rights of victims as never before. In doing so, they must be aware of the strengths *and* weaknesses of such an approach. The main strength is that victims' voices are heard, acknowledged and disseminated, again as never before. Core weaknesses are outlined below.

This section addresses in turn the prism on truth and reconciliation provided by narrow, one-dimensional victim and perpetrator identity positions; discourses that I would argue offer more potential to link truth to reconciliation (through positive and multiple identities, and identity transformation); the complex implications of identity collectivisation; and the challenges posed by the reification of victimhood in the context of identity politics, nationalism and the conduct of democratic politics.

The decision to focus on victims and perpetrators informed the cast for the narrative of South Africa's past, the template for their stories and the nature of their relationships. Those who saw themselves as creative and resilient activists, as survivors who chose to engage in a just war, tended not to submit statements or testify before the TRC, in part because they did not recognise themselves in the mirror it held up to the past. Fullard (interview 27/8/2002) claims that victims often constructed themselves as entirely innocent, passive and devoid of agency. The classic victim was a person caught up in violence, in events they had little role in or control over. The result was 'cleansed, purified' stories, told to present the narrator in the best possible light: 'It is regrettable the Commission did not make space for people to feel that the entirety of their experience was acceptable'. De Ridder (interview 3/8/1998; de Ridder 1997) confirms this tendency, noting that within counselling people classified as victims by the TRC often acknowledged that they were also perpetrators. She points out the danger that the TRC was creating a 'nation of victims, not survivors – in other words, a continued dependency'. Not only did victims construct their own identities in this way but, as we saw in Chapter 2, those who contested the victim designation were reconstructed by others in its image. An established criticism of victimhood is that individuals become passive objects of pity defined purely in terms of their suffering, and are thereby rendered dependent and subject to external interventions (Marks and Clapham 2005: 403–7).

Subject to their own strait-jacket, perpetrators in turn modified narratives to meet the conditions for amnesty, such as demonstrating a political motive. While perpetrators more often embraced a past characterised by agency and choice, black perpetrators felt frustration that their complex identities were not recognised (liberation fighter, perpetrator, victim – Abrahamsen and van de Merwe 2005; see Chapter 1 and the discussion of *amnesty for truth*). Across the board, I would argue, the chosen identity coordinates (one-dimensional victims and perpetrators; passive dependency versus active agency; adversarial relationships) impoverished truth and provided a poor basis for reconciliation and nation-building.[8]

Is there a solution to this conundrum? Human rights discourse provides a greater range of identity options than is utilised by truth commissions and many human rights organisations. It is a dual discourse of violence and violations (victims, perpetrators), and of idealism and resistance. The latter echoes Cronin's (1998; 1999) affirmation of the 'little freedom fighter' in all South Africans, the spirit of collective self-reliance and the just struggle, affirmed by the TRC in abstract but barely present in the detail. Surely such identity coordinates, alongside inquiries into the role of the 'righteous', rescuers and cosmopolitans working across manufactured societal divides, have at least as much potential to link truth to reconciliation as violations-based identities? They open on to identity work emphasising full citizenship and the equal embrace of rights and responsibilities. But this is also an area where commissions need to reach beyond human rights, to draw on complementary identity-related discourses.

A useful example is provided in a pre-TRC piece by Foster and Skinner (1990), suggestively titled 'Detention and Violence: Beyond Victimology'. Contesting a focus on individual victims and the psychological 'effects' of detention (there are clear parallels here between psychological discourse and human rights, both narrowly defined), the authors interpret detention in social and political terms as a relatively rare intergroup encounter in which, despite the violence and power inequalities, all parties are active agents. Group relations can be altered, social change nurtured. This approach recognises damage but also coping strategies, resistance and even a form of dialogue; it also recognises that an 'effects' discourse that assists in creating victims can become part of the problem rather than part of the solution (229). Extending the analysis from detention to imprisonment, the transformation of Robben Island from 'hell-hole' to 'university', and specifically reconfigured relations among the prison population and between prisoners and warders, provides a concrete example of an intergroup encounter that produced extraordinary social change inside and outside the prison (Gready 2003: 64–70). How intergroup dynamics were worked through *then*, in adversity, is surely relevant to possibilities *now*.

Building on these insights, Foster *et al.*'s (2005) study of protagonists from different sides in the South African conflict argues that political violence is a relational phenomenon, meaning that identities and actions are co-constructed. The term 'protagonist' is preferred to 'perpetrator', and used alongside 'positionings' in an attempt to escape simplistic binaries (victim–perpetrator). In this terrain people have multiple identities and can move between a range of identities, such as those suggested by the passage between criminal and political violence. Further 'grey areas' in the perpetrator designation include perpetrators who are also victims, informers and bureaucratic functionaries; 'horizontal' violence within black communities; the fact that few perpetrators regard themselves as perpetrators; and more (4–7). To capture the multi-sided nature of political violence the more ambiguous figure of the protagonist is seen as an actor in a 'theatre' or 'arena' of violence (also see TRC 1998, Vol. 5: 259–303).

The point is a broader one, that the cast of the past, their narratives and relationships depend on the questions asked and the identities assigned, and that the victim question is important, but does not warrant a monopoly on the past. Before rushing to alter our prism on the past, however, modes of analysis have to be mapped onto forms of intervention. Complex identity formulations may provide a more accurate reflection of the truth and a more cogent link between truth and reconciliation. They are unlikely, however, to aid prosecutions, which usually require that the perpetrator is drawn in one-dimensional rather than three-dimensional terms, hence the imperative of a well-founded triangulation between analysis, interventions and objectives.

A second, related, solution lies beyond the insistence on diverse and multiple identities, in possible sources of identity transformation. Victims (and perpetrators) are a necessary part of a truth commission's starting point, but they cannot be its sole destination. Change requires facilitative processes: the search for meaning, often found in religious and political beliefs (Scheper-Hughes 1999); gaining greater control over and reconstituting one's life and social environment; seeking and securing justice; economic opportunities and empowerment; challenging past categorisations and stereotypes; and so on. The 'victims turned survivors' mantra has become something of a cliché, and can feel like a form of revictimisation for the vulnerable if prematurely applied – hence, the outcomes of such facilitative processes are best left relatively open.[9] While the TRC may have sought to go beyond significant, symbolic moments to be such a process, it was not a cogent process of 'working through'; it lacked the flexibility and resources to meet diverse needs and, crucially, its chosen tools were too crude. As noted above, for example, public hearings do not constitute therapy. A number of the truth-telling sites discussed later in this chapter provide insightful correctives to these shortcomings.

As an example of the TRC's transformative shortcomings, its adoption of an 'all are victims' and 'all are perpetrators' approach took the path of least resistance to reconciliation. The definition of gross violations of human rights, and therefore victims, was drawn both too narrowly (gross civil and political rights abuses, individual victims and perpetrators) and too broadly. The TRC report stated that apartheid damaged and wounded all South Africans; Tutu repeatedly articulated the view that all South Africans were victims of apartheid, marshalling *ubuntu* as his creed and arguing that dehumanising relationships affect all partners to the relationship (TRC 1998, for example Vol. 1: 22; Tutu 1999: 35, also see 78–91). The ANC also contested the TRC's reparations regime on the grounds that South Africa is a nation of victims. Thus, the 'all are victims' claim served various purposes.

Perpetrators too were drawn too narrowly and too broadly. As part of the call for wider societal acknowledgement of responsibility, the TRC conceded that its focus had been on the exceptional at the expense of the commonplace: 'The result is that ordinary South Africans do not see themselves as represented by those the Commission defines as perpetrators, failing to recognise the "little perpetrator" in each one of us' (TRC 1998, Vol. 1: 133). All victims, all perpetrators are the ingredients for reconciliation lite. Inclusion on such terms embraces a moral relativism or balance in pursuit of short-term transitional accommodation, which undermines the prospects for longer-term structural or identity transformation. Various commentators contested the marriage of truth and reconciliation suggested by this vision of history.

Mamdani (1996, 1998, 2000; also see Chapter 1), for example, argues that social or systemic justice and social reconciliation need to look beyond an elite group of perpetrators and minority victims, state agents and political activists, and more generally beyond the terms of the 1994 political compromise and political reconciliation (an inaccurate view of the TRC's core constituency), to address a society more broadly conceived as majority victims and beneficiaries (an important recasting of the TRC's mandate and objectives). In short, for societal reconciliation to occur a majority truth and justice, addressing structures of power and dispossession, is required. By adopting the narrower framework, Mamdani asserts, the TRC invited beneficiaries to embrace victimhood by claiming ignorance about apartheid abuses and to join in the outrage against perpetrators. The 'great equalisation[s]' (Maluleke 1999: 108) obscured the fact that while apartheid perpetrators have lost power, apartheid beneficiaries have not. White beneficiaries revolted against any sense of responsibility; black victims were enraged by this impoverished response.

As this analysis begins to suggest, truth commissions reconfigure both individual and collective identity. The implications of individualisation for victims can be positive, for example providing 'an opportunity to make their "collective" experience "individual"', to acknowledge and address their own pain beyond collective or political agendas (de Ridder interview 3/8/1998; and de Ridder 1997). But if individual narratives converge around incidents of human rights abuse and victimhood, so too can collective narratives – a similar isolation and reification of suffering occurs, especially if truth-telling, identity and victimhood become one.

> [F]ollowing the work of the Truth and Reconciliation Commission, the claims to absolute victimhood were translated into a myth of secular reason: I suffer(ed) therefore I am. The 'I am' of the formulation folds into itself the right to speak as a South African.
>
> (Quayson 2004: 14)

What is being played out in victim claims through truth-telling is the politics of recognition (Taylor 1994). As collective identities are thrown into flux by political transition, collective claims for recognition ('We suffer[ed] therefore we are') came from diverse groups and in multiple forms. Victim claimant groups in South Africa include (members of) the Afrikaans community, for example. A powerful example of an Afrikaner claim for recognition is Krog's *Country of My Skull* (1998). For Krog (1998: 277–79, also 1995), the TRC 'kept alive the idea of a common humanity' and created a space for belonging: 'all voices, all victims ... forgive me / You whom I have wronged, please / take me / with you'. Such claims seek safe passage into the future and reach back into the past as justification. Giliomee in *The Afrikaners: Biography of a People* (2003: 662) takes a long historical view to root an explanation for apartheid in the nexus of victimhood and ethnic survival:

> History had happened to the Afrikaners. Their forebears were both colonisers and a colonised people. They had defeated blacks in war but had suffered a shattering defeat at the hands of the British [in the South African War of 1899–1902]; they had known poverty and contempt for their culture; they had won power and had experienced the corruption of power.

Genuine and more problematic grievance, the TRC process and contested views of the past, placed victimhood claims at the heart of a transitional politics of recognition.

Collective victim narratives present a range of challenges, with regard to identity politics, nationalism and democracy (see Cohen 1995: 180, 1996: especially 15).

The allure of victimhood is part of a wider post-modern identity-politics, linked to social movements rendering the personal political. Special interests and identities seek protection by generating new human rights and victim claims, some genuine, some spurious. As for nationalism, reverberating through conflicts in Northern Ireland, Israel/Palestine, Rwanda, the Balkans and indeed South Africa, the 'victim-reversal myths of ethnic nationalism' (Cohen 2001: 96) fuel violence and history itself. As Dawson (2003) and Smyth (2003) document that in Northern Ireland, it is not unusual for those on opposing sides of a conflict to claim the mantle of victim, or for constituencies with different attitudes to peace agreements to categorise victims differently, creating a contested politics of victimhood. At worst, collectives refract their pasts into histories of suffering, claiming uniqueness. From the moral high ground 'victim's licence' can be claimed, and sometimes granted, under which the permanent victim is endowed with a moral authority that is permanently blameless, that can do no wrong (Monbiot in Marks and Clapham 2005: 407). Victimhood as misdirected identity politics and narrow nationalism is clearly problematic.

Victimhood unleashed as a form of partisan politics can be exclusive, intolerant and competitive, with the potential to fracture communities and undermine reconciliation: 'Does the appropriation of victimisation as the core moral stance create a paradox in that it becomes a means to revivify the fragments of communities, one that works against reconciliation and rebuilding?' (Das and Kleinman 2002: 25). Truth commissions clearly need to provide alternative modes of self-imagining and narrative framing, for individuals *and* collectives. Empirical research can help to question and shift firmly held community perceptions (Gibson 2004; Smyth 2003). It would also be useful to plunder the social science literature for relevant conceptual frameworks. Oppressed groups could be encouraged to see themselves as multi-faceted and fluid entities, for example by using the typology of communities of suffering (violence, victimhood, resistance), moral communities (mutual welfare, internal giving, collective provision) *and* aesthetic communities (cultural knowledge, creativity, passion) (for example, P. Werbner 1997). Again, this would require a focus on more than the negative past; an embrace of multiple and transformative identities at a collective level; and joined-up thinking about analysis, interventions and objectives.

A final point is that a public culture of victimhood is a poor foundation for democracy. A cacophony of special pleadings, exclusive groups and competitive suffering subverts democratic politics and citizenship. Victimhood needs to be acknowledged and redress offered because it is right to do so, but also so that victimhood does not become a foundational means of securing influence, resources and rights, in short of conducting politics, in the new order. Otherwise the politics of the present will never be free of the politics of the past. This also entails people assuming forms of power beyond their status as victims.[10] This section argues that the TRC set up a key victim-related tension that pervades the truth template. The TRC privileged victims, mapped an incoherent and inaccurate conceptualisation of victimhood – at once too broad and too narrow – and placed claims to victimhood at the heart of the right to voice and the politics of recognition in the new South Africa. This was a mistake, but it is an error that others have sought to rectify.

Sites of truth-telling

A proliferation of TRC-informed sites of truth-telling can be identified in South Africa. Narratives of self drew on, and in turn appropriated, modified and critiqued, the public narratives and truth template of the TRC. Examples of such sites range from the Internal Reconciliation Commission at the University of the Witwatersrand Faculty of Health Sciences (see Chapter 6) to the National Speak Out on Poverty Hearings (Budlender 1998); from support groups, life story documentation and oral history training projects, to community projects and museums and memorials; from theatrical productions to films, art, novels and forms of popular culture; and across a range of impromptu settings such as church services and conferences.

Questions explored in the following case studies refer back to the five strands of the truth-telling template. How are human rights abuses, violence and suffering defined and understood? What is the relationship between past and present, and in which predominant temporal direction does the testimony face? What are the profiles of silence and exposure, and how do these profiles differ from those of the apartheid past and the TRC hearings? What is the relationship between speaking truth to reconciliation and truth to power? And, finally, who is categorised as a victim or a survivor, and more generally, which identities and modes of self-identification emerge in post-apartheid and post-TRC narration? The overarching question is how, if at all, is truth linked to reconciliation? The case studies featured below are support groups, memorials (speaking truth to place), and public culture and novel truths.

Support groups: encounters and transformations

Civil society groups, working at least initially within an ethos of support and complementarity vis-à-vis the TRC, often embraced truth-telling as an important part of their work and continued their narrative emphasis beyond the brief life-span and limited reach of the Commission. Two examples are discussed below: the Cape Town-based Institute for Healing of Memories (IHM) and the Khulumani Support Group, which has national, provincial and local structures.

Institute for Healing of Memories

The IHM grew out of the Healing of Memories Chaplaincy Project at the Trauma Centre for Victims of Violence and Torture in Cape Town, and was established in 1998.[11] It is deeply informed by the experiences and ethos of its Director, Father Michael Lapsley, a former ANC chaplain in exile, who lost an eye and both his hands in a letter bomb explosion in Zimbabwe in 1990 (Worsnip 1996). IHM's core work brings together South Africans from different backgrounds in a weekend workshop setting, seeking to provide a 'safe space' for interactions across racial and class divides. Such spaces remain scarce in South Africa. Truth-telling can be prompted by drawings and visual representations of participants' lives or a series of questions about experiences in the apartheid years (What have you done? What was done to you? What have you failed to do?, etc.). There is an emphasis, guided by facilitators, on the emotional and spiritual: 'It is not that important for us to know what actually happened, we are not fact finding. We want to get into feelings and emotions' (Mngese, interview 4/4/2005; on the role of facilitators, see Karakashian 2007). Participants share their stories of the past in a 'testimonial dialogue', an exercise in talking and listening or witnessing rather than confrontation. Story-telling is seen as a means to establish new forms of social interaction. The IHM prefers to frame this as an opportunity for individual healing and for South Africans to 'encounter one another', rather than purely as promoting 'reconciliation'.

IHM is informed by a vision that all South Africans have been damaged, if not identically and equally, by apartheid – all have a story to tell, and every story needs a listener. This echoes the TRC's 'all are victims' paradigm, but seeks to operationalise a response by allowing a broad range of South Africans to participate in the workshops. A 'community of suffering' is conceived as a way of transcending other differences. Narrative healing seeks to deal with anger, bitterness and pain in such a way that victims do not become victimisers. This extends the 'all are victims', 'all are potential perpetrators/victimisers' prism (the latter also features in the IHM's discourse), by adding a transformative and temporal dimension: past victims could become victimisers in the future if the necessary steps are not taken. In the transition from 'victim to being a survivor to becoming a victor', forgiveness is seen as a means of taking control, as empowerment. A recognition of multiple identities extends to a complex spectrum of identity positions – victim, victimiser, victor; attempts to draw on 'the redemptive' from the past; and seeking to modify the [black] victim versus [white] perpetrator binary by identifying 'grey zones' of human interaction.

IHM has expanded its work to new constituencies (youth, refugees, prisoners, persons with HIV/AIDS), and countries (Southern Africa, other post-conflict settings), while struggling to recruit white participants for its workshops. In open narrative settings South African workshop participants began to raise issues such as HIV/AIDS, poverty and ongoing violence, linking the past and present and testifying to 'multiple woundedness'. The healing of memories intervention remains a very close twin of the TRC and its speaking truth to reconciliation paradigm: strongly influenced by, but seeking to extend its appeal beyond, Christian values and ritual (the workshops end with a liturgy or celebration, a symbolic reorientation towards hope); emphasising forgiveness and a largely one-off intervention using a narrative cleansing ethos (described by the IHM as one step on a journey, but nevertheless questions must remain about whether benefits are sustainable). Such truth-telling work raises certain questions. Can the emotional and spiritual be the grounds for transformation and new forms of subjectivity? How can impacts be scaled up beyond the individual to communities? Ultimately, the IHM's major contribution is to provide an interactive setting for truth-telling, rendering it and identity formation consciously relational, and the attempt to operationalise a transformative identity agenda that engages with the past, acknowledges the past in the present, and prepares for the future.

Khulumani Support Group

Formed in 1995, the activities of the Khulumani (meaning 'speak out' in Zulu) Support Group have varied over time, and in different provinces.[12] It has a membership of 54,000 – which is overwhelmingly African, female and poor, and well over double the number who made victim statements to the TRC. Of these, 74 per cent are unemployed, and 90 per cent were not included in the TRC process and therefore did not receive reparations (because they did not know how to reach or engage with the Commission; many did not hear about its existence until too late; some may not have qualified as 'victims' on the TRC's terms). Khulumani seeks to extend the constituency of the TRC in two ways. First, it claims that the TRC only reached a small percentage of the victims that met its qualification criteria. Second, situated between the categorisations of narrowly drawn victims of gross human rights abuses and the expansive 'all are victims' thesis, Khulumani works with a recognisable human rights discourse but renders it more inclusive (for example, accepting within its fold victims of economic and social human rights abuses). While organisationally it has at times struggled, it has unquestionably done important work.

Khulumani's main initial objective was to facilitate participation in the TRC through education, assisting people to submit statements, and providing support before and after hearings. It also lobbied the TRC about the rights and concerns of victims and the families of victims. Khulumani, post-TRC, has moved on to address the needs of its members by campaigning on unfinished business such as apartheid-era prosecutions and reparations. Alongside local campaigns the court case *Khulumani et al.* v. *Barclays et al.* was filed in the United States against several foreign companies accused of aiding and abetting the apartheid regime (see Chapter 6). Other priority areas include organisational capacity-building, economic livelihoods, grassroots, victim-led histories, and, more generally, 'civic competence' or active citizenship (Madlingozi 2010: 215–21).

Enabling victims to find their voice, and giving more victims of apartheid a platform to tell their stories, has been an ongoing priority (using group counselling, meetings and events, films, theatrical productions and exhibitions, local histories, through their website, and so on). Group members have placed great emphasis on a solidarity in suffering, created by Khulumani, breaking their isolation (Makupe, interview 11/9/1998; Mozikare, interview 2/9/1998). Khulumani groups have also made use of the IHM workshops and methodologies. Unlike IHM, however, where truth-telling is governed by an ethic of confidentiality and stories are not routinely documented, within Khulumani there is a strong documentation and dissemination drive.[13]

In a study of the Khulumani (Western Cape) Support Group, Colvin (2000) noted that while Khulumani engaged in political advocacy, for example for reparations and structural economic change, story-telling was at this time an important component of support group meetings. Here truth-telling was to a relatively homogenous audience of black African victims where the emphasis was often less psychological and more on nurturing a social space and relationships. It dealt more consistently than IHM workshops with human rights abuse, although women, as before the TRC, frequently spoke about the experiences of male loved ones. A template or formula was evident:

> All of these stories ... tend to begin with a brief introduction of the speaker, continue through a summary of key events and people and end on a distinctly tense and unresolved note. These stories are 'tight' in their construction, reduced to the essential elements needed to make the point – what happened, to whom, where and when. There is little exploration of why these things might have happened or of what life is like at the present.
> (Colvin 2000: 10)

This sounds like a human rights researcher's dream testimony, and mirrors the TRC's narrow focus and quest for detail. Facilitators, like TRC commissioners at HRV hearings, set the scene at the start, and through questioning and providing links to broader truths and the present, assisted in bringing the testimony to a conclusion. There were few interventions during the testimony itself. Colvin argues that story-telling was framed predominantly in terms of individual *and* group healing; reconciliation was seen primarily and increasingly in economic/ structural and political terms. Frustration had grown at the inability of the former to secure access to the latter. This has contributed to the emphasis on story-telling declining over time. The currency of truth-telling for the most marginalised seems to have depreciated in value, at least as a stand-alone intervention. Colvin's study (2000: 13–14) suggests that a persuasive argument made by Khulumani has been to identify not truth but justice, defined as reparations, related concerns such as special pensions, and more broadly as 'justice-as-transformation', as the priority and as a precondition for reconciliation.

In conclusion, how do the debates from the truth template play out in support groups? In both of these case studies truth provides no easy route to reconciliation. Truth-telling is linked to personal healing and group or social thickening. Access to truth-telling is extended to wider constituencies; suffering is seen as a source of community or solidarity. That said, IHM and Khulumani configure 'the group' very differently – across race and class divides (as deliberative) versus poor, marginalised Africans, especially women (as participatory). While the IHM's approach is dialogic, relational, seeking to traverse social and racial divisions in society and very much speaking truth to facets of the TRC's understanding of reconciliation, Khulumani's stance is increasingly adversarial, shifting to a position where its main public voice on behalf of the still-marginalised speaks truth to state and corporate power ('bad victims'). The danger with this approach is that unlike the IHM, which provides some potentially self-driven, transformative routes out of victimhood and the past, Khulumani's approach may instil an investment in victimhood, trapping members in the past and a transformative ethos that is more dependent on others. Such a burden-allocation is entirely understandable and legitimate, but has its costs. An emphasis on victims telling their own stories and histories, and organisational and economic capacity-building, is a potential rejoinder to this concern. For me, the IHM's transformation toolkit actually feels slight (emotion, forgiveness) and tolerant of factual silences, when placed alongside Khulumani's emphasis on justice and a more inclusive conception of human rights. At stake here are very different discourses of speaking truth to reconciliation (as emotional and spiritual journey, or political and economic struggle). But in both cases reconciliation is trumped by other concepts and hedged with preconditions ('encounter one another', 'justice-as-transformation'), suggesting that as a reference point its purchase may have diminished in the aftermath of the TRC.

Memorials: speaking truth to place

> The effectivity of the commemorative experience lies largely with the power of oral testimony and the notion of witnessing that both 'survivors' and 'place,' in different ways, can offer.
>
> (Coombes 2003: 88)

Speaking truth to place is an important component of transitional truth-telling, and a driving force behind the upsurge in public history described in Chapters 1 and 2. This is because '[a]ll memories have a geography. We recall memories, in part, through specific sites and attach our recollections to particular places' (Nevins 2005: 268).

Truth commissions are often aware of the importance of place. Offices and archives are established or hearings held in symbolically important sites, such as former prisons (e.g. see TRC 1998, Vol. 4: 199); commissions create their own memorial as a way of disseminating and continuing their work; recommendations include memorials as a component of symbolic reparations (Bickford 2005). That said, memorials remain somewhat on the margins of truth commission and transitional justice work.[14]

While context and locale are for obvious reasons crucial, speaking truth to place has local, national and international dimensions.[15] Interviews with personnel involved in memorialisation in South Africa revealed a set of challenges that resonate on all these levels. How to ensure that an appropriate geographical, political and cultural range is covered (heritage spans grand architecture to small community projects)? How should the layered history of memorialisation, from both pre- and post-oppression or -conflict eras, be dealt with? Can memorials be both private sites of mourning, healing and reflection and public sites of civic engagement, local ownership and democratic debate, and encompass victim/survivor truth-telling and multiple perspectives on the past (Brett *et al.* 2008)? How much heritage can a country sustain? How to resolve a possible tension between the needs of local communities and the potential for memorials to drive development and tourism? This section focuses on a subset of challenges: those raised by the truth template. Memorials navigate these choppy waters in different ways. One insightful example is Constitution Hill in Hillbrow, central Johannesburg, which is analysed in some detail below.[16]

Constitution Hill

In a former life Constitution Hill was a large prison complex, consisting of the Old Fort (for white males), Number Four (for black males), a Women's Jail (for black and white women) and an Awaiting Trial Block. The Constitutional Court's decision in 1996 to base itself at the Old Fort prison complex ended years of neglect, dating back to the closure of the prisons in 1983. The intervention was also designed to drive inner-city regeneration, in what remains a run-down and impoverished part of the city. The decision was made that Constitution Hill as a 'campus for human rights', home of not just the Constitutional Court but also a number of Chapter 9 institutions and NGOs, should represent a vision of civil society engagement with the Constitution – in short, it should represent 'democracy at work'. The Constitutional Court opened on 21 March 2004, the memorial site shortly thereafter.

Carrying little baggage by way of a pre-established narrative from the past, Constitution Hill offered an unprecedented opportunity to depart from established, official memorial templates (nation-building, speaking truth to reconciliation). To a degree it has done so, and at its heart is a conceptualisation of human rights that is in important ways at odds with that championed by the TRC. To substantiate this claim, what follows maps the various ways the site speaks truth to place and engages with the truth template, through (1) internal transformation, (2) external orientation, and (3) process dynamics.

Internally, the human rights present and future have literally been physically constructed from the bricks and mortar of an abusive past. The Awaiting Trial Block was sacrificed to provide space for the Constitutional Court, but it has been commemorated rather than erased – for example, a stairwell was incorporated into the Court's lobby. The Commission on Gender Equality occupies the Women's Jail. Place has been both preserved *and* transformed in the attempt to create a 'living' memorial. To the extent that this involved making some modifications to the physical infrastructure, the changes met with resistance from some former prisoners. Former prisoners often regard places of incarceration as 'sacred', and one of the challenges for the process dynamics of memorial-making here (and elsewhere) has been to manage the tension between, and harness the energy generated by, the site's 'living' and 'sacred' dimensions (Gevisser 2004: 516; Gevisser in Segal *et al.* 2006: 131). I will argue that human rights need to be similarly conceived.

Constitution Hill's vision of human rights is complex. The visitor is invited to embrace both a violations and a struggle version of human rights. At this site there is an explicit acknowledgement that human rights is a dual discourse of violations, violence and victimhood ('done to') but also of idealism and resistance ('fighting against and striving for') (see Brett *et al.* 2008: 10 and 29, for a wider call for memorials to be framed in this way). At the bottom end of Number Four, two adjacent rooms contrast 'power and punishment' on the one hand and 'resistance and resilience' on the other. The latter includes such softer rubrics as blanket sculptures and song. It is this expanded vision of human rights that the TRC failed to capture.

Constitution Hill also widens the frame of analysis by troubling the binaries on which human rights and transitional justice are often predicated (criminal/political, human rights abuse/structural violence, legal/illegal). Criminals and political offenders were held in the prison, mixing for example in Number Four's large communal cells. In this sense it was a prison of the people, as almost all black families in the city would have had a family member incarcerated here for one reason or another. It also captured apartheid's contradictions, as for example resistance against the pass laws was considered political while arrest under their terms was not. Homage is paid to different eras of political resistance and political prisoners held in the prison – the 1956 treason trialists, PAC pass resisters in the 1960s, students in the aftermath of the uprisings in 1976, ANC activists accused of treason in the 1980s. But by also focusing on the legalisation of oppression, the criminalisation of the everyday and the politicisation of the criminal (criminal prisoners voiced their desire for freedom in political terms, in their graffiti for example: Gevisser in Segal *et al.* 2006: 194), Constitution Hill challenges the boundaries of legality/illegality, criminal/political and the human rights prism, opening up a series of debates that the TRC largely sidelined. The visitor is asked questions such as: 'Who is a criminal?' This is not to say that there are no distinctions – returning political prisoners often speak as survivors, proud of their resistance and imprisonment; criminals more usually still see themselves as victims. But by adopting an expansive notion of human rights, and questioning its frontiers, a range of identity-related questions are asked, and a range of identity positions are being opened up from which to testify.[17]

External orientation is just as crucial to the memorial's message as internal transformation.[18] The view from the rampart, situated on a hill in the centre of Johannesburg, provides a commentary on the challenges that human rights, and the Constitutional Court, face in contemporary South Africa. The past knocks on the door of the present internally, as binaries are challenged, but also in the extremes and contrasts of the urban environment over which Constitution Hill casts its shadow. To the south is the run-down central business district (CBD), with hawker-filled streets overlooked by empty office space, subject to determined urban regeneration efforts; to the east is Hillbrow, vibrant but essentially a violent urban slum, home to many immigrants from elsewhere in the continent; to the west is Braamfontein, a bustling area where government, the University of the Witwatersrand, NGOs and shops sit cheek by jowl; to the north are the suburbs, sanctuary of the white and now black middle class as well as business, seeking security behind walls and barbed wire and in gated communities. Constitutional Hill is a confident proclamation of change that also sits nervously, insecure in its message and basic safety, surveying a landscape in which there is indeed change but not all of it by any means is on message. Constitution Hill's greatest challenge will be to reach out to its hinterland, for all four points of the compass to meet and feel ownership of the site and to see themselves, and their interests and actual lives, reflected in its human rights-based vision.

Both internal transformation and external panorama suggest that if it is to remain relevant in the present, the orientation of Constitution Hill will in time have to shift from a past–present orientation (a repeatedly used technique is that of counterposing new rights enshrined in the Constitution with conditions and laws under apartheid) to an ideal–reality trajectory in the present, as the apartheid past recedes as the dominant comparative benchmark. The most obvious form the ideal–reality trajectory takes at the moment is the 'We the People' exhibition, which each year will ask a different artist to respond to the question: 'How has the Constitution changed the lives of South Africans?' A reorientation to the ideal–reality axis would cast the present in a less flattering light and augment speaking truth to reconciliation with speaking truth to power. Is the Constitutional Court an effective means of furthering social justice? What discourses and strategies beyond human rights are needed to serve this end?[19]

Constitution Hill is a multi-dimensional site (heritage, tourism, business), seeking to build partnerships between government, the private sector and civil society. It has various project strands (including exhibitions, lekgotlas [gatherings or discussions] and educational work), and some of the public programmes do suggest a more provocative questioning of the present, e.g. 'encounter lekgotlas' between decision-makers such as politicians or judges and the public, or 'rapid response lekgotlas' responding to current controversies and issues raised by the Constitutional Court. Memorials do potentially provide a space for democratic strengthening (Brett *et al.* 2008), particularly if they can combine official, top-down and unofficial, local, community or grassroots inputs; partnership-based and more conflictual state–civil society relations; and reflections on continuities as well as change with reference to the past. At the moment the more conflictual ethos, challenging the realities rather than the ideals of the present, is not so visible in the physical memorial space itself, and remains generally undeveloped. Constitutional Hill will need to adapt if it wants to be an instigator as well as a register of change. In short, it is human rights, not just the site itself, that need to be understood as both sacred and living.

The third facet of speaking truth to place is the process dimension of memorial-making, which encompasses various kinds of truth-telling. Process dynamics at Constitution Hill consist of two components. The first is the set of narrative processes that contributed to the formation of the site, and the translation of prison and prisoner stories into exhibitions. A 'We the People Campaign' sought to bring the people to Constitution Hill, specifically those with historical relationships with the site, and take the Hill to the people. The latter outreach particularly targeted those who live and work in neighbouring areas, but also involved a broader canvassing of views on how the Constitution had impacted on people's lives in the first decade of democracy (the results of this road trip featured in the first 'We the People' exhibition).

Ex-political prisoners (in groups defined by factors such as the era when they were held, gender and political affiliation), ordinary criminal offenders and warders were invited to Constitution Hill for on-site workshops and to tell their stories. Using devices such as a 'narrative walkthrough', designed to evoke memories and enable individuals to spark off one another as well as space and place, generating elements of performance and re-enactment within processes of narration, a thick description of prison geography, history, life and culture began to emerge (Segal *et al.* 2006: 133–68). The translation of stories into representational forms extended beyond voice and text to include, for example, blanket and soap sculptures made for the exhibition by former prisoners. Time pressures and delivery dates coexisted with a desire to embrace an inclusive process (ibid.: 169–96).

The second process dynamic involves the visitor and visitor stories, and the efforts made to nurture an open site in terms of both access and ongoing formation. The site is envisaged as a way-station and not simply a destination, a place where people meet and through which they pass in their daily lives. Such openness resonates very powerfully with the ethos of the prison-become-memorial and the workings of institutions such as the Constitutional Court, but competes with forms of closure, notably those deemed necessary by security concerns, and the limited reach of human rights into the site's immediate and more distant surrounds. Seeking to duplicate the relationship created for returning prisoners between physical place, movement and narration, a further visitor-related process dynamic is the stress on structuring a memorial space that is interactive and evolving, premised on the site creating 'an endless flow of story' (Gunn, interview 21/2/2006). In the 'Response Room' the visitor is shown the process of making the exhibition and, whether a former prisoner or member of the public, invited to record his or her own memories and responses. An attempt to achieve inclusive process dynamics and the motif of passage or journey, in inhospitable terrain, underpin Constitutional Hill as physical site, narrative engine and, I would hope, as human rights vision.[20]

Memorials face many similar challenges to truth commissions when confronted with the task of representing history. To seek closure or ongoing debate, the complexities of balancing inclusive process against other demands, and the tensions captured in the truth template, are shared dilemmas. Constitution Hill has wrestled with core challenges and come up with some answers that differ from those reached by the TRC. Chiefly, its conceptualisation of human rights is broader, and it also questions certain human rights assumptions. By embracing a violations *and* struggle conception of human rights and unsettling a series of human rights-related binaries (criminal/political, human rights abuse/structural violence, legal/illegal), Constitution Hill not only provides a different lens on the past but also suggests an alternative set of subject positions from which former prisoners, visitors and the place itself can speak. For such innovation to continue, human rights must be both a sacred and a living creed, worthy of celebration but not infallible, granted a monopoly on progressive intent, nor silent about the shortcomings of the present. In essence, human rights, and memorials, must speak truth to reconciliation and to power in contemporary South Africa.

Public culture and novel truths

> Popular culture – film, theatre, music, and literature – often leads the way in helping a society face uncomfortable truths.
>
> (Cole and Barsalou 2006: 5)

Public culture has if anything outstripped public history in its engagement with the TRC.[21] Cultural production has used and recontextualised TRC testimony and itself provides a space for new truth-telling. The use of testimony is a familiar device in South African culture – for example, there is a long, oppositional tradition of testimony- and workshop-based theatre (Kruger 1999: 154–90) – but the TRC amplified this voice. Influence extended beyond 'high culture' to popular genres such as TV game shows, talk shows and soap operas: 'The ostensibly liberating practice of granting public platforms to the formerly silenced appears to have become a cathartic and defusing ritual in South African culture' (Lewis 2000: 175; also see Flockemann 2000: 144, and Nuttall and Michael 2000: 308–10). As well as the powerless being granted a voice in the public sphere, the private entered the public sphere in new ways. This has not always been edifying or substantial: the already cited culture of victimhood flourished; short-term catharsis did not translate into altered everyday lives; and so on.

More positively, in taking up and taking on the TRC, culture has meditated upon and deconstructed its keywords (truth, justice, reconciliation), reflected upon violence, violation and resistance, and reinvented its meta-narratives and metaphors – for example, bringing to the fore metaphors such as the cracked vase and textile images (quilting, tapestry, weaving), suggesting ongoing processes of reworking and the presence of the past in the present, rather than, say, the rainbow nation (de Kok 1998; Samuelson 2003). Cultural production has challenged the silences of apartheid and the TRC alike, and harboured its own silences (on cartoons, for example, see Verwoerd and Mabizela 2000: 2–3). It has reflected upon ambiguity and complexity, interrogating grey areas of experience and identity. Further, unlike official education and memorialisation, which reflect rather than pioneer attitude change, cultural responses can surface quickly to ask difficult questions and raise controversial issues. As such, TRC-related culture has redrawn the contours of South African culture (Fainman-Frenkel 2004), and provided its own commentary on the TRC's truth template.

While in Chapter 2 I recorded my disillusionment with the relativist stance towards truth adopted by many in the literary and cultural studies fraternity, I turned back to the work of individual artists and writers because of their ability to shed light on 'uncomfortable truths' and make a contribution to the TRC's 'unfinished business' agenda. I was particularly intrigued by post-apartheid fiction, because it addressed such a range of provocative themes over a sustained period of time. 'Novel truths' venture into areas that human rights and truth commission reports struggle to address due to resource constraints, methodological shortcomings or political sensitivities. By novel truths I mean the unique truth practices and repertoire available to the novel as a genre, asking questions rather than seeking answers, rooting out ambiguity, as distinct from genres such as the human rights report, state inquiry or official history.

Transitional South African literature has been preoccupied with the past. 'In postapartheid literature, the future has little future, whereas the future of the past is reasonably secure', write Attwell and Harlow (2000: 4). One outcome of the presence of the past has been an outpouring of autobiographical and historical fiction, autobiographies and memoirs, and generically hybrid texts; and one key trigger was the TRC. As elsewhere, the TRC's speaking truth to reconciliation discourse was duplicated and contested, and the debates of the truth template fully engaged. Here I will examine briefly five sub-groups of novels: (1) Elleke Boehmer's *Bloodlines* (2000) and Sindiwe Magona's *Mother to Mother* (1998) duplicate the speaking truth to reconciliation paradigm; (2) J. M. Coetzee's *Disgrace* (2000) and Achmat Dangor's *Bitter Fruit* (2004) contest the paradigm by documenting the enduring appeal of revenge and retribution; (3) a further pair of novels – Gillian Slovo's *Red Dust* (2000) and Jann Turner's *Southern Cross* (2002) – tackle spying and betrayal on both sides of the political spectrum, issues inadequately addressed by the TRC and, therefore, a legacy from the past that needs to be considered in other forums and spaces; (4) Sarah Penny's *The Beneficiaries* (2002) and Eprile's *The Persistence of Memory* (2005) address the similarly neglected question of a wider white complicity in apartheid's crimes; (5) while Zoë Wicomb's *Playing in the Light* (2006) unpacks one complex identity-related issue for blacks, broadly defined, namely situations where those designated 'coloured' under apartheid 'played white'.

Speaking truth to reconciliation

Elleke Boehmer's *Bloodlines* (2000) and Sindiwe Magona's *Mother to Mother* (1998) embrace forms of interpersonal, relational reconciliation through narrative.

Among the striking similarities between them are plots circling around black, in the inclusive sense, perpetrator/s and white victim/s, with the former clearly depicted as both perpetrator and victim. While neither mentions the TRC, both novels, set in the early 1990s and presumably written while the TRC was in full flow, can be understood as conducting their own mini-truth and reconciliation exercise.

Bloodlines opens with a bomb explosion outside a Natal beach-front supermarket, resulting in six white deaths. The everyday is shattered by the extraordinary. Joseph Makken, the bomber, is given a life sentence. Anthea Harding, journalist and girlfriend of one of the victims, Duncan Ferguson, seeks understanding and alternative remedies, '[a] story from the other side' (112), 'a story that will bring things together, create a pattern I can understand' (67). She approaches Dora Makken, the coloured mother of the bomber, who is initially reluctant to awaken, or give up ownership of, her family's resented, partially known past. The story they eventually unravel together reaches back to the Anglo-Boer War, to Afrikaner and Irish anti-Imperial struggles against the British and the collaboration between the two in the Anglo-Boer War. While the source of family shame is Joseph Macken, Dora's grandfather, an Irishman who fought with Afrikaners in the Anglo-Boer War, the reconciling story is that of her grandmother, Dollie Makken: 'the blank space in our hoped-for network of links and connections between Europe and Africa, then and now, between the different warring sides' (193).

Particular notions of history pervade this story: 'a different pattern of connection' moving away from cyclical repetition to the complex, shared mixing of '[a] ravelling web, a thicker story, bigger pictures' (128). Dora Makken and Anthea Harding search for a 'new story' (113), a 'different script … and not only among leaders and parties, but one to one' (128). The process raises provocative questions about the roles of the narrative collaborators and the dynamics of control, and the limits of narrative (What does history change? Is anger alleviated by being passed on?) as well as its possibilities (catharsis; the idea that Joseph can be saved by history, in that his part-Irish origins might assist in the appeal against the life sentence). In short, the novel suggests a possible transition within life story narration itself, from the violently collaborative narrative relations of apartheid to more cooperative collaboration, spanning the interpersonal (as here) and state–citizen interactions (as within the TRC), and the links between the two (Gready 2003: 10, 279, 283–84).

Sindiwe Magona's *Mother to Mother* (1998), a story told by the perpetrator's mother (Mandisa) to the mother of the victim, can be understood in similar terms. Provoked by a real incident, the killing of Amy Biehl, an American Fulbright scholar attacked by a group of youths in Guguletu, Cape Town, in August 1993, the account again seeks to provide an understanding of the perpetrator's (Mxolisi's) world and context. In a story that is at once hers and his, Mandisa details a past scarred by personal hardship, misfortune and trauma; dispossession, forced removal and police raids; the collapse of education and fraught intergenerational relations; and the slide of the townships into violence and ungovernability. Mother speaks to mother:

> But now, my Sister-Mother, do I help him hide? Deliver him to the police? Get him a lawyer? Will that mean I do not feel your sorrow for your slain daughter? Am I your enemy? Are you mine? What wrong have I done you ... or you me? ... Mother of the Slain, you whose heart is torn, know this: I have not slept since. Food turns to sawdust in my mouth. All joy has fled my house and my heart bleeds, it sorrows for you ... My Sister-Mother, we are bound in this sorrow ... We did not choose, we are the chosen.
> (Magona 1998: 198, 199, 201)

Son and daughter, linked as call and response: 'Your daughter. The imperfect atonement of her race. My son. The perfect host of the demons of his' (201); 'My son, the blind but sharpened arrow of the wrath of his race. Your daughter, the sacrifice of hers. Blindly chosen. Flung towards her sad fate by fortune's cruellest slings' (210). As with *Bloodlines*, *Mother to Mother* seeks a way forward by attempting to understanding the perspective of another, through connections rather than division, and via transformation (creating new identities, histories, power relations). Through such forms of speaking truth to reconciliation, relational reconciliation can be made real and societal fabric thickened.

Revenge and retribution

Coetzee's *Disgrace* (2000) revisits the central themes of this chapter, but in an altogether different tone. Testimony, truth-telling and apology are stifled and displaced. First, a committee of inquiry, with clear parallels to the TRC, hears a complaint of sexual harassment made by a student, Melanie Isaacs, against Professor David Lurie, and a second related charge of inaccurate record-keeping. Lurie pleads guilty. He puts forward a dry legal plea, rejecting the compromise of confession, acknowledgement, apology and counselling. He refuses offers to fully tell his side of the story, and rejects what he sees as the discourse of public debasement:

> I appeared before an officially constituted tribunal, before a branch of the law. Before that secular tribunal I pleaded guilty, a secular plea. That plea should suffice. Repentance is neither here nor there. Repentance belongs to another world, to another universe of discourse.
> (Coetzee 2000: 58)

But Lurie's 'universe of discourse' is no longer enough – 'These are puritanical times. Private life is public business. Prurience is respectable, prurience and sentiment. They wanted a spectacle ... I wouldn't oblige' (66). He is asked to resign.

Setting off for his daughter Lucy's smallholding near Salem in the Eastern Cape, he enters an old, yet also altogether new, frontier world. During his stay, a similarly evasive account of his actions, this time to his daughter, is interrupted by the arrival of three African strangers who rape his daughter, set him alight, rob them and shoot several dogs. In the aftermath of this violation, Lucy too will not tell the 'whole story' (110), the story of her rape, to him or to the police. For her it is a private matter; the right she claims is the right not to tell her story, not to have to defend or justify herself or her actions. And yet: 'Like a stain the story is spreading across the district. Not her story to spread but theirs: they are its owners' (115). In time, Lucy talks to her father on her own terms, trying to explain her decision to stay on.

Lurie visits George, in the Western Cape, delivering another elusive version of his side of the story and providing an apology to Melanie Isaac's father. He also prostrates himself before her mother and sister. Back in Cape Town his house has been ransacked – '[b]ooty; war reparations; another incident in the great campaign of redistribution' (176) – and he returns to a life in disarray and disgrace. News that Lucy is pregnant from the rape takes him back to the smallholding. One of the rapist-robbers moves onto the farm, a boy to whom Petrus – the African co-proprietor, neighbour, conspirator, potential protector/patron – has family obligations. Lucy agrees to a union with Petrus under which her land and child become his in exchange for protection. She states:

> I agree, it is humiliating. But perhaps that is a good point to start from again. Perhaps that is what I must learn to accept. To start at ground level. With nothing ... No cards, no weapons, no property, no rights, no dignity.
>
> (205)

In Coetzee's *Disgrace* the violence of the past informs the violence of the present. The right to remain silent is as important as the right to speak; speech is partial and occurs at unexpected times, in unexpected places. It will not appear on demand. There are no straightforward victims or perpetrators. Responsibility is repeatedly distorted: David takes on too little, Lucy too much, while, in an ironic twist, Petrus becomes the bystander and beneficiary, looking the other way (Nagy 2004). Truth and its dissemination are the servants of power. In contemporary South Africa there are many 'universes of discourse', and in this novel redistribution and reparation, and even a dreadful rite of passage required to remain and belong, are conducted through hatred, rape and robbery. The divide between races and generations is, if not absolute, at least stark. This is not a universe where truth speaks to reconciliation. In the context of the templates and contagions described in this chapter Coetzee's is an alien world; yet in the new South Africa it is very real.

Achmat Dangor's novel, *Bitter Fruit* (2004), revolves around the themes of memory, confession and retribution. Silas Ali encounters François du Boise in a shopping mall 19 years after the former security policeman raped his wife, Lydia, while he was made to listen. When he shares the news with his wife, the webs of containment that have formed within the family and everyday life through intersecting political and personal silences, secrets, denials and forgettings, around multiple layers of pain and betrayal, are broken open. Or more accurately they are reformulated alongside memory and confession as the narrative unfolds, new layers added on old.

Family life and history are saturated in the discourse and debates of the TRC, and society is firmly in a 'new liberated Age of Truth and Confession' (95). Silas, former member of an Umkhonto we Sizwe (MK) counter-intelligence unit, now works liaising between the Ministry of Justice and the TRC. But the TRC is a backdrop to the novel, providing one vocabulary among many to deal with political and personal pasts. The novel's characters betray an enduring scepticism about its ethos and speaking truth to reconciliation, in all spheres of life:

> We'll learn, all of us, to live in our spheres of silence, not saying the unsayable, denying everyone the pleasure of seeing us suffer the divine virtue of the brave new country: truth. We have to learn to become ordinary, learn how to lie to ourselves, and to others, if it means keeping the peace, avoiding discord and strife, like ordinary people everywhere in the world.
> (Dangor 2004: 138)

The novel concludes with the publication of the TRC report set against one of the alternative vocabularies of transition, revenge, in the form of a double murder. Mikey/Michael, the son of Silas and Lydia, murders two rapists. The first is Johan Viljoen, veteran of the struggle and father of Vinu, a friend who confesses to Michael that her father has raped her since she was 14. The second, having read his mother's diary and discovered he is a child of rape, is du Boise, whose death interrupts two other forms of closure, his amnesty application and death from cancer. This is Michael killing his past. His future lies elsewhere, Islam and India, as he searches for a new beginning.

Bitter Fruit is one of a number of recent South African novels that examine violence that is folded into intimate, interpersonal, everyday relationships. If relationships are damaged, marked by betrayal, then the past enters the present as 'poisonous knowledge'. Such violence is often dealt with by a descent into everyday life, by learning to inhabit the world and relationships again through the everyday work of recovery and repair (Das 2001). This is a useful framework with which to examine post-TRC novels that deal with the issues of spying and betrayal.

Spying and betrayal

In Gillian Slovo's *Red Dust* (2000), the town of Smitsrivier, near Port Elizabeth, is turned upside down by the arrival of the TRC: 'Every rule by which all

Smitsrivier had once lived out its life seemed to have been vanquished' (84). Dirk Henricks, a former security policeman, has applied for amnesty in connection with an assault on Alex Mpondo, now a member of parliament, in 1985. Hendricks is in jail for his role in another death, which is the subject of a separate amnesty application.

Red Dust plots the multiple reversals of a slowly unfolding TRC amnesty hearing. While Hendricks remembers to save himself, Mpondo has until this moment survived by forgetting, but is now forced against his will to revisit his past. The white policeman applies for amnesty and, therefore, has to answer questions; the torture victim interrogates his torturer, now a prisoner. The former reveals a betrayal, that Mpondo divulged where weapons were stored; the latter forces Hendricks to divulge information not in his amnesty application. Both confront the intimacy of their relationship, the violence of their shared knowledge (183–201). The torturer as victim faces the victim robbed of everything, even of his anger. The victim withdraws from the amnesty hearing: 'It was such a struggle to free myself from that man's clutches … I won't be his victim again … I am not and I will not be, their victim'. The perpetrator's victim, the TRC's victim: the difference is that Mpondo can now choose to refute this identity (128–32, 220–21, 316).

Publicly, community heroes, black and white, are turned into pariahs or fallen icons. The layers of solidarity and betrayal, within the security police *and* political opposition, in the past *and* present, are complex. Intimate knowledge, role reversals and betrayal, real and imagined, blur the victim/perpetrator divide. In *Red Dust* the truth is compromised/compromising and incomplete, truths mixed with lies. There is a vague and ambiguous sense of moving on, but reconciliation is unable to shake itself free from power, old and new. Poisonous knowledge abounds.

Jann Turner's *Southern Cross* (2002) casts Paul Lewis and Anna Kriel as lovers and part of the same underground cell, a political and propaganda unit of the ANC in South Africa. Lewis, along with fellow cell member Jacob Oliphant, is shot dead in April 1987 while on a mission, their bodies found on the road between Mafikeng and Vryburg. Kriel's personal quest for truth and justice eventually spans testifying before a HRV hearing of the TRC, and interviews with Colonel Ignatius Du Preez, an imprisoned former death squad member clearly modelled on Eugene de Kock, and other policemen. Among this latter group is former security police captain Frans Nel, whose amnesty application/hearing for the killings is also part of the narrative.

The quest quickens as allegations are made that Lewis was a policeman and security police spy. This news casts a shadow over Kriel's life – '*My life has not been a lie*' (171) – and over her work at the Ministry of Safety and Security. Gradually the evidence of betrayal becomes irrefutable, augmented by the revelation that Lewis had been having an affair with Frans Nel's wife:

> Here was a poisonous truth … dismantling the house of her spirit, cornerstone after cornerstone crumbling to dust until there was nothing left … Her

| 186 | Speaking truth to reconciliation |

entire life was a lie ... All the innocence and purity and idealism of her life and her love for Paul were destroyed ... Everything had to be revisited, everything mistrusted.

(179, 186, 207)

As Kriel closes in on the truth, it becomes clear, as she is followed and others shot at and killed, that someone does not want her to succeed in her quest. The trail leads to her former underground cell commander, Joe Dladla, now Assistant Police Commissioner and Kriel's lover, who it transpires was also a security police captain and double agent in the past. Dladla was Lewis's handler. He ordered and carried out his murder because Lewis was about to hand himself over to the ANC and tell them everything. More poison; many shades of grey in the new, as in the old, South Africa.

And the truth was more awful and more familiar than she cared to know. The truth was no acid pellet of knowledge delivered to the Commission for sanitising and sealing and disposing in the dustbin of history. It was a dull mirror, which showed the dirt that clung to everyone, instead of cleansing and absolving all.

(Turner 2002: 300)

But the consoling thread of the narrative is that Kriel resurrects herself from self-doubt and recrimination by hunting down a truth that ultimately frees her from the past, that reactivates stalled time so she can inhabit the present and embrace the future: 'She had restored [her future] to herself' (309).

Beneficiaries

In two post-apartheid South African novels, perhaps as a statement of what ought to have happened more often in reality, white beneficiaries are drawn into the TRC process and towards a re-engagement with South Africa. Because of the TRC's narrow focus on victims and perpetrators, white beneficiaries, as we have seen, were able to condemn apartheid and distance themselves from any complicity in its abuses.

In Penny's *The Beneficiaries* (2002), Laeticia ('Lally'), while growing up, has some initial awakenings about the delusional character of her life which question authority and apartheid and, as a result, begins to stumble towards an alternative regime of language and truth (45–69, 94–107). In this state of personal transition, as a 16-year-old girl, she becomes 'the almost-spectator/almost-participant of a backwater murder mystery' (203). As the novel closes she is drawn back to South Africa from her desultory and transitory émigré life in London by a TRC investigation into the incident she witnessed.

Pim, a fellow searcher for the truth in *The Beneficiaries* – unlike Lally, he maintains his distance and stays in England – and Sweetbread in Tony Eprile's *The Persistence of Memory* (2005), are both white males traumatised by military service and their participation in the war in countries neighbouring South Africa. In the army, Sweetbread remains on the margins, a cook and then a cameraman. Nevertheless, as witness and combatant he can no longer remain a mere bystander, or expect others to do his dirty work for him. From the start he is challenged by Captain Lyddie: 'So what did you do about it? ... you think your silent objection means you have no responsibility. All you had to do was say *Stop it!* and that's what I would have done' (133); 'I hate that look that says, *I don't like this, but I'm not going to get involved.* You're part of this, old son, like it or not. So now you know' (136). Sweetbread has the 'poisoned gift' (10, 255) of perfect memory in a land where history is fluid, imagined, disputed and eventually fashionable. He is a model citizen, therefore, of the new South Africa, a one-man metaphor for a country obsessed with the past but uncertain about the future. The 'gift' is put to work as he testifies at an amnesty hearing, contesting Captain, now Major, Lyddie's amnesty application, while he himself seeks exorcism and spiritual succour through an African diviner.

Novels foregrounding what might be termed progressive beneficiaries shed light on the interface between beneficiaries' lives and the TRC's remit, sites of 'suspended responsibility' (Boehmer 2000: 7), unveiling a spectrum of complicities and resistances, alienations and belongings, and subtle reflections on the TRC's methodologies. Sweetbread, for example, who believes that white beneficiaries should be challenged to recognise what was done on their behalf and make amends, remarks: 'Sure, lies trap you into more lies, into doing things you wouldn't believe of yourself, but I'm not at all sure the reverse is true [that the truth sets you free]' (Eprile 2005: 259–60, also see 219–20, 276). If the aim of truth commissions is to facilitate both the fullest possible accountability and a new sense of unity and belonging, individuals such as the protagonists in these novels need to be engaged too (to stay on in their home country as the two main characters here do, rather than emigrate, for example).

Complex black identities

Whites were not the only ones whose complicity was complex and untouched by the TRC. In Wicomb's *Playing in the Light* (2006), Marion Campbell's inquiry into her past is sparked by a newspaper story featuring the testimony of Patricia Williams at the TRC about her persecution and torture at the hands of the security police – her face is a call to remember, a bearer of resemblances. Delving into her family past Marion discovers that Williams is a family member, and uncovers stories of both resistance and complicity. She is a coloured from a 'play-white' family which sought rebirth through obliteration of their past under apartheid (the exact opposite of the TRC's rationale). Playing white is beautifully drawn as a condition of hiding rather than playing, of constant vigilance, betrayal of family, doing the best for one's children, of internalised bigotry and even resistance. As such, in this novel personal historical inquiries into playing white shine a distinctive spotlight on the past, highlighting overlooked forms of violence, complex identities, difficult relationships between the past and present, and particular forms of disclosure and secrecy.

These novels embark on new conversations about, and explore fresh ways of recounting, violence, human rights and history. As such they add their own voice to the truth template debates. Perhaps their major contribution is in providing alternative grammars of transition, speaking to silences, 'uncomfortable truths' and the 'unfinished business' of the TRC: revenge and retribution, spying and betrayal, the complicities of all races in apartheid. With greater depth than the TRC, fiction plots the passage of the public, political and performative into the private and intimate, the past into the present, and journeys in the opposite direction. Such rites of passage can be profoundly unsettling, even damaging, as well as truth-bearing and cathartic. Novel truths also escape the previous rigid certainties, stereotypes and characterisations of the struggle and struggle novels (Gready 2003), and the related identity oppositions and homogenisations of the TRC. Characterisation and identity are cast in shades of grey devoid of absolute divides between eras and actors, reflecting ambiguity and complexity. Yet as micro-level studies, the novels generally escape sweeping, banal statements of equivalence and relativisations of truth. Speaking truth to reconciliation or power is similarly presented in a nuanced light. Truth is as much beholden to as spoken to power. While the TRC is a strong presence in all of these novels, the real work of speaking truth to reconciliation, where it happens at all, takes place off-stage. Truth-telling is partial, fragmentary and evolves according to an unpredictable calendar. Reconciliation is ultimately rooted in the rhythms of everyday life, the opportunities and disappointments of becoming ordinary.

Conclusion

The TRC initiated a societal debate about the past, but also about the dynamics and plausibility of speaking truth to reconciliation, in a range of different sites and spaces. Here, as elsewhere, the TRC had a rather rudimentary conceptual framework which has been affirmed, critiqued and elaborated on by others. On this broad stage, over time, anything but the standardisation or formalisation of institutional modes of truth-telling has occurred. It is worth returning briefly to the five strands of the truth template in the light of the case studies examined in this chapter.

Much civil society truth-telling revolves around violence, and indeed gross violations of human rights under apartheid, but the narrative terrain extends to other kinds and eras of violence, and to continuities as well as discontinuities between past and present. More broadly, there is a sense that many injustices, and the structural violence, of the past, are very much alive in the present. As such, the present is increasingly seen in a more critical light. The pendulum is perhaps swinging back from speaking truth to reconciliation to speaking truth to power, as epitomised by the journey travelled by the Khulumani Support Group from TRC support structure to an advocacy group, or even social movement, championing economic justice.

Profiles of silence and public discourse are reworked rather than reversed. The IHM, for example, focuses on the emotional and spiritual truth and not fact-finding. Novels reveal the messy afterlife of betrayal and complicity in all political camps and racial groups, in personal lives, and in both the past and present. Novels register various 'universes of discourse', including some passed over by the TRC (e.g. revenge). Finally, testimonial sites mobilise the identity of victimhood, but also map grey and multiple identities, provide some mechanisms facilitating identity transformation, and increase the range of identity positions and places from which people can speak. One outcome has been a questioning of the effects of truth-telling and the emergence of different understandings of reconciliation (emotional and spiritual journey; political and economic struggle). The TRC's success has been to inspire and legitimise these sites which may assist it in achieving its goals, but may also nurture counter-discourses.

One reading of possible futures would suggest the following. Civil society actors and communities are engaged in the making and taking of safe and public spaces for voice as/and action (Gready 2003a: 7–10). In such sites or spaces, claiming the right to voice, a right to be heard on one's own terms – Werbner's 'right of recountability' (1998: 1) – takes us closer to Friedman's (2006) rights-based participation, Cornwall's (2004) 'popular' spaces of governance, and Pells's lived participation (2009; see Chapter 2). This is a form of political action, reclaiming history, justice and the social fabric of communities. There is a momentum at work. Voices creating space for other voices, political struggles create space for other struggles (Sanford 2003: 180–231, 2003a; Minow 1998: 101–2). This represents a further, less media-driven pattern of dissemination and suggests a political future in which the TRC's truth template is turned on the present and the ANC's failure to tackle the inequality, poverty and social/criminal violence which are now the most enduring legacies of the apartheid past. In the terms of Das and Kleinman (2002), with which we began, genuine political recognition and citizenship require no less.

The TRC's reconciliation lite, as well as the shortcomings of some of the sites discussed in this chapter, indicates the need to combine truth-telling with other initiatives seeking to ground reconciliation in everyday life, socio-economic improvement and hopes for the future rather than the tragedies of the past. This second reconciliation paradigm is the subject of the next chapter.

Notes

1 Others have conceived of the relationship between truth and reconciliation differently. Gibson (2004) specifically tackles the research question: has truth led to reconciliation in South Africa? He argues that the TRC's main objective was reconciliation, and

identifies its four strands as interracial reconciliation, political tolerance, support for the principles of human rights and the rule of law, and the legitimacy of political institutions. As such:

> A reconciled South African is one who respects and trusts those of other races, who is tolerant of those with different political views, who supports the extension of human rights to all South Africans, and who extends legitimacy and respect to the major governing institutions of South Africa's democracy.
>
> (4)

This definition is in the thin reconciliation camp, concerned with 'broader socio-political aspects of the reconciliation of all South Africans, not just victims and perpetrators' (14). Truth is understood as an authoritative account or collective memory of the past (not individual truth-telling), leading to the hypothesis that those who accept the TRC's version of the past are more likely to be reconciled. On these terms, Gibson concludes that the TRC process did contribute to reconciliation (see Chapters 1 and 2 for further discussion of Gibson's work).

2 Chapter 2 questions the truth–reconciliation linkage from a different perspective (examining the interpretation and reception of testimony in an increasingly globalised public sphere). A far-reaching critique, assessing the relationship between truth and peace, is provided by Mendeloff (2004). Mendeloff (ibid.: 356) argues:

> Claims about the peace-promoting effects of formal truth-telling mechanisms rest far more on faith than on sound logic or empirical evidence. The literature has done a poor job of specifying the logic of truth-telling arguments, defining and clarifying key concepts, operationalising key variables, indicating the conditions under which proposed relationships hold, providing compelling empirical evidence to support core assumptions, and testing claims systematically against competing explanations … In short, truth-telling advocates claim more about the power of truth-telling than logic or evidence dictates.

A rigorous deconstruction follows of truth claims: that truth encourages social healing and reconciliation, promotes justice, facilitates a historical record, serves a public education function, aids institutional reform, promotes democracy, and pre-empts and deters future atrocity. These arguments chime with a core observation of this book, that claims made on behalf of the keywords of transitional justice, and their interrelationships, often lack conceptual coherence and empirical support.

3 There are various manifestations of the collective, and it should be noted that it is as unhelpful to overlook collectives/communities as it is to automatically conflate the collective with the nation. There is undoubtedly a collective and social dimension to suffering/perpetration and recovery/responsibility.

4 Similar criticisms have been made of interventions informed by the diagnosis and standard verbal treatment methodologies of post-traumatic stress disorder (Honwana 1999, writing about Angola and Mozambique). Claims of cultural inappropriateness have not had a high profile in relation to the South African TRC and its testimonial ethos, although the importance of culturally sensitive readings of testimony has been emphasised (Krog *et al.* 2009). The question of appropriateness has emerged as an important issue in a number of African contexts where secrecy and evasiveness may characterise social exchange, or ritual may be at the heart of reconciliatory dynamics. With reference to the Sierra Leone Truth and Reconciliation Commission, see Shaw (2005: 9) on social forgetting as a route to reconciliation: 'Social forgetting is a different process from individual forgetting, in that people still have personal memories

of the violence. But speaking of the violence – especially in public – was (and is) viewed as encouraging its return'. In a similar vein, Buckley-Zistel (2006) argues in relation to Rwanda that while certain features of the past are remembered (the event of the genocide, as rupture), others are forgotten (the causes of the genocide, and decades of tensions between Hutu and Tutsi) as a form of 'chosen amnesia', seen as essential for local coexistence.

5 To plot patterns of continuity and change, this template should be placed alongside another, devised by the author in an earlier work developing a theory of life story-praxis in the context of political struggle (imprisonment, exile and homecoming: Gready 2003). One noteworthy observation is that this earlier template stresses agency and resistance, while that inaugurated by the TRC focuses on suffering and victimhood (also see Nuttall and Michael 2000, on victimhood as the autobiographical register most likely to be heard in this later era).

6 International jurisprudence defining the attributes of, and boundaries around, the relevant groups that need to be targeted for the act of genocide to have been committed has taken a different position, considering the perceptions of victims (self-perception) and perpetrators (perceptions of others), thereby acknowledging that identities are contested, social constructs (Verdirame 2000).

7 Providing one example of these dividends, the rights of victims to justice, truth and reparation are detailed in the Basic Principles and Guidelines on the Right to a Remedy and Reparation for Victims of Gross Violations of International Human Rights Law and Serious Violations of International Humanitarian Law, adopted and proclaimed by UN General Assembly resolution 60/147 of 16 December 2005, UN Doc. A/RES/60/147. In South Africa there is now an effective victims' lobby in relation to crime which has successfully campaigned for recognition of core victims' rights (see Chapter 4). The *Service Charter for Victims of Crime in South Africa* and *Minimum Standards on Services for Victims of Crime* (available at: www.doj.gov.za), for example, recognise seven rights: the right to be treated with fairness and with respect for one's dignity and privacy; the right to offer information; the right to receive information; the right to protection; the right to assistance; the right to compensation; and the right to restitution. Victims/survivors of apartheid-era human rights abuses, unfortunately, have not been afforded the same entitlements.

8 Among the other commentators who have attempted to problematise victims/perpetrators as human rights categories and characterisations in South African history, Borer (2003) highlights differences within and overlaps between the categories, and questions of scope and degree (direct/indirect, active/passive, omission/commission, individual/group–institution–sector–community). In a general discussion, Huyse (2003: 54–55, 67–68) distinguishes between individual/collective, direct/indirect, and first- and second-generation victims, as well as primary/indirect and individual/collective offenders.

9 Tshepo Madlingozi, from the Khulumani Support Group, makes an interesting distinction between 'good victims' and 'bad victims' (Madlingozi 2009 and 2010: 220–21). The former are frequently invited to tell their stories, which emphasise moving on from the past and catharsis for the nation. In contrast, the latter continue to struggle for reparations and social justice, denouncing the 'elite compromise' that brought about South African's transition. Different facilitative process yield different identity-related outcomes, not all of which are necessarily or immediately transformative.

10 In *The Guilt of Nations: Restitution and Negotiating Historical Injustices*, Elzar Barkan (2000) makes the interesting counter-argument that the emergence of the discourse of restitution, broadly defined, represents the increased salience of victim *and* perpetrator identities in contemporary politics and provides a framework or mechanism for debate and democratic deepening.

11 The discussion which follows draws on the following sources: Kayser (2001); Lapsley (1997, 2002); Mngese and Lonzi (interview 29/8/2002); Mngese (interview 4/4/2005, 11/12/2009); also see Kayser (1999, 2001a); TRC (1998, Vol. 5: 431–32) and TRC (2003, Vol. 6: 158). Karakashian (2007) includes an evaluation of IHM's work; the IHM website is a further useful resource: www.healingofmemories.co.za.
12 In addition to those cited in the text, this discussion draws on interviews with Gunn (27/8/2002, 5/4/2005, 21/2/2006); Khalipha (7/4/2005); Kumalo (4/9/1998, 15/8/2002, 17/8/2002, 22/8/2003, 22/4/2005); and Shezi (4/9/1998, 22/4/2005). Also see the Khulumani Support Group website: www.khulumani.net and TRC (2003, Vol. 6: 156–59).
13 See, for example, the work of the Western Cape branch of the Khulumani Support Group described in Chapter 2; and the publication *Katorus Stories*. The latter was the result of an art and memory workshop held by the Khulumani Support Group in Katorus on the East Rand in February and March 2007, which was designed to explore and record memories of repression and violence in the area.
14 Barsalou and Baxter (2007: 9) argue that truth commission recommendations relating to memorialisation are largely an 'afterthought':

> To date, truth commissions have not articulated in much detail what memorialisation means, how it should be connected to other transitional justice processes, who should take charge, and other specific points of consideration. By not taking into greater account the role of memorialisation and the educational processes that should accompany it, truth commissions are losing an important opportunity to extend their impact.
> (Barsalou and Baxter 2007: 10; also see Brett *et al.* 2008: especially 29, on the need to link memorialisation to broader transitional justice strategies)

15 There are a number of reference points for place-based sites in South Africa. The list below is by no means exhaustive. As already mentioned, place occupies a particular niche in the discourse and delivery of reparations. Thus, among the reference points for post-apartheid memorialisation in South Africa has been the TRC's call for symbolic reparations (TRC 1998, Vol. 5: 188–90). The government's National Legacy Project scheme, officially constituted in 1996 and overseen by the Department of Arts, Culture, Science and Technology, is a second spur, partly framed in terms of symbolic reparations. This operates very much to a unifying, nation-building remit. Initial projects included Freedom Park and Constitution Hill, both of which are discussed below (Xaba and Monis, interview 28/4/2005). A third pillar of memorialisation is the legislative framework, provided by the National Heritage Resources Act (No. 25 of 1999), which established the South African Heritage Resources Agency (SAHRA: see www.sahra.org.za/) to oversee management of the heritage resources of the country and provide for heritage management at all levels of government. Fourth, there are a number of global conduits for memorialisation – these include transitional justice discourse; the International Coalition of Historic Site Museums of Conscience (of which Constitution Hill and District Six Museum are members: www.sitesofconscience.org/) and UNESCO's World Heritage sites (which include Robben Island: http://whc.unesco.org/).
16 I owe a debt for insights into the above-mentioned challenges, and into memorialisation practice more generally, to interviews with Gunn (21/2/2006), Hlongwane (26/4/2005), Itzkin (25/4/2005), Kgomommu (29/4/2005), Layne (8/4/2005), Naidu (25/4/2005), Ndlovu (24/4/2005), O'Donoghue (31/3/2006), Rassool (7/4/2005), and Seleti (7/3/2006). The discussion on Constitution Hill is based on interviews with Segal (28/4/2005 and 7/3/2006) and numerous visits to Constitution Hill.

Also see Gevisser (2004), Segal *et al.* (2006), and the website at www.constitutionhill.org.za/.

17 Other memorials have grappled with which forms of violence and identities to feature. Freedom Park hosts a Wall of Names, part of the Sikhumbuto memorial, which while organised around episodes of violence – eight conflicts dating back to pre-colonial wars, a time frame that significantly expands on the TRC's historical range – celebrates not victims, but the struggles of heroes and heroines who fell in the fight for freedom and humanity. Freedom Park's discourse of reconciliation draws on that of the TRC (reparation, healing), and on emancipating an indigenous African spirituality and voice informed by former President Mbeki's African Renaissance philosophy (Seleti, interview 7/3/2006; also see www.freedompark.co.za/). Some see this as another, homogenising, top-down meta-narrative, but it provides a different lens on the histories, violence and identities thought to link truth and reconciliation.

18 A number of South African memorials resonate provocatively with the landscape around them. At the Hector Pieterson Memorial and Museum, the visitor both 'walks through the narrative' and 'talks to the landscape outside', through strategically placed windows that identify key places in the Soweto-led uprisings of 1976 and the community's political history (Hlongwane, interview 26/4/2005; Ndovu, interview 24/4/2005). Another, equally evocative, example is the Apartheid Museum, a Johannesburg-based museum charting the rise and fall of apartheid: www.apartheidmuseum.org/. The Krok brothers, who in part made their money from skin-lightening creams, were required to fund its construction as a condition for being granted the licence to build the gambling haunt, Gold Reef City, which is the museum's proximate neighbour. It is hard to know whether the irony of this juxtaposition is delicious or obscene. Dubow (2004: 377) writes wryly: 'There's a PhD waiting to be written about an emerging pattern in the new South Africa: the thesis that good works tend to happen more quickly, or happen only, if the pursuit of a gaming licence is involved'.

19 The issue of whether memorials sever the past from the present or explore the legacies of the past in the present plays out differently in different contexts. A related issue is whether an intervention should be a definitive statement and form of closure, or interactive, an unfinished account and part of an ongoing debate. The Hector Pieterson Memorial and Museum is an example of a site that through community engagement, ongoing research and a fundamental sense of non-resolution about the issues addressed, is likely to be a lightning rod for ongoing disagreements about the role of various actors (youth, at the fore in the memorial at present, ANC, PAC, etc.) in the 1976 uprisings (Hlongwane, interview 26/4/2005; Ndlovu, interview 24/4/2005). Furthermore, the narrative told by the Memorial and Museum is cut off in the 1970s specifically to leave its message 'raw and unresolved', and avoid the cliché that arrival in the present of reconciliation has become (Ndlovu, interview 24/4/2005). Others feel that it leaves the visitor in a 'time warp' and represents a missed opportunity to engage with the Soweto community and youth, and the issues they face today (Segal, interview 28/4/2005).

20 Process-related debates must tackle the tricky question of reasonable limits to participation, especially if participation is framed as rights-based. Many NGO and civil society 'how to' manuals privilege process, especially the need to involve victims/survivors and local communities in the making of public history, as a means of providing acknowledgement, catharsis and empowerment (Barsalou and Baxter 2007; Brett *et al.* 2008; Naidu 2004, 2004a; and Suttner 2006 on the 'democratic stream' in South African politics and heritage). To operationalise this process agenda is easier said than done, however. For projects involving national, provincial or local government an alternative discourse of 'delivery', within budget and on time for the opening on a particular commemorative day, has at times prevailed (Kgomommu, interview 29/4/2005).

For artists and architects the internal prerogatives of their trade may dominate. NGOs may also be too inclined to lead rather than follow. There is already a contested politics of memorialisation and a second generation of post-apartheid memorials, replacing ill-conceived first attempts. Two Cape Town examples are the replacement memorials for the Guguletu Seven and the Trojan Horse killings in Athlone, both commemorating apartheid-era shooting incidents – which testify to the fact that the means are as important as the ends in memorialisation, as in all facets of transitional justice.

21 A sense of TRC-related cultural output can be gained from a snapshot of its volume and range. In the art world, there were noteworthy exhibitions, for example the 'Faultlines' exhibition was staged in the Castle of Good Hope in Cape Town (1996), while 'Truth Veils' was held at the Gertrude Posel Gallery at the University of the Witwatersrand (1999). There have also been powerful individual contributions: these include Sue Williamson's interactive artworks *Truth Games* and *Can't Forget, Can't Remember* (Williamson 2002), and Judith Mason's haunting triptych *The Blue Dress*, now part of the Constitutional Court collection (www.constitutionalcourt.org.za/). On TRC-related art, see Bester (2004); Coombes (2003: 243–78); and Rassool *et al.* (2000: 118–21). Cartoonists had a field day with the contradictions and sometimes plain lunacy of TRC proceedings (Verwoerd and Mabizela 2000), while photography captured a complex landscape of surfaces and subtexts – examples include the photographic essay 'Unfinished Business' (Grundlingh *et al.* 2000) and Jillian Edelstein's book *Truth and Lies* (2001). Documentary films such as *The Gugulethu Seven* (dir. Wilson, 2000), *Long Night's Journey into Day* (dir. Reid and Hoffman, 2000) and the corpus of Mark Kaplan on disappearances (*Where Truth Lies, Between Joyce and Remembrance* and *Betrayal*) are forms of record, investigation, and provide both commentary on, and critique of, the TRC. Feature or drama films from *Forgiveness* (dir. Gabriel, 2004) to *In My Country* (dir. Boorman, 2004, based on Krog's *Country of My Skull*) and *Red Dust* (dir. Hooper, 2004, based on Gillian Slovo's novel of the same name) fictionalised and dramatised the real. Theatrical productions too have flourished, *Ubu and the Truth Commission* (Taylor 1998) being perhaps the best-known example, while *Truth in Translation* (www.truthintranslation.org), which highlights the role of interpreters in truth commission work, is also a notably contribution. Victims and survivors themselves contributed to this rich theatrical vein, notably in *The Story I am About to Tell – Indaba Engizoyixoxa*, featuring three members of the Khulumani Support Group, and *He Left Quietly*, developing the life story of one of their number, Duma Kumalo. See Chapter 2 for more on Khulumani's cultural work.

Chapter 6

Reconciliation, relationships and the everyday

This chapter shifts attention from alternative public spheres to the repair of relationships, and specifically community and economic relationships. It does so because these are the structural relationships, relatively unexamined and untouched by the TRC process, which still undermine the project of reconciliation at all levels of South African society.[1] As such they lie at the heart of what I will term the recovery and reimagining of the everyday. At the outset this agenda requires a three-pronged argument: defining the everyday, making the case for a focus on relationships, and situating reconciliation within post-conflict repair and reconstruction.

Reconciliation and the everyday

In a collection of essays entitled *South African Literature and Culture: Rediscovery of the Ordinary* (1994), Njabulo Ndebele called on black South African literature to move on from too narrow a focus on politics and protest. He critiqued a superficiality in fiction that did not probe beyond 'the interaction of surface symbols' and a clichéd cast of characters (28). Apartheid was dealt with on its own, often binary, terms with scant regard for 'processes in character development or in social evolution' (32). A preoccupation with spectacle was surface symbol's twin:

> The spectacular documents; it indicts implicitly; it is demonstrative, preferring exteriority to interiority; it keeps the larger issues of society in our minds, obliterating the details; it provokes identification through recognition and feeling ... it calls for emotion rather than conviction ... it confirms without necessarily offering a challenge. It is the literature of the powerless identifying the key factor responsible for their powerlessness.
>
> (Ndebele 1994: 49)

The TRC can be placed within an established South African tradition of the symbolic and the spectacular. An urgent task was deferred: 'Tomorrow the everyday work of daily stories' (Boehmer 2000: 112). As noted in earlier chapters, the implications of this approach were in some instances more positive, notably in its dramatic impact on the public sphere and media. But the impact of the public sphere and media on the everyday was uneven.

While the spectacular tradition reifies the individual and the symbolic, the everyday resituates the individual in webs of relationships, and nurtures the mechanisms and imaginative capacities to go beyond patterns of rediscovery to create social relationships and ordinariness anew (Ross 2003: 133–61; van der Merwe 2003). Reconciliation situated within the everyday is understood in this chapter as a series of reorientations or transformations: from the extraordinary, spectacular and individual to the ordinary and social processes of change; from binary to multi-dimensional identities and ways of viewing the world; from suffering to living; and from the past (rediscovery) to the present and future (creation).

In *The Cry of Winnie Mandela: A Novel*, Ndebele (2003) practices what he preaches, retelling the story of Winnie Madikisela-Mandela, whose later life and appearance before the TRC exemplifies a 'culture of political posture' (62), surface symbol and spectacle (Boraine 2000: 221–57; Krog 1998: 243–60; Meredith 1999: 221–70; TRC 1998, Vol. 2: 555–82). In part this is done through a gendered narrative template: departure, waiting, return and the 'zone of absence without duration' (Ndebele 2003: 6–7), 'a great South African story not yet told' (1; also see TRC 2003, Vol. 7: 9). This is also a great human rights story, a template for disappearances, itself often untold and here rearticulated for everyday structures of oppression. The template is applied to the lives and through the stories of four women; it spans the ordinary and the extraordinary, everything from migrancy to various forms of political activism. Each woman in turn enters into conversation with and questions Madikisela-Mandela, whose life was so publicly stamped with the same template. She responds, and engages in self-reflection and internal dialogue. In the process, Madikisela-Mandela is folded back into the everyday through a narrative journey that is intimate, multi-dimensional, relational, transformative and deeply unsettling.

This chapter also argues that reconciliation is intrinsically relational. It is 'a relationship that is restored [or created anew] to the extent that the parties can move on in peace while accepting each other's integrity' (Van Zyl Slabbert 2000: 70). A capacity to restore and create relationships in an ongoing way is essential to the fabric of the everyday. It involves a double-take, and gradual reorientation, between reclaiming and a fresh start, continuity and change, past and future. If reconciliation is relational, it requires personal encounters and dialogue embedded in a social process. An ability to speak *and* to listen is rooted in a sense of self at a crossroads, at once sufficiently empowered, self-reflective and empathetic, risk-taking and trustful; and a sense of the other that includes a desire to understand their perspectives, fears and hopes, and a capacity to put yourself in their shoes.[2] Such interactions can be transformative, founded on collaboratively examining the stereotypes, identities, histories/narratives and power relations that fuelled past divisions, on being prepared to raise one's eyes to consider altered horizons of possibility without yet knowing the ultimate destination. Over time, in difficult processes and problem-solving in daily lives, new relationships and social networks emerge.[3] It is precisely this social, relational facility, especially across races, that the TRC neglected and South Africa still lacks.[4]

A third, and final, scene-setting argument is that reconciliation needs to be seen as part of a broader programme of post-conflict repair and reconstruction.[5] Some route maps are available. Fletcher and Weinstein (2002; also see Stover and Weinstein 2004) propose an 'ecological model' of social breakdown and social reconstruction, influenced particularly by the forms of collective, mass violence seen in Rwanda and the former Yugoslavia in the 1990s. In contrast to what the authors see as the dominant transitional justice discourse, which has a misplaced faith in criminal trials as agents of social repair and reconciliation, this approach to social reconstruction envisages a multi-dimensional, synchronised frame of analysis and response. In this setting reconciliation is 'a process', requiring empathy, forgiveness and altruism, 'that takes place on an individual level and may not be mandated, but rather interventions may lay the foundation for reconciliation to occur in the future, if at all'. It draws on 'higher order' needs (safety, love, esteem, self-actualisation) that cannot be addressed until more basic needs are met (Fletcher and Weinstein 2002: 623–25).

This model is emblematic of the rise of holistic approaches within transitional justice. Yet, as noted in the introduction, there is now a need to move beyond such wish-lists to investigate more difficult questions about how interventions can be prioritised and sequenced in resource-constrained and politically contested environments. Nevertheless, the model does provide a conceptualisation and contextualisation of reconciliation – as needing to engage a broad range of actors, as a process/objective requiring that certain prerequisites are fulfilled or basic needs met, and as one, interactive, component of social reconstruction.

Providing further assistance, Galant and Parlevliet's (2005: 114–18) four dimensions of human rights can be applied so as to identify the multi-dimensional nature of reconstruction, and the specific role of reconciliation therein. Hence:

- frameworks of rules (laws, codes of conduct, customary rights, etc.), provide guidance for problem-solving and legitimise outcomes;
- structures and institutions (courts, commissions, policies, and community or street committees) manage access to rights and remedies, and the distribution of power and resources;
- relationships (vertical and horizontal relationships between groups, individuals and the state) are of assistance if they are built on justice, equality and dignity, and framed in terms of rights and responsibilities;
- human rights principles – equality, non-discrimination, participation, accountability, empowerment – are embedded in the process requirements of interventions; processes conceived in this way enhance the validity and sustainability of outcomes.

Rules and structures/institutions are usually thought of, in the first instance, as the remit of peace negotiations, peace-building, post-conflict reconstruction, institution- or capacity-building, good governance, and so on. But they will assist reconciliation insofar as they themselves are the product of positive processes and relationships (imperfect examples include political agreements such as the South African negotiated settlement and the Oslo peace process involving Israel and the Palestinian Liberation Organisation [PLO]), and if they provide an enabling context and model for the empowerment, trust, leaps of faith and encounters on which societal reconciliation depends.[6] Thus, democratic processes and reconciliation can be linked, as can macro- and micro-level change (Bloomfield *et al.* 2003;[7] Cockburn 1998). While level-disjuncture frequently blights new democracies – one key challenge is how reconciliation can be decentralised beyond elite pacting and political actors – democracy and reconstruction ideally encompass the above-mentioned four dimensions of human rights, provides the infrastructure and a set of tools for managing ongoing conflict in non-violent ways, and the security and equity needed to push relationships beyond non-violent coexistence to thicker forms of interaction.

In short, reconciliation can best be defined as the work of (re)constructing relationships through enlightened processes, at a variety of levels (social, interpersonal, political, institutional, economic). The goal is to recover and reimagine the everyday (see the discussion of lived participation: chapter 2). Before moving on to apply the conception of reconciliation as the everyday to a series of case studies, one final definitional component is required.

Reconciliation and risk

There is a compelling need to theorise reconciliation in a manner that takes it beyond easy feel-good statements, thinly veiled attempts to pacify and preserve the status quo, and formulations that routinely exact primary demands upon victims/survivors. In short, reconciliation needs both an acknowledgement of risk and an apportioning of that risk in a manner that itself feeds reconciliation. The TRC frequently acknowledged that reconciliation, and associated processes such as forgiveness, are not without cost and pain (TRC 1998, Vol. 1: 17–19; Vol. 5: 307, 349, 380, 435) – for example, reconciliation requires economic justice and acknowledgement of beneficiary responsibility. But risk was at no stage built into a broader conceptualisation of reconciliation. What might such a conceptualisation look like?

Three propositions provide a useful starting point. The first concept draws on Hoddie and Hartzell's (2005) notion of 'costly signals of conciliatory intent'. They argue that the stages of building power-sharing institutions within peace negotiations to resolve civil wars – namely initiating negotiations, designing institutions and signing a settlement, and implementing the settlement provisions – all involve costs. Of particular note is the loss of power in relation to a former enemy and the potential loss of credibility or stature within one's own group. There is a direct link between a willingness to bear these costs, which provide 'signals of conciliatory intent', and perceived credibility with, and reassurance for, other parties (28).

Costly signalling within and across stages as a two-way process between competing groups builds confidence and trust. Relationships and reconciliation are again seen as crucial to institution-building. This is an idea with broader applicability.

The second concept draws on an argument about reconciliation and risk made by Christodoulidis (2000), in which the author argues that there is a fundamental incompatibility between law and reconciliation that rendered the TRC, as a hybrid body, schizophrenic and incoherent. The law entails an institutional foreclosing of risk through a generalised and rule-bound reflex to categorise and fix meaning. Reconciliation, in contrast, requires a discursive and reflexive embrace of contingency and risk. Select examples suffice to make the point. At a procedural level, as we have seen, legal challenges wrapped the HRV hearings in procedural requirements inimical to reconciliation. At a temporal level, there is a disjuncture between the time of law and the time of reconciliation. Confronting the future as risk, the law's 'always–already' draws on the past to determine and control the future, while reconciliation is 'not yet', and as such allows a future possibility to inform, and unsettle, the present.

Third, reconciliation, as already mentioned, is transformative, whether in relation to identities, histories/narratives and/or power relations. While the future may be unknown, the need for change and new beginnings is clear. Linking these three concepts together, the risk of reconciliation can be summarised as processes of costly signalling, embracing openings on to an unpredictable future, and the necessity of transformative change. A good place to start when looking to apply this thesis is the potential call and response of apology and forgiveness.

Apology and forgiveness

Truth commissions have largely been a 'non-Western affair', and Howard-Hassmann and Gibney (2008: 1) argue that 'apology has become the West's own version of the truth commission'. An international culture of apology (Cunningham 1999; Gibney and Roxstrom 2001; Minow 1998: 112–17) amply illustrates the need for risk-taking. Apologies, in what Brooks (1999) calls 'the age of apology' and Cohen (2001) 'political times for instant virtual apology' (247), can do precisely the opposite, side-stepping risk by assuaging guilt, masking errors and seeking to reclaim the moral high ground in the most pernicious traditions of spectacle or gesture politics.[8]

As a measure of authenticity, both political and interpersonal apologies require an element of risk and a preparedness to transform. An initial risk is that the apology will be rejected. The full panoply of risks include the unknown futures opened up by full acknowledgement, truth-telling and owning responsibility; the prospect of legal suits, justice and/or reparation; and potential challenges to power imbalances and inequitable relationships. So, in essence, a genuine apology requires living with danger and a wider context of action and change. Embracing the full spectrum of risk would make an apology more challenging, possibly more unlikely, but also more meaningful.

Unpredictability, therefore, is inherent in genuine apology. Apologies are often campaigned for from below rather than simply bestowed from above. The processes and campaigns seeking apology may be more valuable than any specific campaign outcome, notably in providing opportunities for testimonial truth-telling (Minow 1998: 91–117). Unintended effects can also germinate in the space created by top-down symbolic gestures, public rituals of atonement and examples of genuine leadership. Chilean President Patricio Aylwin's televised apology to the victims of Pinochet's repression, to mark the release of the Chilean truth commission report to the public, is one example; West German Chancellor Willy Brandt going down on his knees to apologise in the former Warsaw ghetto is another.

In South Africa, the apartheid-era political leadership, notably former Presidents P. W. Botha and F. W. de Klerk, has been heavily criticised for failing to make an unequivocal apology for apartheid.[9] Furthermore, amnesty was not conditional on apology or an indication of remorse. Difficult calculations about the authenticity of apologies were bypassed, but as an uncomfortable example of unpredictability successful applicants could reel off a catalogue of barbarities without contrition. The issue of whether reconciliation in South Africa can bypass individual and collective white apology remains unresolved (Cronin 1999: 11; R. Wilson 2001: 101–2).[10]

If a genuine apology is a 'costly signal of conciliatory intent' then forgiveness is a form of reciprocation, albeit that such a response cannot simply be expected or demanded. Forgiveness is often understood to imply the forgoing of anger, bitterness and hatred towards an offender, a resurrection of the human being(s) from the inhuman act. Note what should be agreed through the reciprocal exchange: that a wrongful act has been committed; that certain actors have a particular relationship to that act (victim, perpetrator, intellectual author); that the conduct merits moral judgement and requires repair; and that the truth should be told, privately and possibly publicly. Given that in many conflicts such issues are foundational to disputes and divisions, agreement along these lines can involve profound transformations of moral world-view, identity, history, status and power. This is the potential set in motion by *apology as truth*, which provides the facts as well as acknowledgement of moral wrongdoing and moral/material redress. As such, the apology–forgiveness nexus potentially provides an opening onto an unpredictable, and more positive, future. A number of commentators help to fill out this analysis.

A temporal, transformative facility is clearly articulated in Arendt's (1958: 230–47) conceptualisation of forgiveness, as is a sense of risk. On the one hand, the power to forgive can provide release from the irreversibility of the past. Unlike vengeance, which perpetuates a negative cycle by 're-acting':

> the act of forgiving can never be predicted; it is the only reaction ... which does not merely re-act but acts anew and unexpectedly, unconditioned by

the act which provoked it and therefore freeing from its consequences both the one who forgives and the one who is forgiven.

(241)

On the other hand, the power of promise (contracts, treaties) supplies the remedy for the unpredictability of the future. Arendt argues that both forgiveness and promise are relational. In concert they secure a renewed, ongoing capacity to act, an ability to break cycles of violence and a temporal reorientation towards the future.

In her meditation on apology and forgiveness, Gobodo-Madikizela (2003: especially 94–103) argues that a 'genuine apology' has certain characteristics. It focuses on the feelings of the other, not the potential benefits for the self; names the deed, provides full acknowledgement, a recognition of pain, and remorse, without any attempt to justify, deflect or erase; and expresses a desire to 'right the relationship' that has been damaged. Apology has the transformative potential 'to begin reconstructing the broken connections between two human beings' (98–99). Such an apology can inspire forgiveness, by encouraging a focus on the perpetrator's humanity (the person rather than their deeds) on the one hand, and by acknowledging the victim's humanity on the other (albeit that it does so based on reciprocal feeling, emotion and sympathy, here defined as empathy). The outcome can be mutual moral recognition.

Forgiveness in turn is conceived as 'a vehicle for shifting the power dynamic' (100) between two people. Where forgiveness is empowering for the victim – 'victims' extraordinary power to forgive' (79) – enacted from a position of strength, it represents a choice to let go of bitterness and anger, an expression of inhabiting a sense of one's agency and rights, and a 'gatekeeper' role with regards to perpetrator desires (117). In short, it marks a moment of self-realisation and rehumanisation. Enabling conditions are both internal and external (available symbols and vocabulary in the public sphere, supportive institutional spaces). Naturally, in the absence of these conditions, forgiveness can be disempowering (for example, see 101–2).[11]

This leads into a third set of arguments from those who advocate unilateral, non-relational forgiveness. Tutu's (1999) Christian understanding of forgiveness is the archetype. While acknowledging the context of risk, and the assistance provided by apology and reparation, Tutu argues that abandoning violent reciprocity and dependency is liberating: 'If the victim could forgive only when the culprit confessed, then the victim would be locked into the culprit's whim, locked into victimhood, whatever her own attitude or intention. That would be palpably unjust' (220). Arguably, victims/survivors have more control over forgiveness as a form of moving on, than reconciliation. And it is indeed important that the victim/survivor's power resides in a capacity to initiate as well as respond. But a number of caveats are necessary. There is a possibility that devoid of apologies, reparations or other enablers, such forgiveness can take on the mantle of a one-sided obligation. It is also a profound error to generalise from the admirable but exceptional, while many people's sense of self-worth, dignity and power will be predicated on a different world-view. Finally, unilateral forgiveness is not, on its own, a form of reconciliation because it implies no relational dimension. In this chapter a relational understanding of forgiveness and reconciliation is preferred, predicated on relationally determined sequencing and social process, costly signals and perhaps equally costly withdrawals, that may fall back from or ultimately go beyond apology and forgiveness.

These commentaries outline various ways of linking apology/forgiveness and risk. One might say reading Arendt's (1958) analysis, for example, that the TRC had the potential to hold unpredictability and promise in a productive tension, but, alas, over time too many promises have been broken (prosecutions, reparations). Apology and forgiveness played a central role in the rhetoric of the TRC (TRC 1998, Vol. 5: 371–400; also Gobodo-Madikizela 2003 and Tutu 1999).[12] As already noted in Chapter 5, the TRC placed great emphasis on the belief that people would or could forgive if they knew what had occurred and why, whom to forgive, and if perpetrators apologised. The degree of emphasis is in some ways surprising as its founding Act does not mention apology or forgiveness. It is also surprising in that few victims at hearings mentioned forgiveness as a priority – 'the TRC was far from a forgiveness fest … the deponents who came to the public hearings were more oriented to truth and justice than to forgiveness and reconciliation' (Chapman 2008b: 68; see 67–75) – and the majority of this group were unwilling to forgive or attached conditions to forgiveness. In essence, the TRC raised expectations and, with the media, publicised high-profile examples of interpersonal reconciliation in a manner that was unrepresentative, and largely decontextualised the individual and symbolic from the systemic and social. Alongside the lack of political leadership mentioned above, there were, in fact, relatively few instances of interpersonal apology and forgiveness.

A further subset of concerns merit attention within and beyond the South African setting. The sequencing that facilitates forgiveness, of which an apology is only one pillar, is poorly understood. In addition, interpersonal forgiveness needs to be distinguished from forms of political forgiveness which address systemic responsibilities (political leaders, intellectual authors, political regimes and institutions) (see Chapman 2008b). Further, a shared societal script may or may not be present in any given setting (Minow 1998: 18–19). Much can be lost where there is no shared narrative of responsibility (Chapman 2008b: 74), or in translation, for example between different religious and cultural understandings of forgiveness, and between the religious and the secular (Auerbach 2005; Bar-On 2006, Part II; Gopin 2001; Shriver 1995). Ongoing, strong readings, against the grain, for forgiveness from victims and survivors (for an example, see Krog *et al.* 2009), and a facile, unaccountable culture of easy forgiveness provide a final set of warnings. Mbembe (2006: 3) has written the following with regard to contemporary South Africa: 'A culture of corruption, impunity and non-accountability is fast becoming the norm. In the aftermath of the Truth and

Reconciliation Commission (TRC), public and private lives are conducted as if forgiveness was an inalienable right'.

Several themes from this discussion play out in the film *Forgiveness* (dir. Gabriel, 2004), a brief analysis of which concludes this section. In the film a former policeman, Tertius Coetzee, still traumatised despite being granted amnesty by the TRC, journeys to the fishing community of Paternoster on the Cape west coast to seek forgiveness from the family whose son, Daniel Grootboom, he tortured and murdered in detention. This costly signal is initially rebuffed, but forgiveness takes place over time, built on reciprocal signalling and through a series of often very difficult encounters. Important messages contained in the film are that forgiveness never completely displaces a host of other responses (despair, rage, resentment), and that its preconditions are person- and context-specific.

Sannie, Daniel's sister, calls three of his comrades who travel across country bent on revenge, but her response shifts from trying to keep Coetzee in Paternoster so that retribution can be exacted to encouraging him to leave to save himself. The currency of forgiveness is rooted in the ordinary and everyday. Coetzee does not apologise and although he recounts the events leading up to Daniel's death, the account is ended when Ernest, Daniel's brother, attacks Coetzee. But more positive outcomes are suggested as Coetzee is seen by Sannie collecting and laying shells (flowers of the sea) on Daniel's grave; snoek run again offshore, after a long absence, and the father lands a large catch; Daniel's mother emerges from housebound depression and mother and father dance together, as in their youth, after Coetzee invites the family to a local hotel for dinner. As the by-line to the film states, 'it's not only about the truth'. In such small intimacies, coincidences and reclamations, forgiveness gains a foothold.

The effect of Coetzee's quest, however, is to open doors onto a web of unresolved complicity and guilt. As he himself comments: 'Once you start something like this it doesn't end'. Within the community Daniel Grootboom's parents stuck to the state version of events that their son died in a car hijacking, embarrassed to have a 'terrorist' in the family. The father blames himself for paying for the car and university education that led to Daniel becoming involved in politics. One of Daniel's friends among the group travelling to Paternoster gave his name to the police. The film concludes as the family and Coetzee congregate at the grave so that they all can ask Daniel for forgiveness. At the graveside forgiveness and revenge meet. The three former combatants arrive and one of them, Zuko, possessed by anger (his brother's spine was broken by Coetzee, leaving him in a wheelchair) and guilt (he was the one who betrayed Daniel in custody), shoots and kills Coetzee.

Here we see all the ingredients of reconciliation as the everyday, in a series of reorientations towards the ordinary, complex identities and world-views, living beyond suffering, and to face the present and future. Such reorientations are accompanied by risk. Costly signally as part of a process leads to transformative change, but this does not quench the risk that is also part of the process.

Change and opening on to an unknown future is in this case ultimately partly tragic. In such complex stories there are few simple happy endings.

The second half of this chapter applies the theory of reconciliation developed above (predicated on the everyday, relationships, processes and risk) to community and economic reconciliation, to explore its potential to reconfigure structural or systemic relationships.

Community reconciliation

A number of commentators stress that reconciliation must be primarily rooted in domestic and local values and social processes, a bottom-up process that can be assisted but not led by external intervention (Pankhurst 1999; Sarkin and Daly 2004). While the work of the TRC may have generated discussion about, and tools for, community reconciliation, it is usually understood to have privileged individual and especially national reconciliation over, and even at the expense of, community reconciliation.[13] As noted in previous chapters, academics, victim/survivor groups and NGOs have begun to supplement and critique the community analyses and impacts of the TRC in relation to local dynamics of violence. Reconciliation in this setting requires the (re)construction of local social networks and political relationships, longer-term engagement and inclusive participation; in short, bottom-up processes which attend to local priorities in their own right rather than as windows on a national picture. That said, sustainability and 'scaling-up' interventions may require top-down support too. Finally, reconciliation within and between communities faces the challenge of addressing issues that remained on the margins of the TRC's work (allegations about informing, the return and reintegration of ex-combatants).

There have been a host of community reconciliation and restorative justice initiatives in post-TRC South Africa (see Chapters 2 to 5). This chapter will focus on the Centre for the Study of Violence and Reconciliation's (CSVR's) victim–offender mediation intervention, which emerged out of research with survivors and amnesty applicants who participated in the TRC amnesty process (some survivors did not themselves participate, but the relevant perpetrator appeared at a hearing). The research revealed a need and desire for (further) dialogue among both constituencies (Abrahamsen and van der Merwe 2005; Phakathi and van der Merwe 2008). In 2003–4, CSVR, in collaboration with various partners, devised a pilot restorative justice mediation project to facilitate dialogue between ex-combatants, survivors and their communities (Ramírez-Barat and van der Merwe 2005). Eleven cases were selected (of which seven eventually went to mediation), from the 27 earlier amnesty interviews conducted with perpetrators. All cases involved black, male ex-combatants engaged in the liberation struggle.

The pilot tested whether restorative justice approaches could be applied to mediations initiated by perpetrators (rather than victims/survivors), to politically motivated and serious violations of human rights, and to the broader objective of contributing to forward-looking processes of democratic strengthening (reconciliation, ex-combatant reintegration, building peace and a human rights culture).

Mediations themselves were structured around story-telling, starting with the perpetrator/mediation initiator and followed by the victim/survivor. An offence was understood as harm done to interpersonal and community relationships, and to all parties, while resolution was conceived as repair of the harm, its causes and consequences, and thereby a restoration of relationships. Alongside the desire to rebuild and construct new relationships, other project goals chime with the arguments of this chapter:

1 The need for equity and redressing of power imbalances. Interesting in this regard, the pilot evaluation recommended that the structure of mediations strengthen the victim's role in shaping the dialogue, by enabling victims to go beyond the offence, and forms of clarification and response, to narrate the whole story of their victimisation.
2 Social transformation through mutual understanding – i.e. reciprocal 'processes of moral learning', about motivations for violent actions but also their consequences on people's lives, alongside challenging one-dimensional, non-relational identities – and the reintegration of both parties into communities and the new democratic order.
3 A reorientation from the past to the present/future, through fulfilment of goals (1) and (2), apology and forgiveness as process, and material or symbolic compensation.

An evaluation of the initial pilot project was predominantly positive (Ramírez-Barat and van der Merwe 2005). On this basis the initiative was expanded in 2005 beyond victims and offenders to focus more explicitly on community reconciliation and ex-combatant reintegration (Greenbaum 2006). The case study of Bonteheuwel, explored below, is part of the expanded programme. It uses a set of interventions that both draw on and critique the TRC's discourse on reconciliation and restorative justice.

Bonteheuwel, a coloured township to the north of Cape Town, was created in the 1960s to receive people forcibly removed from Cape Town under apartheid segregationist policies. By the mid- to late 1980s, and the era of rolling States of Emergency, a 'total strategy' was introduced by the apartheid state which combined repression and modest reform to deal with a perceived 'total onslaught'. Such measures encountered resistance, often led by the youth. Bonteheuwel was a hotbed of student-led activism and crime, one of many townships at the forefront of an upsurge in violence. The main goals of the Bonteheuwel Military Wing (BMW), formed in the mid-1980s, were to protect the community, resist the apartheid state and render Bonteheuwel ungovernable. There are differing accounts about the origins, structure and political affiliations of the BMW. Its relations with Umkhonto we Sizwe (MK), the ANC's armed wing, and more generally with the United Democratic Front (UDF) and ANC allies, are unclear and contested. As elsewhere in the country, however, the youth-led rebellion – most of the BMW's members were between 14 and 18 years old – represented a revolt against both apartheid and an older generation seen as compliant, and even complicit in its longevity. By late 1986 and early 1987 Bonteheuwel had been rendered ungovernable. The state's response was swift and violent. Between June 1987 and January 1988 over 40 members of the BMW were detained and brutally tortured in an attempt to gather information to facilitate further arrests and convictions (on the BMW see TRC 1998, Vol. 3: 482–85; Vol. 4: 278–81). In a short time the organisation was effectively destroyed. While members of the BMW approached the TRC, much was left unresolved by the Commission's work.[14]

The first Bonteheuwel mediation in early April 2005 had been preceded by a series of preparatory meetings, including two with each of the individuals party to the mediation (S and W).[15] Costly signalling begins at this preliminary stage of the process. On the Saturday of the mediation itself an edgy, uncertain silence in the meeting room seems to hold as much threat as promise. Eyes shift uneasily, rarely meeting. Seating positions shift. Messages are being sent. After a long wait the mediator, M, suggests that other possibly attendees are probably not coming; we should begin. There are seven people from Bonteheuwel present. S (the 'offender') has requested an opportunity to reconcile with W (the 'victim'). Perhaps oddly, given these labels, the group coheres around S, while W is unaccompanied and alone. After introductions, M starts by framing the mediation in inclusive, positive terms. The BMW and MK were allies, sharing a common goal in the past, the liberation of communities; beyond liberation there is a common goal in the present, uplifting communities. From the distant to the immediate, from the past to the present, we arrive at the objective of the mediation: to 'heal broken relationships', and, more generally, peace and reconciliation linked to community development.

S's 'side of the story' is governed by two linked narratives, a claim for recognition and a reflection on unforgiving times, past and present. From the start, he argues that he was with MK, in a senior unit with well-known activists, a commander and leader: 'one of the most daring guerrillas ever in the Western Cape'. Shifting to the latter narrative, a code of conduct existed to the effect that sell-outs or informers would be eliminated. As Bonteheuwel was a no-go area for the security forces, the only people who could give them information came from within the community. At this time a court case took place in which S was one of the accused and W was thought to be a state witness, although S admits that he lacked 'clear evidence'. After the case a rumour spread in the community that W was an informer for the police. S was instructed to 'silence' him and in a field behind a church W was interrogated, beaten and stabbed. S left the scene to go and buy petrol with which to set W alight, but on his return was informed that people in the church had intervened, rescuing W.

Following several questions from M that shift the moral compass, beginning to open up space for W to talk (Did you verify information about informers?

Did some comrades prefer other methods of dealing with informers?), the mediator asks what made S seek mediation. A charismatic orator, S combines the two threads of his narrative, laying claim to a difficult past (torture and harassment) and present (marginalisation), before privileging strength over vulnerability. From the latter heights S sends a complex 'signal of conciliatory intent', at once asking for and offering forgiveness.

> I am one of the guys that achieved great things ... I am a free person. Who am I not to ... reconcile with a comrade from the BMW? ... I realised the security police branded people as informers, this became clearer through the work of the TRC ... In that regard it would be right for me to ask forgiveness from W for all the harm I personally did to him. Also to tell him that I forgive him ... It was not me who branded W an informer, it was me who acted on the information. I'm here to correct this, I believe it is right ... This can be a platform to resolve this matter.

One ambivalent note in this narrative is noteworthy. S oscillated between referring to W as 'Mr' and 'Comrade', with the former a distancing, even disowning term, and the latter an indication of inclusion and belonging. This tension was ultimately unresolved. On these linguistic terms it is unclear if S is offering forgiveness.

'I remember it as clearly as if it were yesterday', W begins his response. He is referring to the attack, on which he focuses immediately. The only violence he mentions is that a concrete slab was thrown on his back. He continues:

> You asked for my forgiveness. There is nothing to forgive. My anger was towards the security police for spreading the rumour that I was an informer. From the time I went to hospital I had already forgiven ... you. I knew you had no idea what you were doing.

In a preparatory meeting, W also mentioned that the matter went to the TRC and S had already apologised. The terms of the mediation are at this point unclear; this does not feel like a reciprocal signal: S has asked for *and* offered forgiveness; W has stated that forgiveness has already been granted *and* is unnecessary; neither has apologised. There is agreement that the real perpetrators were the security police, but they are not part of the mediation.

W's account now spans outwards, recalling that his movement between two areas, Bonteheuwel and Bridge Town, made him difficult for the security police to find but also made it easy for them to label him as an informer and easy for the community to believe this labelling. He refutes the charge of being a state witness on the grounds that he received a summons to appear in court in connection with another case, claiming that he still has the summons to prove it. W's is a narrative of virtue (continued political activity, even after the attack) and misunderstandings (he was framed as an informer), which concludes in much more understated terms than the narrative of S: 'I am glad for us, for things to work out for the better'.

The meditation is then snapped open, faced with an almost infinite unravelling of interrelated incidents. First, it becomes clear that there are several narratives of betrayal relating to W. F, another BMW member, for example, states that W had been labelled an informer because he failed to follow the code of conduct that if a person was tortured and divulged information they must tell their comrades immediately. This is a slightly more subtle interpretation of the code of conduct than had been aired previously. It is also a different reason for W having been labelled an informer.[16] Second, many of those present have at some time been labelled informers and assaulted. S too had been attacked – at the preparatory stage it became clear that S was seeking mediation in part to clear his own name of such allegations, while S had attacked W not once but twice in relation to separate incidents. These allegations provoke the most strident disagreement of the mediation and raise familiar challenges for reconciliation, such as how to confront but also contain uncertainty and risk. Judiciously, M intervenes, to lay out lines of agreement about the first incident.

While wrapping up, M takes the opportunity to identify as the real villain the security police and 'dark forces' in the past, and the potentially related, partially different authors of informer rumours and threats in the present. He stresses the need to heal rifts with the community and families and for an ongoing commitment to community development. A range of further mediations are suggested: a BMW meeting with the community, and thereafter a meeting between the BMW and former commander N, as the latter is seen as a major source of politically motivated informer labelling. At the close, S and W are asked by M to shake hands. They do so, to applause.[17]

Analysis of this mediation reveals four core conclusions: a reframing of the link between truth and reconciliation; the unresolved and ongoing importance of informers; the complex, fractious micro-dynamics of community politics; and, underpinning all these issues, continuities between the past and present.

From the first mediation it is clear that factual truth is not always a precondition for reconciliation. In relation to the initial claim that W was a state witness, no one showed any interest in asking W to produce the summons he claimed to still possess, or in consulting the court records to verify his story. Key factual questions remained unresolved. Was W in fact a state witness and informer? To what extent was he set up by the security police? The truth that was required was a negotiated, flexible truth with which all parties could live (everyday or relational truth), not brittle-edged, accusatory, factual truth. Outcomes were restorative in the sense that the mediation's role was to re-establish relationships as part of a social and political process.[18]

Second, informing in the past, and its relationship to ongoing insecurity in the present, clearly still fragments communities. Community relations echo post-apartheid novels in highlighting the damage caused by the 'poisonous knowledge' of betrayal, as the past folds into the present. Such violence is often dealt with most effectively at the level of relationships and the everyday (Das 2001). Allegations of informing were commonplace in the late 1980s in South Africa. Several participants in the mediation had tried to kill other participants on these grounds. M returned to the issue of verification of, and responses to, informer allegations on a number of occasions, stating incredulously at one point: 'You just went out and started attacking each other? ... can you realise the damage done to all of you? ... to families and the Bonteheuwel community?' In an environment of extreme pressure, and as structures to check allegations did not exist or ceased to function, real and alleged informing were used to devastating effect by the state. The grounds for taking someone out were as tenuous as 'if a person talked too much, too loud'. As already mentioned, the label of informer still has currency in communities such as Bonteheuwel, influencing political belonging, access to resources and personal security. Specific names were cited of rumour-mongers (including the former BMW commander, N). Several times the claim was made that a divisive 'third force' is still operating. Ongoing divisions were in part ascribed to these continuities with the past.

Third, Richard Records identifies two narratives about the origins and formation of the BMW. The absence of resolution between these narratives directly impacts on ongoing conflicts and the politics of recognition in the community. The tension is between the claim that the BMW was a local student creation driving a mass-based social movement, a unit with significant autonomy but also links to, and characterised by some movement of personnel into, MK (narrative 1); and the counter-claim that MK embedded itself in Bonteheuwel as trained MK operatives entered the community and recruited members from the student bodies, and recruits in turn set in motion a process that resulted in the creation of a series of cells and were responsible for broader mass mobilisation (narrative 2). Further complicating matters, certain BMW leaders, such as N, joined MK and went into exile; others joined MK and remained in South Africa; another group did not join MK at all. A larger cohort remained outside all structures but as 'the masses' provided forms of active and indirect support. Like informer labelling, conflicts rooted in micro-discourses of resistance involving different organisational structures and leaders, people who went into exile and those who remained, and structure-based and mass-based activism, have material and security implications in the present.

The TRC in its report (TRC 1998, Vol. 3: 482–85; Vol. 4: 278–81) essentially sides with the first narrative, without alluding to a tension between competing narratives or its ongoing implications. Among its findings is the following statement:

> that the group received endorsement and facilitation from the UDF, albeit at local level, and that MK operatives furthered this endorsement in the provision of arms and military training. The Commission criticises both the UDF and ANC for its expedient encouragement of this group of very young

people who were all under the age of eighteen, finding it inappropriate that such youth were mobilised into organised violence.

(TRC 1998, Vol. 3: 485)

The TRC's account appears to have done little to settle the disputes that still simmer in the community. A fourth, and final, overarching challenge to reconciliation is the damaging continuity that exists between the past and present, as the people of Bonteheuwel struggle to live their lives and maintain relationships under the strain of poverty, criminal and social violence, divisive politics and allegations of informing.

CSVR's community reconciliation programme in Bonteheuwel, and elsewhere, has ended as a result of factors including funding constraints, the organisation's own changing priorities and external political developments, e.g. the cloud of possible prosecutions diminished the willingness of perpetrators to take part in mediations. In Bonteheuwel some signals of intent were sent, mediation as a process began, but sustainable reconciliation remains elusive. Embracing risk and an unpredictable future can have some very challenging outcomes, most obviously an endless vista of need. This in itself requires a transformation, from dependency to local ownership. While CSVR sought to train local mediators, strengthen local capacities, and build relations with community structures and the state to ensure sustainability (Greenbaum 2006), ultimately neither the local community (bottom-up) nor the state (top-down) had the capacity and/or will to take the initiative forward as CSVR withdrew.

On the plus side the CSVR intervention, unlike the TRC, represents a cogent attempt to marshal restorative justice to further reconciliation in a transitional justice setting. The combination of principle and pragmatism suggests potential routes beyond a stark distinction between restorative justice and human rights (see Chapter 3). Despite their shortcomings – uneven preparatory work, follow-up and outcomes – the Bonteheuwel mediations indicate the advances that can be made by engaging all parties and focusing on longer-term processes, relationships and locally defined, everyday harms. The project unpacked the different kinds of, and reasons for, informing, and recognised diverse forms of participation in the struggle. Similarly, it acknowledged complex identities beyond victim/survivor and perpetrator, at the very least registering that many are both. Divergent views were expressed, discussed and, in part, understood. There is potential for securing transformative change through such interventions.

Economic reconciliation

In this new world order, the power of capital looms over the rhetoric of reconstructed and 'people-driven' programmes devised by governments of national unity in recently liberated states. Thus the critical question to be asked of an official ideology of reconciliation, with its language of consensus and settlement, is that it is deployed within social formations that remain fissured by class divisions and conflicts. In which case, is it not premature to command concord when the circumstances making for discord remain in place? And is it not inequitable for governments and intellectuals to entreat gestural atonement from the strong, whose privileges are intact, while the aspirations of the dispossessed, who are enjoined to pardon their expropriators and exploiters, continue to be unappeased? The problem ... then presents itself not as one of aligning reconciliation and remembrance, but rather of joining remembrance of the past with a critique of the contemporary condition.

(Parry 1995: 95)

Transitional justice mechanisms, including the TRC, have been weak in their economic analysis and interventions. Material continuities between the past and present undermine capacities to achieve the reorientations of everyday reconciliation, from the extraordinary and spectacular to the ordinary and social processes of change, from binary to multi-dimensional identities, from suffering to living, from the past to the present and future, because for too many little or nothing has changed. The argument of this section is that it is the economic realm that provides the structural underpinnings of sustainable reconciliation, and that while relational economic reconciliation will be resisted by many and is difficult to operationalise, it has a vital contribution to make to a redistributive agenda in South Africa and elsewhere.

To make such an argument requires an exploration of several, linked themes: (1) the enduring economic divide in South Africa; (2) the global meta-discourses that shape patterns of post-conflict continuity and change in this terrain (neo-liberalism, a focus on civil and political rights, the liberal peace); (3) why and how economic and social rights need to be addressed in transitional contexts and by truth commissions, featuring the case studies of land reform and reparations; (4) the complex relationship between reconciliation and transformation; and, finally, (5) the possible value added of what I have termed relational reconciliation, in the economic domain.

One snapshot helps to set the scene. In February 2006, when I was in South Africa conducting fieldwork, President Mbeki's State of the Nation address and Finance Minister Trevor Manuel's budget, as well as most press and pundit commentary on the economy, were decidedly upbeat. And yet, the reality was a complex one, a story of two separate, yet interdependent, economies. On the one hand, over 75 straight months of economic growth and a GDP growth rate of 5 per cent for 2005, combined with declining inflation and a very low budget deficit, were interpreted by many to mean that the basic foundations of the economy were strong. The black middle class had more than doubled in size in a decade, and there were notable achievements in service delivery (water, electricity, housing). Much attention was given to the latest economic initiative and acronym, the Accelerated Shared Growth Initiative (ASGI), a R370bn set of state interventions to boost public sector infrastructure and economic growth. On the other hand, certain telling problems persisted. Chief among these were poverty, inequality and unemployment (at over 25 per cent). Despite a significant expansion of social grants, many lacked access to employment or social security. HIV/AIDS had become a multi-dimensional catastrophe for the country (human, economic, political). Another huge challenge was that of translating policies into delivery, given capacity and skills shortages, and systemic corruption. After over a decade of benign global economic conditions and strong domestic growth, South Africa has been caught up in the global downturn post 2008, suggesting more difficult times ahead.

A double-headed narrative is required to explain this scenario. Like other countries in transition, South Africa has been incorporated into two dominant strands of contemporary globalisation. The first is an important but partial human rights discourse, privileging liberal paradigms of civil and political rights through an emphasis on elections, procedural liberalism, constitutionalism and the rule of law, and various backward-looking truth and justice measures. This is the domain of national/political or 'thin' reconciliation. The second is market-driven, neo-liberal economics. South Africa's Reconstruction and Development Programme (RDP) effectively lasted two years, superseded in 1996 by the Growth, Employment and Redistribution (GEAR) macro-economic framework that in fact merely entrenched the already dominant neo-liberal economic strategy. Certain caveats need to be acknowledged in the South African case. The South African Constitution (No. 108 of 1996), contains state-of-the-art economic and social rights provisions, but these have partially humanised rather than radically critiqued or replaced the market. Further, the President Zuma era (post 2009) has brought with it a populist questioning of both civil–political rights and market orthodoxies. The TRC, as we have seen, failed to adequately address systemic economic abuses and legacies, as it privileged a narrow civil and political rights focus. Despite the above-mentioned caveats a congregation of post-apartheid policies resulted in entrenched, even increasing, inequality (Terreblanche 2002: especially 95–149). The two strands of globalisation are interlinked, with the rule of law and its allies now widely held to provide an enabling context for free markets.

Internationally this policy prescription is often described as the liberal peace thesis, which has come to dominate the various aftermaths subsumed under the rubrics of transitional justice, peace-building and post-conflict reconstruction (e.g. Paris 2004). The thesis, although it comes in no single, agreed form, essentially maintains that political democracy and market economics are the foundations of sustainable peace, both within countries and between states. Critics determinedly bark along the borders of these assumptions. Among the most pertinent criticisms are that processes of democratisation and market liberalisation are themselves conflict-generating, exacerbating social tensions and competition at a juncture when a country is ill equipped to contain these developments within peaceful limits (Cramer 2006; Lund 2006; Thoms and Ron 2007). Whether described in terms of 'pathologies' (Paris 2004: 8, also 151–78) or 'dialectically linked integration *and* fragmentation' (Lipschutz 1998: 14), such processes endanger the sustainability of peace.

In South Africa, anger at enduring poverty and inequality is such a 'pathology', as is violent crime. For some, the thesis merely requires modification. Paris (2004: 5–8, also 179–211), for example, in his study of 1990s peace-building in the aftermath of civil wars, argues for 'institutionalization before liberalization'. The former anticipates and manages the destabilising effects of the latter, and the liberal peace is phased in rather than fast-tracked. For some, the liberal peace is more fundamentally flawed. One argument made by such critics is that it is predicated on an elite pact, designed to insert and enrich a national elite within the global economy, and that as such it overlooks the structural causes of conflict, broader issues of social justice, and the need for thicker relational bonds of trust and civility in society (or social reconciliation) (Lipschutz 1998). These and other criticisms of the liberal peace resonate with the South African transition; and with the broader thrust of this book.

South Africa suggests a twist in the tail of this narrative: from RDP through GEAR to the developmental state (from 2005). Responding to the desire for growth *and* equity, the ANC government revisited the need for a strong, effective, interventionist state (hence the ASGI). Troublingly, drawing as it does on the East Asian economic model, this policy reroute raises questions about the purported democracy-development trade-off (Southall 2006). Interestingly, parallels can be mapped between post-1994 economic and justice policy, including the shift from progressive rhetoric to conservative realities, and ultimately movement towards a hybrid and more locally informed policy trajectory (the 'policy pendulum'). Further, service delivery figures are as incendiary as crime statistics, simultaneously difficult to measure, contested and subject to defensive responses and manipulation (Hemson and O'Donovan 2006).

In fairness, the TRC recognised the importance of addressing poverty and inequality to furthering reconciliation, but deflected the responsibility for doing so by arguing that this realm lay outside its mandate. Apartheid was thus misrepresented, human rights rendered divisible rather than indivisible, and a range of actors from beneficiaries to business were handed narratives facilitating self-exculpation rather than self-recognition ('we did not perpetrate gross violations of human rights as you interpret the term', 'we are all victims'). On the occasions when the TRC strayed into the economic arena, most notably during the business and labour sector hearings, the insights gleaned were not integrated into the mainstream work of the Commission (TRC 1998, Vol. 4: 18–58; also see Nattrass 1999). A more sophisticated analysis of collaboration and accountability, for example – identifying three different orders of involvement: first-order involvement in the design and implementation of apartheid policy, second-order involvement through profiteering from cooperating with state security structures and activities that promoted state repression, and third-order involvement as ordinary business benefited indirectly from operating under apartheid – was left to languish in an institution-specific chapter.

In post-apartheid South Africa, it is clearly not the TRC that bears the greatest responsibility for failing to tackle structural poverty and inequality. But that it and transitional justice mechanisms generally have to date fitted so seamlessly into this mainstream paradigm and shared similar conceptions about the preconditions for peace and reconciliation (there is a clear fit, for example, between the liberal peace and 'thin' reconciliation) surely warrants pause for thought. Whose interests are being furthered and what kind of transformation is being sought? What continuities are sanctioned and what conflicts fuelled?

To move beyond these rather broad-brush statements requires an assessment of why truth commissions should do more on economic and social rights, and what they might usefully and realistically do.[19] There are four main responses to the 'why' question. First, if truth commissions are a victim-centred enterprise, economic and social rights matter because they are often prioritised by victims and local populations (for example, see Robbins 2009 on Nepal, and Vinck and Pham 2008 on eastern Democratic Republic of Congo). Surveys of the views of victims and local populations suggest that an appropriate sequencing might be as follows: security and basic needs as immediate priorities, with truth, justice and reconciliation coming later. Second, a socio-economic focus would enhance the potential of truth commissions to address the root causes of conflict, and hence optimise their preventive role. In their analysis of whether human rights abuses cause internal conflict, Thoms and Ron (2007) argue that economic and social rights violations, and discrimination, function as the underlying, structural causes of conflict (creating grievances and group identities). Civil and political violations are the proximate causes or immediate triggers of conflict (regime change, violations of personal integrity and security rights) (also see Arbour 2006, and Mani 2002). Third, human rights itself has moved on to stress the equal importance and indivisibility of civil–political and socio-economic rights. One example of indivisibility in the transitional justice sphere is that impunity for violations across these categories of rights can clearly be mutually reinforcing (Carranza 2008). Fourth, the 'springboard thesis' argues that highlighting economic and social rights could act as a 'springboard' for the embedding of such rights, and a fuller conception of justice, in new democracies (Arbour 2006). To summarise, local ownership, prevention, better analysis and the 'springboard thesis' are the reasons why economic and social rights matter.

The question of how transitional justice mechanisms, and specifically truth commissions, should work on economic and social rights is more difficult to answer. Truth commissions in Kenya, Liberia, Peru, Sierra Leone and Timor Leste have begun to more seriously investigate and/or make recommendations on economic, social and cultural rights, and the indivisibility of rights (Arbour 2006; Duthie 2008). But these rights remain second-class citizens, as they are in human rights work more generally. Returning to the main arguments of this book, attempts to recreate the public sphere (truth commissions as acts of public description and constituency-building) and reimagine human rights (as indivisible and hybrid) suggest some points of departure:

> Public description: Economic and social rights can be addressed either directly, as important in their own right, or indirectly, through civil and political rights.[20] I would argue for both for the prioritisation of public description (testimony and analysis) over infinitely expanding recommendations; and for further development of an emerging targeted approach to public description (identifying gateway rights that impact on other rights; pinpointing the engines of conflict, such as war economies, corruption and land-related grievances; shining a light on the indivisibility of human rights abuses and damaging continuities between past and present). Painting a broad, yet strategically informed, human rights canvas would lay bare a fuller account of the past and the causes of conflict, alter relations between the past and present, and suggest a wider framework of responsibility. Diverse constituencies (state and non-state, different practitioner communities) would then be in a position to debate and advocate for appropriate responses. This leads neatly to the next point of departure.
>
> Constituency building: in essence, the methodological choice in this sphere of human rights work is between adapting the problem to your skill set (in the case of human rights, a growing repertoire, including naming and shaming, lobbying for policy change, and human rights training and education), or adapting your skill set to the problem. There is a role for traditional methods, such as naming and shaming, in the economic sphere, but there is in my view clearly also a need for new skills. Innovative methods are being developed to work on economic and social rights (e.g. budget monitoring, the use of indicators and benchmarks to monitor the progressive realization of rights). Some of these tools can be adapted to the truth commission task of public description. An equally challenging methodological horizon, and one that will require new skills and strategic borrowing, is the more process oriented goal of constituency building. Truth commissions, for example, could draw on the hybrid methodologies of rights-based approaches to development, notably rights-based participation, building the capacities of rights holders and duty bearers (bottom-up and top-down rights work), and emphasising the importance of power relations and the underlying causes of problems (Gready 2009). Facilitative processes are required for the voices of victims and the marginalized to be heard on a more sustainable basis, and on issues about which new dispensations are likely to remain ambiguous (such as poverty and inequality).

Certain qualifications are in order. I hope I have not fallen too squarely into the trap of expecting truth commissions to solve every problem under the sun. I think a contextualised history, and a more inclusive analysis and voicing of violations, is a realistic aim, whereas informed, strategic recommendations on everything from torture to education is not. This agenda also requires that the human rights community relinquish its near monopoly of the transitional justice agenda. The reforms envisaged require more than just a 'reskilling' of human rights practitioners; they require a radical influx of new ideas, approaches and personnel. This shake-up could in part be informed by sequencing: as noted above, development and meeting basic needs may well be a necessary precondition for traditional transitional justice measures. Finally, the grass is not always greener on the other side of the disciplinary or practitioner fence. Humility about the potential of human rights for transformative change needs to be combined with a lack of romanticism about alternative discourses (development can hardly be said to have cracked the challenge of participation, for example).

Land reform in South Africa provides a revealing case study of some of the dangers of framing an economic issue as a human rights concern. Although land reform was overseen by its own institutional architecture, rather than by the TRC, it provides interesting lessons for future truth commission forays into socio-economic rights (James 2007; Ntsebeza 2004; Walker 2006, 2008).[22] Land ownership remains racially skewed, and thus far has only been partially redressed by a grindingly slow land reform programme. Land reform focuses on land restitution, redistribution and tenure reform, all of which can be framed in relational terms. Restitution is a policy response to racially based land dispossession and forced removals, and allows restoration of original land, provision of alternative land or other state benefits, or financial compensation. The most recent state target for completing the land restitution process is 2011, with an overall reform-related target of transferring 30 per cent of farmland to black owners by 2025. The main (re)distributive mechanism adopted by the South African government was the market-based policy of willing seller–willing buyer. Progress on this front has been unsatisfactory, leading to discussion about a more robust enforcement mechanism.

Aims as diverse as providing redress for past wrongs and establishing a class of viable African commercial farmers have proved to be contradictory. Processes of reform are also inhibited by tensions within the double narrative described in the main body of the chapter (the market and/vs human rights). Over time, as the ANC government's embrace of market economics became more transparent, the right to property has trumped human rights as a broader programme of restoring citizenship, and future-oriented development and (African) commercial property rights have trumped past-oriented redress and anti-poverty agendas. In short, the market has prevailed. Here again the practice of rights has been about balancing and weighing interests, this time with less conducive outcomes for social justice. In a familiar pattern, NGO activists and human rights lawyers moved into and then out of government positions in parallel with these events, but still combine strategies of working with the state (especially at local and provincial levels) and critique (at a national level) (James 2007: 27–51).

Human rights informed a master narrative of 'loss and restoration' (restitution) that ultimately proved to be too narrow to span the diverse land-related needs of South Africa, or to drive forward far-reaching transformation:

The problem is that the narrative is too simple – the elements it assembles are incomplete. It does not tell the full story, or enough of the story, to sustain a satisfactory resolution of the plotline it sets up. Thus it isolates the history of forced removals under apartheid and before as a story on its own, instead of an important chapter in a much larger and more complex history not only of dispossession but also of social change.

(Walker 2008: 16)

The warning is a clear one, and becomes all the more stark as commissions, such as the Kenyan Truth, Justice and Reconciliation Commission, begin to include land-related issues in their mandates. Truth commission expansion into socio-economic concerns could simply reproduce the weaknesses of human rights on a broader canvas (too narrow a focus on redress, decontextualisation, etc.), and in the process fail to provide an adequate response to the transitional needs of justice-based transformation combined with forward-looking development. As noted above, what is needed is a contextualised history, and an inclusive analysis and voicing of violations.

A second interesting commentary on transitional justice and economic justice is provided by reparations interventions in post-TRC South Africa. Reparations can take a variety of forms, some of which feature in the land reform discussion above: restitution (restoration to an original situation); compensation (appropriate and proportional economic damages); rehabilitation (medical and psychological care as well as legal and social services); and satisfaction and guarantees of non-repetition (covering many components of a holistic understanding of transitional justice) (OHCHR 2008: 7–8).[22] Measures can be material as well as symbolic, individual as well as collective, directly or indirectly reparative, costly or inexpensive (changing place or street names), and target purely civil and political rights or a broader range of rights violations. There are genuine debates to be had about the balance between reparations for the few and reconstruction and development for the majority: in South Africa, between the TRC's victims and a nation of victims (see chapter 3). One concern is that human rights practitioners will reduce recommendations relating to economics, or development, to reparations, which are not delivered on a sufficient scale to facilitate a transformative redistribution of wealth or power at a macro level, but may do so on a more micro level (Miller 2008; Roht-Arriaza and Orlovsky 2009).

I would argue that the primary transformative potential of human rights lies elsewhere, with rights-based participation. Arguably reparations are the only transitional justice measure that directly targets victims and attends to their needs: 'While prosecutions and to some extent vetting are, in the end, a struggle *against* perpetrators, and truth-seeking and institutional reform have as their immediate constituency society as a whole, reparations are explicitly and primarily carried out *on behalf of* victims' (ibid.: 2–3). Such recognition has the potential to transform victims into citizens and rights holders (the right to reparations) and build trust between citizen and state (ibid.: 30–31). The potential for shifts in wealth and power relations resides mainly in the fact that reparations programmes usually evolve and are contested over time, from below, as a result of civil society and victim/survivor mobilisation. Herein lies the possibility for rights-based participation, constituency-building and the acquisition of new skills, and fresh patterns of engagement with the state through and beyond reparations campaigns (Roht-Arriaza and Orlovsky 2009). Truth commissions can play a major role in mobilising and channelling these transformative energies.

In South Africa, the interim Constitution (No. 200 of 1993), the Promotion of National Unity and Reconciliation Act (No. 34 of 1995) and the AZAPO judgment all held out the promise of reparations. Statutory obligations created what the TRC called a 'legitimate expectation' giving rise to 'legally enforceable rights' (TRC 2003, Vol. 6: 99), for those identified as victims by the TRC. Reparations were necessary to counterbalance the amnesty provision and facilitate reconciliation. One of the main contracts on which the success of the TRC hinged paired individualised, conditional mechanisms for the granting of amnesty on the one hand and reparations on the other (reparations were conceived more broadly than in purely individual and financial terms, but much of the controversy initially revolved around individual reparations grants).[23] The TRC itself used the carrot of financial reparations as an inducement to increase the initially disappointing number of victim statements, and suggested that the government was on board with its policy proposals (Buur 2003: 154–57). For this contract to be perceived as just, the two processes needed to take place simultaneously or, ideally, reparations should have preceded amnesty. The reality was amnesty first, as the TRC's Amnesty Committee had the power to make binding amnesty decisions, and financial reparations a grudging, partial, much delayed second, authorised by a reluctant ANC government as the TRC's Reparation and Rehabilitation Committee could only make recommendations.[24]

The TRC recognised the potential damage that delayed and diminished reparations could cause to its legacy, for example undermining positive experiences testifying before the victims' hearings. What had been a concise reparations policy statement in the initial reports (TRC 1998, Vol. 5: 170–95) became a meta-narrative and concerted lobbying effort in the codicil report. Legal arguments were fleshed out (marshalling domestic and international evidence in support of the victim's 'right to reparation'), voices and requests of 'witnesses' or victims added, and the call for business and civil society as well as the state to play their part amplified (TRC 2003, Vol. 6: 92–180). The net effect of a meagre and poorly coordinated reparations policy, and ongoing tensions between the ANC government, TRC and victim–survivor groups, is that reparations have largely failed to make even a micro contribution to economic justice, either at an individual or more collective level, and this failure has undermined some of the non-material achievements of the TRC.

Tensions have been exacerbated because although the TRC's process of drawing up its reparations policies and recommendations was consultative (TRC 1998, Vol. 5: 177), if not uncontested, the ANC's actual implementation, notably around individual reparation grants, was another consultation blind spot (see Chapter 2).

> In the beginning the government promised to give us reparation, but at the end the government now is trying to play hide and seek. They don't give us an opportunity to express our views. They don't call us into their commissions, to present our ideas or our feelings about the whole thing – they just sum up, and go and take decisions on their own.
>
> (Xolile Dyabooi in TRC 2003, Vol. 6: 135)

As such, the delivery of and mobilisations for reparations have not fulfilled their transformative potential, essentially because they have been predominantly against the state rather than involving a more enabling combination of collaboration and critique.

In this context, there is the danger that South Africa will be, perhaps already has been, redivided by language and the keywords of transition. Reconciliation becomes the vocabulary of perpetrators and beneficiaries, and reconstruction, reparation and transformation that of victims/survivors and the impoverished. An interesting reflection on these issues is provided by Colvin's (2000) already cited study of the Khulumani Support Group in the Western Cape (see Chapters 2 and 5). Justice (defined here as reparations and special pensions, and more broadly in terms of 'justice-as-transformation' or altering economic, political and social structures) has become the priority, not reconciliation. Without these preconditions, reconciliation is premature ('too much, too early'; 'no reconciliation without justice'; ibid.: 13–14). This philosophy is at the heart of their victim-centred and victim-driven approach to reconciliation. Emphases such as these run counter to the dominant, TRC-influenced reconciliation paradigms, for example moving away from an intra-subjective, healing-based focus (whether using the rubrics of medicine, psychology and trauma or religion and forgiveness), to an insistence on situating these ideals in material contexts, and reconfiguring the landscape of sacrifice and gain.

> Group members have been shifting the burden for reconciling from their own healing transformation to the moral redemption of the perpetrator (through confession and repentance) and the establishment of structural, economic changes that will secure victim's material and social well-being. The effect has been to encourage a separation of the process of healing and the process of reconciliation in the work and discourse of the group.
>
> (Colvin 2000: 17)

It is the fight for reparations that galvanised this shift, as a result of which reconciliation has become first and foremost an economic and political struggle.

The debate about whether reconstruction, reparation and transformation on the one hand, and reconciliation on the other, have to be prioritised/sequenced or can be mutually constitutive, is clearly key. An already alluded to two-stage reconciliation thesis often assumes that the former basket of interventions comes first, as a precondition, with the higher-order need of reconciliation building on the fulfilment of certain basic needs. This debate fed differences between Tutu and Mbeki.

> Where reconciliation for Tutu is the beginning of a transformative process (one must be able to transcend one's selfish inclinations before one can transform oneself and one's society) – for Mbeki reconciliation is a step that can follow only after total transformation has taken place.
> (Krog 1998: 110)

The former, rather like unilateral forgiveness, can be admirable but cannot be an expectation because it is an individual act of faith or solidarity; the latter can also be admirable and is more likely to be translated into a goal for public policy. That said, there is evidence that transformation and reconciliation can be mutually constitutive and supporting.

For example, the Internal Reconciliation Commission (IRC) at the University of the Witwatersrand Faculty of Health Sciences (FHS) was explicitly devised as a two-phase process, with submissions, hearings and a report followed by dissemination, debate, a public assembly (including a public apology) and deeper transformative change and redress (for example, seeking to change the racial composition of the student body and faculty). Max Price, then Dean of the Faculty of Health Sciences (interview, 7/3/2006), argued that the relationship between transformation and reconciliation was dialectical. For whites in power, an appreciation of the need for reconciliation was a precondition before they could or felt obliged to support transformation; for blacks feeling excluded, the reverse was true. The IRC sought to address both sides of the equation, to bring parties from different directions to the reconciliatory relationship, and this model has broader applicability (Goodman and Price 2002).[26]

Finally, I want to address the question of what a relational perspective and placing poverty and inequality within the framework of reconciliation add to the debate, if anything. In short, I would argue that without an implied or explicit relationship there is no sense of responsibility and therefore no possibility of reconciliation, and this logic applies in the economic realm as elsewhere. Beyond interpersonal relationships, the economic relationships to be reconciled need to be recast as both vertical and horizontal; and, in Mamdani's terms (1996, 1998, 2000), as seeking to engage majority victims and beneficiaries rather than minority victims and perpetrators. The TRC, in passing, presented economic inequality and poverty in relational terms, on occasion quite creatively identifying beneficiary responsibility and obligations (for example, introducing the notion of 'unjust enrichment' as a source of legal obligation: 'the impoverished party acquires a legal right to claim that the extent of the other's enrichment be restored to him/her if it was acquired at his/her expense' [TRC 2003, Vol. 6: 155]). But they missed the opportunity to present this as a meta-narrative of the apartheid past and the reconciliation sought in the future. Relevant recommendations were also not cogently presented in relational terms.[27] Finally, the TRC did nothing of substance to contest the shift in economic policy from the relational (redistribution) to the non-relational (growth).

What then might relational reconciliation in the economic sphere look like? This chapter concludes with two examples. At a conceptual level, Doxtader argues that the 'relationship between reconciliation and reparation is the abiding question of how to invent the potential for beginning in relation' (2004: 118). It is precisely in concert that these terms have the potential to rework identities and material circumstances, the symbolic and the real. Relative priority is less important than that each should help constitute the other:

> the potential of the reconciliatory and the reparative is frequently explained through accounts that obscure their interdependence. On one side, reconciliation is held out as a creature of the symbolic and the dialogic. Its potential is thought to be actualised in words that give voice to experience, garner acknowledgement and direct animosity towards shared oppositions that allow estranged parties to find common ground ... On the other side, reparation is typically held to turn on the exchange of goods that return capacity. The debt that is paid is not simply a recognition of desert but a way to (re)create the work of life. When set into the context of transition, however, the relationships undertaken through reconciliation appear to constitute the referent for material exchange and the materiality of reparation underpins and supports the capacity for expression. More than truth-finding, reconciliation entails speech that opens and teaches ways of seeing that which requires repair. On the other side of the coin, the provision of material goods may provide the time, energy and resources needed to speak and be heard (more than once).
>
> (Doxtader 2004: 135)

These tensions and debates Doxtader calls the struggle for recognition. To see reconciliation and reparation as mutually constitutive, as part of a process, is a useful contribution to understandings of economic reconciliation.

A second, more concrete, example illustrates that appropriate channels can be found to render economic reconciliation real. Such channels require an implicit or explicit relationship and through such a relationship the assumption of some kind of responsibility. The example relates to a well-known incident, already discussed in Chapter 2. Ambush tactics adopted in the Trojan Horse shootings on 15 October 1985 in Athlone, Cape Town, whereby security police concealed themselves in a moving vehicle before opening fire on a crowd without warning, resulted in the deaths of Michael Cheslyn Miranda, Shaun Magmoed and Jonathan Claasen. Parallel to an officially funded process devising a new memorial for the deceased in 2005, an initially unfunded process was initiated to erect tombstones on what were unmarked graves. Shirley Gunn from the

Human Rights Media Centre, which was facilitating the memorial project, identified the need for the tombstones and the opportunity to create an appropriate channel for funding:

> Many lawyers had worked on and benefited from this case over the years. I started by making a list of the lawyers, told them about the unmarked graves and asked them to contribute to the tombstones. One after the next they said of course they will contribute. Then one bright lawyer told me that one of the lawyers representing the security forces had been the soft underbelly of their team. Could he send the letter to him? In the end we got money not only from members of the security force's legal team but from members of the security forces too. Working with schools in Athlone, we also raised money. You need channels, and at present they are lacking.
> (Gunn, interview 21/2/2006)

But the particular – specific relationships or incidents – must be complemented by the systemic for economic reconciliation to really make its mark. The TRC did not do the necessary groundwork on systemic violence and different orders of responsibility to begin to shift white, beneficiary self-perceptions and identities. Rather the reverse, as it ignored the majority of blacks and vindicated the majority of whites. In this context it is not surprising that interventions gesturing in this direction, however clumsily, such as the business recommendations and Home for All Campaign, failed.[27] Collective guilt is an unpopular concept. But it must be recognised that an individualised focus on a narrow range of abuses provides an equally distorting picture of reality. Alternative tools for gauging responsibility and securing redress, such as the orders of involvement detailed in the business report, need to be developed and applied. Without them, mutually reinforcing transformation and reconciliation at the level of the ordinary and everyday will not occur, and neither will an enduring sense of belonging or citizenship for all.

This final section argues that the innovative mapping of relationships, responsibilities and appropriate channels of redress has a contribution to make to economic reconciliation and redistribution. Transitional justice mechanisms have barely entered this terrain. In South Africa, through the reluctance of white beneficiaries and business to send costly signals of reconciliatory intent, the ANC's economic and reparations policies, and the unwillingness of the TRC to see the structural and economic as part of its mandate, the transitional era has essentially entrenched divisions. Race and class cleavages endure. The past cannot be set aside because structural injustices and inequities ensure that the past retains its imprint on the present, constraining the potential of the future to inform and unsettle the present with its promise. Multi-dimensional, new identities cannot be assumed for similar reasons. The warning, ultimately, is a stark one: either poverty is relational, a shared responsibility, or it will become the subject of political struggles and adversarial relationships. The growing prevalence of the latter reality is not the TRC's responsibility alone, but it is a part of its harvest.

Conclusion

These two chapters on reconciliation represent an attempt to define reconciliation and apply the chosen definition to concrete case studies, and thereby rescue the keyword from cycles of excessive optimism followed by disappointment and even rejection. The term has travelled on the wing of globalisation in the aftermath of the TRC, blown by its very vagueness and seemingly cost-free, feel-good ambiance. To replace it with another term does not necessarily solve the problem, it merely relocates it. Reconciliation, it is argued here, requires both forms of public truth-telling and the (re)creation of relationships. The former can create the bridge for the latter meeting to take place. But it is only one such bridge, if reconciliation is understood as the work of (re)constructing relationships through enlightened processes. Processes can take many forms, the ultimate goals of which are a series of reorientations that can only be achieved in the thick textures of everyday life: reorientations towards the ordinary, more complex identities and world-views, living beyond suffering, to face the present and future, and encompassing a preparedness to embrace risk. The risk of reconciliation is premised on costly signalling, embracing openings onto an unpredictable future, and the necessity of transformative change. Understood in these ways, reconciliation still has a useful role to play in transitional justice discourse.

This chapter seeks to apply the relationships-based portion of the reconciliation model to apology and forgiveness, and to a set of structural relationships that remained at the margins of the TRC's work (communities and the economy). The structural case studies provide valuable insights into the processes of relational reconciliation. The Bonteheuwel study reveals that restorative justice has a contribution to make to such processes but also highlights the fact that many communities in South Africa remain caught in a downward spiral of poverty, violence and divisive informer labelling. Levels of risk are such that they often impede risk-taking and the reorientations necessary for reconciliation. While the economic realm is resistant to a relationship-based understanding of reconciliation, even here I argue that if the necessary will exists there are appropriate, relational channels of redress at interpersonal and structural levels. But for these to be opened up requires acknowledgement of broad-based responsibility and similarly framed redistribution and redress. Some important lessons can be identified. Can we argue (with Price) that transformation and reconciliation are mutually constitutive, that the one cannot succeed without the other? Or (with Doxtader) that a similar argument applies to reparations and reconciliation? Interventions with two stages or parts (voice/values and other forms of action; reconciliation and transformation; reconciliation and reparation; basic needs and higher-order needs) seem ultimately to rely on each intervention shaping the other (mutually constitutive), rather than absolute trade-offs; and to be dependent on the complex sequencing and signalling needed to draw in a range of parties to the reconciliatory relationship.

Structural considerations remained on the margins of the TRC in part because reconciliation in this guise involves challenging the present as well as the past in ways that truth commissions rarely entertain. Nevertheless, reviewing the examples discussed in this chapter it is clear not only that the TRC's immediate reconciliatory reach was relatively shallow, but also that in these cases, as in those cited in the previous chapter, it initiated and legitimised a public debate and ripple effect of interventions which used, adapted and critiqued its mode of operation. Its aftermath in this sense is more significant than it might at first seem. But again a crossroads has been reached, both in South Africa and for the transitional justice enterprise, with regard to the desired depth of transformation and challenge to the status quo. This unresolved note is an appropriate one on which to move to the conclusion.

Notes

1 Other relevant structural relationships include those involving professional groups and institutions (on the TRC's sector hearings, see TRC 1998, Vol. 4; the TRC's work informed a number of spin-off initiatives: TRC 1998, Vol. 5: 431–34). The Internal Reconciliation Commission (IRC) at the University of the Witwatersrand Faculty of Health Sciences (FHS) is an interesting example (Goodman and Price 2002). In relation to testimony-based hearings, Goodman and Price (212) write: 'A phenomenon that remains unexplored is the way in which this innovation permeated deeper levels of South African society and enabled different institutions to use a similar model to facilitate internal transformation'.

2 Halpern and Weinstein (2004: 568) distinguish between empathy and sympathy: 'Sympathy is about experiencing shared emotion; empathy involves imagining and seeking to understand the perspective of another person'. Empathy entails resonating emotionally, curiosity about the other's perspective and an ability to tolerate emotional ambivalence (581). This tolerance of difference is a more resilient, less static, basis for ongoing relationships. The authors argue that empathy, deeply informed by social context and process in the face of perceived fears about ostracism, is crucial to a process of individualisation and rehumanisation and, therefore, to reconciliation. Beyond often decontextualised and idealised moments of sympathy (exemplified in many of the TRC's reconciliatory encounters), empathy needs to be rooted in everyday life, and the interweaving of individual and social change (for a commentary that is referred to in the above article and often conflates sympathy and empathy, see Gobodo-Madikizela [2003], describing interactions between Eugene de Kock on the one hand and his victims and herself on the other).

3 My conception of relationships and reconciliation echoes those found elsewhere. Two examples suffice. Bar-On's (2006, Part III) parameters of reconciliation, derived from work on the Holocaust and Israel–Palestinian conflict, can be summarised along three axes, more emotionally acknowledged complexity, less power asymmetry and the combination of top-down and bottom-up processes. The parameters are: confidence and trust-building; reflectivity (inner dialogue) and interpersonal dialogue; identity reconstruction (notably of collective identities); a long-range temporal dimension (top-

down peace-making can be relatively quick, bottom-up processes often take longer – there is a need to strategise for this time lag); challenging links between subjective language/narratives about the past, asymmetric power relations and attempts to maintain the status quo; inclusion of target populations (e.g. women); better understanding and coordination of unilateral, bilateral and external initiatives; and maintaining hope, not illusions. In Cockburn's (1998) work on women's groups, operating across ethnic or national divides in Bosnia-Hercegovina, Israel–Palestine and Northern Ireland, she argues that key to structuring the 'space between us' is the intersection between democratic and identity processes. Six core principles are outlined (224–28): affirmation of difference; non-closure on identity (including judging people by what they do, not who they are); reduction of polarisation by emphasising other differences; acknowledgement of injustices done in the name of identity; defining the agenda (issues that are safe to address, or not, and changes over time); and inclusive group process.

4 Commentators suggest that in South Africa certain racial boundaries have been eroded (leading largely to coexistence and functional cooperation), while others remain. Fanie du Toit (interview, 4/4/2005) makes the distinction between the formal sector (the workplace, schools, etc.), where there is far more interaction than under apartheid, and the informal, social sector, where people socialise in their own groups. Colvin (2000: 19) writes:

> South Africans of all ethnic and racial classifications work together, watch sport together, share similar public and media spaces together, but the number of white South Africans who have crossed the more difficult linguistic and geographic boundaries in a significant way remains extremely small.

Gibson's (2004: 117–75) empirical survey substantiates the claim that interracial contact is crucial to reconciliation, but indicates that racial isolation is still widespread, especially among blacks, and that workplace contact has no significant impact on reconciliation. The latter finding may be due in part to hierarchical workplace interactions.

5 Useful insights on reconciliation can be gleaned from a range of literatures in which it now features, such as peace-building (Lederach 1997) and post-war reconstruction (Barakat 2005).

6 Rasmussen (2001) argues that processes of brokering official agreements, and the terms and implementation of such agreements, i.e. processes and outcomes, should explicitly nurture reconciliation and relationship-building. In this way peace agreements become a 'blueprint' for the future. At present this is a rarity, and in the light of the rise of intrastate violence and the failures of realist approaches to conflict resolution, change, the author suggests, is required:

> The historical frailty of negotiated settlements and the risks associated with adopting power sharing as a strategy for peaceful sociopolitical change suggests strongly that the manner in which power sharing formulas are engineered and applied should require attention to the processes of relationship building and reconciliation.
>
> (104)

7 This International Institute for Democracy and Electoral Assistance handbook, edited by Bloomfield *et al.* and entitled *Reconciliation After Violent Conflict*, argues that democratic compromise, or politics, is the process of addressing the *issues* in conflict, while reconciliation is the parallel process through which *relationships* at all levels are reworked (Bloomfield *et al.* 2003: 11–12).

8 For lists of apologies see Cunningham (1999: 285–87); *Index on Censorship* (1998); Minow (1998: 112–14); also the Political Apologies and Reparations website: http://political-apologies.wlu.ca/. Minow (114) states that

> public acknowledgements of wrongdoing and statements of contrition reflect a growing international interest in restorative steps towards justice, and perhaps the mounting influences of television talk shows on a public culture of private feelings. Apologies are actual actions officials can take to promote reconciliation and healing in the contexts of political and interpersonal violence. They may also be the most inexpensive and least difficult actions available to them.

For an entertaining satire on the contemporary culture of unaccountable apology, see Jay Rayner's novel *The Apologist* (2004). The reader enters a world driven by self-serving, emotional feel-good excess, in which the UN sets up an Office of Apology and Reconciliation, and 'penitential engagement' becomes a dominant paradigm in international diplomacy.

9 For a variety of views on this issue and de Klerk's apology to the TRC, see Boraine (2000: 156–71, 188–220, 365, 371–72, 441); Giliomee (2003: 650–54); Govier and Verwoerd (2004: 251–53); Krog (1998: for example, 105, 107, 125–31, 157–58); Meredith (1999: 179–99); Nagy (2004: 716–19); Tutu (1999: 17, 146, 195–203).

10 Former apartheid-era Law and Order Minister Adriaan Vlok embarked upon a spate of apologies in 2006, accompanied by the symbolic foot-washing of Frank Chikane, then Director General of the President's Office (Chikane was targeted for poisoning during Vlok's term in office), and the mothers and widows of the Mamelodi Ten (a disappearance case, in which the bodies have been exhumed and identified). Vlok's pilgrimage reawakened debate about whether whites have done enough to atone for the past and on the requirements for a genuine apology and forgiveness. Vlok has been accused, among other things, of not making a full disclosure. It is also worth remembering that this is not the first time that Vlok has been at the centre of an apology-related controversy (see Sarkin 2004: 217, 221). Vlok, with others, pleaded guilty to attempting to murder Chikane in an August 2007 court case and received a suspended sentence under new prosecution guidelines (see Chapter 3).

11 Power dynamics are complex in this terrain. Is forgiveness a vehicle to shift power or are shifts in power a precondition for forgiveness? Similarly, the precise components of power need clarification. It is open to question whether power relations can be significantly altered through shared emotion.

12 Among its recommendations, the TRC called for the liberation movements to apologise to those who were victims of their human rights abuses (TRC 1998, Vol. 5: 347); a public apology to be made to the people of neighbouring states for past violations (TRC 1998, Vol. 5: 348–49); and, finally, for the President to apologise to all victims on behalf of members of the security forces of the former state and armed forces of the liberation movements who committed gross violations of human rights (TRC 2003, Vol. 6: 728).

13 The lack of emphasis on community reconciliation is not universal among truth commissions. In Timor Leste, for example, a Community Reconciliation Process was facilitated by the Commission for Reception, Truth and Reconciliation to deal with lower-level offences at community level.

14 Twelve statements were made to the TRC by BMW members. The violations focus of the TRC report entries on the BMW is exclusively on torture and severe ill treatment, often of a sexual nature: 'The consequences of participating in the violent activities of the BMW – prolonged detention, brutal torture and imprisonment with common criminals – will be felt by the individuals concerned, their families and friends and the

community of Bonteheuwel for decades' (TRC 1998, Vol. 4: 280). The shift in emphasis from the TRC report (torture) to the mediation (informing) is significant in terms of identifying what is of paramount importance in rebuilding everyday lives and relationships.
15 This section owes a considerable debt to Richard Records at CSVR, and it is informed by his notes on the Bonteheuwel mediations and several conversations with him on the subject. The analysis which follows mainly focuses on the first mediation which I attended at the CSVR offices in Cape Town.
16 It is striking in this context what W omitted from his mediation testimony, possibly because most of those present already knew these details about his past. Later on in proceedings he mentioned that he was 11 years old when he became involved in the struggle, and yet even as one of the youngest members of the BMW he was detained and tortured several times.
17 Several further mediations were carried out in 2005 (also see Greenbaum 2006). The first two were those proposed at the close of the initial session. At a meeting of former members of BMW, their parents and Bonteheuwel community representatives, accounts of S and W's reconciliation were well received but the parents and community leaders went on to express their own desire for recognition for the role they played, and the hardships they endured, in the struggle. A further, highly charged, mediation took place between N and other BMW members. As noted in the text, N is at the centre of community tensions surrounding the political manipulation of the informer label, and is charged with having abused his role as gatekeeper to state resources and personal security. For example, tensions exist over who made it on to relevant 'lists' for special pensions or to enter the South African National Defence Force (SANDF) or South African Police Service (SAPS) (while N became a major in the SANDF, many others are unemployed). Further poisoning discussions, claims have also been made that N himself was an informer. According to CSVR this third meeting cannot be considered successful as no resolution or reconciliation occurred. N expressed an unwillingness to attend further mediations, stating that people must get on with their lives and move forward. One further interpersonal mediation took place in 2005. CSVR organised for members of the BMW to see the film *Red Dust*, a viewing designed to feed into a workshop discussion about informers. Afterwards two people approached CSVR with a request to mediate between them. One had been accused of being an informer and state witness by the other. This mediation broke down as the participants could not agree on what was said at the court hearing. The group of mediations detailed above also led to workshops on memory and memorialisation, as a potential route to broad-based recognition and capacity-building (advocacy skills; information about how to set up a non-profit organisation). Participants were asked to come up with ideas for an exhibition and a community development project.
18 This is not to say that important truths did not emerge in the Bonteheuwel mediations (for example, about how rumours concerning informers were spread and their impacts), or that factual truth never matters. The last mediation referred to in note 17, featuring allegations that another member of BMW was an informer and state witness, resulted in a major disagreement about what was said at the court hearing. And in this case an unsuccessful attempt was made to locate the court record. Here it appears that factual truth was necessary for reconciliation to be a possibility. The point, in short, is that within any given mediation there are no set rules on this issue, only party-dependent contingency.
19 Commentary on transitional justice and economic concerns is recent, but gathering momentum. Mani (2002) argued for an integrated approach to justice after conflict (legal justice or the rule of law, rectificatory justice and redistributive justice). Early contributions to the debate also came from Alexander (2003) and Arbour (2006). In

228 Reconciliation and the everyday

2008 the *International Journal of Transitional Justice* published a special issue on transitional justice and development (Volume 2, Number 3), and a year later the International Center for Transitional Justice and the Social Science Research Council released the volume, *Transitional Justice and Development: Making Connections* (de Greiff and Duthie 2009).

20 In an early formulation, Alexander (2003) argued that transitional justice mechanisms could contribute to poverty reduction in two main ways: by helping to secure the *necessary conditions* for poverty reduction and through their *direct impacts* on the material and non-material well-being of those identified as victims. Indirect measures would include strengthening the rule of law, building civic trust and strengthening mechanism of participation.

21 Although the TRC did not seriously engage with the land question, among the illuminating parallels between land restitution and the TRC are the triumph of symbol over substance; the poor take-up by victims; the low financial commitment to redress; the clash between a focus on individual victims and other public interests; the use of oral testimony to make claims; and the highly personalised experience of the process, notably with regard to achieving closure on the past (Walker 2006, 2008).

22 In addition to OHCHR's (2008) rule-of-law tool on reparations, also see de Greiff 2006; the Updated Set of Principles for the Protection and Promotion of Human Rights through Action to Combat Impunity, UN Doc. E/CN.4/2005/102/Add.1, February 2005; and the Basic Principles and Guidelines on the Right to a Remedy and Reparation for Victims of Gross Violations of International Human Rights Law and Serious Violations of International Humanitarian Law, adopted and proclaimed by UN General Assembly resolution 60/147 of 16 December 2005, UN Doc. A/RES/60/147.

23 Urgent interim reparations were granted to certain victims starting in July 1998. The TRC recommended a range of reparation and rehabilitation measures in its final report – urgent interim reparations, individual reparation grants, symbolic reparation/ legal and administrative measures, community rehabilitation programmes, institutional reform (TRC 1998, Vol. 5: 170–95) – including payments of between R17,000 and R23,000 (in the region of $2,700) per year for six years by way of individual reparation for victims of gross human rights violations. As with other recommendations, critics have voiced concerns about these measures, highlighting, for example, their vagueness, and the lack of costings (beyond individual grants) and prioritisation (Colvin 2006: 197–98).

24 In November 2003 the government began to implement a much more modest reparations policy for individuals than that recommended by the TRC, a one-off, final reparations payment of R30,000 (about $4,000) to those identified as victims. Another possible route to reparations are lawsuits in the US, the most important of which is the one filed in November 2002 by the Khulumani Support Group and others against several foreign companies accused of aiding and abetting the apartheid regime. The lawsuit, *Khulumani et al. v. Barclays et al.*, is based on the Alien Tort Claims Act and common law principles of liability. The ANC government initially opposed this and other lawsuits, but under President Zuma has withdrawn its opposition; former TRC commissioners are supporting the claims. Considered together, the apartheid lawsuits are still working their way through the US courts. See www.khulumani.net/. This limited financial portfolio does not exhaust the reparation possibilities as parliament has approved four categories of recommendations: financial reparations for victims; symbols and monuments; rehabilitation of communities; and medical and other forms of assistance. For an overview of the reparations issue in South Africa, see Colvin (2006); and Seekoe (2006). Civil society initiatives in the realms of reparation and recognition continue undeterred by the as yet unsatisfactory state response to the

TRC's recommendations. One hitherto unmentioned example is the Heritage Project of the *Sunday Times* newspaper, launched to mark its 100th year of publication in 2006. Public 'story art' and memorials are being commissioned to record and recognise notable people and events that made the 'news century' (see www.sundaytimes.co.za/heritage). Also see Khulumani's Charter for Redress (www.khulumani.net/).

25 The transformation–reconciliation conundrum clearly exists elsewhere, and is invariably underpinned by power differentials. The following quote comments upon meetings between peace-leaning Israelis and Palestinians:

> Israelis participating in joint activities desire to normalize relations with the Palestinian participants ... the desire for normalization emanates from the belief that peace and peacemaking should be based on mutual acceptance and recognition ... on the other hand, Palestinian desire for normalization is preconditioned on their call for justice ... normalization is a bargaining chip that should not be handed over until the occupation is terminated and a Palestinian state is established.
>
> (Dajani and Baskin 2006: 100)

I am grateful to Ron Dudai for making me aware of this quotation. Some research on transformation and reconciliation is taking place in South Africa. The Institute for Justice and Reconciliation's Political Analysis Programme assesses reconciliation, transformation and development through its SA Reconciliation Barometer (public opinion surveys of attitudes to sociopolitical transformation and national reconciliation), and a Transformation Audit. The former uses the following criteria to measure reconciliation: human security (physical, economic, cultural); political culture (the legitimacy and accountability of institutions, structures and values); cross-cutting political relationships; dialogue; historical confrontation (an ability to confront and address the past); and race relations (cross-racial contact, perceptions, social distance). For the relevant reports, see: www.ijr.org.za/politicalanalysis/.

26 With regard to business, the TRC encouraged contributions to the President's Fund, and recommended the establishment of a Business Reconciliation Fund and that a range of other measures be considered, including a wealth tax. Recommendations have largely not been implemented, and while business leaders identified the Business Trust as a reparative organ contributions to the trust have been derisory (TRC 1998, Vol. 5: 318–20; also see Vol. 4: 54–58, Vol. 6: 140–44, 162). Implicit in these recommendations is a call for a reparative gesture from all business to all disadvantaged South Africans, in short a systemic notion of perpetrator and beneficiary. As Nattrass (1999: 375) notes:

> the TRC proposed that all business (regardless of their different levels of involvement) should be liable for punitive taxation. In so doing, the TRC shifted from a focus on individual perpetrators, to a systemic analysis that equated any profitable activity with prospering under apartheid and drew a link between benefiting from the system and moral culpability for it.

This was out of tune with both the individualised focus of its other work and jarred with the subtle three-tiered index of involvement it had devised for business – in effect, blanket recommendations stressed the TRC's third order of involvement (benefiting from the apartheid economy). While an understanding of the systemic nature of apartheid is necessary for beneficiary acknowledgement of responsibility, and would increase the potential for relational reconciliation in this field, in the

TRC's analysis it remains unevenly and incoherently delivered. Any temptation to believe that such debates go away of their own accord, rather than venue-hopping, can be swiftly set aside if one considers the contemporary discourse around corporate social responsibility (CSR) in South Africa. Business favours concepts such as 'corporate social investment' and 'corporate citizenship' because they 'ask no questions about legacy, memory, history, justice, or moral and ethical responsibilities' (Fig 2005: 601). In sum, businesses use CSR to redefine responsibility and 'manufacture amnesia' (617 – in a similar vein, contributions to the Business Trust were in the name of nation-building rather than reparations).

27 The Home for All Campaign (which later became the Home to All Campaign) called upon South Africans to sign a declaration acknowledging that whites were beneficiaries of the past, that racism and the damage done endures, and that a failure to accept responsibility inhibits reconciliation and transformation; it asked for the personal sharing of skills and resources, linking redress to belonging.

Conclusion

Transitional justice, impaled on the dilemma of whether to pursue an idealistic course or to compromise and embrace pragmatism, constitutes an extraordinarily compelling story within contemporary politics. If one adds the fact that it situates complex national histories and priorities within various strands of globalisation, the plot thickens. As such, 'the era of transitional justice' is a good place to start if you want to find out what really matters in politics and international relations today. What are the key debates? Who is shaping the debates? Beyond big ideas and policy prescriptions what gets implemented, and what subset of interventions actually work? What are the counter-discourses? This is also a good place to start for activists seeking to orientate themselves within contemporary politics, and reshape it. Transitional justice is a field in which non-governmental actors have both profoundly influenced discussions and outcomes, and yet remain marginal to decision-making about major, structural issues, e.g. the economy, criminal justice.

By way of a conclusion I revisit the main arguments of the book – conceptualising keywords; reimagining human rights; engaging the past and the present; and remaking the public sphere – by posing four questions that those debating or proposing transitional justice interventions, and particularly truth commissions, should consider before getting their hands dirty.[1]

Question 1: Do human rights 'occupy the field of emancipatory possibility' (Kennedy 2002: 108)?

This question speaks to the perceived dominance of human rights in global activism. Human rights can be isolationist, fundamentalist, arriving at the gate of adjacent territory bearing gifts rather than seeking to learn. Questions do indeed need to be asked about the expansion and tone of the human rights project. Has human rights become 'an object of devotion rather than calculation', with the latter implying a pragmatic and strategic approach (Kennedy 2002: 102)? What are the costs, as well as the benefits, of privileging human rights? Is a one-size-fits-all emancipatory practice emerging? Such dominance directs resources, carves out privileged ways of being heard, frames issues in certain ways and for certain audiences, and legitimises a subset of ideas and interventions while delegitimising alternatives. There is some truth to the claim that human rights dominates transitional justice discourse through an often unthinking and uncritical justice and legal reflex. A concrete example of occupation is the way in which human rights colonised other ways of framing the past and alternative research methodologies, within the genre colony of the TRC's reports (Chapter 1). The emergence of transitional justice as an industry and its embrace of holistic understandings of its remit resonate with this criticism, although one could argue that much of the expansion is into areas less associated with human rights than criminal prosecutions and rule of law measures. The emergence of hybrid moral arguments and ways of working also render the claim of occupation less convincing.

One of the most interesting facets of transitional politics is that it fosters so many ways in which different ideas and intervention strategies coexist. Hybridity now pervades almost all facets of truth commission work: methodologies (e.g. development discourse informs process dynamics such as participatory approaches); outputs (Chapter 1 argues that truth commissions produce reports that are a hybrid genre, and have moved beyond report fetishisation); and activism (the need to combine social action and legal action, and move beyond legal fetishism, is reflected in various chapters in this book). It is in this context that I advocate the reimagining of human rights and remaking of the public sphere.

The former includes the indivisibility of civil–political and socio-economic rights (still new terrain for transitional justice), identity coordinates beyond the binary of victim and perpetrator (positive identities associated with just resistance, for example), and human rights as a means of balancing interests and weighing values. All these innovations will gain from creative borrowing. They also recognise that human rights cohabits with other discourses, whether it be in the genre colony of truth commission reports or the complex intersections between human rights and restorative justice or development. Remaking the public sphere requires a hybrid approach to both broad-based public description and dissemination, and constituency-building and rights-based participation.

Movement towards hybridity in the methodologies, outputs and activism of truth commissions positions them on the front line of human rights innovation. As noted above, human rights, as manifest in international law and through international NGOs, often resists collaboration and ploughs its own lonely furrow. It occupies or it ignores. Within truth commissions, human rights has been drawn into collaboration, in a way that is emblematic of challenges facing human rights in the contemporary world. Whether in development, humanitarianism, public health or transitional justice, human rights is gaining a foothold but not a monopoly. The challenge is to tie multiple ways of working and moral vocabularies into a steadfast knot (for example, analysis stressing complex identities may undermine conventional human rights interventions such as prosecutions). While there remains an impulse towards fundamentalism and colonisation within human rights in certain quarters, its hybrid forms suggest that it does not, and should not, occupy the field of emancipatory possibility.

Question 2: Is there a danger of co-option?

One of the main arguments of this book is that transitional justice discourse, and its use of human rights, is itself in danger of being, and in some cases has already been, co-opted by more powerful elements in societies and the dominant strands of globalisation (Chapter 6). Transitional agendas are usually set by elites and the heavyweight strands of globalisation (neo-liberal economics, punitive responses to violent crime). The discourse and tool-kit of transitional justice often fail to question this policy compact that has become an orthodoxy, and may even ease its passage. A related danger is that transitional justice is consigned to those institutions that are least likely to make a difference. Would it not be advisable to also concentrate on integrating its priorities into the economic and political powerhouses at national and international levels? Victims and survivors of human rights abuse are invariably marginalised as transitions stall and power holders regroup. As it currently stands, for example, transitional politics oversees amnesty and impunity for perpetrators far more effectively than justice and reparations for victims/survivors. For a supposedly victim-centred intervention, truth commissions in particular have a long way to go to deliver on their promise. In short, as transitional justice is currently operationalised it has too little effect on the marginalised, in part because it is subsumed within structural processes and continuities that often result in their remarginalisation. It is in this setting that the complex relationships between past and present, and human rights and power, take centre-stage.

Some will argue that a preoccupation with the present and future, and with such a broad economic and political canvas, is not an appropriate or realistic priority for transitional justice. It is essentially a backward-looking exercise, confronting human rights violations from the past. But as we have seen, the past is not an island. There is a need to more clearly link human rights concerns in the present to structural continuities with the past (poverty, inequality, social and criminal violence), and to anticipate that the past often affects the present not as straightforward repetition, but in modified, evolving ways, through complex processes of continuity and change. A forward-looking emphasis on non-repetition and prevention demands such an approach. Big-picture blindness is not an option. One potential outcome of big-picture blindness, among NGO activist and others, is that whole communities of practitioners and policy-makers will sleepwalk into at best unintended effects, and at worst catastrophe. Sceptics should read Peter Uvin's book *Aiding Violence: The Development Enterprise in Rwanda* (1998), which plots in devastating detail how 'development' in fact contributed to structural violence and genocide in Rwanda. What, then, is the solution? I have argued that as broad-based exercises in public description, truth commissions will become more political, in that they will criticise injustice in the past and present. By nurturing rights-based participation, truth commissions will create links between democratic principles and the legacies and contingencies of power in such a way that the former have more chance of becoming an enduring challenge to the latter.

The relationship between human rights and power raises equally daunting challenges. Human rights is a site on which compromise is forged, privilege defended and radical change envisaged. As we saw in Chapter 1, the TRC employed human rights to tell unpopular truths to all political parties and emphasise the importance of legal equality. But it stepped back from fully delivering on this promise, as it ultimately balanced speaking truth to power with speaking truth to reconciliation to ease the passage of the new democracy. Rights-based law spoke truth to specific powers, but power also mobilised the law to contain the agendas of truth and justice, protecting perpetrators rather more effectively than victims. Further, a narrow human rights reporting discourse marginalised individual subjectivity and political context, and overlooked structural violence and broader notions of accountability. Thus, human rights can be critiqued for speaking decontextualised, partial truths to similarly selective constructs of power. This critique applies to civil–political rights (Chapters 1 and 2), and their socio-economic counterparts (Chapter 6).

Another way of addressing this problem is to say that transitional justice provides an entry-point into understanding human rights as a way of balancing law and politics, and balancing interests, weighing values and prioritising demands, as well as making absolute claims and right-versus-wrong adjudications. Some of the balancing acts are important and constructive (recognising the rights of victims as well as perpetrators; addressing all parties to a conflict), others, usually where equivalence is claimed or very narrow understandings of rights prevail, are more problematic (all voices should be heard; we are all victims, and all perpetrators; property trumping other rights). A related ambivalence is that human rights is elevated, even fetishised, at the expense of mainstream politics and economics (where previously we had resistance, now we have human rights), the implication being that the struggle is over, and its fallout can be arbitrated by the neutral intervention of law. Nothing is further from the truth. While this book explores ways of countering the ambivalent relationship human rights has with power, through public description based on the indivisibility of rights and rights-based participation, for example, human rights will always reflect as well as challenge broader political and power dynamics.

Two final points are worth making on the issue of co-option. First, no social justice discourse is intrinsically or inevitably pro-poor. How much development aid or humanitarian assistance is creamed off by elites, for example? Discourses advocating social justice enter the political firmament, and are shaped by its contours even as they seek to change them. Co-option is invariably contested. As long as transitional justice and human rights are being claimed by victims and survivors, adapted and critiqued from below as well as imposed from above, it remains imperative to try to keep their radical edge sharp. A second point relates to questions 1 and 2: can human rights be both particularly adept at co-option and particularly susceptible to co-option? It is hard to imagine anything as simplistic as human rights scooping up all social justice discourses (co-opting) and delivering them to the door of the rich and powerful (co-opted). Critics cannot have it both ways. Human rights cannot be all-powerful and powerless.

Question 3: Is too much or too little being attempted?

Question 1 is one variant of the 'too much' critique. Perhaps the most pertinent charge is that transitional justice promises more than it can deliver, with little by way of evidential base for its claims. The development of a transitional justice industry, utilising holistic understandings of its field and keywords, runs precisely this risk. One objective of this book has been to provide clearer definitions of transitional justice keywords, and fresh insights into the relationship between human rights and transitional justice, while avoiding both excessive ambition and its alter ego, uncalled-for pessimism. While broadly in agreement with some of the more sanguine recent evaluations of the TRC, I have identified core weaknesses (its failure to engage with economic realities and social and criminal violence) as well as hitherto underappreciated strengths (the TRC's impact on public culture and public history). I hope that the insights provided can be used to help design truth commissions, and shape a sense of what these important institutions can realistically achieve.

Transitional justice and human rights are accused of doing too little when they focus on symptoms (torture, killings) rather than causes (structural violence), on the state and public violence rather than non-state actors and abuses in the private realm, and on the past rather than the present. Partial critiques of power detailed in Chapters 1 and 2 fall into this camp: in South Africa, 'truth as content' (civil–political abuses) and 'truth as process' (liberal proceduralism) failed to comprehensively challenge the power that still presides over injustice. Arguably, the chosen framing of reconciliation (stressing national, and to a lesser degree individual and interpersonal, reconciliation) had a similar effect (Chapters 5 and 6). In short, both problems and solutions can be conceived too narrowly.

And yet, much the same criticism (doing too little, promising too much) could be made of any social justice discourse. Which one of these does not over-promise to acquire donor funding or community support? Who can claim to unerringly address structural, root causes of problems and achieve sustainable solutions? My own suggestion that truth commissions should describe broadly and nurture rights-based participation as a means of facilitating structural change will be seen as wildly ambitious by some, as will the argument that transitional justice measures need to be tied more closely to criminal justice reform (too much). My suggestion that recommendations should be modest and strategically targeted will increase their effectiveness in my view; but others will see this as downgrading an essential advocacy tool (too little). These tensions are inescapable.

International human rights law is a statement of ideals, not realities; its practice is about attempting to close the gap between the two. Whether this is happening is a question all practitioners must continually ask themselves. And yet critics (again) cannot have it both ways. Human rights and/or transitional justice cannot simultaneously be attempting too much *and* too little.

Before moving on, one aspect of the attempting too much/little debate deserves to be highlighted more clearly. Transitional justice commentary is oddly silent about its relationship with democracy (for an exception, making connections between transitional justice, and specifically the TRC, and citizenship, see Nagy 2004a; nation-building is something different, as it does not necessarily foster democracy: McEachern 2002; R. Wilson 2001). As currently configured, democracy takes the shape of a global, liberal template. Processes of democratisation often appear to be little more than exercises in box-ticking, designed to appease the international community (elections held, market forms introduced, certain laws passed, a truth commission established), while structural violence and inequalities are left largely intact. A conventional transitional justice repertoire of public voicing/debate, the rule of law and strengthening state institutions can be valuable, but largely reinforces this narrow conception of democracy. As such, democracies are fractured, uneven, partial, and so are human rights protections. To address structural violence (poverty, crime), the most damaging legacy of conflicts and oppression, and deepen democracy, requires more.

I have appropriated the notion of rights-based participation to suggest an alternative. It offers a way to link local, national and perhaps even global levels of decision-making, transitional justice and processes of democratisation, and powerful articulatory moments with more enduring forms of public decision-making. Societal innovation and collective action within civil society will clearly vary enormously from place to place, depending on national circumstances and histories. But if a portion of this resource can be incorporated into public forms of decision-making (and avoid co-option), particularly on issues about which the new dispensation equivocates (human rights, economic redistribution), there is potential for a two-way process of democratic thickening and for state–society relations to be genuinely remade. Receptiveness and innovative design will be required and could be aided by both the activities of a truth commission and its recommendations. As hybrid institutions, set between the state and civil society, official truth commissions, in particular, are perfectly positioned to perform this role. What kinds of groups, beyond NGOs, might step forward as civil society partners? New organisational forms emerging from transitional frustrations and opportunities lead the way. In South Africa, social movements came to the fore alongside the TRC, with the latter barely giving the former a sideways glance. Donor and development discourses favouring participation and decentralisation have fostered public responses, some of which are robust. Similarly, long-established strands of mobilisation – women's groups, trade unions – are often under-utilised. Church groups may have deep roots, and could be less threatening for the state.

Certain patterns in state–civil society relations can be repeatedly observed in post-apartheid South Africa, in fields ranging from transitional justice to criminal justice and land reform: an emphasis on human rights and progressive change is marginalised over time; NGOs and other actors move from collaboration to critique, while still trying to combine both registers in their engagements with the state; top-down and bottom-up interventions fail to fully capitalise on each other's strengths. There may be times when bottom-up programmes wish to, or have to, stand alone. Ideally, however, the dissemination and scaling up of best practice, and sustainability, requires a partnership between the local and national, civil society and state (post-apartheid restorative justice initiatives provide both more and less encouraging examples: see Chapters 4 and 6). For some, this will be a quintessential example of attempting too much. I don't think transitional justice has any choice. What are truth, justice and reconciliation about, ultimately, if not what we mean by democracy? Without rights-based participation the legacies of truth commissions are likely to unravel; without deeper forms of democracy, commissions are likely to merely scratch the surface of injustice.

Question 4: Can the prioritisation/sequencing and interlinking of interventions be mapped on to patterns of continuity and change in society?

Prioritising within the basket of transitional justice interventions is inevitable. Doing everything and helping everyone is not possible, certainly not within the constrained confines of what normally constitutes transition. Many of the countries emerging from conflict and authoritarian rule are among the poorest countries in the world; often they are what are now termed fragile or failed states. The question is whether prioritisation, sequencing and interlinking of interventions can take place in a way that keeps open, and even generates momentum towards, other supplementary interventions, or whether policy choices close off alternatives.

Such choices need to keep an eye on a range of temporal registers. Public culture will perhaps be quickest in facing uncomfortable truths about the past, truths that truth commissions may shy away from (betrayal and informing; the desire for revenge and retribution). Truth commissions are designed as up-front measures to generate greater consensus about history. Educational reform and official memorialisation are slower, usually reflecting rather than pioneering change. Amnesty, often seen as the ultimate in the closing-off of future options, has recently become less absolute. While amnesty may shut off certain justice avenues in the short term, its restrictions have on occasion been circumvented in the longer term as political circumstances change and judicial assertiveness grows. Reconciliation may require basic needs and security as a precondition; reparations policies invariably emerge several years into transitions. Transitional justice, therefore, has its own temporality which suggests that policy choices have commonsense parameters as well as aspects which strain the strategic guile of activists and the political strength of new democracies.

Underwriting this temporality are broader dynamics of continuity and change. Continuities take various forms, from impunity, to patterns of violence and hard-line responses to violence; from elite pacting, authoritarian attitudes and decision-making 'blind spots' to deliberative and material inequalities. Not all continuities are problematic, but this particular cohort diminishes democracy. Similarly, not all change is good. And change can be brought about by the methodical accretion of sequencing and momentum, but also by eruptions (an arrest-of-Pinochet-in-London moment), that dramatically shift the political balance of power. The 'policy pendulum' is also a temporal process marking continuity and change, and one which attempts to chart evolving policy responses to issues such as the economy and criminal justice. To integrate prioritisation and sequencing into these patterns of continuity and change in order to enhance social justice is the ultimate goal of transitional justice. For policy ideas to resonate, in short, requires an anticipatory faculty along these lines.

As we have seen, questions surrounding prioritisation, sequencing, preconditions, momentum and interlinking apply across a number of transitional justice debates – institutionalisation and liberalisation; amnesty and reparations; justice and peace; apology and forgiveness; reconciliation and transformation; bottom-up and top-down approaches. Despite frequent bold claims and certitudes in the literature, these processes remain opaque and poorly understood. There is some evidence in the preceding chapters that interventions are indivisible, mutually constitutive, rather than requiring trade-offs: in fact, suggestions that both measures may be necessary as one alone will not succeed. Rather than seeing sequencing as purely a problem it can be understood as an opportunity, providing the flexibility for the call and response needed to draw a range of parties, via a range of routes, into taking the risks required by the transitional justice enterprise.

An answer to question 4 can draw on positive insights, but ultimately must also acknowledge that trade-offs are inevitable. Doing everything, helping everyone, is not even possible over time. It is important not to reinvent a different kind of holism, with its ambition merely stretched vaguely over a longer period of time; or to promise too much, again. Human rights has an inbuilt resistance to prioritisation, largely because it has traditionally meant civil–political rights gaining the upper hand over economic, social and cultural rights. But absolute assertions of indivisibility can be disempowering in resource-scarce environments, and prioritisation becomes less threatening if it is not a formulaic exercise. Where might one begin? Facilitating locally informed choices, working on gateway rights that bolster other rights, evading an evaluative focus that solely privileges 'results', nurturing momentum and honing an anticipatory faculty, are admirable and more realistic goals. The choices that need to be made could potentially be a foundation lesson in participation and democracy for transitional governments and societies, not least in deciding what matters most and why, and in negotiating divisions of labour between state, civil society and the international community.

Alas, there are no easy answers to these questions. There is a debate to be had and a set of highly political outcomes to be contested. But it is important that self-reflective activists and academics, committed to social justice and well versed in a range of moral vocabularies and ways of working (including but going beyond human rights), are part of the debate. Without them transitional injustice will prevail; with them transitional justice still just might.

Note

1 This discussion draws on David Kennedy's (2002) article, 'The International Human Rights Movement: Part of the Problem?', but is far from a comprehensive summary of its contents.

Interviewees

Details provided indicate the profession or affiliation of each interviewee at the time of the interview, and/or a previous profession/affiliation that was the subject of discussion. The date of the interview(s) is given in brackets.

Mike Batley, Restorative Justice Centre (28/4/2005)
Fanie du Toit, Institute for Justice and Reconciliation (4/4/2005)
Madeleine Fullard, TRC researcher; Head of the Missing Persons Task Team, National Prosecuting Authority (27/8/2002, 21/4/2005)
Shirley Gunn, Human Rights Media Centre and Khulumani Support Group (27/8/2002, 5/4/2005, 21/2/2006, 26/8/2009)
Ali Hlongwane, Chief Curator, Hector Pieterson Museum (26/4/2005)
Eric Itzkin, Deputy Director for Immovable Heritage, City of Johannesburg (25/4/2005)
Zukiswa Khalipha, Khulumani Support Group (7/4/2005)
Thabo Kgomommu, South African Heritage Resources Agency (29/4/2005)
Antjie Krog, broadcaster, poet (23/7/1998)
Duma Kumalo, Khulumani Support Group (4/9/1998, 15/8/2002, 17/8/2002, 22/8/2003, 22/4/2005)
Themba Lonzi, Institute for Healing of Memories (29/8/2002)
Mabel Makupe, Khulumani Support Group (11/9/1998)
Thembi Mgonjeni, Treatment Action Campaign (29/4/2005, telephone interview)
Mongezi Mngese, Institute for Healing of Memories (29/8/2002, 4/4/2005, 11/12/2009)
Alicia Monis, Heritage: Legacy Projects, Department of Arts and Cultures (28/4/2005)
Ntambi Mozikare, Khulumani Support Group (2/9/1998)
Irene Mxinwa, mother of one of the Guguletu Seven (30/7/1998)
Ereshnee Naidu, Centre for the Study of Violence and Reconciliation (25/4/2005)
Sifiso Ndlovu, historian, Hector Pieterson Memorial and Museum (24/4/2005)
Bridget O'Donoghue, Environmental Planner, City of Cape Town (31/3/2006)

Wendy Orr, TRC Commissioner (19/4/2005)
Deborah Posel, historian (14/8/2002)
Max Price, Dean of the University of the Witwatersrand Faculty of Health Sciences (7/3/2006)
Ciraj Rassool, historian (7/4/2005)
Trudy de Ridder, psychologist (3/8/1998)
Jeremy Sarkin, legal academic (11/4/2005)
Lauren Segal, Constitution Hill (28/4/2005, 7/3/2006)
Yonah Seleti, Head of Heritage Department, Freedom Park Trust (7/3/2006)
Thandi Shezi, Khulumani Support Group (4/9/1998, 22/4/2005)
Ann Skelton, lawyer, children's law expert (28/4/2005)
Yasmin Sooka, TRC Commissioner (20/4/2005)
Vivi Stavrou, psychologist (17/8/1998)
Hugo van der Merwe, Centre for the Study of Violence and Reconciliation (10/3/2005)
Elrena van der Spuy, criminologist (8/4/2005)
Brian Xaba, Heritage: Legacy Projects, Department of Arts and Cultures (28/4/2005)

Bibliography

Abrahamsen, T. and van der Merwe, H. (2005) *Reconciliation Through Amnesty? Amnesty Applicants' Views of the South African Truth and Reconciliation Commission*. Johannesburg: Centre for the Study of Violence and Reconciliation.

Afghanistan Independent Human Rights Commission (AIHRC) (2005) *A Call for Justice: A National Consultation on Past Human Rights Violations in Afghanistan*. Available at: www.aihrc.org.af (accessed 17 May 2010).

AfriMAP and the Open Society Foundation for South Africa (2005) *South Africa: Justice Sector and the Rule of Law*. Cape Town: Open Society Foundation for South Africa.

Alexander, J. (2003) *A Scoping Study of Transitional Justice and Poverty Reduction: Final Report*. London: DFID, January.

Altbeker, A. (2004) 'Guns and Public Policy in South Africa'. In *Justice Gained? Crime and Crime Control in South Africa's Transition*, ed. B. Dixon and E. van der Spuy. Cape Town: University of Cape Town Press, 58–82.

Amnesty International (2007) *Truth, Justice and Reparation: Establishing an Effective Truth Commission*. London: Amnesty International.

Anthonissen, C. (2006) 'Critical Discourse Analysis as an Analytical Tool in Considering Selected, Prominent Features of TRC Testimonies'. *Journal of Language and Politics* 5, 1: 71–96.

Arbour, L. (2006) 'Economic and Social Justice for Societies in Transition'. Second Annual Transitional Justice Lecture hosted by the Center for Human Rights and Global Justice at New York University School of Law and the International Centre for Transitional Justice. New York University Law School, New York, 25 October.

Arendt, H. (1958) *The Human Condition*. Chicago: University of Chicago Press.

Arias, A. (ed.) (2001) *The Rigoberta Menchú Controversy*. Minneapolis: University of Minnesota Press.

Ashforth, A. (1990) *The Politics of Official Discourse in Twentieth-century South Africa*. Oxford: Clarendon Press.

Ashworth, A. (2002) 'Responsibilities, Rights and Restorative Justice'. *British Journal of Criminology* 42: 578–95.

Asmal, K., Asmal, L. and Roberts, R. S. (1997) *Reconciliation through Truth: A Reckoning of Apartheid's Criminal Governance*. 2nd ed. Cape Town: David Philip.

Aspen Institute (1989) *State Crimes. Punishment or Pardon?* New York: Aspen Institute.

Attwell, D. and Harlow, B. (2000) 'Introduction: South African Fiction after Apartheid'. *Modern Fiction Studies* 46, 1: 1–9.

Auerbach, Y. (2005) 'Forgiveness and Reconciliation: The Religious Dimension'. *Terrorism and Political Violence* 17: 469–85.

Backer, D. (2003) 'Civil Society and Transitional Justice: Possibilities, Patterns and Prospects'. *Journal of Human Rights* 2, 3: 297–313.

Baker, B. (2002) 'Living with Non-state Policing in South Africa: The Issues and Dilemmas'. *Journal of Modern African Studies* 40, 1: 29–53.

Baldwin-Ragaven, L., de Gruchy, J. and London, L. (eds) (1999) *An Ambulance of the Wrong Colour: Health Professionals, Human Rights and Ethics in South Africa*. Cape Town: University of Cape Town Press.

Ball, P., Spirer, H. and Spirer, L. (eds) (2000) *Making the Case: Investigating Large Scale Human Rights Violations Using Information Systems and Data Analysis*. Washington DC: AAAS.

Bar-On, D. (2006) 'Reconciliation Revisited: Parts I–III'. *Newropeans Magazine*, 14–16 March. Available at www.newropeans-magazine.org/ (accessed 17 May 2010).

Barakat, S. (2005) 'Seven Pillars for Post-war Reconstruction'. In *After the Conflict: Reconstruction and Development in the Aftermath of War*, ed. S. Barakat. London: I. B. Tauris, 249–70.

Barkan, E. (2000) *The Guilt of Nations: Restitution and Negotiating Historical Injustice*. Baltimore: Johns Hopkins University Press.

Barsalou, J. and Baxter, V. (2007) *The Urge to Remember: The Role of Memorials in Social Reconstruction and Transitional Justice*. Stabilization and Reconstruction Series No. 5. Washington DC: United States Institute of Peace, January.

Bell, C. and Keenan, J. (2004) 'Human Rights Nongovernmental Organizations and the Problems of Transition'. *Human Rights Quarterly* 26, 2: 330–74.

Berat, L. (1995) 'South Africa: Negotiating Change?'. In *Impunity and Human Rights in International Law and Practice*, ed. N. Roht-Arriaza. New York: Oxford University Press, 267–80.

Beristain, C. M. (1998) 'The Value of Memory'. *Forced Migration Review* 2: 24–26.

——(1998a) 'Guatemala: *Nunca Más*'. *Forced Migration Review* 3: 23–26.

Bester, R. (2004) 'Spaces to Say'. In *A Decade of Democracy, South African Art 1994–2004: From the Permanent Collection of Iziko: South African National Gallery*, ed. E. Bedford. Cape Town: Double Storey, 24–33.

Beverley, J. (2001) 'What Happens When the Subaltern Speaks: Rigoberta Menchú, Multiculturalism, and the Presumption of Equal Worth'. In *The Rigoberta Menchú Controversy*, ed. A. Arias. Minneapolis: University of Minnesota Press, pages 219–36.

Bhatia, V. (2004) *Worlds of Written Discourse: A Genre-based View*. London: Continuum.

Bickford, L. (2005) *The Power of Memorials: Human Rights, Justice and the Struggle for Memory*. New York: International Center for Transitional Justice, June.

——(2007) 'Unofficial Truth Projects'. *Human Rights Quarterly* 29, 4: 994–1035.

Bickford, L., Karam, P., Mneimneh, H. and Pierce, P. (2009) *Documenting Truth*. New York: International Center for Transitional Justice.

Blommaert, J., Bock, M. and McCormick, K. (2000) *Narrative Inequality and the Problem of Hearability in the TRC Hearings*. Working Papers on Language, Power and Identity No. 8. London: Gent.

Bloomfield, D., Barnes, T. and Huyse, L. (eds) (2003) *Reconciliation After Violent Conflict: A Handbook*. Stockholm: International Institute for Democracy and Electoral Assistance.

Bock, Z., Mazwi, N., Metula, S. and Mpolweni-Zantsi, N. (2004) 'An Analysis of What Has Been "Lost" in the Interpretation and Transcription Process of Selected TRC

Testimonies'. Paper presented at the Intercultural Communication Conference at Stellenbosch University, 6–8 September.

Boehmer, E. (2000) *Bloodlines*. Cape Town: David Philip.

Bonner, P. and Nieftagodien, N. (2002) 'The Truth and Reconciliation Commission and the Pursuit of "Social Truth": The Case of Kathorus'. In *Commissioning the Past: Understanding South Africa's Truth and Reconciliation Commission*, ed. D. Posel and G. Simpson. Johannesburg: Witwatersrand University Press, 173–203.

Boraine, A. (2000) *A Country Unmasked: Inside South Africa's Truth and Reconciliation Commission*. Oxford: Oxford University Press.

Boraine, A. and Levy, J. (eds) (1995) *The Healing of a Nation?* Cape Town: Justice in Transition.

Boraine, A., Levy, J. and Scheffer, R. (eds) (1994) *Dealing with the Past*. Cape Town: IDASA.

Borer, T. A. (2003) 'A Taxonomy of Victims and Perpetrators: Human Rights and Reconciliation in South Africa'. *Human Rights Quarterly* 25, 4: 1088–1116.

——(2004) 'Reconciling South Africa or South Africans? Cautionary Notes from the TRC'. *African Studies Quarterly* 8, 1: 19–38.

Bosire, L. K. (2006) 'Overpromised, Underdelivered: Transitional Justice in Sub-Saharan Africa'. *Sur – International Journal on Human Rights* 5: 71–107.

Botman, H. R. and Petersen, R. M. (eds) (1996) *To Remember and to Heal: Theological and Psychological Reflections on Truth and Reconciliation*. Cape Town: Human and Rousseau.

Bozzoli, B. (1998) 'Public Ritual and Private Transition: The Truth Commission in Alexandra Township, South Africa 1996'. *African Studies* 57, 2: 167–95.

Brasil: Nunca Maís (1985) *Brasil: Nunca Maís*. Rio de Janeiro: Editora Vozes.

Brett, S., Bickford, L., Ševenko, L. and Rios, M. (2008) *Memorialization and Democracy: State Policy and Civic Action*. New York: FLASCO, International Center for Transitional Justice and the International Coalition of Historic Site Museums of Conscience, July.

Brink, A. (1998) 'Interrogating Silence: New Possibilities Faced by South African Literature'. In *Writing South Africa: Literature, Apartheid, and Democracy, 1970–1995*, ed. D. Attridge and R. Jolly. Cambridge: Cambridge University Press, 14–28.

——(1998a) 'Stories of History: Reimagining the Past in Post-apartheid Narrative'. In *Negotiating the Past: The Making of Memory in South Africa*, ed. S. Nuttall and C. Coetzee. Oxford: Oxford University Press, 29–42.

Bronkhorst, D. (1998) 'Naming Names: Identity and Identification in Human Rights Work'. *Netherlands Quarterly of Human Rights* 16, 4: 457–74.

Brooks, R. (1999) 'The Age of Apology'. In *When Sorry Isn't Enough: The Controversy over Apologies and Reparations for Human Injustice*, ed. R. Brooks. New York: New York University Press, 3–11.

Browde, J., Mokhoba, P. and Jassat, E. (1998) *Internal Reconciliation Commission, Report Submitted to the Dean*. Johannesburg: University of the Witwatersrand, Faculty of Health Sciences, November.

Buckley-Zistel, S. (2006) 'Remembering to Forget: Chosen Amnesia as a Strategy for Local Coexistence in Post-genocide Rwanda'. *Africa* 76, 2: 131–50.

Budlender, D. (1998) *The People's Voices: National Speak Out on Poverty Hearings, March–June 1998*. Johannesburg: SANGOCO.

Bundy, C. (2000) 'The Beast of the Past: History and the TRC'. In *After the TRC: Reflections on Truth and Reconciliation in South Africa*, ed. W. James and L. van de Vijver. Cape Town: David Philip, 9–20.

Burgess, P. (2006) 'A New Approach to Restorative Justice – East Timor's Community Reconciliation Processes'. In *Transitional Justice in the Twenty First Century: Beyond Truth Versus Justice*, ed. N. Roht-Arriaza and J. Mariezcurrena. Cambridge: Cambridge University Press, 176–205.

Burton, M. (2000) 'Reparation, Amnesty and a National Archive'. In *After the TRC: Reflections on Truth and Reconciliation in South Africa*, ed. W. James and L. van de Vijver. Cape Town: David Philip, 109–14.

Buur, L. (2001) 'The South African Truth and Reconciliation Commission: A Technique of Nation-state Formation'. In *States of Imagination: Ethnographic Explorations of the Postcolonial State*, ed. T. Hansen and F. Stepputat. Durham: Duke University Press, 149–81.

——(2002) 'Monumental Historical Memory: Managing Truth in the Everyday Work of the South African Truth and Reconciliation Commission'. In *Commissioning the Past: Understanding South Africa's Truth and Reconciliation Commission*, ed. D. Posel and G. Simpson. Johannesburg: Witwatersrand University Press, 66–93.

——(2003) ' "In the Name of the Victims": the Politics of Compensation in the Work of the South African Truth and Reconciliation Commission'. In *Political Transition: Politics and Cultures*, ed. P. Gready. London: Pluto Press, 148–64.

Buur, L. and Jensen, S. (2004) 'Introduction: Vigilantism and the Policing of Everyday Life in South Africa'. *African Studies* 63, 2: 139–52.

Caldeira, T. (2000) *City of Walls: Crime, Segregation, and Citizenship in São Paulo*. Berkeley: University of California Press.

Carothers, T. (2002) 'The End of the Transition Paradigm'. *Journal of Democracy* 13, 1: 5–21.

Carranza, R. (2008) 'Plunder and Pain: Should Transitional Justice Engage with Corruption and Economic Crimes?'. *International Journal of Transitional Justice* 2, 3: 310–30.

Chapman, A. (2008) 'Truth Recovery Through the TRC's Institutional Hearings Process'. In *Truth and Reconciliation in South Africa: Did the TRC Deliver?* ed. A. Chapman and H. van der Merwe. Philadelphia: University of Pennsylvania Press, 169–88.

——(2008a) 'The TRC's Approach to Promoting Reconciliation in the Human Rights Violations Hearings'. In *Truth and Reconciliation in South Africa: Did the TRC Deliver?* ed. A. Chapman and H. van der Merwe. Philadelphia: University of Pennsylvania Press, 45–65.

——(2008b) 'Perspectives on the Role of Forgiveness in the Human Rights Violations Hearings'. In *Truth and Reconciliation in South Africa: Did the TRC Deliver?* ed. A. Chapman and H. van der Merwe. Philadelphia: University of Pennsylvania Press, 66–89.

Chapman, A. and Ball, P. (2001) 'The Truth of Truth Commissions: Comparative Lessons from Haiti, South Africa, and Guatemala'. *Human Rights Quarterly* 23, 1: 1–43.

——(2008) 'Levels of Truth: Macro-truth and the TRC'. In *Truth and Reconciliation in South Africa: Did the TRC Deliver?* ed. A. Chapman and H. van der Merwe. Philadelphia: University of Pennsylvania Press, 143–68.

Chapman, A. and van der Merwe, H. (eds) (2008) *Truth and Reconciliation in South Africa: Did the TRC Deliver?* Philadelphia: University of Pennsylvania Press.

Cherry, J. (2000) 'Historical Truth: Something to Fight For'. In *Looking Back, Reaching Forward: Reflections on the Truth and Reconciliation Commission of South Africa*, ed. C. Villa-Vicencio and W. Verwoerd. Cape Town: University of Cape Town Press, 134–43.

Cherry, J., Daniel, J. and Fullard, M. (2002) 'Researching the "Truth": A View from Inside the Truth and Reconciliation Commission'. In *Commissioning the Past: Understanding South Africa's Truth and Reconciliation Commission*, ed. D. Posel and G. Simpson. Johannesburg: Witwatersrand University Press, 17–36.

Christodoulidis, E. (2000) ' "Truth and Reconciliation" as Risks'. *Social and Legal Studies* 9, 2: 179–204.
Chubb, K. and van Dijk, L. (2001) *Between Anger and Hope: South Africa's Youth and the Truth and Reconciliation Commission*. Johannesburg: Witwatersrand University Press.
Clapham, A. (2007) *Human Rights: A Very Short Introduction*. Oxford: Oxford University Press.
Cochrane, J., de Gruchy, J. and Martin, S. (eds) (1999) *Facing the Truth: South African Faith Communities and the Truth and Reconciliation Commission*. Cape Town: David Philip.
Cock, J. (2006) 'Guns and the Social Crisis'. In *State of the Nation: South Africa 2005–2006*, ed. S. Buhlungu, J. Daniel, R. Southall and J. Lutchman. Cape Town: HSRC Press, 333–49.
Cockburn, C. (1998) *The Space Between Us: Negotiating Gender and National Identities in Conflict*. London: Zed Books.
Coetzee, J. M. (2000) *Disgrace*. London: Vintage.
Coetzee, M. (2003) 'An Overview of the TRC Amnesty Process'. In *The Provocations of Amnesty: Memory, Justice and Impunity*, ed. C. Villa-Vicencio and E. Doxtader. Cape Town: David Philip, 181–94.
Cohen, S. (1995) *Denial and Acknowledgement: The Impact of Information About Human Rights Violations*. Jerusalem: Center for Human Rights, The Hebrew University.
——(1996) 'Crime and Politics: Spot the Difference'. *British Journal of Sociology* 47, 1: 1–21.
——(2001) *States of Denial: Knowing about Atrocities and Suffering*. Cambridge: Polity Press.
Cole, E. and Barsalou, J. (2006) *Unite or Divide? The Challenges of Teaching History in Societies Emerging from Violent Conflict*. Washington DC: United States Institute of Peace, Special Report 163, June.
Colvin, C. (2000) *'We are Still Struggling': Storytelling, Reparations and Reconciliation after the TRC*. Johannesburg: Centre for the Study of Violence and Reconciliation.
——(2006) 'Overview of the Reparations Program in South Africa'. In *The Handbook of Reparations*, ed. P. de Greiff. Oxford: Oxford University Press, 176–214.
Comaroff, J. and Comaroff, J. (2004) 'Policing Culture, Cultural Policing: Law and Social Order in Postcolonial South Africa'. *Law and Social Inquiry* 29, 3: 513–45.
——(2004a) 'Criminal Justice, Cultural Justice: The Limits of Liberalism and the Pragmatics of Difference in the new South Africa'. *American Ethnologist* 31, 2: 188–204.
Cooke, B. and Kothari, U. (eds) (2001) *Participation: The New Tyranny?* London: Zed Books.
Coombes, A. (2003) *History after Apartheid: Visual Culture and Public Memory in a Democratic South Africa*. Durham: Duke University Press.
Cornwall, A. (2004) 'New Democratic Spaces? The Politics and Dynamics of Institutionalised Participation'. *IDS Bulletin* 35, 2: 1–10.
Cramer, C. (2006) *Civil War is Not a Stupid Thing: Accounting for Violence in Developing Countries*. London: Hurst.
Crocker, D. (2000) 'Truth Commissions, Transitional Justice, and Civil Society'. In *Truth v. Justice: The Morality of Truth Commissions*, ed. R. Rotberg and D. Thompson. Princeton: Princeton University Press, 99–121.
Cronin, J. (1998) 'Tutu's Report Tells the Truth, but Not the Whole Truth'. *Sunday Independent*, 26 December.
——(1999) 'A Luta Dis-continua? The TRC Final Report and the Nation Building Project'. Paper presented at the Truth and Reconciliation Commission: Commissioning the Past conference, a joint project of the History Workshop of the University of the Witwatersrand and the Centre for the Study of Violence and Reconciliation, Johannesburg, 11–14 June.

Cunningham, M. (1999) 'Saying Sorry: The Politics of Apology'. *The Political Quarterly*, 70, 3: 285–93.
Dajani, M. and Baskin, G. (2006) 'Israeli–Palestinian Joint Activities: Problematic Endeavour, but Necessary Challenge'. In *Bridging the Divide: Peace-building in the Israeli–Palestinian Conflict*, ed. E. Kaufmann and W. Salem. London: Lynne Rienner, 87–110.
Dangor, A. (2004) *Bitter Fruit*. London: Atlantic Books.
Das, V. (2001) 'The Act of Witnessing: Violence, Poisonous Knowledge, and Subjectivity'. In *Violence and Subjectivity*, ed. V. Das, A. Kleinman, M. Ramphele and P. Reynolds. New Delhi: Oxford University Press, 205–25.
Das, V. and Kleinman, A. (2002) 'Introduction'. In *Remaking a World: Violence, Social Suffering, and Recovery*, ed. V. Das, A. Kleinman, M. Lock, M. Ramphele and P. Reynolds. New Delhi: Oxford University Press, 1–30.
Dawson, G. (2003) 'Mobilising Memories: Protestant and Unionist Victims' Groups and the Politics of Victimhood in the Irish Peace Process'. In *Political Transition: Politics and Cultures*, ed. P. Gready. London: Pluto Press, 127–47.
de Greiff, P. (ed.) (2006) *The Handbook of Reparations*. Oxford: Oxford University Press.
de Greiff, P. and Duthie, R. (eds) (2009) *Transitional Justice and Development: Making Connections*. New York: Social Science Research Council and the International Center for Transitional Justice.
de Klerk, F. W. (1996) 'Submission to the Truth and Reconciliation Commission by Mr. F. W. de Klerk, leader of the National Party, 1996'.
de Kok, I. (1998) 'Cracked Heirlooms: Memory on Exhibition'. In *Negotiating the Past: The Making of Memory in South Africa*, ed. S. Nuttall and C. Coetzee. Cape Town: Oxford University Press, 57–71.
de Ridder, T. (1997) 'The Trauma of Testifying: Deponents' Difficulty Healing Process'. *Track Two* 6, 3 and 4.
Deacon, H. (1998) 'Remembering Tragedy, Constructing Modernity: Robben Island as a National Monument'. In *Negotiating the Past: The Making of Memory in South Africa*, ed. S. Nuttall and C. Coetzee. Cape Town: Oxford University Press, 161–79.
Derrida, J. (1996) *Archive Fever: A Freudian Impression*. Chicago: University of Chicago Press.
Dieltiens, V. (2005) *Learning Anew: Truth and Reconciliation in Education*. Johannesburg: Centre for the Study of Violence and Reconciliation.
Dixon, B. (2004) 'Cosmetic Crime Prevention'. In *Justice Gained? Crime and Crime Control in South Africa's Transition*, ed. B. Dixon and E. van der Spuy. Cape Town: University of Cape Town Press, 163–92.
——(2004a) 'Introduction: Justice Gained? Crime, Crime Control and Criminology in Transition'. In *Justice Gained? Crime and Crime Control in South Africa's Transition*, ed. B. Dixon and E. van der Spuy. Cape Town: University of Cape Town Press, ix–xxxvii.
Dixon, B. and Johns, L.-M. (2001) *Gangs, Pagad and the State: Vigilantism and Revenge Violence in the Western Cape*. Johannesburg: Centre for the Study of Violence and Reconciliation.
Doxtader, E. (2004) 'The Matter of Words in the Midst of Beginnings: Unravelling the "Relationship" between Reparation and Reconciliation'. In *To Repair the Irreparable: Reparation and Reconstruction in South Africa*, ed. E. Doxtader and C. Villa-Vicencio. Cape Town: David Philip, 115–48.
du Pisani, J. and Kim, K.-S. (2004) 'Establishing the Truth about the Apartheid Past: Historians and the South African Truth and Reconciliation Commission'. *African Studies Quarterly* 8, 1. Available at http://web.africa.ufl.edu/asq/v8/v8i1a5.htm (accessed 17 May 2010).

du Plessis, A. and Louw, A. (2005) 'The Tide is Turning: The 2003/04 SAPS Crime Statistics'. *SA Crime Quarterly* 12: 1–8.

du Toit, A. (1999) 'Perpetrator Findings as Artificial Even-handedness? The TRC's Contested Judgements of Moral and Political Accountability for Gross Human Rights Violations'. Paper presented at the Truth and Reconciliation Commission: Commissioning the Past conference, a joint project of the History Workshop of the University of the Witwatersrand and the Centre for the Study of Violence and Reconciliation, Johannesburg, 11–14 June.

——(2000) 'The Moral Foundations of the South African TRC: Truth as Acknowledgement and Justice as Recognition'. In *Truth v. Justice: The Morality of Truth Commissions*, ed. R. Rotberg and D. Thompson. Princeton: Princeton University Press, 122–40.

Dubow, N. (2004) 'On Monuments, Memorials and Memory: Some Precedent Towards a South African Option'. In *To Repair the Irreparable: Reparation and Reconstruction in South Africa*, ed. E. Doxtader and C. Villa-Vicencio. Cape Town: David Philip, 359–78.

Dudai, R. (2006) 'Advocacy with Footnotes: The Human Rights Report as a Literary Genre'. *Human Rights Quarterly* 28, 3: 783–95.

——(2009) ' "Can You Describe This?" Human Rights Reports and What They Tell Us About the Human Rights Movement'. In *Humanitarianism and Suffering: The Mobilization of Empathy*, ed. R. Wilson and R. Brown. Cambridge: Cambridge University Press, 245–64

Dugard, J. (1997) 'Retrospective Justice: International Law and the South African Model'. In *Transitional Justice and the Rule of Law in New Democracies*, ed. A. J. McAdams. Notre Dame: University of Notre Dame Press, 269–90.

——(1997a) 'Is the Truth and Reconciliation Process Compatible with International Law? An Unanswered Question – *AZAPO v. President of the Republic of South Africa*'. *South African Journal on Human Rights* 13, 2: 258–68.

——(2001) *From Low Intensity War to Mafia War: Taxi Violence in South Africa (1987–2000)*. Johannesburg: Centre for the Study of Violence and Reconciliation.

——(2001a) 'Drive On? Taxi Wars in South Africa'. In *Crime Wave: The South African Underworld and its Foes*, ed. J. Steinberg. Johannesburg: University of the Witwatersrand Press, 129–49.

Duthie, R. (2008) 'Toward a Development-sensitive Approach to Transitional Justice'. *International Journal of Transitional Justice* 2, 3: 292–309.

Dyzenhaus, D. (1998) *Judging the Judges, Judging Ourselves: Truth, and the Apartheid Legal Order*. Oxford: Hart.

Edelstein, J. (2001) *Truth and Lies: Stories from the Truth and Reconciliation Commission in South Africa*. London: Granta.

Ellis, S. (1998) 'The Historical Significance of South Africa's Third Force'. *Journal of Southern African Studies* 24, 2: 261–99.

——(1999) 'The New Frontiers of Crime in South Africa'. In *The Criminalization of the State in Africa*, ed. J.-F. Bayart, S. Ellis and B. Hibou. Oxford: International Africa Institute in association with James Currey, 49–68.

Eprile, T. (2005) *The Persistence of Memory*. Cape Town: Double Storey.

Ernest, C. (ed.) (2007) with papers by K. Oh and T. Edlmann. *Reconciliatory Justice: Amnesties, Indemnities and Prosecutions in South Africa's Transition*. Paper 2 in *After the Transition: Justice, the Judiciary and Respect for the Law in South Africa*, ed. Centre for the Study of Violence and Reconciliation. Johannesburg: Centre for the Study of Violence and Reconciliation.

Fainman-Frenkel, R. (2004) 'Ordinary Secrets and the Bounds of Memory: Traversing the Truth and Reconciliation Commission in Farida Karodia's *Other Secrets* and Beverley Naidoo's *Out of Bounds*'. *Research in African Literatures* 35, 4: 52–65.

Falk, R. (2004) 'Human Rights and Global Civil Society: On the Law of Unintended Effects'. In *Fighting for Human Rights*, ed. P. Gready. London: Routledge, 33–53.

Feitlowitz, M. (1998) *A Lexicon of Terror: Argentina and the Legacies of Torture*. New York: Oxford University Press.

Fig, D. (2005) 'Manufacturing Amnesia: Corporate Social Responsibility in South Africa'. *International Affairs* 81, 3: 599–617.

Fletcher, L. and Weinstein, H. (2002) 'Violence and Social Repair: Rethinking the Contribution of Justice to Reconciliation'. *Human Rights Quarterly* 24: 573–639.

Fletcher, L. and Weinstein, H. with Rowen, J. (2009) 'Context, Timing and the Dynamics of Transitional Justice: A Historical Perspective'. *Human Rights Quarterly* 31: 163–220.

Flockemann, M. (2000) 'Watching Soap Opera'. In *Senses of Culture: South African Cultural Studies*, ed. S. Nuttall and C.-A. Michael. Oxford: Oxford University Press, 141–54.

Foster, D. and Skinner, D. (1990) 'Detention and Violence: Beyond Victimology'. In *Political Violence and the Struggle in South Africa*, ed. N. Chabani Manganyi and A. du Toit. London: Macmillan, 205–33.

Foster, D., Haupt, P. and de Beer, M. (2005) *The Theatre of Violence: Narratives of Protagonists in the South African Conflict*. Oxford: James Currey.

Foucault, M. (1991) 'Truth and Power'. In *The Foucault Reader: An Introduction to Foucault's Thought*, ed. P. Rabinow. London: Penguin, 51–75.

Frank, C. (2007) *Quality Services Guaranteed? A Review of Victim Policy in South Africa*. ISS Monograph No. 137. Pretoria: Institute for Security Studies, July.

Friedman, S. (2006) *Participatory Governance and Citizen Action in Post-apartheid South Africa*. Decent Work Programme, Discussion Paper, DP/164/2006. Geneva: International Institute for Labour Studies.

Fullard, M. (2004) *Dis-placing Race: The South African Truth and Reconciliation Commission and Interpretations of Violence*. Johannesburg: Centre for the Study of Violence and Reconciliation.

Fullard, M. and Rousseau, N. (2003) 'Truth, Evidence and History: A Critical Review of Aspects of the Amnesty Process'. In *The Provocations of Amnesty: Memory, Justice and Impunity*, ed. C. Villa-Vicencio and E. Doxtader. Cape Town: David Philip, 195–216.

Galant, G. and Parlevliet, M. (2005) 'Using Rights to Address Conflict: A Valuable Synergy'. In *Reinventing Development? Translating Rights-based Approaches from Theory into Practice*, ed. P. Gready and J. Ensor. London: Zed Books, 108–28.

Gallinetti, J. (2006) 'What Happened to the Child Justice Bill? The Process of Law Reform Relating to Child Offenders'. *SA Crime Quarterly* 17: 7–12.

Gallinetti, J., Kassan, D. and Ehlers, L. (eds) (2006) *Child Justice in South Africa: Children's Rights under Construction*. Cape Town: Open Society Foundation for South Africa and the Child Justice Alliance, Conference Report, August.

Garman, A. (1997) 'Media Creation: How the TRC and the Media Have Impacted on Each Other'. *Track Two* 6, 3 and 4.

Garton Ash, T. (2000) *History of the Present: Essays, Sketches and Despatches from Europe in the 1990s*. London: Penguin.

Gastrow, P. (2001) *Organised Crime in the SADC Region: Police Perceptions*. Monograph Series, No. 60. Pretoria: Institute for Security Studies, August.

—— (ed.) (2003) *Penetrating State and Business: Organised Crime in Southern Africa – Volume 2*. Monograph Series, No. 89. Pretoria: Institute for Security Studies, November.

Gear, S. (2002) *Wishing us Away: Challenges Facing Ex-combatants in the 'New' South Africa*. Johannesburg: Centre for the Study of Violence and Reconciliation.

Geschier, S. (2005) 'Beyond Experience: The Mediation of Traumatic Memories in South African History Museums'. *Transformation* 59: 45–65.

Gevisser, M. (2004) 'From the Ruins: The Constitution Hill Project'. *Public Culture* 16, 3: 507–19.

Gibney, M. and Roxstrom, E. (2001) 'The Status of State Apologies'. *Human Rights Quarterly* 23, 4: 911–39.

Gibson, J. (2004) *Overcoming Apartheid: Can Truth Reconcile a Divided Nation?* New York: Russell Sage Foundation.

Giliomee, H. (2003) *The Afrikaners: Biography of a People*. London: Hurst.

Gilligan, G. and Pratt, J. (eds) (2004) *Crime, Truth and Justice: Official Inquiry, Discourse, Knowledge*. Cullompton, Devon: Willan.

Gobodo-Madikizela, P. (2003) *A Human Being Died that Night: A Story of Forgiveness*. Cape Town: David Philip.

Goldblatt, B. and Meintjes, S. (1998) 'South African Women Demand the Truth'. In *What Women Do in Wartime: Gender and Conflict in Africa*, ed. M. Turshen and C. Twagiramariya. London: Zed Books, 27–61.

Goodman, T. and Price, M. (2002) 'Using an Internal Reconciliation Commission to Facilitate Transformation at a Health Sciences Faculty in Post-apartheid South Africa: The Case of Witwatersrand Health Sciences Faculty'. *Health and Human Rights* 6, 1: 211–27.

Gopin, M. (2001) 'Forgiveness as an Element of Conflict Resolution in Religious Cultures: Walking the Tightrope of Reconciliation and Justice'. In *Reconciliation, Justice, and Coexistence: Theory and Practice*, ed. M Abu-Nimer. Lanham: Lexington Books, 87–99.

Gordon, D. (2006) *Transformation and Trouble: Crime, Justice, and Participation in Democratic South Africa*. Ann Arbor: University of Michigan Press.

Gottschalk, K. (2005) *Vigilantism v. the State: A Case Study of the Rise and Fall of Pagad, 1996–2000*. ISS Paper 99. Pretoria: Institute for Security Studies.

Govier, T. and Verwoerd, W. (2004) 'The Promise and Pitfalls of Apology'. In *To Repair the Irreparable: Reparation and Reconstruction in South Africa*, ed. E. Doxtader and C. Villa-Vicencio. Cape Town: David Philip, 242–55.

Grandin, G. (2005) 'The Instruction of Great Catastrophe: Truth Commissions, National History, and State Formation in Argentina, Chile, and Guatemala'. *The American Historical Review* 110, 1: 46–67.

Gready, P. (2003) *Writing as Resistance: Life Stories of Imprisonment, Exile, and Homecoming from Apartheid South Africa*. Lanham: Lexington Books.

—— (2003a) 'Introduction'. In *Political Transition: Politics and Cultures*, ed. P. Gready. London: Pluto Press, 1–26.

—— (2008) 'The Public Life of Narratives: Ethics, Politics, Methods'. In *Doing Narrative Research*, ed. M. Andrews, C. Squire and M. Tamboukou. London: Sage, 137–50.

—— (2009) 'Reasons to be Cautious about Evidence and Evaluation: Rights-based Approaches to Development and the Emerging Culture of Evaluation'. *Journal of Human Rights Practice* 1, 3: 380–401.

Gready, P. and Kgalema, L. (2003) 'Magistrates under Apartheid: A Case Study of the Politicisation of Justice and Complicity in Human Rights Abuse'. *South African Journal on Human Rights* 19, 2: 141–88.

Greenbaum, B. (2006) *Evaluation of the 2005 Ex-combatants' Dialogues*. Johannesburg: Centre for the Study of Violence and Reconciliation, February.

Grundlingh, G., Reynolds, P. and Ross, F. (2000) 'Unfinished Business'. In *After the TRC: Reflections on Truth and Reconciliation in South Africa*, ed. W. James and L. van de Vijver. Cape Town: David Philip.

Gumede, W. (2005) *Thabo Mbeki and the Battle for the Soul of the ANC*. Cape Town: Zebra Press.

Gunn, S. (2007) *If Trees Could Speak: The Trojan Horse Story*. Cape Town: HRMC.

Gunn, S. and Krwala, S. (eds) (2008) *Knocking On ... Mothers and Daughters in Struggle in South Africa*. Johannesburg: Centre for the Study of Violence and Reconciliation, and Cape Town: Human Rights Media Centre.

Gunn, S. and Tal, M.-M. (eds) (2003) *Torn Apart: Thirteen Refugees Tell Their Stories*. Cape Town: Human Rights Media Centre.

Halpern, J. and Weinstein, H. (2004) 'Rehumanizing the Other: Empathy and Reconciliation'. *Human Rights Quarterly* 26: 561–83.

Hamber, B. and van der Merwe, H. (1998) 'What is this Thing Called Reconciliation?'. Paper presented at the Goedgedacht Forum, After the Truth and Reconciliation Commission, Goedgedacht Farm, Cape Town, 28 March.

Hamber, B. and Wilson, R. (2002) 'Symbolic Closure through Memory, Reparation and Revenge in Post-conflict Societies'. *Journal of Human Rights* 1, 1: 35–53.

Hamilton, C., Harris, V., Taylor, J., Pickover, M. Reid, G. and Saleh, R. (eds) (2002) *Refiguring the Archive*. Dordrecht: Kluwer.

Harries, P. (2004) 'Zero Hour and Beyond: History in a Time of Change, 1994–2004'. Paper presented at the conference, Looking at South Africa 10 Years On, hosted by the Institute of Commonwealth Studies and the School of Oriental and African Studies, London, 10–12 September.

Harris, B. (2001) *'As for Violent Crime that's Our Daily Bread': Vigilante Violence during South Africa's Period of Transition*. Johannesburg: Centre for the Study of Violence and Reconciliation.

——(2001a) *A Foreign Experience: Violence, Crime and Xenophobia during South Africa's Transition*. Johannesburg: Centre for the Study of Violence and Reconciliation.

——(2005) *Between a Rock and a Hard Place: Violence, Transition and Democratisation – A Consolidated Review of the Violence and Transition Project*. Johannesburg: Centre for the Study of Violence and Reconciliation.

Harris, V. (2006) 'Archives' (lead contributor to the debate). In *Truth and Reconciliation in South Africa: 10 Years On*, ed. C. Villa-Vicencio and F. du Toit. Cape Town: David Philip, 53–58.

Hartman, G. (2000) 'Memory.com: Tele-suffering and Testimony in the dot com Era'. *Raritan* 19, 3: 1–18.

Harvard Law School Human Rights Program and The World Peace Foundation (1997) *Truth Commissions: A Comparative Assessment (An Interdisciplinary Discussion Held at the Harvard Law School, May 1996)*. Cambridge MA: Harvard Law School Human Rights Program.

Hayner, P. (2002) *Unspeakable Truths: Facing the Challenge of Truth Commissions*. New York: Routledge.

——(2009) *Negotiating Justice: Guidance for Mediators*. Geneva: Centre for Humanitarian Dialogue and the International Center for Transitional Justice, February.

Hegarty, A. (2003) 'The Government of Memory: Public Inquiries and the Limits of Justice in Northern Ireland'. *Fordham International Law Journal* 26, 4: 1148–92.

Hemson, D. and O'Donovan, M. (2006) 'Putting Numbers to the Scorecard: Presidential Targets and the State of Delivery'. In *State of the Nation: South Africa 2005–2006*, ed. S. Buhlungu, J. Daniel, R. Southall and J. Lutchman. Cape Town: HSRC Press, 11–45.

Henri, Y. (2000) 'Where Healing Begins'. In *Looking Back, Reaching Forward: Reflections on the Truth and Reconciliation Commission of South Africa*, ed. C. Villa-Vicencio and W. Verwoerd. Cape Town: University of Cape Town Press.

——(2003) 'Reconciling Reconciliation: A Personal and Public Journey of Testifying before the South African Truth and Reconciliation Commission'. In *Political Transition: Politics and Cultures*, ed. P. Gready. London: Pluto Press, 262–75.

Herman, J. L. (2001) *Trauma and Recovery: From Domestic Abuse to Political Terror*. London: Pandora.

Hickey, S. and Mohan, G. (eds) (2004) *Participation: From Tyranny to Transformation? Exploring New Approaches to Participation in Development*. London: Zed Books.

Hoddie, M. and Hartzell, C. (2005) 'Signals of Reconciliation: Institution-building and the Resolution of Civil Wars'. *International Studies Review* 7: 21–40.

Hofmeyr, I. (1988) 'Introduction: Exploring Experiential Testimony – a Selection of History Workshop Papers'. *Social Dynamics* 14, 2: 1–5.

Holston, J. and Caldeira, T. (1998) 'Democracy, Law, and Violence: Disjunctions of Brazilian Citizenship'. In Fault Lines of Democracy in Post-transition Latin America, ed. F. Agüero and J. Stark. Miami: University of Miami North–South Center Press, 263–96.

Honwana, A. (1999) 'The Collective Body: Challenging Western Concepts of Trauma and Healing'. *Track Two* 8, 1: 30–35.

Howard-Hassmann, R. and Gibney, M. (2008) 'Introduction: Apologies and the West'. In *The Age of Apology: Facing Up to the Past*, ed. M. Gibney, H. Howard-Hassmann, J.-M. Coicaud and N. Steiner. Philadelphia: University of Pennsylvania Press, 1–9.

Human Rights Media Centre (HRMC) (2006) *The Story is Yours, the Choice is Yours: Media Ethics for Storytellers*. Cape Town: HRMC.

Huyse, L. (2003) Chapters on 'Victims' and 'Offenders'. In *Reconciliation After Violent Conflict: A Handbook*, ed. D. Bloomfield, T. Barnes and L. Huyse. Stockholm: International Institute for Democracy and Electoral Assistance, 54–66, 67–76.

Index on Censorship (1998) 'Apologies: Who's Sorry Now?' compiled by Emily Mitchell. *Index on Censorship* 3: 46–47.

Ignatieff, M. (1994) *Blood and Belonging: Journeys into the New Nationalism*. London: Vintage.

——(1996) 'Articles of Faith'. *Index on Censorship* 25, 5: 110–22.

——(2001) *Human Rights as Politics and Idolatry*, ed. A Gutmann. Princeton: Princeton University Press.

International Center for Transitional Justice (ICTJ) and CDD-Ghana (2004) *Truth Commissions and NGOs: The Essential Relationship (The 'Frati Guidelines' for NGOs Engaging with Truth Commissions)*. ICTJ Occasional Paper Series. New York: ICTJ, April.

International Center for Transitional Justice (ICTJ) and the Human Rights Center, University of California Berkeley (2004) *Iraqi Voices: Attitudes Toward Transitional Justice and Social Reconstruction*. ICTJ Occasional Paper Series. New York: ICTJ, May.

International Council on Human Rights Policy (ICHRP) (2003) *Crime, Public Order and Human Rights*. Geneva: ICHRP.

James, D. (2007) *Gaining Ground? 'Rights' and 'Property' in South African Land Reform*. London: Routledge.

Jeffery, A. (1999) *The Truth About the Truth Commission*. Johannesburg: South African Institute of Race Relations.
Johnston, L. and Shearing, C. (2003) *Governing Security: Explorations in Policing and Justice*. London: Routledge.
Karakashian, S. (ed.) (2007) *Reflecting on Journeys to Healing and Wholeness: Toolkits for Facilitators*. Conference Report, 12–14 October 2007. Cape Town: Institute for Healing of Memories.
Kayser, U. (1999) 'To be Considered … a Post-TRC Age?' Paper presented at the conference, The Truth and Reconciliation Commission: Commissioning the Past, a joint project of the History Workshop of the University of the Witwatersrand and the Centre for the Study of Violence and Reconciliation, Johannesburg, 11–14 June.
——(2001) *Creating a Space for Encounter and Remembrance: The Healing of Memories Process*. Johannesburg: Centre for the Study of Violence and Reconciliation.
——(2001a) *What Do We Tell Our Children? The Work of the Centre for Ubuntu in Cape Town (Formerly the Religious Response to the Truth and Reconciliation Commission)*. Johannesburg: Centre for the Study of Violence and Reconciliation: Johannesburg.
Keck, M. and Sikkink, K. (1998) *Activists Beyond Borders: Advocacy Networks in International Politics*. Ithaca: Cornell University Press.
Keightley, R. (1993) 'Political Offences and Indemnity in South Africa'. *South African Journal on Human Rights* 9, 3: 334–57.
Kennedy, D. (2002) 'The International Human Rights Movement: Part of the Problem?' *Harvard Human Rights Journal* 15: 101–25.
Kent, L. (2005) 'Community Views of Justice and Reconciliation in Timor-Leste'. *Development Bulletin* 68 (October): 62–65.
Kiss, E. (2000) 'Moral Ambition Within and Beyond Political Constraints: Reflections on Restorative Justice'. In *Truth v. Justice: The Morality of Truth Commissions*, ed. R. Rotberg and D. Thompson. Princeton: Princeton University Press, 68–98.
Klaaren, J. (1998) 'The Truth and Reconciliation Commission, the South African Judiciary, and Constitutionalism'. *African Studies* 57, 2: 197–208.
——(2007) 'Institutional Transformation and the Choice Against Vetting in South Africa's Transition'. In *Justice as Prevention: Vetting Public Employees in Transitional Societies*, ed. A. Mayer-Rieckh and P. de Greiff. New York: Social Science Research Council, 146–79.
Kleinman, A., Das, V. and Lock, M. (1997) 'Introduction'. In *Social Suffering*, ed. A. Kleinman, V. Das and M. Lock. Berkeley: University of California Press, ix–xxvii.
Klug, H. (2000) *Constituting Democracy: Law, Globalism and South Africa's Political Reconstruction*. Cambridge: Cambridge University Press.
Kollapen, N. and Sekhonyane, M. (2002) 'Combating Crime and Respecting Human Rights: An Illusive Balance or the Search for a Durable Solution'. International Council on Human Rights Policy – Crime, Public Order and Human Rights Project. Review Seminar: Carnegie Council on Ethics and International Affairs, New York, 21–22 October.
Krabill, R. (2001) 'Symbiosis: Mass Media and the Truth and Reconciliation Commission of South Africa'. *Media, Culture and Society* 23, 5: 567–85.
Krog, A. (1995) 'The South African Road'. In *The Healing of a Nation?* ed. A. Boraine and J. Levy. Cape Town: Justice in Transition, 112–19.
——(1998) *Country of My Skull*. Johannesburg: Random House.

Krog, A., Mpolweni, N. and Ratele, K. (2009) *There Was This Goat: Investigating the Truth Commission Testimony of Notrose Nobomvu Konile*. Scottsville: University of KwaZulu-Natal Press.

Kruger, L. (1999) *The Drama of South Africa: Plays, Pageants and Publics Since 1910*. London: Routledge.

Kynoch, G. (2003) 'Apartheid Nostalgia: Personal Security Concerns in South African Townships'. *SA Crime Quarterly* 5: 7–10.

——(2005) 'Crime, Conflict and Politics in Transition-era South Africa'. *African Affairs* 104, 416: 493–514.

Lalu, P. and Harris, B. (1996) 'Journeys from the Horizons of History: Text, Trial and Tales in the Construction of Narratives of Pain'. *Current Writing* 8, 2: 24–38.

Landman, T. (2006) *Studying Human Rights*. London: Routledge.

Langlois, A. (2001) *The Politics of Justice and Human Rights: Southeast Asia and Universalist Theory*. Cambridge: Cambridge University Press.

Laplante, L. (2007) 'The Peruvian Truth Commission's Historical Memory Project: Empowering Truth-tellers to Confront Truth-deniers'. *Journal of Human Rights* 6: 433–52.

Lapsley, M. (1997) 'Healing the Memory: Cutting the Cord Between Victim and Perpetrator' (interview by H. Siebert). *Track Two* 6, 3 and 4.

——(2002) 'The Healing of Memories: An Interview with Fr Michael Lapsley' (conducted by C. White, J. Speedy and D. Denborough). *International Journal of Narrative Therapy and Community* Work 2; also available on the Dulwich Centre website: www.dulwichcentre.com.au (accessed 17 May 2010).

Lax, I. (2004) 'Amnesty, Reparation and the Object of Reconciliation in the Context of South Africa's Truth and Reconciliation Commission'. In *To Repair the Irreparable: Reparation and Reconstruction in South Africa*, ed. E. Doxtader and C. Villa-Vicencio. Cape Town: David Philip, 224–41.

Lederach, J. P. (1997) *Building Peace: Sustainable Reconciliation in Divided Societies*. Washington, DC: USIP.

Leggett, T. (2005) 'The State of Crime and Policing'. In *State of the Nation: South Africa 2004–2005*, ed. J. Daniel, R. Southall and J. Lutchman. Cape Town: HSRC Press, 144–76.

Leman-Langlois, S. and Shearing, C. (2004) 'Repairing the Future: The South African Truth and Reconciliation Commission at Work'. In *Crime, Truth and Justice: Official Inquiry, Discourse, Knowledge*, ed. G. Gilligan and J. Pratt. Cullompton, Devon: Willan, 222–42.

Lewis, D. (2000) 'Prized Pleasures: TV Game Shows'. In *Senses of Culture: South African Cultural Studies*, ed. S. Nuttall and C.-A. Michael. Oxford: Oxford University Press, 155–77.

Lipschutz, R. (1998) 'Beyond the Neoliberal Peace: From Conflict Resolution to Social Reconciliation'. *Social Justice* 25, 4: 5–19.

Llewellyn, J. (2004) 'Doing Justice in South Africa: Restorative Justice and Reparation'. In *To Repair the Irreparable: Reparation and Reconstruction in South Africa*, ed. E. Doxtader and C. Villa-Vicencio. Cape Town: David Philip, 166–83.

Lund, M. (2006) 'Human Rights: A Source of Conflict, State Making and State Breaking'. In *Human Rights and Conflict: Exploring the Links between Rights, Law, and Peacebuilding*, ed. J. Mertus and J. Helsing. Washington, DC: USIP, 39–61.

Lundy, P. and McGovern, M. (2006) 'A Truth Commission for Northern Ireland?'. *Research Update* 46 (October), available at: www.ark.ac.uk (accessed 17 May 2010).

Lutz, E. and Sikkink, K. (2001) 'The Justice Cascade: The Evolution and Impact of Foreign Human Rights Trials in Latin America'. *Chicago Journal of International Law* 2, 1: 1–33.

Lyons, B. (1999) 'Getting to Accountability: Business, Apartheid and Human Rights'. *Netherlands Quarterly of Human Rights* 17, 2: 135–60.

McEachern, C. (2002) *Narratives of Nation Media, Memory and Representation in the Making of the New South Africa*. New York: Nova Science Publishers.

McEvoy, K. (2008) 'Letting Go of Legalism: Developing a "Thicker" Version of Transitional Justice'. In *Transitional Justice from Below: Grassroots Activism and the Struggle for Social Change*, ed. K. McEvoy and L. McGregor. Oxford: Hart, 15–45.

McEvoy, K. and Eriksson, A. (2007) 'Restorative Justice in Transition: Ownership, Leadership and "Bottom-up" Human Rights'. In *A Handbook of Restorative Justice*, ed. D. Sullivan and L. Tift. New York: Routledge, 321–37.

McEvoy, K. and McGregor, L. (eds) (2008) *Transitional Justice from Below: Grassroots Activism and the Struggle for Social Change*. Oxford: Hart.

——(2008a) 'Transitional Justice from Below: An Agenda for Research, Policy and Praxis'. In *Transitional Justice from Below: Grassroots Activism and the Struggle for Social Change*, ed. K. McEvoy and L. McGregor. Oxford: Hart, 1–13.

McGreal, C. (1999) 'Foes Pay Tribute as Mandela Begins Long Goodbye', *Guardian*, 27 March.

Madlingozi, T. (2009) 'Khulumani: "Bad Victims" Empowering Themselves'. Paper presented at the Justice for Apartheid Crimes: Corporations, States and Human Rights conference, Oxford Transitional Justice Research, Oxford, 31 January.

——(2010) 'On Transitional Justice Entrepreneurs and the Protection of Victims'. *Journal of Human Rights Practice* 2, 2: 208–28.

Maepa, T. (2005) 'The Truth and Reconciliation Commission as a Model of Restorative Justice'. In *Beyond Retribution: Prospects for Restorative Justice in South Africa*, ed. T. Maepa. ISS Monograph series No 111. Pretoria: ISS with the Restorative Justice Centre, February, 66–75.

——(ed.) (2005a) *Beyond Retribution: Prospects for Restorative Justice in South Africa*. ISS Monograph Series No. 111. Pretoria: ISS with the Restorative Justice Centre, February.

Magona, S. (1998) *Mother to Mother*. Cape Town: David Philip.

Maluleke, T. S. (1999) 'The Truth and Reconciliation Discourse: A Black Theological Evaluation'. In *Facing the Truth: South African Faith Communities and the Truth and Reconciliation Commission*, ed. J. Cochrane, J. de Gruchy and S. Martin. Cape Town: David Philip, 101–13.

Mamdani, M. (1996) 'Reconciliation without Justice'. *Southern African Review of Books* 46 8, 6.

——(1998) 'A Diminished Truth'. *Siyaya!* 3: 38–40.

——(2000) 'The Truth According to the TRC'. In *The Politics of Memory: Truth, Healing and Social Justice*, ed. I. Amadiume and A. An-Na'im. London: Zed Press, 176–83.

Mani, R. (2002) *Beyond Retribution: Seeking Justice in the Shadows of War*. Cambridge: Policy Press.

Marks, S. and Clapham, A. (2005) *International Human Rights Lexicon*. Oxford: Oxford University Press.

Marlin-Curiel, S. (2002) 'The Long Road to Healing: From the TRC to TfD'. *Theatre Research International* 27, 3: 275–88.

Matear, A. (2004) 'The Pinochet Case: The Catalyst for Deepening Democracy in Chile?'. In *Fighting for Human Rights*, ed. P. Gready. London: Routledge. 117–33.

Mayer-Rieckh, A. and de Greiff, P. (eds) (2007) *Justice as Prevention: Vetting Public Employees in Transitional Societies*. New York: Social Science Research Council.

Mbembe, A. (2006) 'South Africa's Second Coming: The Nongqawuse Syndrome'. 15 June, available at www.openDemocracy.net (accessed 17 May 2010).

Menchú, R. (1984) *I, Rigoberta Menchú: An Indian Woman in Guatemala*. Ed. and introduced by Elizabeth Burgos-Debray; trans. Ann Wright. London: Verso.

——(2001) 'Those Who Attack Me Humiliate the Victims, Interview by Juan Jesús Aznárez'. In *The Rigoberta Menchú Controversy*, ed. A. Arias. Minneapolis: University of Minnesota Press, pages 109–18.

Mendeloff, D. (2004) 'Truth-seeking, Truth-telling, and Postconflict Peacebuilding: Curb the Enthusiasm?'. *International Studies Review* 6, 3: 355–80.

Meredith, M. (1999) *Coming to Terms: South Africa's Search for Truth*. New York: PublicAffairs.

Mertus, J. (2003) 'The Politics of Memory and International Trials for Wartime Rape'. In *Political Transition: Politics and Cultures*, ed. P. Gready. London: Pluto Press.

Meyer, D. (2000) *Dead at Daybreak*. London: Coronet Books.

——(2007) *Devil's Peak*. London: Hodder and Stoughton.

Miller, Z. (2008) 'Effects of Invisibility: In Search of the "Economic" in Transitional Justice'. *International Journal of Transitional Justice* 2, 3: 266–91.

Minkley, G. and Rassool, C. (1998) 'Orality, Memory, and Social History in South Africa'. In *Negotiating the Past: The Making of Memory in South Africa*, ed. S. Nuttall and C. Coetzee. Cape Town: Oxford University Press, 89–99.

Minow, M. (1998) *Between Vengeance and Forgiveness: Facing History after Genocide and Mass Violence*. Boston: Beacon Press.

——(2000) 'The Hope for Healing: What can Truth Commissions Do?'. In *Truth v. Justice. The Morality of Truth Commissions*, ed. R. Rotberg and D. Thompson. Princeton: Princeton University Press, 235–60.

Mongia, R. (2004) 'Impartial Regimes of Truth: Indentured Indian Labour and the Status of the Inquiry'. *Cultural Studies* 18, 5: 749–68.

Mutua, M. wa (1997) 'Hope and Despair for a New South Africa: The Limits of Rights Discourse'. *Harvard Human Rights Journal* 10: 63–114.

Mutz, D. (2006) *Hearing the Other Side: Deliberative* versus *Participatory Democracy*. Cambridge: Cambridge University Press.

Nagy, R. (2004) 'The Ambiguities of Reconciliation and Responsibility in South Africa'. *Political Studies* 52, 4: 709–27.

——(2004a) 'After the TRC: Citizenship, Memory, and Reconciliation'. *Canadian Journal of African Studies* 38, 3: 638–53.

Naidu, E. (2004) *Empowerment Through Living Memory: A Community-centred Model for Memorialisation*. Johannesburg: Centre for the Study of Violence and Reconciliation.

——(2004a) *Symbolic Reparations: A Fractured Opportunity*. Johannesburg: Centre for the Study of Violence and Reconciliation.

Nattrass, N. (1999) 'The Truth and Reconciliation Commission on Business and Apartheid: A Critical Evaluation'. *African Affairs* 98: 373–91.

Ndebele, N. (1994) *South African Literature and Culture: Rediscovery of the Ordinary*. Manchester: Manchester University Press.

——(1998) 'Truth, Memory, and the Triumph of Narrative'. In *Negotiating the Past: The Making of Memory in South Africa*, ed. S. Nuttall and C. Coetzee. Cape Town: Oxford University Press, 19–28.

——(2000) 'Of Lions and Rabbits: Thoughts on Democracy and Reconciliation'. In *After the TRC: Reflections on Truth and Reconciliation in South Africa*, ed. W. James and L. van de Vijver. Cape Town: David Philip, 143–56.

——(2003) *The Cry of Winnie Mandela: A Novel*. Cape Town: David Philip.
Neild, R. (2003) 'Human Rights NGOs, Police and Citizen Security in Transitional Democracies'. *Journal of Human Rights* 2, 3: 277–96.
Nevins, J. (2005) 'The Abuse of Memorialized Space and the Redefinition of Ground Zero'. *Journal of Human Rights* 4: 267–82.
Ntsebeza, L. (2004) 'Reconciliation, Reparation and Reconstruction in Post-1994 South Africa: What Role for Land?'. In *To Repair the Irreparable: Reparation and Reconstruction in South Africa*, ed. E. Doxtader and C. Villa-Vicencio. Cape Town: David Philip, 197–210.
Nuttall, S. and Coetzee, C. (eds) (1998) *Negotiating the Past: The Making of Memory in South Africa*. Cape Town: Oxford University Press.
Nuttall, S. and Michael, C.-A. (2000) 'Autobiographical Acts'. In *Senses of Culture: South African Cultural Studies*, ed. S. Nuttall and C.-A. Michael. Oxford: Oxford University Press, 298–317.
Nuttall, T. and Wright, J. (2000) 'Probing the Predicaments of Academic History in Contemporary South Africa'. *South African Historical Journal* 42: 26–48.
Office of the United Nations High Commissioner for Human Rights (OHCHR) (2006) *Rule-of-Law Tools for Post-conflict States: Truth Commissions*. New York and Geneva: United Nations.
——(2007) *Making Peace Our Own: Victims' Perceptions of Accountability, Reconciliation and Transitional Justice in Northern Uganda*. New York and Geneva: United Nations.
——(2008) *Rule-of-Law Tools for Post-conflict States: Reparations Programmes*. New York and Geneva: United Nations.
Omar, A. M. (1996) 'Foreword'. In *Confronting Past Injustices: Approaches to Amnesty, Punishment, Reparation and Restitution in South Africa and Germany*, ed. M. Rwelamira and G. Werle. Durban: Butterworths, vii–xii.
Oomen, B. (2004) 'Vigilantism or Alternative Citizenship? The Rise of *Mapogo a Mathamaga*'. *African Studies* 63, 2: 153–71.
——(2005) 'Donor-driven Justice and its Discontents: The Case of Rwanda'. *Development and Change* 36, 5: 887–910.
Orentlicher, D. (1991) 'Settling Accounts: The Duty to Prosecute Human Rights Violations of a Prior Regime'. *Yale Law Journal* 100: 2537–2615.
——(2007) ' "Settling Accounts" Revisited: Reconciling Global Norms with Local Agency'. *International Journal of Transitional Justice* 1: 10–22.
Panizza, F. (1995) 'Human Rights in the Processes of Transition and Consolidation of Democracy in Latin America'. *Political Studies* XLIII: 168–88.
Pankhurst, D. (1999) 'Issues of Justice and Reconciliation in Complex Political Emergencies: Conceptualising Reconciliation, Justice and Peace'. *Third World Quarterly* 29, 1: 239–56.
Paris, R. (2004) *At War's End: Building Peace After Civil Conflict*. Cambridge: Cambridge University Press.
Parker, P. (1996) 'The Politics of Indemnities, Truth Telling and Reconciliation in South Africa: Ending Apartheid without Forgetting'. *Human Rights Law Journal* 17, 1–2: 1–13.
Parry, B. (1995) 'Reconciliation and Remembrance'. *Pretexts* 5, 1–2: 84–96.
Pells, K. (2009) ' "No One Ever Listens to Us": Challenging Obstacles to the Participation of Children and Young People in Rwanda'. In *A Handbook of Children's Participation: Perspectives from Theory and Practice*, ed. B. Percy-Smith and N. Thomas. London: Routledge: 196–203.

Penny, S. (2002) *The Beneficiaries*. London: Penguin.
Peterson, T. H. (2005) *Final Acts: A Guide to Preserving the Records of Truth Commissions*. Baltimore: Johns Hopkins University Press.
Phakathi, T. and van der Merwe, H. (2008) 'The Impact of the TRC's Amnesty Process on Survivors of Human Rights Violations'. In *Truth and Reconciliation in South Africa: Did the TRC Deliver?* ed. A. Chapman and H. van der Merwe. Philadelphia: University of Pennsylvania Press, 116–40.
Phelps, T. Godwin (2004) *Shattered Voices: Language, Violence, and the Work of Truth Commissions*. Philadelphia: University of Pennsylvania Press.
Pigou, P. (2002) 'False Promises and Wasted Opportunities? Inside South Africa's Truth and Reconciliation Commission'. In *Commissioning the Past: Understanding South Africa's Truth and Reconciliation Commission*, ed. D. Posel and G. Simpson. Johannesburg: Witwatersrand University Press, 37–65.
——(2003) 'Degrees of Truth: Amnesty and Limitations in the Truth Recovery Project'. In *The Provocations of Amnesty: Memory, Justice and Impunity*, ed. C. Villa-Vicencio and E. Doxtader. Cape Town: David Philip, 217–36.
——(2009) 'Accessing the Records of the Truth and Reconciliation Commission'. In *Paper Wars: Access to Information in South Africa*, ed. K. Allan. Johannesburg: University of the Witwatersrand Press, 17–55.
Posel, D. (2002) 'The TRC Report: What Kind of History? What Kind of Truth?'. In *Commissioning the Past: Understanding South Africa's Truth and Reconciliation Commission*, ed. D. Posel and G. Simpson. Johannesburg: Witwatersrand University Press, 147–72.
Posel, D. and Simpson, G. (eds) (2002) *Commissioning the Past: Understanding South Africa's Truth and Reconciliation Commission*. Johannesburg: Witwatersrand University Press.
——(2002a) 'The Power of Truth: South Africa's Truth and Reconciliation Commission in Context'. In *Commissioning the Past: Understanding South Africa's Truth and Reconciliation Commission*, ed. D. Posel and G. Simpson. Johannesburg: Witwatersrand University Press, 1–13.
Quayson, A. (2004) 'The Enchantment of a False Freedom'. *The WISER Review* 1 (July): 14.
Quinn, J. and Freeman, M. (2003) 'Lessons Learned: Practical Lessons Gleaned from Inside the Truth Commissions of Guatemala and South Africa'. *Human Rights Quarterly* 25, 4: 1117–49.
Ramírez-Barat, C. and van der Merwe, H. (2005) *Seeking Reconciliation and Reintegration: Assessment of a Pilot Restorative Justice Mediation Project*. Johannesburg: Centre for the Study of Violence and Reconciliation.
Rasmussen, J. L. (2001) 'Negotiating a Revolution: Toward Integrating Relationship Building and Reconciliation into Official Peace Negotiations'. In *Reconciliation, Justice, and Coexistence: Theory and Practice*, ed. M. Abu-Nimer. Lanham: Lexington Books, 101–27.
Rassool, C., Witz, L. and Minkley, G. (2000) 'Burying and Memorialising the Body of Truth: the TRC and National Heritage'. In *After the TRC: Reflections on Truth and Reconciliation in South Africa*, ed. W. James and L. van de Vijver. Cape Town: David Philip, 115–27.
Rauch, J. (2004) *Police Transformation and the South African TRC*. Johannesburg: Centre for the Study of Violence and Reconciliation.
Rayner, J. (2004) *The Apologist*. London: Atlantic Books.

Redpath, J. (2004) *The Scorpions: Analysing the Directorate of Special Operations*. Pretoria: Institute for Security Studies, Monograph Series, No. 96, March.

REHMI (1998) *Guatemala: Nunca Más*, 4 volumes. Guatemala City: Oficina de Derechos Humanos del Arzobispado de Guatemala.

Risse, T., Ropp, S. and Sikkink, K. (eds) (1999) *The Power of Human Rights: International Norms and Domestic Change*. Cambridge: Cambridge University Press.

Robbins, S. (2009) 'Whose Voices? Understanding Victims' Needs in Transition' (review essay). *Journal of Human Rights Practice* 1, 2: 320–31.

Roche, D. (2002) 'Restorative Justice and the Regulatory State in South African Townships'. *British Journal of Criminology* 42: 514–33.

Roht-Arriaza, N. (2005) *The Pinochet Effect: Transnational Justice in the Age of Human Rights*. Philadelphia: University of Pennsylvania Press.

Roht-Arriaza, N. and Mariezcurrena, J. (eds) (2006) *Transitional Justice in the Twenty First Century: Beyond Truth Versus Justice*. Cambridge: Cambridge University Press.

Roht-Arriaza, N. and Orlovsky, K. (2009) 'A Complementary Relationship: Reparations and Development'. In *Transitional Justice and Development: Making Connections*, ed. P. de Greiff and R. Duthie. New York: Social Science Research Council and the International Center for Transitional Justice, 170–213.

Rolston, B. and Scraton, P. (2005) 'In the Full Glare of English Politics: Ireland, Inquiries and the British State'. *British Journal of Criminology* 45: 547–64.

Rombouts, H. (2002) *The Legal Profession and the TRC: A Study of a Tense Relationship*. Johannesburg: Centre for the Study of Violence and Reconciliation.

Rombouts, H. and Parmentier, S. (2002) 'The Role of the Legal Profession in the South African Truth and Reconciliation Commission'. *Netherlands Quarterly of Human Rights* 20, 3: 273–98.

Ross, F. (2003) *Bearing Witness: Women and the Truth and Reconciliation Commission in South Africa*. London: Pluto Press.

——(2003a) 'The Construction of Voice and Identity in the South African Truth and Reconciliation Commission'. In *Political Transition: Politics and Cultures*, ed. P. Gready. London: Pluto Press, 165–80.

——(2003b) 'On Having Voice and Being Heard: Some After-effects of Testifying Before the South African Truth and Reconciliation Commission'. *Anthropological Theory* 3, 3: 325–41.

——(2005) 'Codes and Dignity: Thinking about Ethics in Relation to Research on Violence'. *Anthropology Southern Africa* 28, 3 and 4: 99–107.

Ruden, S. (1999) 'Country of My Skull: Guilt and Sorrow and the Limits of Forgiveness in the New South Africa'. *Ariel* 30, 1: 165–79.

SAHA (2003) *SAHA Update: The TRC Codicil and Archives/Recordkeeping*. South African History Archive, 6 May, available at www.saha.org.za/research (accessed 17 May 2010).

Samuelson, M. (2003) 'Cracked Vases and Untidy Seams: Narrative Structure and Closure in the Truth and Reconciliation Commission and South African Fiction'. *Current Writing* 15, 2: 63–76.

Sanford, V. (2003) *Buried Secrets: Truth and Human Rights in Guatemala*. New York: Palgrave Macmillan.

——(2003a) '"What is Written in Our Hearts": Memory, Justice and the Healing of Fragmented Communities'. In *Political Transition: Politics and Cultures*, ed. P. Gready. London: Pluto Press, 70–89.

Sarkin, J. (1996) 'The Trials and Tribulations of South Africa's Truth and Reconciliation Commission'. *South African Journal on Human Rights* 12, 4: 617–40.

—— (2004) *Carrots and Sticks: The TRC and the South African Amnesty Process*. Antwerp: Intersentia.

Sarkin, J. and Daly, E. (2004) 'Too Many Questions, Too Few Answers: Reconciliation in Transitional Societies'. *Columbia Human Rights Law Review* 35, 3: 661–728.

Schabas, W. (2006) 'The Sierra Leone Truth and Reconciliation Commission'. In *Transitional Justice in the Twenty-first Century: Beyond Truth Versus Justice*, ed. N. Roht-Arriaza and J. Mariezcurrena. Cambridge: Cambridge University Press, 21–42.

Schaffer, K. and Smith, S. (2004) *Human Rights and Narrated Lives: The Ethics of Recognition*. New York: Palgrave Macmillan.

Schärf, W., Saban, G. and Hauck, M. (2001) 'Local Communities and Crime Prevention: Two Experiments in Partnership Policing'. In *Crime Wave: The South African Underworld and its Foes*, ed. J. Steinberg. Johannesburg: Witwatersrand University Press, 65–85.

Scheper-Hughes, N. (1999) 'Un-doing: Social Suffering and the Politics of Remorse'. In *Remorse and Reparation*, ed. M. Cox. London: Jessica Kingsley, 145–70.

Schönteich, M. (1999) 'How Organised is the State's Response to Organised Crime?'. *African Security Review* 8, 2: 3–12.

Scott, J. (1990) *Domination and the Arts of Resistance: Hidden Transcripts*. New Haven: Yale University Press.

Seekoe, M. (2006) 'Reparations' (contributor to the debate). In *Truth and Reconciliation in South Africa: 10 Years On*, ed. C. Villa-Vicencio and F. du Toit. Cape Town: David Philip, 36–45.

Segal, L., Martin, K. and Cort, S. (2006) *Number Four: The Making of Constitution Hill*. London: Penguin.

Segal, L., Pelo, J. and Rampa, P. (2001) 'Into the Heart of Darkness: Journeys of the *Amagents* in Crime, Violence and Death'. In *Crime Wave: The South African Underworld and its Foes*, ed. J. Steinberg. Johannesburg: Witwatersrand University Press, 95–114.

Sekhonyane, M. and Louw, A. (2002) *Violent Justice: Vigilantism and the State's Response*. Monograph Series 72. Pretoria: Institute for Security Studies.

Shaw, M. (2002) *Crime and Policing in Post-apartheid South Africa: Transforming Under Fire*. London: Hurst.

Shaw, R. (2005) *Rethinking Truth and Reconciliation Commissions: Lessons from Sierra Leone*. Special Report 130. Washington, DC: United States Institute of Peace.

Shriver, D. (1995) *An Ethic for Enemies: Forgiveness in Politics*. New York: Oxford University Press.

Sierra Leone Working Group on Truth and Reconciliation (2006) 'Searching for Truth and Reconciliation in Sierra Leone: An Initial Study of the Performance and Impact of the Truth and Reconciliation Commission' (February).

Sikkink, K. and Booth Walling, C. (2006) 'Argentina's Contribution to Global Trends in Transitional Justice'. In *Transitional Justice in the Twenty-first Century: Beyond Truth Versus Justice*, ed. N. Roht-Arriaza and J. Mariezcurrena. Cambridge: Cambridge University Press, 301–24.

Simpson, G. (2001) 'Shock Troops and Bandits: Youth, Crime and Politics'. In *Crime Wave: The South African Underworld and its Foes*, ed. J. Steinberg. Johannesburg: Witwatersrand University Press, 115–28.

—— (2002) ' "Tell No Lies, Claim No Easy Victories": A Brief Evaluation of South Africa's Truth and Reconciliation Commission'. In *Commissioning the Past: Understanding*

South Africa's Truth and Reconciliation Commission, ed. D. Posel and G. Simpson. Johannesburg: Witwatersrand University Press, 220–51.
——(2004) '"A Snake Gives Birth to a Snake": Politics and Crime in the Transition to Democracy in South Africa'. In *Justice Gained? Crime and Crime Control in South Africa's Transition*, ed. B. Dixon and E. van der Spuy. Cape Town: UCT Press, 1–28.
Skelton, A. (2002) 'Restorative Justice as a Framework for Juvenile Justice Reform: A South African Perspective'. *British Journal of Criminology* 42: 496–513.
——(2004) 'For the Next Generations: Remaking South Africa's Juvenile Justice System'. In *To Repair the Irreparable: Reparation and Reconstruction in South Africa*, ed. E. Doxtader and C. Villa-Vicencio. Cape Town: David Philip, 111–23.
——(2005) 'The Child Justice Bill from a Restorative Justice Perspective'. In *Beyond Retribution: Prospects for Restorative Justice in South Africa*, ed. T. Maepa. Monograph Series, No. 111. Pretoria: Institute for Security Studies, February, 127–35.
——(2006) 'The South African Child Justice Bill: Transition as Opportunity'. In *Juvenile Law Violators, Human Rights and the Development of New Juvenile Justice Systems*, ed. E. Jensen and J. Jepsen. Oxford: Hart, 65–80.
Skelton, A. and Batley, M. (eds) (2006) *Charting Progress, Mapping the Future: Restorative Justice in South Africa*. Pretoria: Institute for Security Studies.
Skelton, A. and Gallinetti, J. (2008) 'A Long and Winding Road: The Child Justice Bill, Civil Society and Advocacy'. *SA Crime Quarterly* 25, September: 3–10, pages 3–9.
Slovo, G. (2000) *Red Dust*. London: Virago.
Slye, R. (2000) 'Amnesty, Truth, and Reconciliation: Reflections on the South African Amnesty Process'. In *Truth v. Justice: The Morality of Truth Commissions*, ed. R. Rotberg and D. Thompson. Princeton: Princeton University Press, 170–88.
——(2000a) 'Justice and Amnesty'. In *Looking Back Reaching Forward: Reflections on the Truth and Reconciliation Commission of South Africa*, ed. C. Villa-Vicencio and W. Verwoerd. Cape Town: University of Cape Town Press, 174–83.
Smyth, M. (2003) 'Putting the Past in its Place: Issues of Victimhood and Reconciliation in Northern Ireland's Peace Process'. In *Burying the Past: Making Peace and Doing Justice after Civil Conflict*, ed. N. Biggar. Washington, DC: Georgetown University Press, 125–53.
Smythe, D. and Parenzee, P. (2004) 'Acting against Domestic Violence'. In *Justice Gained? Crime and Crime Control in South Africa's Transition*, ed. B. Dixon and E. van der Spuy. Cape Town: University of Cape Town Press, 140–62.
Snodgrass Godoy, A. (2005) '*La Muchacha Respondona*: Reflections on the Razor's Edge Between Crime and Human Rights'. *Human Rights Quarterly* 27: 597–624.
Sooka, Y. (2006) 'The TRC's Unfinished Business: Prosecutions'. In *Truth and Reconciliation in South Africa: 10 Years On*, ed. V. Villa-Vicencio and F. du Toit. Cape Town: Institute for Justice and Reconciliation and David Philip, 17–22.
Southall, R. (2006) 'Introduction: Can South Africa be a Developmental State?'. In *State of the Nation: South Africa 2005–2006*, ed. S. Buhlungu, J. Daniel, R. Southall and J. Lutchman. Cape Town: HSRC Press, xvii–xlv.
Spivak, G. (1988) 'Can the Subaltern Speak?'. In *Marxism and the Interpretation of Culture*, ed. C. Nelson and L. Grossberg. Chicago: University of Illinois Press, 271–313.
Standing, A. (2004) 'Out of the Mainstream: Critical Reflections on Organised Crime in the Western Cape'. In *Justice Gained? Crime and Crime Control in South Africa's Transition*, ed. B. Dixon and E. van der Spuy. Cape Town: University of Cape Town Press, 29–57.

——(2005) *The Threat of Gangs and Anti-gangs Policy: Policy Discussion Paper 116*. Pretoria: Institute for Security Studies, August.

Stanley, E. (2001) 'Evaluating the Truth and Reconciliation Commission'. *Journal of Modern African Studies* 39, 3: 525–46.

Stauffer, C. and Hamber, B. (1996) *Putting a Face on the Past: Survivor–Offender Mediation and the Truth and Reconciliation Commission*. Johannesburg: Centre for the Study of Violence and Reconciliation.

Steinberg, J. (2001) 'Introduction: Behind the Crime Wave'. In *Crime Wave: The South African Underworld and its Foes*, ed. J. Steinberg. Johannesburg: University of the Witwatersrand Press, 1–12.

——(2002) *Midlands*. Johannesburg: Jonathan Ball.

——(2004) *The Number: One Man's Search for Identity in the Cape Underworld and Prison Gangs*. Johannesburg: Jonathan Ball.

Stenning, P. and LaPrairie, C. (2004) ' "Politics by Other Means": The Role of Commissions of Inquiry in Establishing the "Truth" about "Aboriginal Justice" in Canada'. In *Crime, Truth and Justice: Official Inquiry, Discourse, Knowledge*, ed. G. Gilligan and J. Pratt. Cullompton, Devon: Willan, 138–60.

Stewart, F. and Wang, M. (2005) 'Poverty Reduction Strategy Papers within the Human Rights Perspective'. In *Human Rights and Development: Towards Mutual Reinforcement*, ed. P. Alston and M. Robinson. Oxford: Oxford University Press, 447–74.

Stoll, D. (1999) *Rigoberta Menchú and the Story of All Poor Guatemalans*. Boulder, CO: Westview Press.

Stout, B. and Wood, C. (2004) 'Child Justice and Diversion: Will Children's Rights Outlast the Transition?'. In *Justice Gained? Crime and Crime Control in South Africa's Transition*, ed. B. Dixon and E. van der Spuy. Cape Town: University of Cape Town Press, 114–39.

Stover, E. and Weinstein, H. (eds) (2004) *My Neighbor, My Enemy: Justice and Community in the Aftermath of Mass Atrocity*. Cambridge: Cambridge University Press.

Suttner, R. (2006) 'Talking to the Ancestors: National Heritage, the Freedom Charter and Nation-building in South Africa in 2005'. *Development Southern Africa* 23, 1: 3–27.

Tarrow, S. (2005) *The New Transnational Activism*. Cambridge: Cambridge University Press.

Taussig, M. (1987) *Shamanism, Colonialism, and the Wild Man: A Study in Terror and Healing*. Chicago: University of Chicago Press.

Taylor, C. (1994) 'The Politics of Recognition'. In *Multiculturalism: Examining the Politics of Recognition*, ed. A. Gutmann. Princeton: Princeton University Press, 25–73.

Taylor, J. (1994) 'Body Memories: Aide-memoires and Collective Amnesia in the Wake of the Argentine Terror'. In *Body Politics: Disease, Desire, and the Family*, ed. M. Ryan and A. Gordon. Boulder, CO: Westview Press, 192–203.

——(1998) *Ubu and the Truth Commission*. Cape Town: University of Cape Town Press.

Taylor, R. (2002) 'Justice Denied: Political Violence in Kwazulu-Natal after 1994'. *African Affairs* 101: 473–508.

Terreblanche, S. (2002) *A History of Inequality in South Africa, 1652–2002*. Pietermaritzburg: University of Natal Press, and Johannesburg: KMM Review Publishing.

Thoms, O. and Ron, J. (2007) 'Do Human Rights Violations Cause Internal Conflict?'. *Human Rights Quarterly* 29, 3: 674–705.

Tomaselli, K. (2003) 'Stories to Tell, Stories to Sell: Resisting Textualization'. *Cultural Studies* 17, 6: 856–75.

Tomuschat, C. (2001) 'Clarification Commission in Guatemala'. *Human Rights Quarterly* 23, 2: 233–58.
Truth and Reconciliation Commission (TRC) (1998) *Truth and Reconciliation Commission of South Africa Report*. Volumes 1–5. Cape Town: Juta Press.
——(2002) *Truth and Reconciliation Commission of South Africa Report*. Volume 7. Cape Town: Juta Press.
——(2003) *Truth and Reconciliation Commission of South Africa Report*. Volume 6. Cape Town: Juta Press.
Turner, J. (2002) *Southern Cross*. London: Orion.
Tutu, D. (1996) 'Foreword'. In *To Remember and to Heal: Theological and Psychological Reflections on Truth and Reconciliation*, ed. H. Russel Botman and R. M. Petersen. Cape Town: Human and Rousseau, 7–8.
——(1999) *No Future without Forgiveness*. London: Rider.
Uvin, P. (1998) *Aiding Violence: The Development Enterprise in Rwanda*. West Hartford, CT: Kumarian Press.
van der Merwe, H. (2001) 'Reconciliation and Justice in South Africa: Lessons from the TRC's Community Interventions'. In *Reconciliation, Justice, and Coexistence: Theory and Practice*, ed. M. Abu-Nimer. Lanham: Lexington Books, 187–207.
——(2002) 'National Narrative versus Local Truths: The Truth and Reconciliation Commission's Engagement with Duduza'. In *Commissioning the Past: Understanding South Africa's Truth and Reconciliation Commission*, ed. D. Posel and G. Simpson. Johannesburg: Witwatersrand University Press, 204–19.
——(2003) 'National and Community Reconciliation: Competing Agendas in the South African Truth and Reconciliation Commission'. In *Burying the Past: Making Peace and Doing Justice after Civil Conflict*, ed. N. Biggar. Washington, DC: Georgetown University Press, 101–24.
——(2008) 'What Survivors Say About Justice: An Analysis of the TRC Victim Hearings'. In *Truth and Reconciliation in South Africa: Did the TRC Deliver?* ed. A. Chapman and H. van der Merwe. Philadelphia: University of Pennsylvania Press, 23–44.
van der Merwe, H., Dewhirst, P. and Hamber, B. (1999) 'Non-governmental Organisations and the Truth and Reconciliation Commission: An Impact Assessment'. *Politikon* 26, 1: 55–79.
van Zyl, P. (1999) 'Dilemmas of Transitional Justice: The Case of South Africa's Truth and Reconciliation Commission'. *Journal of International Affairs* 52, 2: 647–67.
——(2000) 'Justice without Punishment: Guaranteeing Human Rights in Transitional Societies'. In *Looking Back Reaching Forward: Reflections on the Truth and Reconciliation Commission of South Africa*, ed. C. Villa-Vicencio and W. Verwoerd. Cape Town: University of Cape Town Press, 42–57.
Van Zyl Slabbert, F. (2000) 'Truth without Reconciliation, Reconciliation without Truth'. In *After the TRC: Reflections on Truth and Reconciliation in South Africa*, ed. W. James and L. van de Vijver. Cape Town: David Philip, 62–72.
van Zyl Smit, D. (1999) 'Criminological Ideas and the South African Transition'. *British Journal of Criminology* 39, 2: 198–215.
Verdirame, G. (2000) 'The Genocide Definition in the Jurisprudence of the Ad Hoc Tribunals'. *International Comparative Law Quarterly* 49, 3: 578–98.
Verwoerd, W. (1996) 'Continuing the Discussion: Reflections from within the Truth and Reconciliation Commission'. *Current Writing* 8, 2: 66–85.

——(1997) 'Justice after Apartheid: Reflections on the South African Truth and Reconciliation Commission'. Paper delivered at the Fifth International Conference on Ethics and Development, Globalization, Self-determination and Justice in Development, Madras, India, 2–9 January.

Verwoerd, W. and Mabizela, M. (eds) (2000) *Truths Drawn in Jest: Commentary on the Truth and Reconciliation Commission through Cartoons*. Cape Town: David Philip.

Villa-Vicencio, C. (2000) 'On the Limitations of Academic History: The Quest for Truth Demands Both More and Less'. In *After the TRC: Reflections on Truth and Reconciliation in South Africa*, ed. W. James and L. van de Vijver. Cape Town: David Philip, 21–31.

——(2000a) 'Restorative Justice: Dealing with the Past Differently'. In *Looking Back Reaching Forward: Reflections on the Truth and Reconciliation Commission of South Africa*, ed. C. Villa-Vicencio and W. Verwoerd. Cape Town: University of Cape Town Press, 68–76.

——(2003) 'Restorative Justice: Ambiguities and Limitations of a Theory'. In *The Provocations of Amnesty: Memory, Justice and Impunity*, ed. C. Villa-Vicencio and E. Doxtader. Cape Town: David Philip, 30–50.

Villa-Vicencio, C. and Verwoerd, W. (2000) 'Constructing a Report: Writing up the "Truth"'. In *Truth v. Justice: The Morality of Truth Commissions*, ed. R. Rotberg and D. Thompson. Princeton: Princeton University Press, 279–94.

Vinck, P. and Pham, P. (2008) 'Ownership and Participation in Transitional Justice Mechanisms: A Sustainable Human Development Perspective from Eastern DRC'. *International Journal of Transitional Justice* 2, 3: 398–411.

Vladislavić, I. (2006) *Portrait With Keys: The City of Johannesburg Unlocked*. London: Portobello Books.

von Schnitzler, A., Ditlhage, G., Kgalema, L., Maepa, T., Mofokeng, T. and Pigou, P. (2001) *Guardian or Gangster? Mapogo a Mathamaga: A Case Study*. Johannesburg: Centre for the Study of Violence and Reconciliation.

Walker, C. (2006) 'Delivery and Disarray: The Multiple Meanings of Land Restitution'. In *State of the Nation: South Africa 2005–2006*, ed. S. Buhlungu, J. Daniel, R. Southall and J. Lutchman. Cape Town: HSRC Press, 67–92.

——(2008) *Landmarked: Land Claims and Land Restitution in South Africa*. Johannesburg: Jacana.

Weinstein, H. and Stover, E. (2004) 'Introduction: Conflict, Justice and Reclamation'. In *My Neighbor, My Enemy: Justice and Community in the Aftermath of Mass Atrocity*, ed. E. Stover and H. Weinstein. Cambridge: Cambridge University Press, 1–26.

Werbner, P. (1997) 'Essentialising Essentialism, Essentialising Silence: Ambivalence and Multiplicity in the Constructions of Racism and Ethnicity'. In *Debating Cultural Hybridity: Multi-cultural Identities and the Politics of Anti-racism*, ed. P. Werbner and T. Modood. London: Zed Books, 226–54.

Werbner, R. (1998) 'Introduction: Beyond Oblivion: Confronting Memory Crisis'. In *Memory and the Postcolonial: African Anthropology and the Critique of Power*, ed. R. Werbner. London: Zed Books, 1–17.

Weschler, L. (1990) *A Miracle, A Universe: Settling Accounts with Torturers*. New York: Viking Penguin.

Wicomb, Z. (2001) *David's Story*. New York: Feminist Press.

——(2006) *Playing in the Light*. Johannesburg: Umuzi.

Williamson, S. (2002) 'Photo Essay: "Truth Games"'. *Kunapipi* 24, 1 and 2: 182–88.

Wilson, R. (1996) 'The Sizwe Will Not Go Away: The Truth and Reconciliation Commission, Human Rights and Nation-building in South Africa'. *African Studies* 55, 2: 1–20.

——(1997) 'Representing Human Rights Violations: Social Contexts and Subjectivities'. In *Human Rights, Culture and Context: Anthropological Perspectives*, ed. R. Wilson. London: Pluto Press, 134–60.

——(2001) *The Politics of Truth and Reconciliation in South Africa: Legitimizing the Post-apartheid State*. Cambridge: Cambridge University Press.

Wilson, S. (2001) 'The Myth of Restorative Justice: Truth, Reconciliation and the Ethics Amnesty'. *South African Journal on Human Rights* 17, 4: 531–62.

Worsnip, M. (1996) *Priest and Partisan: A South African Journey*. Melbourne, Australia: Ocean Press.

Young, I. (2002) *Inclusion and Democracy*. Oxford: Oxford University Press.

Zehr, H. (1997) 'Restorative Justice: When Justice and Healing Go Together'. *Track Two* 6, 3 and 4.

Index

Amnesty and justice 93–102; administrative and political procedures 96–97; 'as justice' approach 95; broader TRC legitimacy, and 98–99; constitutionality 97; democratic blind spot 94–95; dilemma 93–94; holistic form of justice 94; international crimes 98; international law, and 97–98; maximalist conception 101–2; 'more justice' approach 95; nature of justice, and 95–96; 'no justice' approach 95; practice 96–102; presidential pardons 100–101; prosecutions, and 99–102; rumours as to 99; series of provisions 96; Slye on 94; theory 93–96; TRC recommendations 99; TRC, and 40–41
Apology and forgiveness 199–204; authenticity, and 199–200; forgiveness, conception of 201; *Forgiveness*, film 203; Gobodo-Madikizela on 201; risk, and 202; sequencing 202–3; temporal, transformative facility 200–201; Tutu on 201–2; unpredictability 200
Archives 53–56; functions of 54–55; 'violence of' 53–54
Argentina; CONADEP, *Never Again* 35

Boehmer, Elleke; *Bloodlines* 181

Child Justice Alliance 148
Civil society; meaning 63–64; TRC, and 64–69
Coetzee, J.M.; *Disgrace* 183–84
Cohen, Stan; TRC, on 72
Community reconciliation 204–10; Bonteheuwel 205–8; Bonteheuwel Military Wing 205–8; initiatives 204–5; mediations 204–5; Constitution Hill 175–79; Constitutional Court 175; external orientation 176–77; human rights vision 176; internal transformation 175–77; multi-dimensional site 177–78; narrative walkthrough 178; visitor stories 178–79
Constitutionalism; legal fetishism, and 138
Criminal justice system; TRC, and 102–6
Criminal violence 117–49; ANC, and 120–21; apartheid, and 120; changing patterns of 121; crime and politics 127; currency of past, as 151–52; democratic social control 128; Directorate of Special Operations 133–34; 'dismantling mentality' 131; ex-combatants 123; gangs 119; global patterns 149–50; Guatemala 117–18; human rights, and 130; intrumental authoritarianism, and 130–35; Kwazulu-Natal 124; legal fetishism see Legal fetishism; local contexts 150–51; motives 121–22; National Crime Combating Strategy 133; National Crime Prevention Strategy (NCPS) 133; Operation Crackdown 133; organised crime 124–27; police reform, and 134–35; policing 131–35; policy pendulum, and 131–35; prison gangs 119; public opinion, and 128; razor's edge between political violence and 121–27; repressive measures 128; responses to 127–49; role of TRC, and 118–19; Self-Defence Units 120; Self Protection Units 120; social belonging, and 150; South Africa 118; South African Police, and 132–33; symbolic perceptions of 129–30; strengthening of criminal justice systems 151;

transitional societies, and 117–18; truth commissions, and 150–52; UDF, and 120; vigilantism, and 121

Dangor, Achmat; *Bitter Fruit* 184
Discourse; meaning 28

Economic reconciliation 210–22; ASGI 211–12; human rights, and 212, 216–17; Internal Reconciliation Commision 220; interventionist state 213; justice as transformation 219; land reform 216; liberal peace thesis 212–13; real reconciliation 221; relational perspective 220–21; reparations 217–18; transitional justice mechanisms, and 222; truth commissions, and 214–15
Eprile, Tony, *The Persistence of Memory* 187

Genre; meaning 28
Globalisation; transitional justice, and 7–8
Guatemala; criminal violence 117–18; REMHI 83

Human rights 9–11; balancing process, as 10; broader definition, needs for 10; criminal violence, and 130; economic reconciliation, and 216–17; hybridity, and 10; legal fetishism, and 137–38; reimagining 9–11; restorative justice, and 112–13
Human Rights Media Centre 84–86; methodology 84–85; rights-based ethical code for story-tellers 85–86
Human rights reports 32–44; best-sellers, as 35; decontextualisation 38–39; impact of 36; impacts beyond fetishisation 33–37; interpretive questions 41–42; language of 37; legitimacy, and 33–37; main activity, as 34; methodological scaffolding 33–34; politics of comparison, and 41; speaking truth with and to power 37; state inquiries distinguished 35–36; subtlety, need to read with 39; TRC, and 33; truth impoverishment, and 37–38

Institue for Healing of Memories 170–72; vision of 171
Instrumental authoritarianism; criminal violence, and 130–35

Judges; TRC, and 103–4
Justice; TRC conceptualisations 106–13; understandings of 106–7
Justice cascade; notion of 8
Justice past 93–116
Justice present 117–55

Keywords; conceptualising 9
Khulumani Support Group 172–74; initial objective 172; story telling 173; Western Cape branch 86
Khutwane, Yvonne; testimony of sexual violence 80–81
Krog, Antjie; nature of truth, on 71

Legal fetishism 135–39; apartheid system, and 136; constitutionalism, and 138; human rights, and 137–38; legal measures in new South Africa 136–37; legal pluralism, and 138–39; progressive laws, and 137
Legal profession; TRC, and 104–5
Literature 180–88; preoccupation with past 180

Magona, Sindiwe; *Mother to Mother* 181–82
Mapogo a Mathamaga 144–46
Memorials 174–79
Motsuenyane Commission 40

Naming names 22–23
National Prosecuting Authority 99
NGOs; TRC, and 64–65
Novel truths; public culture, and 179–88

Official history 44–56; challenges, facing 48–49; educational dynamics 47; other forms of history, and 45; sequencing, and 47–48; timing, and 47–48; victor's history, as 45–46
Organised crime 124–27; extreme variant of capitalism, as 126; globalisation of 125–26; regional catalysts 125

PAGAD 142–44
Paralegality 139–47; private security firms 140–42
Penny, Sarah; *The Beneficianies* 186–87
Police reform; TRC, and 134–35
Presidential pardons 100–101
Priority Crimes Litigation Unit 99

Private security firms 140–42; growth in 141; segregation, and 141–42
Public culture 179–88; literature 180–88; novel truths, and 179–88
Public opinion; criminal violence, and 128

Reconciliation 15–16, 156–94; causal assumptions 160; community 16–17; conceptualisation 156–57; definition 222–23; definitional debates 157–58; economic 17; HRV hearings, and 161; narratives of pain and suffering, and 159–60; non-fitting testimonies 162; 'regime of truth' 159; relationship with truth 159; relationships, and 16; relationships-based portion of model 223; social discourses on 158; speaking truth to 158–60; structural considerations 223–24; TRC, and 156–94; TRC debates 162–63; truth, and 156–94; truth-telling, and 15–16; truth telling template 160–63; victimhood, culture of 163–70 see also Victimhood, culture of; victims/survivor agency 162
Reconciliation and risk 198–204; apology and forgiveness 199–204; authenticity, measure of 199–200; costly signals of conciliatory intent 198–99
Reconciliation and the everyday 195–98; human rights, and 197; Njabulo Ndebele 195; post-conflict repair and reconstruction 197; relational nature of reconciliation 196; Winnie Madikisela-Mandela 196
Relationships; reconciliation, and 16
Research hypothesis 2
Restorative justice 147–49; amnesty trumps reparations 11; Child Justice Alliance 148; Child Justice Bill 147–48; genuine encounters 110–11; human rights, and 112–13; instrumental cultural and religious readings 111–12; parallelism 110–11; reluctant perpetrators 110; TRC, and 108–13
Rights based participation 61–92; different forms 63; Friedman on 62; merits of 62

Sites of truth telling 170–74; encounters 170–88; support groups 170–88; transformations 170–88

Skweyiya commission 40
Slovo, Gillian; *Red Dust* 185
Social Justice; TRC, and 107–8
Social truth 61–92; globalisation, and 87–88; media and 87–88; rights based participation, and 61–92
South Africa; compromises 1; crossroads, at 1; transitional violence 15; trend towards public history 48
South African History Archive 54–55
Speaking truth to place 174–79; Constitution Hill see Constitution Hill
Speaking truth to reconciliation; possible futures 189
State inquiries 28–32; Foucault on 30; history in South Africa 29; human rights reports distinguished 35–36; political agendas, and 31

torture, and 29
TRC as 28–32
truth as objectivity 30–31
Testimony in public sphere 76–87; control of 77; globalisation, and 77–78; Guatemala REMHI 83; Human Rights Media Centre 84; official methodologies 82–83; self narration 76; subaltern research methods 82–87; TRC, and 79–82; victims as agents of research 83–84; violation of trust, and 78
Transitional justice; Bosire on 7; cycles of boom and bust 5; core characteristics 5; holistic understandings of 6; 'justice present' 14–15; globalisation, and 7–8; industry, as 5–6; keyword conceptualisation 7; nature of 1; past legacies, and 14; peace versus justice debate 6; political and social processes, and 6–7; success of 5–6
Transitional truths 20–27; naming names 22–23; official acknowledgement 20–21; public acknowledgement 20–21; public debate about nature of justice 21; truth as acknowledgement 20–21
Trojan Horse history project 84
Truth; concept of 9; genre, and see also Truth as genre; genre, as 12–13
Truth and Reconciliation Commission (TRC) 1–2; academic historians, and 46; access to human rights protections 42–43; amnesty process 25–26; ANC,

and 40–41; approach to publishing report 34–35; archive, as 53–56; breadth of mandate 27; civil society, and 64–69; difficulties hindering interaction 66; Dullah Omar, and 64–65; media coverage 67–69; publicity 67–68; transitional contexts 66; transparency 69; universalising impulse of media 68–69; conceptual insights 2; conceptualisations of justice 106–13; contextual analysis 52; contours of partiality 26–27; criminal justice system, and 102–6; fault lines 102–3; judges, and 103–4; legal challenges 103; legal profession, and 104–5; criminal violence, and 118–19; crisis of history, and 46–47; decontextualisation 38–39; definition of factual or forensic truth 44–45; discourse of democratic debate 74–76; disjuncture from education/history 47; discursive redistribution of power, and 75; entry point, as 3; evaluation 2–3; failure to achieve hybrid or synthetic coherence 13; focus on patterns of abuse 24; fourfold categorisation of truth 2, 36–37; genetic confines 56; hearability 79–80; history, and 46–49; human rights report 33; impacts of human rights law 43; incomplete list of victim names 23; interaction with justice 14; interpretive contribution 73; international legal standards, and 40; investigation unit 24; justice, and 21–22, 93–106; language, and 74–75; legal sector hearing 104–5; legality of amnesty provision 42; legitimacy agenda 32; limitations 30; local dynamics of power and violence, and 52; local histories, and 53; meta-narrative 50–51; NGO's, and 64–65; official history, whether 44–56; police reform, and 134–35; policy changes, and 113; political-criminal tension, and 118–19; powers of subpoena, search and seizure 31–32; procedural issues 25–26; procedural liberalism 13–14, 73; public sphere, and 69–76; public victim hearings 79; reconciliation, and 156–94; reframing of testimony 75; report 4; report as historical text 44; research hypothesis 2; restorative justice, and 108–13; amnesty trumps reparations 111; genuine encounters 110–11; human rights, and 112–13; instrumental cultural and religious readings 111–12; Kiss on 109–10; parallelism 110–11; reluctant perpetrators 110; Villa-Vicencio on 109; rights-based participation, and 61–92; shift in focus and working methods 38; shifting values, and 70–71; social justice, and 107–8; state inquiry, as 28–32; testimony, and 79–82; charismatic narrators 81–82; circulation of 81; research methods, and 87; violation of 82

testimony in public sphere 76–87 see also Testimony in public sphere

truth dividend 25–26; truth in historical or political context 72; truth-timidity 31–32; values, consensus on 69–70; voice, significance of 14; women as victims 80; workings of 4

Truth as genre 20–60; complex truths 32; discourse, meaning 28; genre, meaning 28; transitional truths 20–27 see also Transitional truths

Truth commissions; conceptual challenge 56; containing meta-narrative 50; core characteristics 3–4; criminal violence, and 150–52; development of 4–5; economic and social rights 214–15; empirical evidence 73; engaging past and present 11; history, and 49–50; human rights abuses, and 51–52; interpretive framework 50; interpretive repertoire of history, and 55; lack of cooperation from perpetrators 25; methodological challenge 56; objective knowledge 73; participation, need to facilitate 88; priorities 23–24; remaking public sphere 11–12; rights-based participation 12; values, and 71–73

Truth-telling; reconciliation, and 15–16

Turner, Jann; *Southern Cross* 185–86

United Democratic Front; criminal violence, and 120

Victimhood, culture of 163–70; collective narratives 168–69; democracy, and 169–70; human rights, and 165–66;

identity transformation, and 166–67; individualism 168; majority truth and justice, and 167–68; partisan politics, and 169; perpetrators, and 167; politics of recognition 168; political violence as relational phenomenon 166; post-modern identity-politics 169; terminology 164

Vigilantism 121, 142–47; Mapogo a Mathamaga 144–46; motivation 122; PAGAD 142–44; partially understood phenomenon, as 146; partnership policing, and 146–47; taxi wars, and 122–23

Wicomb, Zoe; *Playing in the light* 187–88